Suicide Assessment and Treatment

Dana Worchel, PhD, is an assistant professor at Columbia University, School of Social Work. Dr. Worchel has a wide range of clinical experience working with individuals with mood disorders and suicidality in outpatient, inpatient, and psychiatric emergency room settings. During the past 8 years, Dr. Worchel has conducted research examining risk and protective factors across cultures related to mood disorders and suicidal behavior. Her research has also focused on the development of novel interventions aimed at improving treatment engagement and adherence among suicide attempters. As a principal investigator, Dr. Worchel has received funding for her research, including the American Foundation for Suicide Prevention (AFSP) and the National Alliance for Research on Schizophrenia and Depression (NARSAD). Dr. Worchel currently teaches clinical practice with a special focus on adult mental illness and individuals with suicidality.

Robin E. Gearing, PhD, is an assistant professor at Columbia University, School of Social Work. Dr. Gearing has extensive experience as a clinician, with 15 years of practice in mental health programs. He has provided a wide range of therapeutic and clinical services as a child, adolescent, and family therapist to individuals, groups, and families at an academic children's hospital, in both inpatient and outpatient psychiatric programs. Dr. Gearing has also worked as a psychiatric social worker with the crisis team of a community hospital where he provided adolescents and adults with clinical consultation and crisis risk assessment. Dr. Gearing has been a principal or co-investigator in a number of research studies in the areas of mental health and health, with a specific focus on children, adolescents, and families. Currently, Dr. Gearing is both teaching and investigating evidence-based mental health clinical interventions with a specific focus on improving and enhancing treatment engagement and adherence in children, adolescents, and their families.

Drs. Worchel and Gearing conduct research together and for several years have co-taught advanced seminars on the assessment and treatment of suicidality.

Suicide Assessment and Treatment

Empirical and Evidence-Based Practices

DANA WORCHEL, PhD
ROBIN E. GEARING, PhD

SPRINGER PUBLISHING COMPANY

New York

Springer Publishing Company, LLC
11 West 42nd Street
New York, NY 10036
www.springerpub.com

Acquisitions Editor: Jennifer Perillo
Production Editor: Gayle Lee
Cover Design: TG Design
Composition: Laura Stewart at Apex

ISBN: 978-0-8261-1698-7
E-book ISBN: 978-0-8261-1699-4

10 11 12 / 5 4 3 2 1

The author and the publisher of this Work have made every effort to use sources believed to be reliable to provide information that is accurate and compatible with the standards generally accepted at the time of publication. Because medical science is continually advancing, our knowledge base continues to expand. Therefore, as new information becomes available, changes in procedures become necessary. We recommend that the reader always consult current research and specific institutional policies before performing any clinical procedure. The author and publisher shall not be liable for any special, consequential, or exemplary damages resulting, in whole or in part, from the readers' use of, or reliance on, the information contained in this book. The publisher has no responsibility for the persistence or accuracy of URLs for external or third-party Internet Web sites referred to in this publication and does not guarantee that any content on such Web sites is, or will remain, accurate or appropriate.

Library of Congress Cataloging-in-Publication Data

Worchel, Dana.
  Suicide assessment and treatment : empirical and evidence-based practices / Dana Worchel, Robin E. Gearing.
    p. ; cm.
  Includes bibliographical references and index.
  ISBN 978-0-8261-1698-7 (alk. paper)
  1. Suicidal behavior.   I. Gearing, Robin E.   II. Title.
  [DNLM: 1. Suicide—prevention & control.   2. Suicide—psychology.
3. Self-Injurious Behavior—diagnosis.   4. Self-Injurious Behavior—therapy.
  WM 165 L789s   2010]
  RC569.L59 2010
  616.85'8445—dc22   2010000412

Printed in the United States of America by Hamilton Printing.

To every individual who has struggled with suicidality;
to supportive family and friends who have struggled with them;
and to all mental health professionals, health care
practitioners, and social service clinicians
who work each day in the field.

Contents

13   Depression and Suicide   255

14   Substance-Related Disorders and Suicide   271

PART V: SPECIAL POPULATIONS   289

15   At-Risk Groups   291

Preface

Suicide is an event that cannot be ignored, minimized, or untreated. Each year in the United States over 300,000 individuals will attempt suicide, with approximately 32,000 taking their own lives. Effective assessment and empirically supported treatment of suicidality can directly reduce these rates. However, all too often mental health professionals, health care practitioners, and social service clinicians feel ill prepared to assess and treat this phenomenon. This text is designed to practically transfer the growing empirically supported knowledge and evidence-based treatments to frontline professionals who will often encounter suicidal clients throughout their careers, and to educators teaching and training future clinicians. Although every suicide may not be predicted or prevented, empirical knowledge derived from current research can provide a deeper foundation for mental health professionals who encounter suicidal clients.

While suicide is the ultimate act we work to prevent, practitioners must also effectively intervene with nonfatal suicidal behaviors that occur with higher frequency. These include suicidal ideation or thoughts, intentional self-harm, and suicide attempts. Empirical research on suicidality indicates that nonfatal suicidal behaviors are often most effectively reduced via systematic focus and specialized intervention strategies. Knowledge of these strategies and evidence-based interventions is essential. This research-driven text provides empirically grounded knowledge on suicide identification, assessment, and evidence-based treatments with specific practical and clinically based learning tools and teaching exercises.

This text is designed to provide mental health students and professionals, health care practitioners, and social service clinicians with the essential empirically supported knowledge in the following areas: (1) incidence and prevalence rates of suicidal behaviors in various demographic and diagnostic groups; (2) ethical considerations and implications related to suicidality; (3) the significance of culture, race, and ethnicity on suicidal behaviors; (4) religious, spiritual, and philosophical influences on suicide; (5) risk and identification of suicidal behaviors across the life cycle (children/adolescents, adults, older adults); (6) suicide risk across major diagnostic categories; (7) the components of comprehensive suicide assessments; (8) evidence-based treatment interventions (i.e., crisis intervention, cognitive-behavioral therapy [CBT], dialectical behavior therapy [DBT], interpersonal psychotherapy [IPT]); (9) suicide across at-risk populations; and (10) the impact of suicide on survivors.

CONTENTS OF THIS BOOK

This text comprises 5 parts divided into 16 chapters. Part I, "Introduction," consists of three chapters exploring the roles and influences of ethics, philosophy, culture, race, ethnicity, and religion in relation to suicidality.

In chapter 1, "Ethical and Philosophical Issues in Suicide," ethical considerations and dilemmas related to suicidality are explored. Ethical and philosophical issues and concerns are addressed from multiple perspectives. Specific attention is given to the issues of philosophical perspectives related to suicide, rational suicide, suicide and the law, euthanasia and physician-assisted suicide, professional ethics and suicide, media and suicide ethics, and ethics in the aftermath of a client suicide. Personal and professional conflicts are explored.

Chapter 2, "The Role of Culture, Race, and Ethnicity in Suicide," explores culturally relevant risk and protective factors for suicide. Epidemiological data and contextual findings on suicidality across cultures and nations are presented. International perspectives on suicide risk and assessment is examined as well as the impact of immigration, acculturation, and assimilation on suicide risk. Treatment of suicidality from a culturally competent perspective is described, including differences in attitudes toward suicide and suicide acceptability across cultures.

A client's religious beliefs can impact suicidality. Chapter 3, "Religion and Suicide," intentionally focuses on the key risk and protective factors of religion as it relates to suicidality. An individual's degree of religiosity can potentially serve as a protective factor against suicidal behavior. In order to accurately identify and assess risk of suicide and to determine resources to modify and enhance treatment of suicidal individuals, it is imperative to understand and not ignore the role of religion in relation to suicidality. Perspectives and influences of Christianity, Islam, Hinduism, and Judaism on suicide are described and related to assessing and treating clients with suicidality.

Part II, "Evidence-Based Treatments," comprises five chapters. These chapters focus on assessment and evidence-based treatment from crisis intervention, cognitive-behavioral, dialectical behavioral, and interpersonal perspectives.

Assessment is the cornerstone of effective treatment for individuals with suicidality. Although there is no universal assessment format, there are a number of key components essential to every suicide assessment. Chapter 4, "Assessment," provides a comprehensive structure for assessing suicide risk, including specific questions and recommendations for consideration. Every individual presenting for clinical treatment should be assessed for risk of suicide. Suicide risk assessment must be individualized based on the person, presenting issues, and personal and family history.

Although the vast majority of individuals will experience a crisis at some point or points in their lives, most of these experiences do not result in suicidality. However, when an individual is experiencing a suicidal crisis, crisis intervention may be an appropriate treatment modality. Chapter 5, "Crisis Intervention and Suicide," presents a model of crisis intervention for suicidal individuals. Key stages and strategies are examined. Evidence regarding the effectiveness of crisis intervention is explored. Finally, recommendations for clinical practice when implementing crisis intervention are provided.

In chapter 6, "Cognitive-Behavioral Therapy and Suicide," the development and application of cognitive-behavioral therapy (CBT) in working with suicidality is presented. Core strategies and key techniques from this evidence-based approach are described. Research regarding the effectiveness of CBT for treating suicidality is reviewed.

Chapter 7, "Dialectical Behavior Therapy and Suicide," presents dialectical behavior therapy (DBT) as a treatment model to address suicidal individuals. The theory behind DBT and a thorough description of the key components and strategies are presented. Research examining the effectiveness of DBT across psychiatric disorders and settings is discussed. Lastly, recommendations for clinical practice when implementing DBT are provided.

Chapter 8, "Interpersonal Psychotherapy and Suicide," presents the interpersonal psychotherapy (IPT) approach and its preliminary adaptation as an emergent model of intervention with individuals experiencing suicidality. The core elements and strategies of IPT are examined, and evidence on the effectiveness of this evidence-based practice (EBP) is provided.

Part III, "Suicidality Across the Life Span," includes three chapters that explore suicidality in children and adolescents, adults, and older adults.

The rising rates of suicide attempts and completions in children and adolescents are a significant and growing concern. In order to work with child and adolescent suicidality it is important to understand the epidemiological trends, prevalence, and incident rates of child and adolescent suicidality. Chapter 9, "Child and Adolescent Suicide," investigates the identification of unique and common risk and protective factors to this younger population. In addition, this chapter deconstructs myths and misconceptions related to suicide among children and adolescents and explores the important developmental issues with this population.

Despite increased federal spending on suicide prevention, the overall number of suicides in the United States has remained consistent for several years. Furthermore, rates of suicide attempts and completions among adults continue to rise. It is important to understand the epidemiological trends, prevalence, and incident rates of adult suicidality. These issues are explored in chapter 10, "Adult Suicide." In addition, this chapter deconstructs myths and misconceptions related to suicide among adults.

Currently, older adults, often referred to as the elderly, in the United States have the highest rate of suicide. It is important to understand the epidemiological trends, prevalence, and incident rates of elderly suicidality. Chapter 11, "Older Adult Suicide," focuses on the identification of risk and protective factors unique to the aging population. This chapter also deconstructs myths and misconceptions related to suicide among the elderly.

Part IV, "Suicide and Mental Illness," centers on suicide across high-risk diagnostic categories. This section comprises three chapters examining psychotic disorders, mood disorders, and substance-related disorders.

In chapter 12, "Schizophrenia and Suicide," a focused review of the suicide risk associated with schizophrenia is provided. Special attention to suicide within schizophrenia is critical because the rate of suicide among individuals with schizophrenia is among the highest of all psychiatric illness, and the rate is increasing.

Chapter 13, "Depression and Suicide," continues to examine the relationship between psychiatric illness and risk of suicidality. Mood disorders are the most common psychiatric disorder associated with suicide.

Chapter 14, "Substance-Related Disorders and Suicide," examines the relationship between substance-related disorders and risk of suicidality. Substance use and abuse has been associated with increased risk of suicide attempt and completion. Diagnosed and undiagnosed substance-related disorders are very prevalent in society.

Part V, "Special Populations," highlights suicide among at-risk groups and pays special attention to survivors of suicide.

Several diverse and unique groups within society are at an elevated risk for suicidality. These at-risk groups are frequently isolated from the larger society, either through stigma, being disenfranchised, separateness, exclusion, or due to sociodemographic characteristics. Although a number of at-risk populations exist, chapter 15, "At-Risk Groups," focuses on the following: military personnel; Native Americans; lesbian, gay, bisexual, transgendered/transsexual, and queer/questioning (LGBTQ) persons; the homeless; and incarcerated individuals. The prevalence of risk for each of these populations is highlighted as compared to the larger societal norms. In addition, the population-specific risk and protective factors from evidence-based research are presented.

Finally, Chapter 16, "Survivors of Suicide," explores the impact of completed suicide on family survivors. An understanding of the grief process for this unique group is outlined. Family members are not the only survivors; clinical professionals are also dramatically impacted by the death of a client. A review of the impact and influence of a client suicide on treating clinicians and an examination of important professional considerations following a client suicide is explored.

FEATURES OF THIS BOOK

Throughout the text, several recurring features offer readers a chance to better understand and apply the material with their students, or in their own clinical practice.

- Each chapter begins with a clear set of *Goals and Objectives* that will be covered within that chapter.

- *Individual Exercises* allow readers to consider their personal reactions to the material under discussion and how those reactions might impact their clinical practice.
- *Small Group Exercises* encourage readers to compare their own reactions with others and discuss why and how differences may arise.
- *Case Examples* depict realistic client scenarios that readers may encounter in practice, followed by questions for discussion.
- *Role Plays* offer readers a chance to act out the common (and often difficult) conversations and scenarios that may arise when working with suicidal clients.
- *Key Points* at the end of each chapter summarize the primary issues covered within that chapter.
- *Further Readings* offer a list of additional materials (books, articles, etc.) that complement or add to that which is discussed in the text.
- *Electronic Resources* offer a wide variety of useful Web sites for further information.
- *Knowledge Acquisition Tests* in each chapter offer readers a chance to confirm their comprehension of the material. Each test includes true or false, short answer, and multiple choice questions. The answers are available in the Instructor's Manual. Qualified instructors may e-mail textbook@springerpub.com to request a copy.

In addition to the answer keys, the Instructor's Manual includes sample syllabi, PowerPoint presentations, and other resources for professors who would like to integrate this textbook into a course.

In summary, this text offers readers comprehensive, empirically grounded knowledge regarding suicidality. It is our hope that it provides a strong foundation for mental health professionals and students who may encounter and work with suicidal clients and those interested in this area. It is essential to recognize that this text does not take the place of effective supervision and training, but it can serve as a useful, practical clinical reference.

Introduction

Suicidal behavior is a complex phenomenon that resonates across societal and individual ethics, philosophies, cultures, ethnicities, and religions. It is important for practitioners to consider the influences and implications of the larger systems and contexts in which individual clients function and reside. Part I specifically focuses on how these larger factors relate to suicidal behavior and how they inform clinical practice and treatment. These factors are often overlooked in the assessment and treatment of suicidal individuals. However, the three chapters in Part I illustrate why it is imperative to have a clear awareness of these issues.

Chapter 1, "Ethical and Philosophical Issues in Suicide," examines the important role of ethical considerations and dilemmas related to client suicidality and clinical assessment and treatment. Chapter 2, "The Role of Culture, Race, and Ethnicity in Suicide," highlights how culture, race, and ethnicity can serve as both risk and protective factors for suicide, and it emphasizes treating suicidality from a culturally competent perspective. Chapter 3, "Religion and Suicide," considers the differential impact of Christianity, Islam, Hinduism, and Judaism as they relate to suicidal behavior, assessment, and treatment.

The issues raised in Part I are complex and can be challenging to discuss and explore. However, it is essential for a practitioner to consider not only how these factors impact their clients but also how they inform the manner in which the practitioner experiences, views, and understands the world as this directly influences suicide assessment and treatment.

1

Ethical and Philosophical Issues in Suicide

Ethical considerations and dilemmas related to suicidality are explored in this chapter. Ethical and philosophical issues and concerns are addressed from multiple perspectives. Specific attention is given to the issues of philosophical perspectives related to suicide, rational suicide, suicide and the law, euthanasia and physician-assisted suicide, professional ethics and suicide, media and suicide ethics, and ethics in the aftermath of a client suicide. Personal and professional conflicts are included.

◼ Goals and Objectives of This Chapter

An understanding of:

- The importance of personal ethical, moral, and value beliefs in clinical practice
- The meaning of rational suicide
- The practitioners' legal and ethical responsibilities
- Professional standards of care
- The four types of euthanasia: passive, active, voluntary, and involuntary
- Implications of physician-assisted suicide (PAS)
- Professional ethical principles of autonomy or self-determination, informed consent, duty to protect, beneficence, nonmaleficence, and confidentiality
- The role of the media in suicidality

■ The ethical issues related to professional performance following the suicide of a client
■ The importance of ethics

INTRODUCTION

What do you think, feel, or believe when considering the concept of suicide? Your ethical, moral, and philosophical conceptualization of suicide will have direct and indirect influence on your clinical practice. Suicide is conceptualized across a spectrum. Suicide has been considered noble, an important freedom, as well as unacceptable, morally wrong, an indication of mental illness, a crime, and an offense against God (Mishna, Antle, & Regehr, 2002). In working with the suicidality of individuals it is essential to candidly consider and openly understand your own ethical, moral, and valued beliefs relating to suicide and the impact of these thoughts and attitudes on your own practice.

These questions could remain relegated to a hypothetical, theoretical, or intellectual argument if suicide or suicide attempts were uncommon events rarely experienced by practitioners in their clinical practice. Although it is hoped that suicides are scarce and all can be prevented, the reality is these beliefs are myths. A few studies have begun to research the phenomenon of client suicides. In survey research, 35% of social workers, 86% of community mental health teams, 46% to 67% of psychiatrists, and 22% to 40% of psychologists have reported experiencing one or more patient suicides (Alexander, Klein, Gray, Dewar, & Eagles, 2000; Chemtob, Hamada, Bauer, Kinney, & Torigoe, 1988; Chemtob, Hamada, Bauer, Torigoe, & Kinney, 1988; Kleespies, 1993; Linke, Wojciak, & Day, 2002; Ruskin, Sakinofsky, Bagby, Dickens, & Sousa, 2004).

Research has also found that experiencing a client suicide during professional training is common (Coverdale, Roberts, & Louie, 2007; Dewar, Eagles, Klein, Gray, & Alexander, 2000; Kleespies, 1993; Ruskin et al., 2004). Consequently, it is fundamentally important to be aware of your ethical and philosophical beliefs, conceptualizations, and individual positions, as well as the direct and indirect impact of these beliefs on your practice.

■ Individual Exercise 1.1

1. Develop a list of your personal values and beliefs as they relate to suicide. In considering this list, do you feel people close to you (e.g., colleagues, peers, family) would see these values and beliefs in you?

2. How do you think your values and beliefs influence your clinical practice, both positively and negatively?

Can Suicide Ever be Considered an Acceptable Action?

Can suicide be an act of competency, or does every suicide demonstrate a client's inability to be competent (Pinch & Dougherty, 1993)? Do individuals ever have a right to die by ending their own life? Can suicide or suicide intervention be moral (Lester & Leenaars, 1996)? When, if ever, is suicide ethically acceptable? What is our professional duty to protect a client from himself or herself? Although each practitioner will have different ethical positions on these questions, such questions raise some important ethical and practical considerations.

PHILOSOPHICAL PERSPECTIVES RELATED TO SUICIDE

There are two dominant philosophical paradigms in suicidality: the Kantian and Utilitarian perspectives (Hill, 1983; Maris, Berman, & Silverman, 2000; Mayo, 1984; Regan, 1983). According to the **Kantian perspective**, a person is a rational agent with autonomy of will, and suicide is a violation of one's duty to himself or herself (Maris et al., 2000). Therefore, any agent or individual who commits suicide is acting in violation of the moral law and his/her duty to protect him/herself (Brassington, 2006; Maris et al., 2000).

The **Utilitarian perspective** considers the consequences of the suicide, including the impact on family members, others, and larger society, in determining the moral or ethical judgment of the action (Maris et al., 2000; Mayo, 1984). A client's suicide that reduces pain or suffering to self and others may be morally acceptable; however, if the suicide causes more harm than good, the act is construed as morally wrong.

These philosophical perspectives are generally considered in opposition; many clients, family members, and practitioners have adopted one approach. In clinically practicing with suicidal clients, how does your philosophical stance impact your work?

▨ Individual Exercise 1.2

1. Which philosophical perspective, Kantian or Utilitarian, resonates more with your personal values and beliefs?
2. Which philosophical perspective, Kantian or Utilitarian, resonates more with your professional values and beliefs?
3. How may your personal and professional philosophical perspectives conflict?

RATIONAL SUICIDE

Individuals often argue that suicide is morally wrong and that allowing an individual to suicide or failing to prevent suicide is no different from killing that individual (Donagan, 1977; Hendin, 1982; Heyd & Bloch, 1999; Schwyn, 1976). Such individuals would argue that under no circumstances is suicide an acceptable solution. Furthermore, suicide is generally thought of as an act committed by irrational individuals affected by psychiatric illness or under the influence of an illicit substance. Several studies, in fact, showed that as many as 90% of those studied who committed suicide were mentally ill at their time of death (Barraclough, Bunch, Nelson, & Salisbury, 1974; Brent et al., 1993; Hendin, 1982; Isometsa et al., 1995; Kaplan & Harrow, 1996; Robins, 1981; Strakowski, McElroy, Keck, & West, 1996). Additionally, research indicates that there tends to be a great deal of ambivalence among individuals who attempt suicide (Daigle, 2005; Erazo, Baumert, & Ladwig, 2005; Litman, 1996; Lynch, Cheavens, Morse, & Rosenthal, 2004) and that a suicide attempt is often a means to communicate a problem (Lizardi et al., 2007; Paris, 2002; World Health Organization [WHO], 2007). Is it not imperative, then, to intervene in every instance of attempted suicide given the chances that mental illness may have influenced the decision to commit the suicidal act or the chance that some ambivalence may be present in the individual? Should we not explore the ambivalence and support problem-solving and coping skills?

Despite the evidence, some still argue that suicide may actually be a rational decision and should be a matter of individual choice (Brock, 1985; Fintzy, 1993; Leeman, 2004; Maris, 1982; Motto, 1999; Szasz, 1999; Werth, 1999). The case of Nico Speijers is often referred to exemplify the concept of **rational suicide**. In 1981, Speijers, a suicidologist and suicide prevention advocate, committed suicide. He left behind a suicide note expressing his decision to end his life in the face of terminal illness and debilitating pain. Speijers had just the year prior published a book *Aiding Suicide* (1980), detailing circumstances under which suicide should not be prevented (Motto, 1999). These conditions include when:

1. The decision to commit suicide is not made under pressure but rather as a result of free will
2. The individual is suffering from unbearable pain with no relief expected

3. The wish to end one's life is ongoing
4. The individual is competent at the time the decision is made
5. No unnecessary or preventable harm to others is caused by the act
6. The helper should be a qualified health practitioner or MD if drugs are utilized
7. The helper should seek advice/consultation from colleagues
8. The process of the suicide should be documented and the documents submitted to the proper authorities

Are these conditions sufficient to suggest that intervention should not be taken when a client expresses suicidality? Who should decide the answers to these questions, the client or the practitioner? In considering the concept of rational suicide it is imperative to understand the legality of suicide and one's legal responsibility as a helping professional. Further review of one's professional code of ethics should also contribute to answering these questions.

■ Case Example 1.1

As a mental health clinician within the crisis team in a large and busy urban hospital, you are frequently called into the emergency department to conduct mental health assessments. After being paged to the emergency room (ER), the attending physician informs you that the referred patient has been medically cleared after a significant overdose attempt. The patient, a 64-year-old male, has no prior reported psychiatric history or past suicide attempts. The attempt would have been lethal if his adult daughter and son-in-law, with whom he resides, had not unexpectedly returned home early from visiting friends in a nearby town and discovered the patient unresponsive in his room wearing a suit. Beside him on his nightstand were sealed letters to each of his family members, his organized bank records, and his will. The ER doctor noted that the patient is stable and oriented. He has slept off the effects of the overdose and charcoal he received upon admission. His blood results are fine, and his toxicology report is clear with no trace of alcohol or illicit narcotics.

In reading his medical chart and receiving a more complete update from the attending physician and ER nurse, you learned that the patient has a chronic and deteriorating pain condition. The patient has managed his condition for 21 years. Over the years, his ability to work or engage in functions of daily living has continued to worsen. He is now on exceptionally strong pain medications and can rarely manage to leave his room to eat, watch television, or interact with his family. His condition is terminal and will continue to decline, perhaps for many years. His constant level of pain will continue to escalate. His wife passed away 8 years earlier due to cancer, at which time he moved in with his daughter and her family. The ER nurse stated that the patient, Lee, is a nice and gentle man in a tremendous amount of physical pain. The doctor noted that Lee is a very strong and dignified individual to have managed his pain this well over the years. Also, the doctor stated that beyond his pain condition he was in good health and expected to live for many more years, but the doctor did think he would have to be placed in a nursing home within a year. The doctor noted that if the patient had not been brought into the hospital, he would not have survived another hour or two without treatment.

In the examination room, you find Lee lying in a hospital bed but sitting up with his hair combed, gently talking to his adult daughter, who is sitting in a bedside chair. After introducing yourself and describing your role of conducting an assessment, the daughter, Karen, accounts how her father has always been a strong and independent person until recently. She recounts finding him yesterday after returning early from visiting friends. She noted how fortunate it was that her friend's son had become very ill during their visit, resulting in her and her husband coming home hours before they had intended. Both report that he has never attempted suicide nor experienced any psychiatric or mental health problems. While it is clear that he is in pain, Lee contributes to the assessment. After a few minutes, Lee states in a quite voice how much he loves his daughter and her family and then requests continuing the assessment alone. Karen, holding back tears, kisses her father on his forehead and leaves the room.

Lee states that he had fully intended to die and was disheartened that his daughter had returned unexpectedly early and found him. In fact, he had carefully planned his death for nearly 3 months. He describes suicide as a morally and personally repugnant idea, but it was best for everyone. Twenty-one years ago, when he was diagnosed with his condition, he knew this moment would come. Over the years, he struggled to maintain a normal and productive life, but with each year his condition deteriorated and his pain increased.

When his wife was diagnosed with cancer, they had agreed that he would continue to support their children and grandchildren until he became a burden. After she died, he noted he wanted to end his life, but he insisted on honoring his wife's request to support and care for the family. Four months ago his treating doctor had informed him that he would soon have to be placed in an expensive nursing home. Also, his pain medications, which were becoming increasingly stronger, were no longer blocking much of the pain. Recently, his daughter spoke of quitting her job to take better care of him. Lee stated that she had her own family, and while he loved his daughter and her family, it was time for him to die. Lee stated that he understood your job was to assess him and prevent his suicide. He agreed to accept any treatment options; however, he also noted that regardless of what you planned he would quietly and effectively complete suicide over the next few weeks.

1. Is this an example of rational suicide? Why or why not?
2. Which of Speijers' eight conditions of rational suicide are present in this case example?
3. What action would you take as the professional practitioner in this case example?

4. Would your stance in regard to Lee change if you were his friend? If so, how?
5. Would your personal ethics, values, and beliefs create any potential dilemmas in regard to your professional obligation?
6. How would you support this practitioner if you were his or her supervisor?

■ Role Play 1.1

Using case example 1.1 of Lee, engage in a role play in which you would propose and present a discharge plan and treatment options to Lee.

SUICIDE AND THE LAW

The past 20 years have seen a dramatic shift in malpractice lawsuits regarding suicide from largely focusing on inpatient institutions and practitioners toward an overrepresentation of lawsuits against outpatient practitioners (Jobes & Berman, 1993; Litman, 1982). As a practitioner, it is critical to be aware of the legal and ethical responsibilities related to the role of practitioner, particularly concerning malpractice liability (Feldman, Moritz, & Benjamin, 2005).

Determining Liability

Regardless of personal values or ethics, practitioners are legally expected to actively prevent suicide of a client. Practitioners are expected to uphold their standard of care or duty to care, which includes making reasonable efforts to prevent suicide of a client. The standard of care is legally defined as the duty to employ the degree of skill and care as would be used by a typical practitioner in a similar circumstance (Gutheil, 1992; Jobes & Berman, 1993).

The act of suicide is nearly impossible to predict, and as such, negligence is deemed more than simply a failure to predict suicide. Four key elements must be present for a claim of malpractice to be supported. These are: (1) the presence of a professional relationship, (2) a violation of the standard of care, (3) the violation resulting in damages or harm, and (4) a direct causal relationship between the practitioner's omissions and the suicidal act of the client (Berman, 2006; Bongar, 2002; Bongar & Greaney, 1994; Cantor & McDermott, 1994).

In malpractice suits, the standard of care is evaluated retrospectively via review of clinical records and available testimony. There are several areas that are considered failures of the standard of care that can result in a practitioner being held liable for malpractice (Bongar, Maris, Berman, & Litman, 1992; Gutheil, 1992; Waltzer, 1980). These include failures to

1. Assess risk (this is the most obvious violation of the standard of care).
2. Keep accurate, up-to-date records.
3. Assess for suicide risk at time of the last professional contact.
4. Conduct or refer client for a psychological evaluation.
5. Secure records from prior psychiatric treatment.
6. Develop an adequate treatment plan.
7. Provide adequate treatment.
8. Refer to inpatient hospitalization, voluntarily or involuntarily, when indicated.
9. Protect patient from known danger to self.
10. Possess the training, knowledge, and skill necessary to treat and assess for suicidality.

Recommendations to Minimize Risk of Malpractice

Essential guidelines have developed as a result of the proliferation of suicide malpractice lawsuits in outpatient care settings (Bongar, 1991). Key recommendations that should not be overlooked include:

1. Conduct an assessment of suicide risk with every patient. As suicidal behavior cannot be predicted, no client can be determined to be free of risk without a thorough assessment.
2. Maintain comprehensive records. A lack of documentation can be damaging to a practitioner's defense because there will be no evidence of the standard of care he or she maintained in respect to the client's treatment.
3. Seek records from the client's prior treatment experiences. Proper assessment of suicide risk must include consideration of prior suicidal behavior. Relying on a client's personal report of suicide history is insufficient when it has been established that prior treatment existed.
4. Suicide risk is increased in offspring of individuals with psychiatric illness and a history of suicidality (Brent et al., 1994; Gould, Fisher, Parides, Flory, & Shaffer, 1996; Kovacs, Obrosky, Gatsonis, & Rich-

ards, 1997; Schulsinger, Kety, Rosenthal, & Wender, 1979; Tsuang, 1983; Weissman, Fendrich, Warner, & Wickramaratne, 1992; Wender et al., 1986). Thus, proper evaluation of a client's risk for suicide should include an assessment of the client's history of mental disorders and psychiatric hospitalization.

5. Establish relevant *Diagnostic and Statistical Manual of Mental Disorders* (4th ed.; *DSM-IV*) diagnoses. There is a differential risk of suicide associated with psychiatric illnesses (see Part IV in this book). Comprehensive assessment of *DSM-IV* psychiatric disorder will shed light on the degree of suicide risk in relation to other psychosocial characteristics with which the client presents.

■ Small Group Exercise 1.1

1. In groups of four to five, use case example 1.2 (later in the chapter) to discuss whether the prescribing physician could be considered liable for malpractice.
2. What violations of the standards of care (listed previously) might apply?
3. If you were a mental health practitioner on the physician's team, what steps could you have engaged in to prevent Sam's action?

EUTHANASIA AND PHYSICIAN-ASSISTED SUICIDE (PAS)

There are four types of euthanasia: passive, active, voluntary, and involuntary. **Passive euthanasia** involves the withdrawal or withholding of artificial life support or medical treatments that may prolong life; whereas **active euthanasia** is an act taken to shorten life (Smokowski & Wodarski, 1996). An individual requesting assistance from anyone in ending their life is **voluntary euthanasia**; however, intentionally causing the death of an individual, whether, competent, incompetent, or unaware, without **informed consent** or explicit request is considered **involuntary euthanasia** (Csikai, 1999). Only passive euthanasia is widely accepted by health care practitioners, family members, society, and the law. **Physician-assisted suicide (PAS)** is the provision of suicidal means, such as prescribed medications, to an individual who is otherwise able to suicide (Csikai, 1999; Smokowski & Wodarski, 1996). If a physician administers the lethal dose following the request of the patient, this is considered active voluntary euthanasia (Smokowski & Wodarski, 1996).

Euthanasia, PAS, and the Law

In 1997, the U.S. Supreme Court unanimously ruled (*Washington v Glucksberg*; *Vaccpo v Quill*) that there is neither a constitutional prohibition nor a constitutional right to euthanasia and physician-assisted suicide (Breitbart & Rosenfeld, 1999; Emanuel, 2002). The 9th and the 2nd U.S. Circuit Courts of Appeals in Washington State and New York State have also ruled in lawsuits brought before them that laws prohibiting PAS are unconstitutional (Drickamer, Lee, & Ganzini, 1997). In 1998, Oregon passed the Death with Dignity Act legalizing PAS for state residents with a terminal illness who voluntarily request this action (Quill, Meier, Block, & Billings, 1998; Sullivan, Hedberg, & Fleming, 2000).

Euthanasia, PAS, and Attitudes

Allen and colleagues (2006) found that Americans supported euthanasia and PAS in their analysis of opinion polls between 1936 and 2002. Since 1973, when asked "when a person has a disease that cannot be cured, do you think doctors should be allowed by law to end the patient's life by some painless means if the patient and his family request it?" the majority of polled Americans supported this position (Allen et al., 2006). In a similar survey study among terminally ill patients and their caregivers, a majority supported PAS, but only a small proportion seriously considered taking such action (Emanuel, Fairclough, & Emanuel, 2000). However, it is important to note that the condition or illness that the client is managing will dramatically impact one's attitude. For example, would your personal or professional ethical stance change if the client has a terminal illness, HIV/AIDS, schizophrenia, or depression?

Not relegated to public opinion, the debate over euthanasia and PAS has been waged for many decades across a number of fields, including, but not limited to, medicine, health care, mental health, individual rights, human rights, religion, professional codes of ethics, and the law. Each practitioner holds very specific ethical considerations in regards to euthanasia and PAS. Health care and mental health practitioners may face a number of ethical dilemmas stemming from clients considering euthanasia and PAS and should be aware of these issues and their own personal ethics and values. What you believe will directly and indirectly impact your practice. For example, in a survey on the attitudes of nurses, 75% personally feel that PAS may be justified in select cases, but only 46% would be willing to participate if PAS was legalized (Kowalski,

1997). A similar survey with U.S. oncologists found that a willingness to perform PAS was lower than the support for the procedure (Emanuel, Fairclough, Clarridge, et al., 2000; Hilden et al., 2001).

Individual Exercise 1.3

1. Do you agree with the law regarding PAS? Why or why not?
2. Would you participate in PAS? Why or why not?

Euthanasia, PAS, and Guidelines for Ethical Practice

Many mental health professional organizations, such as the American Psychiatric Association, American Psychological Association, National Association of Social Workers, and American Counseling Association, are beginning to develop guidelines for members working with clients considering PAS (Werth, 1999). However, each organization has a different perspective on addressing these ethical issues. It is important to understand the professional stance of your governing body.

For example, the National Association of Social Workers (NASW) Code of Ethics (2000), Standard 1.02 states that social workers have a responsibility to help clients assert their rights of self-determination (NASW, 1999). According to Mackelprang and Mackelprang (2005), this "suggests that, for terminally ill people who are capable of making decisions, the ethical responsibility to promote self-determination outweighs the social workers' responsibilities to avoid harm" (p. 321). While self-determination is a primary principle, Csikai (1999) iterates that social workers "must be well informed of and comply with the laws of their states concerning end-of-life decisions, including living wills, durable powers of attorney for health care, and laws concerning physician assisted suicide" (pp. 55–56). NASW also dictates that social workers should discuss all options to clients and families in end-of-life situations (Csikai, 1999).

However, the NASW does not articulate clear procedures or guidance for when social workers should become involved or not with terminally ill clients (Allen et al., 2006). Consequently, in working with terminally ill patients considering PAS, social workers may need, at minimum, to: (1) understand the implications of their own personal ethics; (2) determine informed consent; (3) assess the client's self-determination and their individual and family's wishes; (4) review all options with client and family; (5) work with the larger health care team; (5) consult with their supervisor, professional organization, and workplace policy and procedures; (6) understand the laws governing their state; and, if necessary, (7) consult with legal counsel.

PROFESSIONAL ETHICS AND SUICIDE

Clearly, the law overwhelmingly obliges practitioners to intervene to prevent suicidal acts. Professional values, those we accept when we choose to enter a profession, serve as yet another guideline for proper behavior that practitioners are expected to follow. Professional codes of ethics define a practitioner's ethical obligations as helping professionals. Ethical codes consist of multiple principles that serve to protect a client (Rosenbluth, Kleinman, & Lowy, 1995; Wagle, Ede, Craig, & Bottum, 2004) and to guide a practitioner through times of conflict involving morals, values, and beliefs (Sasson, 2000). While differences exist, the fundamental principles proposed by the main codes of ethics of the helping professions (social work, psychology, psychiatry, and medicine) share several fundamental features. The ethical principles most relevant when considering a suicidal patient include **autonomy** or self-determination, informed consent, **duty to protect**, **confidentiality**, **beneficence**, and **nonmaleficence**.

Autonomy

Autonomy is one of the foremost principles that affect a practitioner's course of action regarding a suicidal client. The principle of self-determination involves the client's right to take action rooted in their own goals, desires, and wishes (Reamer, 1983). Suicide often occurs in those with mental illness. Thus, granting autonomy to individuals to act on suicidal thoughts and/or feelings is considered, by some, to be allowing a noncompetent individual to make life-threatening decisions. Respecting one's individual rights might be better served by recognizing their vulnerability and strengthening their resources. In fact, the NASW Code of Ethics (1999) permits social workers to limit client self-determination when their action or potential actions pose a serious, foreseeable, and imminent risk to themselves or to others.

Informed Consent

The principle of autonomy grows directly out of the doctrine of informed consent, having competent understanding of risks, benefits, and alternatives from which a client can make a decision regarding an appropriate course of action (Beauchamp, 1999). The process of informed consent recognizes the importance of autonomy, of individuals making their own decisions (Bell & Clark, 1998). Prevention of suicide is ethically justified by suggesting that the suicidal person is not competent to give informed consent and to make decisions regarding their care (Chadwick & Tadd, 1992) because suicidal behavior is considered to be the by-product of mental illness (Barraclough et al., 1974; Brent et al., 1993; Chadwick & Tadd, 1992; Hendin, 1982; Isometsa et al., 1995; Kaplan & Harrow, 1996; Robins, 1981; Strakowski et al., 1996).

Duty to Protect

In entering a therapeutic relationship with a client, practitioners accept certain responsibilities, including the duty to protect the client from harming himself or herself (Packman & Harris, 1998; Welfel, 2002; Werth & Rogers, 2005). However, how practitioners understand this duty to protect when a client is at risk of self-harm or suicidality varies considerably. It has been argued that practitioners should always intervene to protect when a client raises possibility of self-harm or suicide (Elitzur, 1995). Conversely, psychiatrist Thomas Szasz forwarded the position that clients have a right to decide for themselves whether they wish to die without the protection and intervention of a practitioner (Maris et al., 2000).

Clearly, how one ethically or professionally interprets this duty to protect is interpretable. Werth and Rogers (2005) have provided some guidelines for the determination of this duty. Specifically, they propose: (1) that this duty should apply when a client is engaging in serious self-harm or death within a short period of time, and (2) the best method to protect is to assess for impaired judgment and apply appropriate treatment interventions.

Confidentiality

Confidentiality is a major area for practitioners as far as suicide is concerned. Most codes of ethics require a practitioner to breach confidentiality if the client represents a danger to themselves or others. Therapists are ethically, and in all states legally, obligated to disclose if the client is homicidal. The responsibility of protecting individuals from harm that may be inflicted by another individual does not frequently pose as an ethical dilemma. However, breaching confidentiality when one poses a threat to him/herself, as is the case with suicide, often results in an ethical conflict (Rosenbluth et al., 1995; Wagle et al., 2004). In these instances, the principles of beneficence and nonmaleficence can guide the practitioner.

Beneficence

This principle represents the concept of doing the greatest good possible. Practitioners have an ethical responsibility to strive for the well-being of clients. Beneficence should take precedence over autonomy as the death of an individual would not generally be considered a "good" action (Rosenbluth et al., 1995; Wagle et al., 2004).

Nonmaleficence

Practitioners have a legal and ethical obligation to protect clients from harm. The principle of nonmaleficence, minimizing or preventing harm, requires a practitioner to take whatever action necessary to prevent a client from taking his own life.

The practitioner is obligated to work toward the improvement of a client's quality of life and well-being, and this responsibility often conflicts with a client's ability to be independent and make decisions about their own lives. Such is the case with a suicidal client. Practitioners often find themselves in a paternalistic position (Abramson, 1985; Kelly, 1994). Reamer (1983) provides a framework for making ethical decisions in times of conflict, particularly regarding the conflict between supporting or limiting one's autonomy. He suggests that while social workers should carefully avoid excessive intrusion into the lives of clients, paternalism may be justified in certain circumstances. These circumstances include when: (1) harmful consequences may result from supporting a client's autonomy that may be irreversible; (2) placing temporary restrictions may potentially generate a wider degree of freedom for the client; and (3) the immediate need to rescue a client from harm exists. Suicidal behavior certainly would fall among these categories. Understanding fully one's responsibilities as dictated by law and one's professional code of ethics can guide a practitioner to take action to prevent a client from acting on suicidal impulses and to feel justified in doing so.

▩ Individual Exercise 1.4

1. Rank in order the ethical principles (autonomy or self-determination, informed consent, duty to protect, beneficence, nonmaleficence, and confidentiality) that are most important to least important?
2. Justify your ordering of the ethical principles.

■ Case Example 1.2

Samantha, who prefers to go by Sam, is a 46-year-old White, female widow with no prior psychiatric history. She was admitted to the adult inpatient psychiatry unit of an urban hospital following an attempted suicide. As the social worker on the unit, your role is to conduct meetings with the client and her family about the factors that led up to her inpatient admission. Prior to scheduling a meeting with significant others in Sam's life, you meet with Sam to conduct an assessment to further understand Sam's presenting situation and to determine who would be the most appropriate to invite to a family session. Sam has been on the unit for less than a day when you meet with her in the small interview room on the unit. She is disheveled, makes poor eye contact, and is hesitant to meet with you. After describing your role, Sam's first words to you are, "You've got the wrong gal. I have no one to ask to come to meet with you." Upon further exploration you learn the following:

Sam was an only child. Her parents, now deceased, were her closet friends growing up. Her mother, Anne, a stay-at-home mom, and her father, Benjamin, a tailor, were loving, warm, supportive, hard-working individuals. Sam was encouraged to be hard-working and to value the importance of an education. Neither Sam's mother nor father had attended college, and Sam was groomed to be the first in the family who would do so. Sam, in fact, was very dedicated to her studies and, despite the fact that she held a job, managed to graduate from college in 3 years. College was a very happy time in Sam's life. She recalls having a full social network. College is also where she met Richard, her future husband. Richard was Sam's first serious boyfriend. He was an artist and her complete opposite. She adored Richard and felt he was the "love of her life."

After college, Sam got a job in an investment banking firm. While she did not receive an MBA, she managed to work her way up through the company to the position of Managing Director and earned nearly a million dollars a year. Richard continued with his art. It came as a great surprise to Sam when Richard informed her that he had a "once in a lifetime job opportunity" to run a small art gallery in the Southwest. They knew no one there, and Sam would have to leave her job. It would be the first time in 32 years she would be unemployed. While the idea was scary, she would do anything to support Richard. The move was the "greatest thing that could have happened." Sam, for the first time in her life, felt truly at ease. She decided not to find a job and instead developed her own hobby, literature. Sam became an avid reader and even dabbled at writing.

Sam and Richard lived a very quiet life. They never had any children and never felt like they were missing out on anything, "We were all we needed." They never made any close friends in the town they moved to, but that was also not something they missed. Sam felt they had the "perfect life. But perfect never lasts."

Five years after they moved, Richard became ill and was diagnosed with a terminal illness. The doctors gave him 2–3 years to live, but the illness progressed rapidly and within 8 months of his diagnosis he died. Sam "died that day too." She never recovered from his death, which, at the time of admission, was 2 years earlier. She moved back to the city they had left 7 years prior, but she could not manage to get a job or make any friends. She lived a solitary life; the life built around Richard was gone. She struggled for 2 years to make meaning out of his death and to figure out what she "was being punished for." She could no longer find a reason to live.

Three weeks prior to her admission, Sam decided she would end her life. She came up with an elaborate plan. She went to the dentist and complained of terrible sensitivity to pain in one of her teeth, where she was informed that she needed a root canal. After having the procedure, she saved up the prescribed pain medication. A week later, she called her physician to explain that she had just had a root canal and that her dentist was out of town for the next week but that she continued to experience severe pain. Her doctor prescribed pain medication on the condition that Sam see her dentist upon his return from vacation. She then spent the next week paying all of her bills, reviewing photos of her husband, and mailing his art work to the gallery in the Southwest. Sam became at ease with the idea that her life was going to end and felt she would finally be reunited with Richard. The night prior to her admission, she overdosed on pain medications.

Sam's well-planned suicide would have been successful had her superintendent not entered her apartment to check for a suspected leak in Sam's bathroom. Sam does not regret her attempted suicide and is "angry" that the super interrupted her. She understands that some may find suicide to be the "easy way out," but she feels it "is the only thing that makes sense." Sam explains that there is no one she can call on to attend a family session because "the only people she ever cared about are dead." She understands that medication and therapy can make some people feel better but feels strongly that she has "nothing to feel better about so why bother." She is unwilling to comply with the treatment team's decision to begin medication, and a decision has to be made as to whether or not to seek court-ordered treatment to medicate her against her will.

1. Should a court order mandating treatment be obtained? Why or why not?
2. What professional values and ethics guide your decision?
3. How would your personal ethics, values, and beliefs influence your decision?
4. How can you support Sam's right to self-determination and informed consent while still upholding your professional responsibilities?

■ Role Play 1.2

Using case example 1.2 of Sam, engage in a role play in which you would present the possibility of court-ordered mandated treatment to Sam. One participant plays the role of Sam; the other plays the role of a mental health practitioner discussing the treatment.

MEDIA AND SUICIDE ETHICS

Can a newspaper article, television news story, or video clip on the Internet cause or encourage an individual to attempt suicide? In and of itself, reading or viewing a story about someone else attempting or committing suicide is generally not sufficient to cause an individual to attempt suicide (WHO, 2000). However, research informs us that if an individual has a preexisting vulnerability to suicide, such as a mental illness, he or she may be more sensitive to suicide reporting and may be more inclined to attempt suicide as the result of exposure to a suicide report (Etzersdorfer & Sonneck, 1998; Pirkis & Blood, 2001). Research has also indicated an increase in the rate of suicide as suicide reports in newspapers and television increase (Motto, 1967; Motto, 1970; Phillips, 1974, 1982; Wasserman, 1984). In particular, researchers found a substantial increase of the number of suicides within the 10 days following the highlighting of a suicide in television news. What then is the ethical responsibility of the media in regard to suicide? Can editorial freedom cross the line into an ethical violation?

Clearly, in an era dominated by 24-hour news, the Internet, and Webcasts the media plays a crucial role in the transfer of knowledge. How the media reports information and transfers knowledge has become a source of much contention, particularly as it relates to reports of suicide in both newspapers and television. Concerns center on the detailed accounts of suicide events (attempted suicide and completed suicide) and the fear that such reports will motivate vulnerable individuals to copy those events, often referred to as the contagion or Werther effect (Alvarez, 1975; Phillips, 1974). There is a fear that, in an attempt to grab readers, sensational headlines, photos of the deceased, and glorified accounts of death may lead to more unnecessary deaths by suicide (Blood & Pirkis, 2007; Motto, 1970; Wasserman, 1984). Additionally, in the rush to meet deadlines and put out a story, information may be presented as fact that has not actually been confirmed. Are these ethical violations or just detailed news required in an increasingly competitive market?

The effect of media is not limited to newspapers and television. In this ever-growing electronic era, the impact of the Internet is undeniable (Alao, Soderberg, Pohl, & Alao, 2006; Baume, Cantor, & Rolfe, 1997). Web sites posting specific instructions on how to attempt suicide by various means can be found in multiples. With a simple click of a mouse, an individual can be led to a Web page that accurately describes how to end ones life. Evidence-based research on the influence of the Internet on suicide attempt risk is limited but should be the focus of future research as the Internet continues grow and its influence expands to new and younger audiences.

According to the WHO, minimizing media reporting of suicide is one of its key strategies for suicide prevention. This has prompted several countries to develop media reporting guidelines. The media is in a position to decrease the incidence of tragic deaths due to suicide by reporting suicide in an appropriate and accurate manner (WHO, 2000). Furthermore, the media can report on the warning signs for suicide and convey the means for seeking help. This suggests that when reports of suicide do not follow these guidelines, ethical boundaries are in fact being crossed because the reason for the reporting has shifted from conveying matters of public interest to vying for customers.

Guidelines for Ethical Suicide Reporting in the Media

Professionals in the media should avoid suicide reporting in a manner that could potentially have a negative impact on vulnerable individuals. Several main principals have been proposed as guidelines to follow for ethical reporting of suicide. These include avoiding:

1. Sensationalizing headlines
2. Description of the means employed in the suicide event
3. Mentioning names or publishing photos to limit the perception that suicide is a means to draw attention to oneself
4. Oversimplification of the cause of suicide; suicide is complex and often is the result of a combination on factors
5. Normalizing when mental illness and/or substance abuse are involved
6. Description of the suicide event as a "success" or as a "solution" (Canadian Association for Suicide Prevention, 2003; The Samaritans, 2005; WHO, 2000)

ETHICS IN THE AFTERMATH OF A CLIENT SUICIDE

What happens to the practitioner when a client suicides? While professionals are very effective in assessing and treating suicidal patients, there will be clients in treatment who successfully complete suicide. This phenomenon is often neglected or minimized in practice and the literature regarding how professionals manage a client's suicide (Gitlin, 1999). Following a client's suicide practitioners reactions may vary from grief, shock, denial, distress, depression, isolation, self blame, a sense of failure, strain on their personal and professional lives, fear of another suicide, loss of confidence, and avoidance of triggering stimuli (Alexander et al., 2000; Cooper, 1995; Dewar et al., 2000; Eagles, Klein, Gray, Dewar, & Alexander, 2001; Halligan & Corcoran, 2001; Maltsberger, 1992; Spiegelman & Werth, 2005; Strom-Gottfried & Mowbray, 2006).

Even though the literature is relatively limited on ethically managing this issue, a number of professions, including social workers (Feldman, 1987; Strom-Gottfried & Mowbray, 2006; Ting, Sanders, Jacobson, & Power, 2006), medical doctors (Alexander et al., 2000; Dewar et al., 2000; Eagles et al., 2001; Halligan & Corcoran, 2001; Talseth & Gilje, 2007), nurses (Cooper, 1995; Gilje, Talseth, & Norberg, 2005), and psychologists (Kleespies, 1993; Spiegelman & Werth, 2005), have began to investigate the impact of a client suicide on their practitioners. Confronted with the reality that a majority of professionals will experience working with a client who completes suicide (Alexander et al., 2000), ethically there are a number of areas that warrant professional consideration. How does a practitioner ethically manage the emotional impact of a client suicide? Do you ignore the impact, or seek support form colleagues, family, and/or counseling? Considering the range of practitioners reactions, how might a client suicide affect your work with other clients, both currently and in the future when other clients may present with similar issues as the client who suicided? How much immediate clinical supervision would be helpful? Is it prudent to take a hiatus from direct clinical practice or not? For each practitioner, these ethical issues require both consideration and planning.

■ Individual Exercise 1.5

As a mental health practitioner in an adult outpatient clinic, you arrive to work and learn that one of your clients completed suicide yesterday afternoon. This is a client who you have worked with for several months and have come to like. While the client had a history of low level suicidal ideation, she had no prior attempts and has consistently denied suicidal intent or planning. However, she has reported increased stress over the past few weeks.

1. What would be your reactions to the event?
2. What would be your course of action (be specific)?
3. How would this event impact your ability as a practitioner?

■ Small Group Exercise 1.2

As a mental health practitioner in a child and adolescent outpatient community agency, you are referred a 17-year-old White male client named Jeb. Jeb has recently been released from juvenile detention where he served 7 months for sexual assault. Although the counseling is a mandatory condition of his probation, you find him eager and willing to engage in treatment. According to Jeb, he and his girlfriend, Rachel, had been dating for a few months before their relationship became sexual. However, Rachel, an African American female, is 2 years younger, and when her parents found out, they had Jeb charged with statutory rape. Jeb was later convicted. He noted no further contact with Rachel, but he is convinced that her parents are keeping her away. Jeb notes that he is saddened with the unfair and disappointing way their relationship ended and has begun to think seriously about suicide. He feels there is no way to move forward with his life due to his conviction and lack of contact with Rachel. Although doubtful, he is hoping you can help him.

1. In a group of four to six, discuss what ethics, values, and beliefs may emerge for you (personally and professionally) in treating Jeb?

■ Small Group Exercise 1.3

You have been counseling Jeb (see small group exercise 1.2) for three weeks. You have developed a very positive therapeutic relationship and are hopeful about his prognosis. Yesterday afternoon you were referred another client who has been diagnosed with PTSD and is suicidal. You learn during the assessment interview that her name is Rachel and she was viciously raped by a bully in her neighborhood. Although Rachel's parents had believed her, she had to convince the police and the courts that she had indeed been raped, an experience that further traumatized her. She felt this experience was harder for her because she was African American and the perpetrator was White. However, her account of the crime, the physical evidence, collaborating witnesses, and the physician's testimony were solid and unquestionably convincing. The local bully, Jeb, was charged and convicted of her rape. You refer Rachel to another mental health practitioner and realize that you have an appointment with Jeb the following day.

1. In a group of four to six, discuss what ethics, values, and beliefs may emerge for you (personally and professionally) in treating Jeb?

SUMMARY

The majority of clinical practitioners will encounter a suicidal client in the course of their career. It is essential to be aware of personal values, ethics and philosophical beliefs, professional ethical responsibilities, legal obligations, and the manner in which these factors interact to influence the course of action that you would take when faced with a suicidal client. Ethics matter.

Key Points

1. In working with the suicidality of individuals it is essential to candidly consider and openly understand your own ethical, moral, and valued beliefs relating to suicide and the impact of these thoughts and attitudes on your own practice.
2. Some argue that suicide may be a rational decision under certain circumstances and should be a matter of individual choice.
3. It is critical to be aware of the legal and ethical responsibilities related to the role of practitioner, particularly concerning malpractice liability.
4. Practitioners are expected to uphold their professional standard of care.
5. Regardless of personal values or ethics, practitioners are legally expected to actively prevent suicide of a client.
6. There are four types of euthanasia: passive, active, voluntary, and involuntary.
7. There is neither a constitutional prohibition nor a constitutional right to euthanasia and physician-assisted suicide.
8. The ethical principles most relevant when considering a suicidal patient include autonomy or self-determination, informed consent, duty to protect, beneficence, nonmaleficence, and confidentiality.
9. Minimizing unethical media reporting of suicide is one of the key strategies for suicide prevention.
10. The majority of professionals will experience working with a client who commits suicide. It is essential to recognize the ethical issues related to professional performance after suicide of a client.

FURTHER READINGS

Battin, M. P. (1995). *Ethical issues in suicide.* Englewood Cliffs, NJ: Prentice Hall.

Capuzzi, D. (2004). *Suicide across the life span: Implications for counselors.* Alexandra, VA: American Counseling Association.

Chochilnov, H. M., & Breitbart, W. (2000). *Handbook of psychiatry in palliative medicine.* New York: Oxford University Press.

Gunnell, D. (1994). Reporting suicide. *British Medical Journal, 308*(6941), 1446.

Gutheil, T. G., Bursztajn, H., & Brodsky, A. (1984). Malpractice prevention through the sharing of uncertainty: Informed consent and the therapeutic alliance. *New England Journal of Medicine, 311,* 49–51.

Hawton, K., &Williams, K. (2002). Influences of the media on suicide. *British Journal of Medicine, 325,* 14.

Herlihy, B., & Corey, G. (1996). *ACA ethical standards casebook* (5th ed.). Alexandria, VA: American Counseling Association.

Kitchener, K. S. (2000). *Foundations of ethical practice, research and teaching in psychology.* Mahwah, New Jersey: Lawrence Erlbaum Associates.

Knapp, S., & VandeCreek. L. (1983). Malpractice risks with suicidal patients. *Theory, research & Practice, 20*(3), 274–280.

Maris, R. W. (1981). *Pathways to suicide: A survey of self-destructive behaviors.* Baltimore, MD: Hopkins University Press.

Overholser, J. C. (2006). Treatment of suicidal patients: A risk-benefit analysis. *Behavioral Sciences & The Law, 13*(1), 81–92.

Perr, I. N. (1985). Suicide litigation and risk management: A review of 32 cases. *Bulletin of the American Academy of Psychiatry and Law, 13*(3), 209–219.

Schultz, D. (2000). Defending the psychiatric malpractice suicide. *Health Care Law* (August), 13–26.

Simpson, S., & Stacy, M. (2004). Avoiding the malpractice snare: Documenting suicide risk assessment. *Journal of Psychiatric Practice, 10*(3), 185–189.

Slomski, A. J. (1999). Could you be blamed for a patient's suicide? *Medical Economist, 76*(8), 174–187.

Tribe, R., & Morrisey, J. (2004). *Handbook of professional and ethical practice for psychologists, counselors and psychotherapists.* New York: Brunner-Routledge/Rachel Tribe.

Werth, J. L. (1996). *Rational suicide? Implications for mental health professionals.* Washington, DC: Taylor & Francis.

Wheat, K. (2000). The law's treatment of the suicidal. *Medical and Law Review, 8*(2), 182–209.

Zahl, D., & Hawton, K. (2004) Media influences on suicidal behavior: An interview study of young people. *Behavioural and Cognitive Psychotherapy, 32,* 189–198.

ELECTRONIC RESOURCES

Rational Suicide

American Association of Suicidology: http://www.suicidology.org/
Suicide prevention, awareness, and support: http://www.suicide.org/
Suicide support from Befrienders International: http://www.befrienders.org/

Suicide and the Law

American Association of Suicidology: http://www.suicidology.org/
Articles about suicide: http://www.suicidereferencelibrary.com/index.php
Developments in New York Law: http://tswartz1.typepad.com/new_york_legal_update/2007/07/suicide-and-psy.html
Ethics and malpractice: http://www.kspope.com/ethics/index.php
Practice pointers, The NASW Insurance Trust: http://www.NASWInsuranceTrust.org

Psychiatry and law updates: http://www.reidpsychiatry.com/
Search engine for medical literature: http://www.ncbi.nlm.nih.gov/entrez/query.fcgi

Euthanasia

Compassion and Choices: http://www.compassionandchoices.org
Death with Dignity National Center: http://www.deathwithdignity.org
Euthanasia Research & Guidance Organization: http://www.finalexit.org/
Exit International: http://www.exitinternational.net/
Hemlock Society, USA: http://www.endoflifechoices.org
Voluntary Euthanasia Society of London, England: http://www.dignityindying.org.uk/
World Federation of Right to Die Societies: http://www.worldrtd.net

Code of Ethics

American Psychological Association: http://www.apa.org/ethics/code2002.html
American Psychiatric Association: http://www.psych.org/psych_pract/ethics/ethics.cfm
Australian Code of Ethics: http://www.iap.org.au/ethics.htm
Center on Ethics: http://ethics.stanford.edu/newsletter/June/index.html
Links to additional ethics codes: http://www.kspope.com/ethcodes/index.php
NASW: http://www.socialworkers.org/pubs/code/code.asp
http://www.sp2.upenn.edu/docs/resources/nasw_code_of_ethics.pdf
Principles of Medical Ethics: http://www.sandiegopsychiatricsociety.org/member/
   2005%20%20Principles%20of%20Medical%20Ethics.htm

Media

American Association of Suicidology—Video Evaluation Guidelines: http://www.sui
   cidology.org/displaycommon.cfm?an=1&subarticlenbr=26
American Foundation of Suicide Prevention—Reporting on Suicide: Recommendations
   for the Media: http://www.ohd.hr.state.or.us/ipe/docs/afsmedia.pdf
American Foundation of Suicide Prevention—Suicide Contagion: http://www.afsp.org/
   research/articles/gould.html
BBC Producers' Guideline—Values, Standards and Principles: http://www.bbc.co.uk/
   info/policies/producer_guides/
Canadian Association for Suicide Prevention ° Media Guidelines: http://www.thesup
   portnetwork.com/CASP/mediaguidelines.html
Examples of good and problematic reporting (from American Foundation for Suicide
   Prevention): http://www.afsp.org/education/recommendations/3/index.html
International World Health Organization's resource: http://www.who.int/mental_health/
   resources/suicide/en/
The Media Monitoring Project: A Baseline Description of how the Australian Media
   Report and Portray Suicide and Mental Health and Illness: http://auseinet.flinders.
   edu.au/resources/other/pa6568media.pdf (Full report)
http://auseinet.flinders.edu.au/resources/other/pa6568execsum.pdf (Executive Summary)
New Zealand Youth Suicide Prevention Strategy—The reporting and portrayal of sui
   cide in the media: http://www.moh.govt.nz/moh.nsf/0/a72dcd5037cfe4c3cc256bb
   5000341e9?

The PressWise Trust—Suicide and the media: http://212.100.226.243:11000/display_page.php?id=166

Reporting Suicide and Mental illness: http://www.mindframe-media.info/rsmi_full.pdf (Full report)

http://www.mindframe-media.info/qr_suicide.pdf (Quick reference)

http://www.mindframe-media.info/ (Further information)

Samaritans' Media Guidelines: http://www.samaritans.org.uk/know/media_guide.shtm

Suicide and the Media—a Critical Review: http://auseinet.flinders.edu.au/resources/other/med_suicide.pdf (Full report)

http://auseinet.flinders.edu.au/resources/other/med_execsum.pdf (Executive Summary)

Suicide Sensitive Journalism Handbook (Sri Lanka): http://www.cpalanka.org/research_papers/suicide_report.pdf

Survivors

Clinician Survivors: http://mypage.iusb.edu/~jmcintos/contacts.htm

National Association of Social Workers End-of-Life Care https://www.socialworkers.org/research/naswResearch/EndofLifeCare/

Project on Death in America: http://www.soros.org/death/

Social Workers in End-of-Life and Palliative Care: http://www.swlda.org

▇ Knowledge Acquisition Test

True or False

1. According to the Kantian perspective, a client's suicide that reduces pain or suffering to self and others may be morally acceptable.
2. The majority of those who commit suicide have a mental illness at the time of their death.
3. Experiencing a client suicide during professional training is not common.
4. The Death with Dignity Act of 1998 legalized physician-assisted suicide (PAS) in all states.
5. An individual may be more inclined to attempt suicide as the result of exposure to a suicide report when he or she has a mental illness.
6. Nonmaleficence represents the concept of doing the greatest good possible.
7. Involuntary euthanasia exists only when the client is incompetent.
8. It is acceptable, under certain circumstances, to allow one's personal values to influence one's professional actions.

Short Answer

9. What are the four key elements to support a claim of malpractice?
10. Under what circumstances can you as a practitioner breach confidentiality?
11. Is failure to secure previous records a breach of standard care practices?
12. What are three key ways to minimize risk of malpractice?
13. If someone is going to commit suicide, can media reporting encourage or discourage their decision-making process?

14. Which ethical principles support an individual's right to commit suicide?
15. What is the difference between voluntary and involuntary euthanasia?

Multiple Choice

16. Which of the following is an ethical principle that does not support an individual's right to suicide?
    A. Informed consent
    B. Self-determination
    C. Confidentiality
    D. Duty to protect
    E. None of the above
    F. All of the above

17. Reamer's (1983) framework for ethical decision making proposes that limiting a client's autonomy is justifiable under which of the following circumstances?
    A. The client's family requests the assistance of the practitioner in facilitating the suicidal act
    B. Harmful consequences that may be irreversible are likely to result should the client's autonomy be supported
    C. There is potential that at some point in the future the need to rescue a client from harm potentially may exist
    D. When a colleague expresses that limiting the client's autonomy would be appropriate
    E. None of the above
    F. All of the above

18. Which of the following is a definition of voluntary euthanasia?
    A. An act taken to shorten life
    B. The withdrawal or withholding of artificial life support or medical treatments that may prolong life
    C. An individual requesting assistance from anyone in ending their life
    D. Intentionally causing the death of an individual without informed consent or explicit request
    E. None of the above
    F. All of the above

19. Failure to uphold the standard of care includes:
    A. Keeping accurate, up-to-date records.
    B. Assessing suicide risk during the last clinical contact
    C. Securing records from prior psychiatric treatment
    D. Developing and adequate treatment plan
    E. None of the above
    F. All of the above

20. In considering ethical issues related to suicide, a practitioner must:
    A. Maintain current knowledge of relevant governing laws
    B. Have self-awareness regarding personal ethics, values, and beliefs concerning suicide

C. Possess mastery of professional obligations as defined in relevant professional code of ethics
D. Take adequate steps to minimize risk of malpractice liability should a client suicide
E. None of the above
F. All of the above

Answer key is available in the Instructor's Manual; qualified instructors may e-mail textbook@springerpub.com *to request a copy.*

REFERENCES

Abramson, M. (1985). The autonomy-paternalism dilemma in social work practice. *Social Casework, 66,* 387–393.

Alao, A. O., Soderberg, M., Pohl, E. L., & Alao, A. L. (2006). Cybersuicide: Review of the role of the internet on suicide. *Cyberpsychological Behavior, 9*(4), 489–493.

Alexander, D. A., Klein, S., Gray, N. M., Dewar, I.G., & Eagles, J. M. (2000). Suicide by patients: Questionnaire study of its effect on consultant psychiatrists. *British Medical Journal, 320,* 1571–1574.

Allen, J., Chavez, S., DeSimone, S., Howard, D., Johnson, K., LaPierre, L., et al. (2006). Americans' attitudes toward euthanasia and physician-assisted suicide, 1936–2002. *Journal of Sociology & Social Welfare, 3*(2), 5–23.

Alvarez, A. (1975). Literature in the nineteenth and twentieth centuries. In S. Perlin (Ed.), *A Handbook for the Study of Suicide* (pp. 153–178). New York: Oxford University Press.

Barraclough, B., Bunch, J., Nelson, B., & Salisbury, P. (1974). A hundred cases of suicide: Clinical aspects. *British Journal of Psychiatry, 125,* 355–373.

Baume, P., Cantor, C. H., & Rolfe, A. (1997). Cybersuicide: The role of interactive suicide notes on the Internet. *Crisis, 18*(2), 73–79.

Beauchamp, T. L. (1999). The philosophical basis of psychiatric ethics. In S. Bloch, P. Chodoff, & S. A. Green (Eds.), *Psychiatric ethics* (3rd ed., pp. 25–48). Oxford: Oxford University Press.

Bell, C. C., & Clark, D. C. (1998). Adolescent suicide. *Pediatric Clinics of North America, 45*(2), 365–380.

Berman, A. L. (2006). Risk management with suicidal patients. *Journal of Clinical Psychology, 62*(2), 171–184.

Blood, R. W., & Pirkis, J. (2007). Media reporting of suicide methods: An Australian perspective. *Crisis, 28*(Suppl 1), 64–69.

Bongar, B. M. (1991). Suicide: Legal perspectives. In B. M. Bongar (Ed.), *The suicidal patient: Clinical and legal standards of care* (pp. 33–59). Washington, DC: American Psychological Association.

Bongar, B. (2002). *The suicidal patient: Clinical and legal standards of care* (2nd ed.). Washington, DC: American Psychological Association.

Bongar, B., & Greaney, S. A. (1994). Essential clinical and legal issues when working with the suicidal patient. *Death Studies, 18*(5), 529–548.

Bongar, B., Maris, R. W., Berman, A. L., & Litman, R. E. (1992). Outpatient standards of care and the suicidal patient. *Suicide & Life-Threatening Behavior, 22*(4), 453–478.

Brassington, I. (2006). Killing people: What Kant could have said about suicide and euthanasia but did not. *Journal of Medical Ethics, 32*, 571–574.

Breitbart, W., & Rosenfeld, B. D. (1999). Physician-assisted suicide: The influence of psychosocial issues. *Cancer Control, 6*(2), 146–161.

Brent, D., Perper, J., Moritz, G., Baugher, M., Schweers, J., & Roth, C. (1993). Firearms and adolescent suicide: A community case-control study. *American Journal of Disorders of Childhood, 147*, 1066–1071.

Brent, D. A., Perper, J. A., Moritz, G., Liotus, L., Scheweers, J., Balach, L., et al. (1994). Familial risk factors for adolescent suicide: a case-control study. *Acta Psychiatrica Scandinavica, 89*, 52–58.

Brock, D. W. (1985). Taking human life. *Ethics, 95*(4), 851–865.

Canadian Association for Suicide Prevention. (2003). Media guidelines. Retrieved January 10, 2008, from http://www.thesupportnetwork.com/CASP/mediaguidelines.html

Cantor, C. H., & McDermott, P. M. (1994). Suicide litigation: From legal to clinical wisdom. *Australian & New Zealand Journal of Psychiatry, 28*(3), 431–437.

Chadwick, R., & Tadd, W. (1992). *Ethics and nursing practice*. London: Macmillan Press.

Chemtob, C. M., Hamada, R. S., Bauer, G., Kinney, B., & Torigoe, R. Y. (1988). Patients' suicides: Frequency and impact on psychiatrists. *American Journal of Psychiatry, 145*(2), 224–228.

Chemtob, C. M., Hamada, R. S., Bauer, G., Torigoe, R. Y., & Kinney, B. (1988). Patient suicide: Frequency and impact on psychologists. *Professional Psychology: Research and Practice, 19*(4), 416–420.

Cooper, C. (1995). Patient suicide and assault: Their impact on psychiatric hospital staff. *Journal of Psychosocial Nursing and Mental Health Services, 33*(6), 26–29.

Coverdale, J. H., Roberts, L. W., & Louie, A. K. (2007). Encountering patient suicide: Emotional responses, ethics, and implications for training programs. *Academic Psychiatry, 31*(5), 329–332.

Csikai, E. L. (1999). Euthanasia and assisted suicide: Issues for social work practice. *Journal of Gerontological Social Work, 31*(3–4), 49–63.

Daigle, M. S. (2005). Suicide prevention through means restriction: Assessing the risk of substitution: A critical review and synthesis. *Accident Analysis Prevent, 37*(4), 625–632.

Dewar, I. G., Eagles, J. M., Klein, S., Gray, N., & Alexander, D. A. (2000). Psychiatric trainees' experiences of, and reactions to, patient suicide. *Psychiatric Bulletin, 24*(1), 20–23.

Donagan, A. (1977). *The theory of morality*. Chicago: University of Chicago Press.

Drickamer, M. A., Lee, M. A., & Ganzini, L. (1997). Practical issues in physician-assisted suicide. *Annals of Internal Medicine, 126*(2), 146–151.

Eagles, J. M., Klein, S., Gray, N. M., Dewar, I. G., & Alexander, D. A. (2001). Role of psychiatrists in the prediction and prevention of suicide: A perspective from north-east Scotland. *British Journal of Psychiatry, 178*, 494–496.

Elitzur, A. C. (1995). In defense of life: On the mental-health professions' failure to confront the suicide epidemic *OMEGA: The Journal of Death and Dying, 31*(4), 305–310.

Emanuel, E. J. (2002). Euthanasia and physician-assisted suicide: A review of the empirical data from the United States. *Archives of Internal Medicine, 162*, 142–152.

Emanuel, E. J., Fairclough, D., Clarridge, B. C., Blum, D., Bruera, E., Penley, W. C., et al. (2000). Attitudes and practices of U.S. oncologists regarding euthanasia and physician-assisted suicide. *Annals of Internal Medicine, 133*(7), 527–532.

Emanuel, E. J., Fairclough, D. L., & Emanuel, L. L. (2000). Attitudes and desires related to euthanasia and physician-assisted suicide among terminally ill patients and their caregivers. *Journal of the American Medical Association, 284*, 2460–2468.

Erazo, N., Baumert, J. J., & Ladwig, K. H. (2005). Factors associated with failed and completed railway suicides. *Journal of Affect Disorders, 88*(2), 137–143.

Etzersdorfer, E., & Sonneck, G. (1998). Preventing suicide by influencing mass-media reporting: The Viennese experience 1980–1996, *Archives of Suicide Research 4*(1), 64–74.

Feldman, D. (1987). A social work student's reaction to client suicide. *Social Casework, 68*, 184–187.

Feldman, S. R., Moritz, S. H., & Benjamin, G. (2005). Suicide and the law: A practical overview for mental health professionals. *Women & Therapy, 28*(1), 95–103.

Fintzy, R. T. (1993). The dangers of legalizing physician assisted suicide. *American Journal of Psychiatry, 150*(12), 1901.

Gilje, F., Talseth, A. G., & Norberg, A. (2005). Psychiatric nurses' response to suicidal psychiatric inpatients: Struggling with self and sufferer. *Journal of Psychiatric and Mental Health Nursing, 12*(5), 519–526.

Gitlin, M. J. (1999). A psychiatrist's reaction to a patient's suicide. *American Journal of Psychiatry, 156*(10), 1630–1634.

Gould, M., Fisher, P., Parides, M., Flory, M., & Shaffer, D. (1996). Psychosocial risk factors of child and adolescent completed suicide. *Archives of General Psychiatry, 53*, 1155–1162.

Gutheil, T. G. (1992). *Suicide and clinical practice.* Washington, DC: American Psychiatric Press.

Halligan, P., & Corcoran, P. (2001). The impact of patient suicide on rural general practitioners. *British Journal of General Practice, 51*(465), 295–296.

Hendin, H. (1982). *Suicide in America.* New York: Norton.

Heyd, D., & Bloch, S. (1999). The ethics of suicide. In S. Bloch, P. Chodoff, & S. Green (Eds.), *Psychiatric ethics* (pp. 441–460). Oxford: Oxford University Press.

Hilden, J. M., Emanuel, E. J., Fairclough, D. L., Link, M. P., Foley, K. M., Clarridge, B. C., et al. (2001). Attitudes and practices among pediatric oncologists regarding end-of-life care: Results of the 1998 American Society of Clinical Oncology survey. *Journal of Clinical Oncology, 19*(1), 205–212.

Hill, T. E. (1983). Self-regarding suicide: A modified Kantian view. *Suicide & Life-Threatening Behavior, 13*(4), 254–275.

Isometsa, E., Henrikksson, M., Marttunen, M., Heikkinen, M., Aro, H., Kuoppasalmi, K., et al. (1995). Mental disorders in young and middle aged men who commit suicide. *British Medical Journal, 310*, 1366–1367.

Jobes, D. A., & Berman, A. L. (1993). Suicide and malpractice liability: Assessing and revising policies, procedures, and practice in outpatient settings. *Professional Psychology, Research and Practice, 24*(1), 91–99.

Kaplan, K. J., & Harrow, M. (1996). Positive and negative symptoms as risk factors for later suicidal activity in schizophrenics versus depressives. *Suicide & Life-Threatening Behavior, 26*(2), 105–120.

Kelly, T. B. (1994). Paternalism and the marginally competent: An ethical dilemma, no easy answers. *Journal of Gerontological Social Work, 23*(1/2), 67–84.

Kleespies, P. M. (1993). The stress of patient suicidal behavior: Implications for interns and training programs in psychology. *Professional Psychology: Research and Practice, 24*(4), 477–482.

Kovacs, M., Obrosky, S., Gatsonis, C., & Richards, C. (1997). First-episode major depressive and dysthymic disorder in childhood: Clinical and sociodemographic factors in recovery. *Journal of the American Academy of Child & Adolescent Psychiatry, 36*(6), 777–784.

Kowalski, S. D. (1997). Nevada nurses' attitudes regarding physician-assisted suicide. *Clinical Nurse Specialist, 11*(3), 109–115.

Leeman, C. P. (2004). Commentary on Elger and Harding: Can suicide be rational in persons who are not terminally ill? *General Hospital Psychiatry, 26*(2), 145–146.

Lester, D., & Leenaars, A. A. (1996). The ethics of suicide and suicide prevention. *Death Studies, 20,* 163–184.

Linke, S., Wojciak, J., & Day, S. (2002). The impact of suicide on community mental health teams findings and recommendations. *Psychiatric Bulletin, 26,* 50–52.

Litman, R. A. (1982). Hospital suicides: Lawsuits and standards. *Suicide & Life-Threatening Behavior, 12,* 212–220.

Litman, R. E. (1996). Suicidology: A look backward and ahead. *Suicide & Life-Threatening Behavior, 26*(1), 1–7.

Lizardi, D., Currier, D., Galfalvy, H., Sher, L., Burke, A., Mann, J. J., et al. (2007). Perceived reasons for living at index hospitalization and future suicide attempt. *Journal of Nervous and Mental Disease, 195*(5), 451–455.

Lynch, T. R., Cheavens, J. S., Morse, J. Q., & Rosenthal, M. Z. (2004). A model predicting suicidal ideation and hopelessness in depressed older adults: The impact of emotion inhibition and affect intensity. *Aging and Mental Health, 8*(6), 486–497.

Mackelprang, R. W., & Mackelprang, R. D. (2005). Historical and contemporary issues in end-of-life decisions: Implications for social work. *Social Work, 50*(4), 315–324.

Maltsberger, J. T. (1992). The implications of patient suicide for the surviving psychotherapist. In D. Jacobs (Ed.), *Suicide and clinical practice* (Vol. Clinical Practice Number 21, pp. 169–182). Washington, DC: American Psychiatric Press.

Maris, R. W. (1982). Rational suicide: An impoverished self-transformation. *Suicide & Life-Threatening Behavior, 12,* 3–16.

Maris, R. W., Berman, A. L., & Silverman, M. M. (2000). *Comprehensive textbook of suicidology.* New York: Guilford Press.

Mayo, D. J. (1984). Confidentiality in crisis counseling: A philosophical perspective. *Suicide & Life-Threatening Behavior, 14*(2), 96–112.

Mishna, F., Antle, B. J., & Regehr, C. (2002). Social work with clients contemplating suicide: Complexity and ambiguity in the clinical, ethical, and legal considerations. *Clinical Social Work Journal, 30*(3), 265–280.

Motto, J. (1967). Suicide and suggestibility. *American Journal of Psychiatry, 124,* 252–256.

Motto, J. (1970). Newspaper influence on suicide: A controlled study. *Archives of General Psychiatry, 23,* 143–148.

Motto, J. A. (1999). A psychiatric perspective on rational suicide: 24 points of view. In J. L. Werth (Ed.), *Contemporary perspectives on rational suicide* (pp. 121–125). Philadelphia, PA: Brunner/Mazel.

National Association of Social Workers. (1999). Code of ethics. Retrieved January 13, 2008, from http://www.socialworkers.org/pubs/code/code.asp

National Association of Social Workers. (2000). Code of ethics. Retrieved January 12, 2008, from http://www.socialworkers.org/pubs/code/code.asp

Packman, W. L., & Harris, E. A. (1998). Legal issues and risk management in suicidal patients. In B. Bonger, A. L. Berman, R. W. Maris, M. M. Silverman, E. A. Harris, & W. L. Packman (Eds.), *Risk management with suicidal patients* (pp. 150–186). New York: Guilford Press.

Paris, J. (2002). Chronic suicidality among patients with borderline personality disorder. *Psychiatric Services, 53,* 738–742.

Phillips, D. P. (1974). The influence of suggestion on suicide: Substantive and theoretical implications of the Werther effect. *American Sociological Review, 39*(3), 340–354.

Phillips, D. P. (1982). The impact of fictional television stories on US adult fatalities: New evidence on the effect of the mass media on violence. *American Journal of Sociology, 87,* 1340–1359.

Pinch, W. J., & Dougherty, C. J. (1993). Competency after a suicide attempt: An ethical reflection. *Dimensions of Critical Care Nursing, 12*(4), 206–211.

Pirkis, J., & Blood, R. W. (2001). Suicide and the media part 1: Reportage in nonfictional media. *Crisis, 22*(4), 146–154.

Quill, T. E., Meier, D. E., Block, S. D., & Billings, J. A. (1998). The debate over physician-assisted suicide: Empirical data and convergent views. *Annals of Internal Medicine, 128*(7), 552–558.

Reamer, F. G. (1983). The concept of paternalism in social work. *Social Service Review, 57,* 254–271.

Regan, D. H. (1983). Suicide and the failure of modern moral theory. *Suicide & Life-Threatening Behavior, 13*(4), 276–292.

Robins, E. (1981). *The final months: A study of the lives of 134 persons who committed suicide.* New York: Oxford University Press.

Rosenbluth, M., Kleinman, I., & Lowy, F. (1995). Suicide: The interaction of clinical and ethical issues. *Psychiatric Services, 46*(9), 919–921.

Ruskin, R., Sakinofsky, I., Bagby, R. M., Dickens, S., & Sousa, G. (2004). Impact of patient suicide on psychiatrists and psychiatric trainees. *Academic Psychiatry, 28*(2), 104–110.

The Samaritans. (2005). Media guidelines: Portrayals of suicide. Retrieved January 9, 2007, from http://www.samaritans.org/pdf/SamaritansMediaGuidelines-UK2005.pdf

Sasson, S. (2000). Beneficence versus respect for autonomy: An ethical dilemma in social work practice. *Journal of Gerontological Social Work, 33*(1), 5–16.

Schulsinger, F., Kety, S. S., Rosenthal, D., & Wender, P. H. (1979). A family study of suicide. In M. Schou & E. Stromgren (Eds.), *Origin, prevention and treatment of affective disorders* (pp. 277–287). Orlando, FL: Academic Press.

Schwyn, E. (1976). Ethical norms of suicide prevention and crisis intervention. *Mental Health and Society, 393*(40), 142–147.

Smokowski, P. R., & Wodarski, J. S. (1996). Euthanasia and physician assisted suicide: A social work update. *Social Work in Health Care, 23*(1), 53–65.

Spiegelman, J. S., & Werth, J. L. (2005). Don't forget about me: The experiences of therapists-in-training after a client has attempted or died by suicide. *Women & Therapy, 28*(1), 35–57.

Strakowski, S. M., McElroy, S. L., Keck, P. E., & West, S. A. (1996). Suicidality among patients with mixed and manic bipolar disorder. *American Journal of Psychiatry, 153,* 674–676.

Strom-Gottfried, K., & Mowbray, N. D. (2006). Who heals the helper? Facilitating the social worker's grief. *Families in Society, 87*(1), 9–15.

Sullivan, A. D., Hedberg, K., & Fleming, D. W. (2000). Legalized physician-assisted suicide in Oregon—The second year. *New England Journal of Medicine, 342*(8), 598–604.

Szasz, T. S. (1999). *Fatal freedom: The ethics and politics of suicide.* Westport, CT: Praeger.

Talseth, A. G., & Gilje, F. (2007). Unburdening suffering: Responses of psychiatrists to patients' suicide deaths. *Nursing Ethics: An International Journal for Health Care Professionals, 14*(5), 620–636.

Ting, L., Sanders, S., Jacobson, J. M., & Power, J. R. (2006). Dealing with the aftermath: A qualitative analysis of mental health social workers' reactions after a client suicide. *Social Work, 51*(1), 329–341.

Tsuang, M. T. (1983). Risk of suicide in relative of schizophrenics, manics, depressives, and controls. *Journal of Clinical Psychiatry, 44,* 396–400.

Wagle, R. K., Ede, K., Craig, J., & Bottum, K. (2004). An ethical dilemma: When the family wants the withdrawal of care. *Journal of Psychiatric Practice, 10*(5), 334–336.

Waltzer, H. (1980). Malpractice liability in a patient's suicide. *American Journal of Psychotherapy, 34*(1), 89–98.

Wasserman, I. (1984). Imitation and suicide: A reexamination of the Werther effect. *American Sociological Review, 49,* 427–436.

Weissman, M. M., Fendrich, M., Warner, V., & Wickramaratne, P. (1992). Incidence of psychiatric disorder in offspring at high and low risk for depression. *Journal of the American Academy of Child and Adolescent Psychiatry, 31,* 640–648.

Welfel, E. R. (2002). *Ethics in counseling and psychotherapy: Standards, research, and emerging issues* (2nd ed.). Pacific Grove, CA: Brooks/Cole.

Wender, P. H., Kety, S. S., Rosenthal, D., Schulsinger, F., Ortmann, J., & Lunde, I. (1986). Psychiatric disorders in the biological and adoptive families of adopted individuals with affective disorders. *Archives of General Psychiatry, 43,* 923–929.

Werth, J. L. (1999). Mental health professionals and assisted death: Perceived ethical obligations and proposed guidelines for practice. *Ethics and Behavior, 9*(2), 159–183.

Werth, J. L., & Rogers, J. R. (2005). Assessing for impaired judgment as a means of meeting the "duty to protect" when a client is a potential harm-to-self: Implications for clients making end-of-life decisions. *Mortality, 10*(1), 7–21.

World Health Organization. (2000). Preventing suicide: A resource for media professionals. Retrieved January 9, 2008, from http://www.who.int/mental_health/media/en/426.pdf

World Health Organization. (2007). Preventing suicide in jails and prisons. Retrieved January 12, 2008, from http://www.who.int/mental_health/prevention/suicide/resource_jails_prisons.pdf

2 The Role of Culture, Race, and Ethnicity in Suicide

In order to ensure accurate identification and assessment of suicide risk, it is essential to understand the role of culture, ethnicity, and race. In this chapter, culturally relevant risk and protective factors for suicide are explored. Epidemiological data and contextual findings on suicidality across cultures and nations are presented. International perspectives on suicide risk and assessment are examined as well as the impact of immigration, acculturation, and assimilation on suicide risk. Treatment of suicidality from a culturally competent perspective is described, including differences in attitudes toward suicide and suicide acceptability across cultures.

■ Goals and Objectives of This Chapter

An understanding of:

- The epidemiology of suicide across culture, race, and ethnicity
- Trends in suicide rates across culture, race, and ethnicity
- The impact of immigration on suicide
- The role of acculturation and assimilation in suicide risk
- Transcultural risk factors
- Transcultural protective factors
- Culture-specific risk factors
- Culture-specific protective factors

- International perspectives and attitudes on suicide
- Culturally competent and evidence-based approach to practice with diverse populations

INTRODUCTION

Over the past 50 years, global suicide rates have been steadily increasing and are predicted to increase to 1.53 million by the year 2020 (Khan, 2005). Remarkably, this trend exists despite considerable improvement in the recognition and treatment of depression and other psychiatric disorders; the introduction of safer, more effective psychotropics; and the fact that there are no data on suicide for more than half of the countries in the world. These nonreporting countries include more than 50 developing countries in Asia, Africa, and South America where the majority of the population is Muslim and the populations exceed 100 million individuals, such as Pakistan, Indonesia, and Bangladesh. It is also important to note that attitudes and perspectives toward suicide in these cultures differ greatly from other cultures and may have a direct impact on the rate of suicide.

It is recognized that by the year 2050, Caucasians will no longer be the majority population in the United States (U.S. Census Bureau, 2004). It is also widely acknowledged that in the United States, minorities greatly underutilize mental health services, particularly if they are depressed and suicidal. If culture, race, and ethnicity are overlooked and it is assumed that individuals from all backgrounds experience the world in the same way, intervention and prevention efforts will remain largely unsuccessful at reducing suicide rates. Only by understanding the unique risk and protective factors for suicide among diverse populations and targeting intervention and prevention efforts for specific populations can such efforts be effective.

In addition to understanding universal and culture-specific risk and protective factors for suicide, as a clinician treating suicidal individuals from diverse backgrounds, it is necessary to be aware of any cultural and ethnic preconceptions, stereotypes, and/or biases you may hold. As is explored in this chapter, our personal values and beliefs impact the nature and quality of the interactions we have with our clients. You need to become aware of the beliefs and attitudes you hold in regard to culture, race, and ethnicity to ensure that they do not interfere with effective, professional treatment of your clients.

▓ Individual Exercise 2.1

1. What is your cultural background? How would you describe your degree of *cultural affiliation*/identification?
2. What is the attitude toward suicide from your culture(s) of origin? Is your attitude toward suicide the same as that of your culture(s) of origin? If it differs, how do you reconcile those differences?
3. Is your culture considered a minority or majority culture? How does your culture view individuals from other cultures?
4. Considering your answers to the above questions, how may these factors impact your work with suicidal individuals from diverse backgrounds?

STATISTICS, EPIDEMIOLOGY, AND TRENDS IN SUICIDE BY CULTURE, RACE, AND ETHNICITY

Suicide rates vary by ethnicity and geographic location. To understand the larger contextual issues related to suicidality and culture and ethnicity, it is important to focus on the trends in suicide rates among Caucasians, African Americans, Latinos, and Asians in the United States (due to the high suicide rate among this group, suicidality among Native Americans is discussed in chapter 15). International trends in suicide are subsequently be examined. In addition, theories are presented that provide an understanding for the differences in suicide rates transculturally.

Trends in Suicide Rates Among the Major Ethnic/Cultural Groups in the United States

Caucasians

Caucasian males have a higher rate of suicide than Caucasian females. Caucasian males aged 85 and older have the highest rate of suicide in the United States (Joe, Baser, Breeden, Neighbors, & Jackson, 2006). In general, Caucasians have a higher rate of suicide than African Americans. This trend is more pronounced with age, with elderly Caucasian male suicide rates exceeding elderly Black male suicide rates by more than 2 to 1 (Joe et al., 2006). The trend is even more pronounced with gender; Caucasian male suicide rates exceed African American female suicide rates 18 to 1 (Joe et al., 2006). Among Caucasian adolescents, approximately 20% consider suicide and make a plan, while 8% report making an attempt (Department of Health and Human Services, 2002). Suicide is the third leading cause of death among Caucasian adolescents (Department of Health and Human Services, 2002). Caucasian adolescents have a higher rate of completed suicide than African Americans and Hispanics (Rutter & Behrendt, 2004).

African Americans

Among African Americans, females have a lower rate of suicide than African American males (Joe et al., 2006; Khan, 2005; Khan & Hyder, 2006; Pritchard & Amanullah, 2007). African American females also have a lower rate of suicide than Caucasian females (Joe et al., 2006; Khan, 2005; Khan and Hyder, 2006). Historically, African American youths have had lower suicide rates than have Caucasians, and while this remains true, the gap between the groups appears to be narrowing (Borowsky, Ireland, & Resnick, 2001; Centers for Disease Control and Prevention, 2006; Garlow, Purselle, & Heninger, 2005; Joe & Kaplan, 2001; Joe et al., 2006). This is largely due to a sharp increase in suicide rates among young African Americans aged 15–24 during the last two decades (Borowsky et al., 2001). However, it is important to note that African American females have a much higher rate of suicide attempt than either African American males or Caucasian females (Joe et al., 2006).

Hispanics

As a group, Hispanics have a lower rate of suicide than Caucasians and a higher rate than African Americans. Evidence shows that Hispanics report less suicidal ideation and make lower lethality attempts than non-Hispanics despite having similar suicide intent (Oquendo et al., 2005). Among Hispanic subgroups, rates of suicidal behavior vary greatly. Cuban Americans have the lowest rate of lifetime suicide attempt (2%) followed by Mexican Americans (3%) (Oquendo, Lizardi, Greenwald, Weissman, & Mann, 2004). Puerto Ricans have the highest rate of suicide attempt (9.1%) (Oquendo et al., 2004; Ungemack & Guarnaccia, 1998). Yet, the completed suicide rate for Puerto Ricans is lower than the completed suicide rates for other Hispanic ethnic subgroups and for Caucasians (Oquendo et al., 2001). Mexican Americans also have a lower rate of completed suicide than Caucasians (Oquendo et al., 2001). Among Hispanics, Latina adolescents have the highest rate of suicide attempts of all age groups (Zayas, Lester, Cabassa, & Fortuna, 2005). Despite similar levels of psychopathology, Latina adolescents have a higher rate of suicide attempts than adolescent females from other ethnic groups (Zayas et al., 2005).

Asian Americans

Among Asians, males and older individuals tend to have higher suicide rates. Overall, Asians have a lower rate of suicidal behavior than their Caucasian counterparts (Evans, Hawton, Rodham, & Deeks, 2005). This is especially the case for Asian adolescents (Evans et al., 2005). However, more Asian females engage in suicide than Caucasian and African American females (Shiang et al., 1997). This finding is more pronounced among elderly female Asians than elderly females from other ethnic groups (Shiang et al., 1997). East Asian American woman have the highest suicide rate among all American women over the age of 65 years (McKenzie, Serfaty, & Crawford, 2003).

International Trends in Suicide Rates

Internationally, there is distinct variance in suicide rates. This is in part due to the limited availability of data from many regions regarding the incidence and prevalence of suicidal behavior. For example, suicide rates in the Mediterranean are among the lowest in the world (3.5 per 100,000) (Goldney, 2002; Marusic & Farmer, 2001). Egypt also has a very low rate of suicide (Kahn & Hyder, 2006; Lester, 1997b). Conversely, the suicide rate in Russia has been consistently reported as high (Goldney, 2002; World Health Organization, 1994); it is currently estimated to be three times the suicide rate in the United States (Pridemore & Spivak, 2003). The suicide rate in Hungary has also been consistently high (Goldney, 2002; Lester, 1997b; Schmidtke, 1997).

The suicide rate in China is among the highest in the world with rates approximating 300,000 suicides per year (Phillips, Liu, & Zhang, 1999). China is one of the few countries in which the rate of suicide among females exceeds the rate of suicide among males (Aaron et al., 2004; Baillargeon et al., 2003; Bhugra, Desai, & Baldwin, 1999; Goldney, 2002; Ji, Kleinman, & Becker, 2001; Lester, 1997b; Phillips et al., 1999; Qin & Mortensen, 2001; Raleigh, 1996; Yip, 1996). Rural suicide rates are dramatically higher than urban rates, and suicide rates are lower for adolescent females (Kleinman & Becker, 2001; Phillips et al., 1999; Qin & Mortensen, 2001). Malaysians have a lower rate of suicide than Chinese (Chen, Lee, Wong, & Kaur, 2005), and, in general, South Asian populations have a lower rate of suicidality than other Asian populations (Bhugra, 2002; Burr, 2002).

There is very little information on suicide in most developing countries and specifically in the Indian subcontinent, including India, Pakistan, Nepal, Sri Lanka, Afghanistan, Bhutan, and the Maldives (Khan, 2002). The limited data that does exist indicates that 10% of suicides in this region occur in India, Sri Lanka, and Pakistan (Khan, 2002). In particular, the suicide rate in Sri Lanka is extremely high (Bolz, 2002; Goldney, 2002; Lester, 1997b). The suicide rate among women in this region is high, specifically in India where the male to female ratio of suicides is much smaller compared to that of the rest of the world (Aaron et al., 2004; Khan, 2005; Mayer & Zianian, 2002).

Based on the limited data available, the rate of suicide among Arab populations is quite low (Morad, Merrick, Schwarz, & Merrick, 2005); however, it appears to be on the rise (Pritchard & Amanullah, 2007). This may reflect Islamic cultural beliefs that strongly sanction taking one's own life (Morad et al., 2005) and that regard suicide as a crime (Khan, 2005; Khan & Hyder, 2006; Pritchard & Amanullah, 2007). In Israel, suicide rates in youth and adults are among the lowest in the world (Kohn, Levav, Chang, Halperin, & Zadka, 1997), and in contrast to most other countries, the overall rate of suicide in this country does not appear to be on the rise (Kohn et al., 1997).

Theories Explaining Suicidal Behavior

While there is no universally accepted explanation for suicidality, some theories have been posited to explain the presence or absence of suicidal behavior. For example, Lester (1987) proposed a **physiological theory of suicidal behavior**. According to the theory, differences in suicide rates may be explained by variances in physiology across cultures, specifically regarding the inheritance of psychiatric disorders and concentrations of neurotransmitters. Lester (1987) found an association between blood type and suicidal behavior. Additionally, in another study, biological markers for endogenous depressive disorders in members of eight countries were significantly associated with the suicide rates in those eight countries (Lester, 1991). Thus, as per this theory, differences in rates of suicidal behavior can, at least in part, be due to differences in the physiological make-up of individuals from different cultures.

More recently, a **stress-diathesis model** of suicidal behavior has been proposed (Goldney, 2002; Mann, Waternaux, Haas, & Malone, 1999). This model proposes that at certain times triggers or stressors exist that can be considered state-dependent, or present only during certain periods of time. Additionally, a threshold or diathesis exists that is more trait-dependent, or constantly present. When risk factors from only one of these domains are present, it is not sufficient to elicit suicidal behavior. However, when risk factors from both domains are present, their combined effect increases the likelihood of suicidal behavior. The ensuing suicidal behavior can be seen as the result of either a decrease in internal restraints against such behaviors or as the result of increased external stressors magnifying the suicidal impulse (Malone, Haas, Sweeny, & Mann, 1995).

Individuals who engage in suicidal actions have a vulnerability or lower threshold for such behaviors than those who do not attempt suicide (Malone et al., 1995). This vulnerability may be innate, as a result of genetic or familial factors, such as having a first-degree relative with a history of suicide attempts (Mann et al., 1999; Malone et al., 2000; Pfeffer, Normandin, & Kakuma, 1994; Roy, 1983; Roy & Linnoila, 1986; Roy, Segal, Centerwall, & Robinette, 1991), or it may be the result of trauma early in life, such as parental loss or childhood physical and/or sexual abuse (Adam, Bouckoms, & Streiner, 1982; Briere & Runtz, 1990; Farber, Herbert, & Reviere, 1996; Levi, Fales, Stein, & Sharp, 1966). Other factors may develop later in life, such as alcoholism or substance abuse, which may contribute to this vulnerability (Malone et al., 1995) and may further decrease the threshold for suicidal behavior (Mann et al., 1999). Additionally, research has indicated that trait-related factors such as aggression and impulsivity are related to suicidal behavior (Mann et al., 1999; Malone et al., 1995). Individuals with an aggressive-impulsive trait appear to have a lower threshold for suicidal behavior, which perhaps is an external expression of their self-directed aggressive, destructive thoughts (Malone et al., 1995).

This theory allows for variance in several areas that may account for the differential rates of suicidal behavior seen across cultures and ethnicities. Both state- and trait-related factors are subject to cultural influences. For example, substance abuse, physical abuse, sexual abuse, aggression, impulsivity, unemployment, and undereducation all occur in varying rates across cultures and have a direct influence on an individual's vulnerability toward suicidal acts.

IMMIGRATION AND THE RISK OF SUICIDE

The act and process of moving to another country, or immigrating, is a stressful life event. It is not surprising that **immigration** is associated with increased levels of stress and mental health illnesses

(Shoval, Schoen, Vardi, & Zalsman, 2007) and can even be considered a crisis event (Ponizovsky & Ritsner, 1999). Individuals who migrate from one country to another are faced with not only the transition and the **acculturation** process, but also with a number of potential risk factors and the withdrawal of some previously established protective factors. Immigrants generally lack a well-developed support system and frequently may experience the loss of their previously established support network (Sorenson & Shen, 1996). Also, immigrants tend to earn less money, are less likely to seek mental health care when needed, and may face a number of linguistic barriers (Sorenson & Shen, 1996). Immigrants are also confronted with prejudice and discrimination that may contribute to increased suicide risk (Shoval et al., 2007).

The research on migration and suicide is inconsistent. Although the linkage between suicide and immigration has been studied across a number of countries, the results are conflicting (Shoval et al., 2007). A seminal work by Kushner (1991) found that during the mid-20th century, migration increased the risk of suicide; specifically, foreign-born persons had nearly twice the suicide rate of native-born persons. Kushner proposed that foreign-born persons from countries with higher suicide rates maintain a higher suicide risk after immigration. This association between suicide rate of immigrants and rates of suicide from their country of origin has received further research support (Lester, 1997a, 1998).

In Nordic studies, being foreign-born compared to being native-born was a significant risk factor for suicide in both sexes and in all age groups except for males aged 30 to 49 years (Johansson et al., 1997). Similarly, a Canadian study found an over representation of foreign-born suicide among psychiatric patients, but the study recognized that unemployment and poor social integration may have been confounding factors (Chandrasena, Beddage, & Fernando, 1991). In contrast, another Canadian study found immigrant adolescents had a lower suicide rate than nonimmigrant peers, as well as lower drug use (Greenfield et al., 2006). In a study of Ghanaian immigrants to the United States, a significant association was found between length of residency in the United States and negative suicide attitudes, and also between psychological acculturation and negative suicide attitudes (Eshun, 2006). These findings may indicate that other factors may confound any clear association between immigration and suicide risk.

In their seminal study, Sorenson and Shen (1996) investigated nearly 33,000 death certificates in California between 1970 and 1992 to assess suicide trends and ethnic group risk. Immigration is an important issue to California as it has been the leading state of residence for authorized and unauthorized immigrant populations every year since 1976 (Evans, 1995; Sorenson & Shen, 1996). Sorenson and Shen found that foreign-born persons are generally at lower risk of suicide than U.S.-born persons. Although there was a higher risk for foreign-born Caucasians than for native-born Caucasians, foreign-born Hispanics had lower risk, and foreign-born Blacks and Asians shared similar risks with native-born persons (Sorenson & Shen, 1996). In interpreting their findings, the following four potential hypotheses that may mediate any suicide risk were suggested.

1. **Culture of origin effects** are protective or risk factors derived from an individual's culture of origin that are brought with them to the new culture. For example, Catholicism's belief regarding suicide (values life, views suicide as a sin) and Confucianism's belief regarding suicide (values self-sacrifice, potentially views suicide as a virtue) may mitigate suicide risk among immigrants.
2. Country of destination factors, such as crowded housing arrangements, which may lead to discovering suicide attempts sooner, or availability of suicide method (e.g., firearms) may be protective or risk factors.
3. Personal characteristics of immigrants may be protective factors; for example, immigrants are often healthier and less depressed than the U.S.-born population (Stephen, Foote, Hendershot, & Schoenborn, 1994).
4. **Migration selectivity efforts** recognize that migration is a process in which only certain people elect or are selected to immigrate. Migration selectivity is a more established theory that posits only healthy individuals who have a good chance of succeeding in the new country and may be able to bring over the rest of the family and/or send money back to their country of origin are supported or encouraged to migrate (Sorenson & Shen, 1996). Similarly, individuals who are not likely to succeed may not be selected by the new country as candidates for immigration (Marmot, Adelstein, & Bulusu, 1984). Consequently, individuals prone to suicidality are less likely to immigrate and more likely to return to their country of origin (Sorenson & Shen, 1996).

◼ Small Group Exercise 2.1

Complete the answers first individually, then discuss in groups of two to three.

1. What are some of your personal and/or family's cultural, bicultural, or multicultural customs, traditions, and effects that may positively or negatively impact your ability to integrate into the larger dominant culture?
2. In considering question 1, what are some potential problems (and strengths) that may emerge and how might you manage them?

THE ROLE OF ACCULTURATION AND ASSIMILATION IN SUICIDE

Acculturation is known as the process through which immigrants pass as they move to a new country. It is characterized by the struggle to maintain one's cultural identity, traditions, values, and customs while adapting to mainstream culture to which they have emigrated, their **host culture**. This period can, for some, prove to be a time of great conflict that can result in heightened feelings of depression, anxiety, isolation, and suicidality (Hovey & King, 1997). The resultant distress is often referred to as **acculturative stress** (Berry & Kim, 1988; Hovey & King, 1996, 1997; Padilla, Cervantes, Maldonado, & Garcia, 1988; Williams & Berry, 1991).

In general, suicide rates were positively associated with acculturation stress and negatively with traditional integration (Lester, 1999). Several factors have been identified that may serve as risk or protective factors for acculturative stress and ensuing suicidality. These factors include availability of social supports in the new community, level of familial support from both immediate and extended family networks, socioeconomic status (SES; i.e., work status changes, education, employment), language ability, expectations toward the future, and preimmigration level of cognitive/coping skills (Hovey & King, 1997; Williams & Berry, 1991).

Counterintuitively, evidence suggests that for many ethnicities, individuals with higher levels of acculturation are at more risk for engaging in suicidal behavior than those with lower levels of acculturation. Among Native Americans, for example, acculturative stress is a strong predictor of suicide (Lester, 1999). More so than ethnicity, strong cultural affiliation is a risk factor for suicide attempt among native Hawaiian adolescents (Yuen, Nahulu, Hishinuma, & Miyamoto, 2000).

Acculturative stress has been found to be a risk factor for suicide among Hispanics (Gutierrez, Osman, Kopper, & Barrios, 2000; Vega, Gil, Warheit, Apospori, & Zimmerman, 1993; Zayas, 1987). For example, Mexican Americans born in the United States have higher rates of suicide and suicidal ideation than Mexican Americans born in Mexico (Sorenson & Golding, 1988; Swanson, Linskey, Quintero-Salinas, Pumariega, & Holzer, 1992). High levels of acculturative stress have also been found to be a risk factor for suicide among Central Americans (Hovey, 2000) and Puerto Ricans (Monk & Warshauer, 1974; Oquendo et al., 2004).

On the other hand, some have found that acculturation is related to suicidal ideation but not to suicidal behavior (Kennedy, Parhar, Samra, & Gorzalka, 2005; Lessenger, 1997). Kennedy and colleagues (2005) found that suicidal ideation, plans, and attempts did not vary by generational level or overall ethnic group among European, Chinese, and Indo-Asians.

In summary, it is essential to consider not only the rates and trends in suicide among various ethnic groups, but it is equally important to consider the process of acculturation and degree of cultural affiliation and how these areas are affecting clients. When evaluating and treating suicidal individuals, a comprehensive assessment should be conducted concerning the process of immigration for the individual and their family, the acculturation process and signs of acculturative stress, their degree of cultural affiliation to their culture of origin, and their connection to their host culture.

■ Case Example 2.1

In a large community mental health agency, a family is referred to you for counseling. The parents emigrated from Norway in the early 1980s. He is a skilled computer engineer, and she is a chartered accountant. Both parents are successful and loving. They had three children, Anna, Peter, and Elise, soon after moving to the United States. The family has always been close. Although the family has maintained many cultural traditions from Norway, they consider America their home and are well integrated into mainstream culture. The eldest daughter, Anna, is completing her master's degree out of state. Elisa, the youngest child, is finishing high school and has been accepted to a business program at a nearby college. Peter has been increasingly depressed and has recently experienced some vague suicidal ideation. The entire family, excluding Anna who resides in another state, wants to help and support Peter. Although everyone is busy, they have all agreed to come to family counseling.

1. During your assessment of Peter, what are some questions that you might ask him?
2. What questions might you ask the other family members?
3. How might your assessment differ from an assessment of a native-born U.S. family with a similar problem?

TRANSCULTURAL RISK AND PROTECTIVE FACTORS

Several studies have attempted to identify risk and protective factors that are generalizable across cultures and ethnicities, or transcultural. However, only a few factors have been able to be identified. A history of previous suicide attempt is the most consistent risk factor for further attempts across ethnic groups (Hispanic, African American, and Whites), particularly for males (Borowsky et al., 2001; Colucci & Martin, 2007). Other risk factors that appear to be universal include youth or old age, low socioeconomic standing, substance use, and recent stressful life events. Exposure to family or friend suicide appears to be another universal risk factor for suicide (Colucci & Martin, 2007; Rew, Thomas, Horner, Resnick, & Beuhring, 2001). However, much more research is needed in this area to further demonstrate and understand this relationship. Among adolescents, parent–family connectedness has been identified as a protective factor for attempting suicide that appears to be universal (Borowsky et al., 2001).

Research in this area is fraught with difficulty. Given the tremendous influence that social forces (attitudes toward suicide, gender norms and roles, socioeconomic status, etc.) and interpersonal forces (quality of familial functioning, peer support, marriage, etc.) have on risk of suicidality and how greatly these factors are affected and vary by culture, race, and ethnicity, it is unlikely that many universal risk factors exist. Additionally, it is unlikely that prevention or intervention efforts based solely on **transcultural risk factors** can effectively reduce suicidal behavior.

CULTURE-SPECIFIC RISK AND PROTECTIVE FACTORS

It is essential to consider the unique risk and protective factors among specific ethnic groups to ensure that intervention and prevention efforts target the most prevalent, significant issues.

Caucasians

More often than African American, Caucasians who engage in suicidal behavior are older and have anxiety disorders (Garlow et al., 2005; Vanderwerker et al., 2007). Caucasians also commit suicide more frequently in the context of a major depressive episode than do African Americans (Hollis, 1996; Malone et al., 2000; Oquendo et al., 2001; Shaffer et al., 1996). A major risk factor for suicide among Caucasians is disrupted family environment (Handy, Chithiramohan, Ballard, & Silveira, 1991). Suicide attempts among Caucasians have also been shown to be associated with alcohol use (Groves, Stanley, & Sher, 2007; Vanderwerker et al., 2007), with Caucasians consuming alcohol before committing suicide twice as often as African Americans (Groves et al., 2007). Loss of a family member or friend to suicide (Borowsky et al., 2001; Brent, Bridge, Johnson, & Connolly, 1996; Brent, Perper, & Moritz, 1993), access to firearms (Brent, Perper, Moritz, Baugher, et al. 1993), and female gender (Grossman, Milligan, & Deyo, 1991; Lefebvre, Lesage, Cyr, & Toupin, 1998; Moscicki et al., 1988; Pirkis, Burgess, & Dunt, 2000; Schmidtke et al., 1996; Suominen, Isometsa, Haukka, & Lonnqvist, 2004; Woods et al., 1997) have also been identified as risk factors among Caucasians. Particularly among elderly Caucasians, physical illness has also been shown to be associated with increased risk of suicidality (Vanderwerker et al., 2007).

A major protective factor identified for Caucasian youth is family cohesion (Borowsky et al., 2001). Other protective factors against suicide for Caucasians include marriage, female gender, low levels of aggression and impulsivity, and religiosity (Oquendo et al., 2004, 2005).

African Americans

African American youth who experience parental conflict are approximately seven times more likely to engage in suicidal behavior than those who do not experience parental conflict (Groves et al., 2007). African Americans aged 15 and older are twice as likely as Caucasians to commit suicide via the use of firearms (Joe, Marcus, & Kaplan, 2007). Overall, African Americans are twice as likely as Caucasians to choose a violent method of suicide (Stack & Wasserman, 2005). African Americans who engage in suicidal behaviors are more likely than their Caucasian peers to use cocaine (Garlow, 2002). Interpersonal conflict, male gender, and younger age have been shown to be consistent predictors of suicide among African Americans (Gibbs, 1997; Groves et al., 2007).

In terms of socioeconomic status, lower levels of education have been found to be associated with increased suicide risk (Gibbs, 1997), and African Americans are more likely than Caucasians to have lower levels of education (U.S. Census Bureau, 2004, 2005). Additionally, unemployed individuals have more than twice the suicide risk of employed white-collar workers (Cubbin, LeClere, & Smith, 2000), and both African American males and females are more likely to be unemployed than their Caucasian counterparts (Bureau of Labor Statistics, 2004).

Yet, African Americans in general have a lower rate of suicide than Caucasians and Hispanics and report greater reasons for living than Caucasians, particularly regarding moral objections to suicide and survival and coping-related beliefs (Morrison & Downey, 2000; Yip, Callanan, & Yuen, 2000). Strong religious ties and family cohesiveness have been identified as protective factors (Ali & Maharajh, 2005; Walker, 2007) among African Americans that may explain why their overall rates of suicide are lower than those of Caucasians.

Hispanics

Acculturative stress has been found to be a risk factor for suicide among Hispanics (Vega et al., 1993). The impact of acculturative stress on suicide risk is increased in the presence of substance use (Vega et al., 1993). Young age is a risk factor for suicide among Puerto Ricans and Mexicans. *Fatalism,* or the belief that life is predetermined by fate, is a risk factor for suicide among Hispanics because it places the locus of control outside of the individual and reduces an individual's desire to cope with and manage stressors (Hoppe & Martin, 1986; Hovey & King, 1997; Sorenson & Golding, 1988).

Familism, which emphasizes close relationships with immediate family and extended family networks, serves as a protective factor against suicide for Hispanics (Hovey & King, 1997, Oquendo et al., 2005), and Hispanics have been shown to endorse greater responsibility toward family than their non-Hispanic counterparts (Oquendo et al., 2005). Moral objections to suicide and survival and coping beliefs are also stronger among Hispanics than non-Hispanics (Oquendo et al., 2005). Religious activities in general have been shown to be protective against suicidality (Dervic et al., 2004; Neeleman, Halpern, Leon, & Lewis, 1997) and have been shown to lead to greater coping skills (Morrison & Downey, 2000;

Neeleman & Wessely, 1999). Specifically among Hispanics, religiosity is a protective factor against suicide (Oquendo et al., 2005). Old age is also a protective factor against suicide among Hispanics (Group for the Advancement of Psychiatry, 1989).

Asian Americans

Among Asian adolescents, a diagnosis of depression leads to a four-fold increase in suicidality as compared to other psychiatric disorders (Groves et al., 2007). High parental conflict increases suicide risk by as much as thirty-fold as compared to low parental conflict (Groves et al., 2007; Lau, Jernewall, Zane, & Myers, 2002). A lower level of acculturation is an additional risk factor for suicidality among Asian Americans particularly in the presence of parental conflict (Lau et al., 2002). Hopelessness is predictive of suicide among Chinese (Stewart et al., 2005).

Risk factors for suicide among the Chinese are primarily related to psychiatric illness and poor health (Zhang, Conwell, Zhou, & Jiang, 2004). Secondary predictors include lack of social support, negative life events, lower SES, religious affiliation, and family conflict (Zhang et al., 2004). Some suggest that political and social environment may be more influential risk factors than economic factors for Asian populations (Yip, 1996). Among female Chinese, traditional values of obedience and respect have been found to be protective against suicide attempt, independent of quality of family relationships (Lam et al., 2004). Impulsivity is a risk factor for suicide among Chinese unique to females (Pearson, Phillip, He, & Ji, 2002). Risk factors for suicide in South Asians include domestic violence, negative family environment, and depression (Ahmed, Mohan, & Bhugra, 2007; Hicks & Bhugra, 2003). Academic stress is a risk factor for suicide among Koreans (Dawkins, 1996).

▇ Case Example 2.2

You are scheduled to do an intake with a new client who you learn is a 16-year-old, first-generation Mexican American female. Lourdes was referred by her school guidance counselor after her gym teacher overheard her in the lockerroom at school telling her friend that she felt like killing herself in a very distressed tone. The gym teacher had noticed that lately Lourdes had seemed more withdrawn, less energetic, and lacking in concentration and attention. Upon hearing this statement the gym teacher notified the school guidance counselor, who then met with Lourdes. Lourdes expressed feeling "stressed" over increasing conflicts with her mother that largely centered on their disagreeing over curfews, dating, dropping grades, going to church, and having to take care of her two younger brothers (ages 5 and 11). Lourdes explained that her father was "cool." He understood and cared for her, but her mother was more concerned about what other people would think and did not take the time to understand what Lourdes wanted. "She's too stuck back in Mexico and doesn't realize this is NY!" Lourdes explained that she had great friends and their parents understood them; they didn't have curfews and were allowed to date. She just wished her mom could be like them but because that would never happen, "what's the point." The guidance counselor was sufficiently concerned about the seriousness of Lourdes's suicidal ideation and promptly made a referral for outpatient services.

1. What risk factors are present in the case example?
2. What protective factors are present in the case example?
3. What areas would you target for treatment with this client?

▓ Role Play 2.1

Using case example 2.2 of Lourdes, engage in a role play in which you would assess for culturally relevant risk and protective factors for repeat suicidal behavior. Have one person take on the role of the clinician and the other the role of Lourdes.

INTERNATIONAL PERSPECTIVES AND ATTITUDES ON SUICIDE

Lay theories are intrinsic or common-sense beliefs held by lay persons (Walker, Lester, & Sean, 2006). Lay beliefs of suicide differ across cultural, ethnic, and societal groups (Angermeyer & Matschinger, 1999; Knight, Furnham, & Lester, 2000). In some cultures suicide is a positive moral act, and in other cultures suicide is an unaccepted forbidden act that is equated with a mental disorder.

Cultural differences *within* cultures also exert influence on attitudes and beliefs toward suicide. For example in the Indian subcontinent, female suicide rates are among the highest in the world (Bhugra, 2005; Thompson & Bhugra, 2000). Traditional and cultural beliefs regarding rigid roles and the position of women contribute to their increased suicide risk. Specially, deference to males, arranged marriages, viewing women as the property of males, restricted life opportunities, limited access to mental health services, high rates of domestic violence, and ritual act *Sati*, or burning themselves on their husband's funeral pyre, influence the attitudes toward suicide of women (Bhugra, 2005; Thompson & Bhugra, 2000).

In Japan, where being part of society is more important than being an individual, there is a traditional acceptance of suicide (*jisatsu*) as an acceptable and appropriate behavior in certain circumstances (Pfeffer, 1991). Also, suicide is not interpreted as a denial of life but rather an affirmation of the value of one's moral duty to others (*giri*) (Young, 2002). Also, there is less traditional sanctioning for double suicide (*shinju*) (e.g., parent–child suicide or husband–wife) or youth suicide (Pfeffer, 1991). The collectivist values of Japan are distinctly different from the autonomous values held in North American, thereby influencing the respective cultures' perspectives on suicide.

Ethnic and cultural groups within the United States have different beliefs regarding who controls life (e.g., god, individual, the government) and what circumstances may dictate when suicide is an option (e.g., intrapsychic, interpersonal, or societal difficulties) (Walker et al., 2006). According to Walker and colleagues, European Americans are more likely than African Americans to attribute suicidal thoughts to interpersonal problems (e.g., conflict, work stress, broken home). In addition, European Americans attribute ownership of life to the individual or government, whereas African Americans attribute ownership of life to god (Walker et al., 2006).

This suggests that when working with individuals, irrespective of their origin of birth, it is important to explore and assess the impact of their culture(s) on their beliefs, attitudes, and values toward life and death, specifically in relation to suicide. The process of collecting this information may not only facilitate and strengthen your engagement and therapeutic alliance with the individual, but it can also provide valuable information on potential protective and/or risk factors that may be incorporated into their prevention and treatment.

◾ Small Group Exercise 2.2

Complete the answers first individually, then discuss in groups of four to six.

1. Is your work with a client whose cultural background supports suicide as an acceptable behavior different than your work with a client whose cultural background clearly sanctions suicide? Explain.
2. Is it appropriate to initiate a discussion with clients regarding their cultural beliefs/attitudes toward suicide as an acceptable or unacceptable practice? Explain. If yes, under what circumstances? Explain.

■ Role Play 2.2

Divide into pairs. Have one person take on the role of the clinician and the other the role of client. Role play how you would engage your client in a discussion regarding their cultural beliefs toward suicide.

EVIDENCE-BASED CULTURAL COMPETENCY IN WORKING WITH DIVERSE POPULATIONS

It is estimated that by the year 2050, half of the U.S. population will be people of color (Dalton, 2005). Researchers and practitioners have noted, with regret, the lack of ethnocultural comparative studies that are needed to develop culturally responsive prevention and intervention strategies in the field of suicidality (Colucci & Martin, 2007, p. 222). Evidence-based cultural competency in working with diverse populations is a developing field. Although evidence-based practices (EBP) are increasingly being developed for specific populations (e.g., gender, developmental stage, age) and issues (e.g., diagnosis, presenting problems, social concerns), there is a gap in the development of specific EBPs that uniquely intersect populations, issues, and cultures. Increasingly, however, clinical and intervention researchers are investigating the adaptation of existing EBPs to targeted cultures and groups (see chapters 5–8 for EBPs within suicidality). Researchers in the field of suicidality are finding that each culture exerts positive and negative influences on suicidality, and interventions will need to incorporate these cultural differences as they emerge and are identified (Bhugra & Mastrogianni, 2004). It is also recommended that evidence-based research needs a finer focus on ethnic groups and that research findings need to be placed into a sociopolitical and cultural context (Colucci & Martin, 2007).

Clinicians are increasingly recognizing the importance of practicing with cultural competency. It is essential that clinicians be sensitive to the cultural expectations and issues of clients and of the cultural differences between the client and themselves (Dalton, 2005). According to Derald Sue and colleagues, cultural competence requires practitioners to work toward several goals Sue, Arredondo, & McDavis, 1992; Sue & Sue, 2003; Sue et al., 1982). Specifically, the practitioner:

1. Actively and continually seeks to become aware of their own assumptions, bias, values, and personal limitations

2. Recognizes that their worldview is different from their clients
3. Is in the process of actively developing and practicing appropriate, sensitive, and relevant intervention strategies and skills in working with culturally diverse clients (Sue & Sue, 2003)

Research has indicated that working from a culturally competent perspective remains an area of concern in the field of suicidality. Burr's (2002) work on mental health care professionals' explanations for patterns of suicide in South Asian communities found that stereotypes have been taken as facts, potentially resulting in misdiagnosis and treatment. Cultural competency is an active process in which the practitioner remains engaged with the individual in front of him/her and does not presuppose an understanding of the client based on an awareness of their cultural group. Practitioners and researchers have warned that by emphasizing the cultural differences one may run the risk of increasing prejudice toward different cultures and reinforcing overgeneralizations (Takahashi, 1997).

■ Small Group Exercise 2.3

Complete the answers first individually, then discuss in groups of two to three.

1. List the cultural groups that you are most familiar in working with. Be specific.
2. List the cultural groups that you are least familiar in working with. Again be specific.
3. What are some of the advantages of being familiar/knowledgeable about the cultural groups with which you may work?
4. What are some of the disadvantages of being familiar/knowledgeable about the cultural groups with which you may work?
5. What are some of the advantages of being unfamiliar/less knowledgeable about the cultural groups with which you may work?
6. What are some of the disadvantages of being unfamiliar/less knowledgeable about the cultural groups with which you may work?

■ Small Group Exercise 2.4

After discussing your answers to small group exercise 2.3, consider the following questions.

1. Were there any similarities and/or differences that emerged between your answers?

2. What may account for these patterns or differences?
3. What did you learn or can take away from this exercise?

■ Small Group Exercise 2.5

In a large group, discuss your observations from small group exercises 2.3 and 2.4, including items that you expected or did not expect. How might this knowledge improve your cultural competency?

SUMMARY

Despite increased funding dedicated to suicide prevention efforts and improved treatments for psychiatric illnesses, suicide continues to be a growing problem in the United States and the world. In order for prevention and intervention efforts to be successful, they must take into consideration the impact of culture, race, and ethnicity. Risk and protective factors vary across ethnicities, as do attitudes and perspectives regarding suicide acceptability. Intervention efforts should stem from a culturally competent approach, and prevention efforts should be guided by culturally relevant risk and protective factors for suicide and attitudes toward suicide among the target population.

■ Key Points

1. The overall number of suicides in the United States has remained relatively stable over the past decade, yet suicide rates are shifting among ethnic groups.
2. Global suicide rates over the past 50 years have steadily increased.
3. Globally, prevention efforts remain largely ineffective at addressing the growing problem of suicide.
4. Immigration in a complex phenomenon that has the potential to affect suicide risk.
5. Acculturation stress is a major risk factor for suicide.
6. Attitudes and beliefs toward suicide vary across cultures and ethnicities and exert a direct influence on suicide risk.
7. When assessing for suicide risk with clients, it is essential to consider culture, race, and ethnicity to accurately identify relevant risk factors that may contribute to increased suicidality.
8. Protective factors that promote resilience vary by culture, race, and ethnicity.
9. Evidence-based practices (EBP) are increasingly being developed for specific populations and presenting problems; however, there is a gap in the

development of specific EBPs that uniquely intersect populations, issues, and cultures.

10. Culturally competent practice is an active process on the part of the practitioner that requires remaining engaged with the individual in front of you and not assuming an understanding of your client based on an awareness of their cultural group.

FURTHER READINGS

Advisory Group on Suicide Prevention. (2003). *Acting on what we know: Preventing youth suicide in First Nations*. Ottawa: Health Canada and the Assembly of First Nations.

Chandler, M.J., & Lalonde, C. (1998). Cultural continuity as a hedge against suicide in Canada's First Nations. *Transcultural Psychiatry, 35*(2), 193–211.

Lalonde, C. E. (2005). *Creating an index of healthy Aboriginal communities. Developing a healthy communities index: A collection of papers*. Ottawa: Canadian Institute for Health Information.

Lalonde, C. E. (2006). *Identity formation and cultural resilience in Aboriginal communities*. Ottawa: University of Ottawa Press.

Lalonde, C. E., & Chandler, M. J. (2004). *Culture, selves, and time: Theories of personal persistence in Native and non-Native youth*. Mahwah, NJ: Laurence Erlbaum Associates.

Leach, M. M. (2006). *Cultural diversity and suicide: Ethnic, religious, gender, and sexual orientation perspectives*. New York: Haworth Press.

Pumariega, A. J., Rogers, K., & Rothe, E. (2005). Culturally competent systems of care for children's mental health: Advances and challenges. *Community Mental Health Journal, 41*(5), 539–556.

Pumariega, A. J., Rothe, E., & Pumariega, J. B. (2005). Mental health of immigrants and refugees. *Community Mental Health Journal, 41*(5), 581–597.

Royal Commission on Aboriginal Peoples. (1995). *Choosing life: Special report on suicide among Aboriginal people*. Ottawa.

Sue, D. W. (2006). *Multicultural social work practice*. New York: Wiley.

Sue, D. W., & Sue, D. (2003). *Counseling the culturally diverse: Theory and practice* (4th ed.). New York: Wiley.

White, J., & Jodoin, N. A. (2003). *Aboriginal youth: A manual of promising suicide prevention strategies*. Calgary: Centre for Suicide Prevention.

Wyche, K. F., & Rotheram-Borus, M. J. (1990). *Suicidal behavior among minority youth in the United States*. Thousand Oaks, CA: Sage.

ELECTRONIC RESOURCES

Latinos

Immigration Forum: http//www.immigrationforum.org/
Journal of American Medical Association: http://jama.ama-assn.org/issues/v288n1/abs/jsc10397.html

National Alliance for Hispanic Health: http://www.hispanichealth.org/stateofgirls.pdf
Pacific Clinics: http://www.pacificclinics.org/latino.html
University of Missouri: http://extension.missouri.edu/greene/Alianzas/alianzas.htm

Asian Americans

Asian Nation: http://www.asian-nation.org/headlines/2007/05/when-too-much-pressure-
    leads-to-suicide/
Suicide Prevention Resource Center: http://www.sprc.org/library/asian.pi.facts.pdf
University of Michigan: http://www.sph.umich.edu/apihealth/2006/suicide.htm#definition

Native Americans

Aboriginal Healing Foundation: http://www.ahf.ca
Health Canada: http:// www.hc-sc.gc.ca/fnihb-dgspni/fnihb/cp.htm
National Aboriginal Health organization: http://www.naho.ca/firstnations/english/docu
    ments/NAHO_Suicide_Eng.pdf
Turtle Island Native Network: http://www.turtleisland.org/healing/healing-suicide.htm

Multicultural Resources

Center for Multicultural Human Services: http://www.cmhsweb.org
Mental Health: Race, Culture and Ethnicity A supplement to Mental Health: A Report
    of the Surgeon General: http://www.surgeongeneral.gov/library/mentalhealth/cre/
National Organization for People of Color Against Suicide: http://www.nopcas.com/
Suicide fact sheets specific for four American populations: http://library.sprc.org/browse.
    php?catid=116637

■ Knowledge Acquisition Test

True or False

1. There is one universal theory of suicide that explains suicide rates across cultures.
2. Suicide rates in developing countries are lower than in developed countries.
3. Crowded housing can be a protective factor against suicide for immigrants.
4. First generation immigrants are at greater risk of suicide death than second generation immigrants.
5. Regardless of the culture, suicide is universally perceived of as an unacceptable action.
6. Immigration is a stressful life event.
7. Psychiatric illness is not a universal risk factor for suicide across cultures.
8. There is an association between suicide rate of immigrants and rates of suicide from their country of origin.
9. Old age is a protective factor against suicide across all ethnicities.

Short Answer

10. According to Sorenson and Shen (1996), what are the four possible hypotheses that may mitigate suicide risk in immigrants?
11. In the acculturation process, describe how maintaining elements from your old culture may be both protective and risk factors for suicide?
12. How might an individual's belief regarding who controls life (e.g., god, individual, the government) influence their perception of suicide?
13. What accounts for the lack of suicide data that exists from developing countries?
14. What are the evidence-based universal risk and protective factors for suicide?
15. What is the stress-diathesis model of suicide?

Multiple Choice

16. What will immigrants generally not experience in their new country?
    A. Linguistic barriers
    B. Prejudice and discrimination
    C. A well-developed support network
    D. Equal access to mental health care
    E. None of the above
    F. All of the above

17. Examples of culture of origin effects that may mitigate suicide in immigrants include?
    A. The importance of establishing and maintaining strong social networks
    B. Religious beliefs
    C. Suicide is unacceptable
    D. Help-seeking behavior
    E. None of the above
    F. All of the above

18. The theory of migration selectivity recognizes:
    A. Healthier individuals elect to migrate.
    B. Families promote and support healthier members to migrate.
    C. Individuals who are more likely to succeed are selected to immigrate.
    D. Individuals with mental health problems are less likely to immigrate and/or more likely to return to their home country.
    E. None of the above
    F. All of the above

19. Evidence shows a higher rate of suicide among males as compared to females in all countries *except*:
    A. India
    B. America
    C. China
    D. Australia
    E. England

20. Adolescents from which ethnicity have the highest rate of suicide?
   A. Caucasian
   B. Hispanic
   C. African American
   D. Native American

Answer key is available in the Instructor's Manual; qualified instructors may e-mail textbook@springerpub.com *to request a copy.*

REFERENCES

Aaron, R., Joseph, A., Abraham, S., Muliyil, J., George, K., Prasad, J., et al. (2004). Suicides in young people in rural southern India. *Lancet, 363*(9415), 1117–1118.

Adam, K.S., Bouckoms, A., & Streiner, D. (1982). Parental loss and family stability in attempted suicide. *Archives of General Psychiatry, 39*, 1081–1085.

Ahmed, K., Mohan, R. A., & Bhugra, D. (2007). Self-harm in South Asian women: A literature review informed approach to assessment and formulation. *American Journal of Psychotherapy, 61*(1), 71–81.

Ali, A., & Maharajh, H. D. (2005). Social predictors of suicidal behaviour in adolescents in Trinidad and Tobago. *Social Psychiatry & Psychiatric Epidemiology, 40*(3), 186–191.

Angermeyer, M.C., & Matschinger, H. (1999). Lay beliefs about mental disorders: A comparison between the western and the eastern parts of Germany. *Social Psychiatry & Psychiatric Epidemiology, 34*(5), 275–281.

Baillargeon, J., Ducate, S., Pulvino, J., Bradshaw, P., Murray, O., & Olvera, R. (2003). The association of psychiatric disorders and HIV infection in the correctional setting. *Annals of Epidemiology, 13*(9), 606–612.

Berry, J.W., & Kim, U. (1988). *Acculturation and mental health.* London: Sage.

Bhugra, D., Desai, M., & Baldwin, D.S. (1999). Attempted suicide in west London, I. Rates across ethnic communities. *Psychological Medicine, 29*(5), 1125–1130.

Bhugra, D., & Mastrogianni, A. (2004). Globalization and mental disorders: Overview with relation to depression. *British Journal of Psychiatry, 184*(Suppl), 10–20.

Bhugra, D. (2002). Suicidal behavior in South Asians in the UK. *Crisis: The Journal of Crisis Intervention and Suicide Prevention, 23*(3), 108–113.

Bhugra, D. (2005). Sati: A type of nonpsychiatric suicide. *Crisis: The Journal of Crisis Intervention and Suicide Prevention, 26*(2), 73–77.

Bolz, W. (2002). Psychological analysis of the Sri Lankan conflict culture with special reference to the high suicide rate. *Crisis: The Journal of Crisis Intervention & Suicide Prevention, 23*(4), 167–170.

Borowsky, I.W., Ireland, M., & Resnick, M.D. (2001). Adolescent suicide attempts: Risks and protectors. *Pediatrics, 107*, 485–493.

Brent, D., Bridge, J., Johnson, B.A., & Connolly, J. (1996). Suicidal behavior runs in families: A controlled family study of adolescent suicide victims. *Archives of General Psychiatry, 53*(12), 1145–1152.

Brent, D.A., Perper, J.A., & Moritz, G. (1993). Psychiatric sequelae to the loss of an adolescent peer to suicide. *Journal of the American Academy of Child & Adolescent Psychiatry, 32*, 509–517.

Brent, D., Perper, J., Moritz, G., Baugher, M., Schweers, J., & Roth, C. (1993). Firearms and adolescent suicide: A community case-control study. *American Journal of Disorders of Childhood, 147,* 1066–1071.

Briere, J., & Runtz, M. (1990). Differential adult symptomatology associated with three types of child abuse histories. *Child Abuse and Neglect, 14,* 357–364.

Bureau of Labor Statistics. (2004). *Unemployed persons by marital status, race, Hispanic or Latino ethnicity, age, and sex.* Washington, DC: U.S. Department of Labor.

Burr, J. (2002). Cultural stereotypes of women from South Asian communities: Mental health care professionals' explanations for patterns of suicide and depression. *Social Science & Medicine, 55*(5), 835–845.

Centers for Disease Control and Prevention. (2006). National Center for Injury Prevention and Control. Retrieved March 12, 2008, from http://www.cdc.gov/ncipc/factsheets/suifacts.htm

Chandrasena, R., Beddage, V., & Fernando, M. L. (1991). Suicide among immigrant psychiatric patients in Canada. *British Journal of Psychiatry, 159*(Suppl), 707–709.

Chen, P.C., Lee, L.K., Wong, K.C., & Kaur, J. (2005). Factors related to adolescent suicidal behavior: A cross-sectional Malaysian school survey. *Journal of Adolescent Health, 37*(4), 337.

Colucci, E., & Martin, G. (2007). Ethnocultural aspects of suicide in young people: A systematic literature review part 2: Risk factors, precipitating agents, and attitudes toward suicide. *Suicide & Life-Threatening Behavior, 37*(2), 222–237.

Cubbin, C., LeClere, F. B., & Smith, G. S. (2000). Socioeconomic status and the occurrence of fatal and nonfatal injury in the United States. *American Journal of Public Health, 90,* 70–77.

Dalton, B. (2005). Teaching cultural assessment. *Journal of Teaching in Social Work, 25*(3–4), 45–61.

Dawkins, K. (1996). The interaction of ethnicity, sociocultural factors, and gender in clinical psychopharmacology. *Psychopharmacology Bulletin, 32*(2), 283–289.

Department of Health and Human Services. (2002). *Youth Risk Behavior Survey.* Atlanta, GA: Centers for Disease Control and Prevention.

Dervic, K., Oquendo, M.A., Grunebaum, M.F., Ellis, S., Burke, A.K., & Mann, J.J. (2004). Religious affiliation and suicide attempt. *American Journal of Psychiatry, 161*(12), 2303–2308.

Eshun, S. (2006). Acculturation and suicide attitudes: A study of perceptions about suicide among a sample of Ghanaian immigrants in the United States. *Psychological Reports, 99*(1), 295–304.

Evans, C.A., Jr. (1995). Immigrants and health care: Mounting problems. *Annals of Internal Medicine, 122*(4), 309–310.

Evans, E., Hawton, K., Rodham, K., & Deeks, J. (2005). The prevalence of suicidal phenomena in adolescents: A systematic review of population-based studies. *Suicide & Life-Threatening Behavior, 35*(3), 239–250.

Farber, E.W., Herbert, S.E., & Reviere, S.L. (1996). Child abuse and suicidality in obstetrics patients in a hospital-based urban pre-natal clinic. *General Hospital Psychiatry, 18,* 56–60.

Garlow, S.J. (2002). Age, gender, and ethnicity differences in patterns of cocaine and ethanol use preceding suicide. *American Journal of Psychiatry, 159,* 615–619.

Garlow, S. J., Purselle, D., & Heninger, M. (2005). Ethnic differences in patterns of suicide across the life cycle. *American Journal of Psychiatry, 162,* 319–323.

Gibbs, J. T. (1997). African-American suicide: A cultural paradox. *Suicide & Life-Threatening Behavior, 27,* 68–79.

Goldney, R. D. (2002). A global view of suicidal behaviour. *Emergency Medicine, 14,* 24–34.

Greenfield, B., Rousseau, C., Slatkoff, J., Lewkowski, M., Davis, M., Dube, S., et al. (2006). Profile of a metropolitan North American immigrant suicidal adolescent population. *Canadian Journal of Psychiatry, 51,* 155–159.

Grossman, D. C., Milligan, B. C., & Deyo, R. A. (1991). Risk factors for suicide attempts among Navajo adolescents. *American Journal of Public Health, 81,* 870–874.

Group for the Advancement of Psychiatry. (1989). Suicide and ethnicity in the United States: Committee on Cultural Psychiatry. 1–131.

Groves, S. A., Stanley, B., & Sher, L. (2007). Ethnicity and the relationship between adolescent alcohol use and suicidal behavior. *International Journal of Adolescent Medicine & Health, 19*(1), 19–25.

Gutierrez, P. M., Osman, A., Kopper, B. A., & Barrios, F. X. (2000). Why young people do not kill themselves: The Reasons for Living Inventory for Adolescents. *Journal of Clinical Child Psychology, 29,* 177–187.

Handy, S., Chithiramohan, R. N., Ballard, C. G., & Silveira, W. R. (1991). Ethnic differences in adolescent self-poisoning: A comparison of Asian and Caucasian groups. *Journal of Adolescence, 14*(2), 157–162.

Hicks, M. H. R., & Bhugra, D. (2003). Perceived causes of suicide attempts by U.K. South Asian women. *American Journal of Orthopsychiatry, 73*(4), 455–462.

Hollis, C. (1996). Depression, family environment, and adolescent suicidal behavior. *Journal of the American Academy of Child & Adolescent Psychiatry, 35,* 622–630.

Hoppe, S. K., & Martin, H. W. (1986). Patterns of suicide among Mexican Americans and Anglos, 1960–1980. *Social Psychiatry, 21,* 83–88.

Hovey, J. D. (2000). Acculturative stress, depression, and suicidal ideation among Central American immigrants. *Suicide & Life-Threatening Behavior, 30*(2), 125–139.

Hovey, J. D., & King, C. A. (1996). Acculturative stress, depression, and suicidal ideation among immigrant and second-generation Latino adolescents. *Journal of the American Academy of Child and Adolescent Psychiatry, 35*(9), 1183–1192.

Hovey, J. D., & King, C. A. (1997). Suicidality among acculturating Mexican Americans: Current knowledge and directions for research. *Suicide & Life-Threatening Behavior, 27*(1), 92–103.

Ji, J., Kleinman, A., & Becker, A. E. (2001). Suicide in contemporary China: A review of China's distinctive suicide demographics in their sociocultural context. *Harvard Review of Psychiatry, 9*(1), 1–12.

Joe, S., Baser, R. E., Breeden, G., Neighbors, H. W., & Jackson, J. S. (2006). Prevalence of and risk factors for lifetime suicide attempts among blacks in the United States. *Journal of the American Medical Academy, 296,* 2112–2123.

Joe, S., & Kaplan, M. S. (2001). Suicide among African American men. *Suicide & Life-Threatening Behavior, 31*(Suppl), 106–121.

Joe, S., Marcus, S. C., & Kaplan, M. S. (2007). Racial differences in the characteristics of firearm suicide descendents in the United States. *American Journal of Orthopsychiatry, 77*(1), 124–130.

Johansson, L. M., Sundquist, J., Johansson, S. E., Bergman, B., Qvist, J., & Traskman-Bendz, L. (1997). Suicide among foreign-born minorities and native Swedes: An epidemiological follow-up study of a defined population. *Social Science and Medicine, 44*(2), 181–187.

Kahn, M. M., & Hyder, A. A. (2006). Suicides in the developing world: A case study from Pakistan. *Suicide & Life-Threatening Behavior, 36,* 76–81.

Kennedy, M. A., Parhar, K. K., Samra, J., & Gorzalka, B. (2005). Suicide ideation in different generations of immigrants. *Canadian Journal of Psychiatry, 50*(6), 353–356.

Khan, M. M. (2002). Suicide on the Indian subcontinent. *Crisis: The Journal of Crisis Intervention & Suicide Prevention, 23*(3), 104–107.

Khan, M. (2005). Suicide prevention and developing countries. *Journal of the Royal Society of Medicine, 98,* 459–463.

Khan, M. M., & Hyder, A. A. (2006). Suicides in the developing world: Case study from Pakistan. *Suicide & Life-Threatening Behavior, 36,* 76–81.

Kleinman, J. J., & Becker, A. E. (2001). Suicide in contemporary China: A review of China's distinctive suicide demographics in their sociocultural context. *Harvard Review of Psychiatry, 9*(1), 1–12.

Knight, M. T. D., Furnham, A. F., & Lester, D. (2000). Lay theories of suicide. *Personality and Individual Differences, 29*(3), 453–457.

Kohn, R., Levav, I., Chang, B., Halperin, B., & Zadka, P. (1997). Epidemiology of youth in Israel. *Journal of the American Academy of Child & Adolescent Psychiatry, 36*(11), 1537–1542.

Kushner, H. I. (1991). *American suicide: A psychocultural exploration.* New Brunswick, NJ: Rutger University Press.

Lam, T. H., Stewart, S. M., Yip, P. S., Leung, G. M., Ho, L. M., Ho, S. Y., et al. (2004). Suicidality and cultural values among Hong Kong adolescents. *Social Science & Medicine, 58*(3), 487–498.

Lau, A. S., Jernewall, N. M., Zane, N., & Myers, H. F. (2002). Correlates of suicidal behaviors among Asian American outpatient youth. *Cultural Diversity & Ethnic Minority Psychology, 8*(3), 199–213.

Lefebvre, F., Lesage, A., Cyr, M., & Toupin, J. (1998). Factors related to utilization of services for mental health reasons in Montreal, Canada. *Social Psychiatry and Psychiatric Epidemiology, 33,* 291–298.

Lessenger, L. H. (1997). Use of Acculturation Rating Scale for Mexican Americans-IT with substance abuse patients. *Hispanic Journal of Behavioral Sciences, 19*(3), 387–399.

Lester, D. (1987). National distribution of blood groups, personal violence (suicide and homicide), and national character. *Personality and Individual Differences, 8,* 575–576.

Lester, D. (1991). The association between platelet imipramine binding sites and suicide. *Pharmacopsychiatry, 24,* 232.

Lester, D. (1997a). Suicide in America: A nation of immigrants. *Suicide & Life-Threatening Behavior, 27*(1), 50–59.

Lester, D. (1997b). Suicide in an international perspective. *Suicide & Life-Threatening Behavior, 27*(1), 104–111.

Lester, D. (1998). Suicide rates of immigrants. *Psychological Reports, 82*(1), 50.

Lester, D. (1999). Native American suicide rates, acculturation stress and traditional integration. *Psychological Reports, 84*(2), 398.

Levi, L. D., Fales, C. H., Stein, M., & Sharp, V. H. (1966). Separation and attempted suicide. *Archives of General Psychiatry, 15,* 158–164.

Malone, K. M., Haas, G. L., Sweeny, J. A., & Mann, J. J. (1995). Major depression and the risk of attempted suicide. *Journal of Affective Disorders, 34,* 173–185.

Malone, K. M., Oquendo, M. A., Haas, G. L., Ellis, S. P., Li, S., & Mann, J. J. (2000). Protective factors against suicidal acts in major depression: Reasons for living. *American Journal of Psychiatry, 157,* 1084–1088.

Mann, J. J., Waternaux, C., Haas, G. L., & Malone, K. M. (1999). Towards a clinical model of suicidal behavior in psychiatric patients. *American Journal of Psychiatry, 156,* 181–189.

Marmot, M. G., Adelstein, A. M., & Bulusu, L. (1984). Lessons from the study of immigrant mortality. *Lancet, 1*(8392), 1455–1457.

Marusic, A., & Farmer, A. (2001). Genetic risk factors as possible causes of the variation in European suicide rates. *The British Journal of Psychiatry, 179,* 194–196.

Mayer, P., & Zianian, T. (2002). Suicide, gender, and age variations in India: Are women in Indian society protected from suicide? *Crisis: The Journal of Crisis Intervention & Prevention Suicide, 23*(3), 98–103.

McKenzie, K., Serfaty, M., & Crawford, M. (2003). Suicide in ethnic minority groups. *British Journal of Psychiatry, 183*(2, Suppl), 100–101.

Monk, M., & Warshauer, M. E. (1974). Completed and attempted suicide in three ethnic groups. *American Journal of epidemiology, 130,* 348–360.

Morad, M., Merrick, E., Schwarz, A., & Merrick, J. (2005). A review of suicide behavior among Arab adolescents. *The Scientific World Journal, 5,* 674–679.

Morrison, L. L., & Downey, D. L. (2000). Racial differences in self-disclosure of suicidal ideation and reasons for living: implications for training. *Cultural Diversity & Ethnic Minority Psychology, 6,* 374–386.

Moscicki, E. K., O'Carroll, P., Rae, D. S., Locke, B. Z., Roy, A., & Regier, D. A. (1988). Suicide attempts in the Epidemiologic Catchment Area Study. *Yale Journal of Biology & Medicine, 61,* 259–268.

Neeleman, J., Halpern, D., Leon, D., & Lewis, G. T. (1997). Tolerance of suicide, religion, and suicide rates: An ecological and individual study in 19 Western countries. *Psychological Medicine, 227,* 1165–1171.

Neeleman, J., & Wessely, S. (1999). Ethnic minority suicide: A small geographical study in south London. *Psychological Medicine, 29*(2), 429–436.

Oquendo, M. A., Dragatsi, D., Harkavy-Friedman, J., Dervic, K., Currier, D., Burke, A. K., et al. (2005). Protective factors against suicidal behavior in Latinos. *Journal of Nervous & Mental Disease, 193,* 438–443.

Oquendo, M. A., Ellis, S. P., Greenwald, S., Malone, K. M., Weissman, M. M., & Mann, J. J. (2001). Ethnic and sex differences in suicide rates relative to major depression in the United States. *American Journal of Psychiatry, 158*(10), 1652–1658.

Oquendo, M. A., Lizardi, D., Greenwald, S., Weissman, M. M., & Mann, J. J. (2004). Rates of lifetime suicide attempt and rates of lifetime major depression in different ethnic groups in the United States. *Acta Psychiatrica Scandinavica, 110*(6), 446–451.

Padilla, A. M., Cervantes, R. C., Maldonado, M., & Garcia, R. E. (1988). Coping responses to psychosocial stressors among Mexican and Central American immigrants. *Journal of Community Psychology, 16,* 418–427.

Pearson, V., Phillip, M. R., He, F., & Ji, H. (2002). Attempted suicide among young rural women in the People's Republic of China: possibilities for prevention. *Suicide & Life-Threatening Behavior, 32*(4), 359–369.

Pfeffer, C. R. (1991). Suicide in Japan. *Journal of the American Academy of Child and Adolescent Psychiatry, 30*(5), 847–848.

Pfeffer, C. R., Normandin, L., & Kakuma, T. (1994). Suicidal children grow up: Suicidal behavior and psychiatric disorders among relatives. *Journal of the American Academy of Child & Adolescent Psychiatry, 33*(8), 1087–1097.

Phillips, M. R., Liu, H., & Zhang, Y. (1999). Suicide and social change in China. *Culture, Medicine & Psychiatry, 23*(1), 25–50.

Pirkis, J., Burgess, P., & Dunt, D. (2000). Suicidal ideation and suicide attempts among Australian adults. *Crisis: The Journal of Crisis Intervention & Suicide Prevention, 21*(1), 16–25.

Ponizovsky, A. M., & Ritsner, M. S. (1999). Suicide ideation among recent immigrants to Israel from the former Soviet Union: An epidemiological survey of prevalence and risk factors. *Suicide & Life-Threatening Behavior, 29,* 376–392.

Pridemore, W. A., & Spivak, A. L. (2003). Patterns of suicide mortality in Russia. *Suicide & Life-Threatening Behavior, 33*(2), 132–150.

Pritchard, C., & Amanullah, S. (2007). An analysis of suicide and undetermined deaths in 17 predominantly Islamic countries contrasted with the UK. *Psychological Medicine, 37,* 421–430.

Qin, P., & Mortensen, P. (2001). Specific characteristics of suicide in China. *Acta Psychiatrica Scandinavica, 103*(2), 117–121.

Raleigh, V. S. (1996). Suicide patterns and trends in people of Indian subcontinent and Caribbean origin in England and Wales. *Ethnicity & Health, 1*(1), 55–63.

Rew, L., Thomas, N., Horner, S. D., Resnick, M. D., & Beuhring, T. (2001). Correlates of recent suicide attempts in a triethnic group of adolescents. *Journal of Nursing Scholarship, 33,* 361–367.

Roy, A. (1983). Family history of suicide. *Archives of General Psychiatry, 40,* 971–974.

Roy, A., & Linnoila, M. (1986). Alcoholism and suicide. *Suicide & Life-Threatening Behavior, 16,* 244–273.

Roy, A., Segal, N. L., Centerwall, B. S., & Robinette, C. D. (1991). Suicide in twins. *Archives of General Psychiatry, 48,* 29–32.

Rutter, P. A., & Behrendt, A. E. (2004). Adolescent suicide risk: Four psychosocial factors. *Adolescence, 39,* 295–302.

Schmidtke, A., Bille-Brahe, U., DeLeo, D., Kerkhof, A., Bjerke, T., Crepet, P., et al. (1996). Attempted suicide in Europe: Rates, trends and sociodemographic characteristics of suicide attempters during the period 1989–1992. Results of the WHO/EURO Multicentre Study on Parasuicide. *Acta Psychiatrica Scandinavica, 93*(5), 327–338.

Schmidtke, A. (1997). Perspective: Suicide in Europe. *Suicide & Life-Threatening Behavior, 27,* 127–136.

Shaffer, D., Gould, M., Fisher, P., Trautman, P., Moreau, D., & Kleinman, M. (1996). Psychiatric diagnosis in child and adolescent suicide. *Archives of General Psychiatry, 53,* 339–348.

Shiang, J., Blinn, R., Bonger, B., Stephens, B., Allison, D., & Schatzberg, A. (1997). Suicide in San Francisco CA: A comparison of Caucasian and Asian groups, 1987–1994. *Suicide & Life-Threatening Behavior, 28*(4), 338–354.

Shoval, G., Schoen, G., Vardi, N., & Zalsman, G. (2007). Suicide in Ethiopian immigrants in Israel: A case for study of the genetic-environmental relation in suicide. *Archives of Suicide Research, 11*(3), 247–253.

Sorenson, S. B., & Golding, J. M. (1988). Prevalence of suicide attempts in a Mexican-American population: Prevention implications of immigration and cultural issues. *Suicide & Life-Threatening Behavior, 18,* 322–333.

Sorenson, S. B., & Shen, H. (1996). Youth suicide trends in California: An examination of immigrant and ethnic group risk. *Suicide & Life-Threatening Behavior, 26*(2), 143–154.

Stack, S., & Wasserman, I. (2005). Race and method of suicide: Culture and opportunity. *Archives of Suicide Research, 9*(1), 57–68.

Stephen, E. H., Foote, K., Hendershot, G. E., & Schoenborn, C. A. (1994). Health of the foreign-born population: United States, 1989–1990. *Advanced Data, 14,* 1–12.

Stewart, S. M., Kennard, B. D., Lee, P. W., Mayes, T., Hughes, C. W., & Emslie, G. (2005). Hopelessness and suicidal ideation among adolescents in two cultures. *Journal of Child Psychology & Psychiatry & Allied Disciplines, 46*(4), 364–372.

Sue, D. W., Arredondo, P., & McDavis, R. J. (1992). Multicultural counseling competencies and standards: A call to the profession. *Journal of Counseling and Development, 70*(4), 477–486.

Sue, D. W., Bernier, J. E., Durran, A., Feinberg, L., Pedersen, P., Smith, E., et al. (1982). Position paper: Cross-cultural counseling competencies. *The Counseling Psychologist, 10,* 42–52.

Sue, D. W., & Sue, D. (2003). *Counseling the culturally diverse: Theory and practice.* New York: Wiley.

Suominen, K., Isometsa, E., Haukka, J., & Lonnqvist, J. (2004). Substance use and male gender as risk factors for deaths and suicide—A 5-year follow-up study after deliberate self-harm. *Social Psychiatry & Psychiatric Epidemiology, 39*(9), 720–724.

Swanson, J. W., Linskey, A. O., Quintero-Salinas, R., Pumariega, A. J., & Holzer, C. E. (1992). A binational school survey of depressive symptoms, drug use, and suicidal ideation. *Journal of the American Academy of Child and Adolescent Psychiatry, 31,* 669–678.

Takahashi, Y. (1997). Culture and suicide: From a Japanese psychiatrist's perspective. *Suicide & Life-Threatening Behavior, 27*(1), 137–145.

Thompson, N., & Bhugra, D. (2000). Rates of deliberate self-harm in Asians: Findings and models. *International Review of Psychiatry, 12*(1), 37–43.

U.S. Census Bureau. (2004). *More diversity, slower growth.* Washington, DC: U.S. Department of Commerce.

U.S. Census Bureau. (2004). *Educational attainment of the population 15 years and over, by age, sex, race, and Hispanic origin.* Washington, DC: Author.

U.S. Census Bureau. (2005). *Educational attainment of the population 15 years and over, by age, sex, race, and Hispanic origin.* Washington, DC: Author.

Ungemack, J. A., & Guarnaccia, P. J. (1998). Suicidal ideation and suicide attempts among Mexican Americans, Puerto Ricans and Cuban Americans. *Transcultural Psychiatry, 35,* 307–327.

Vanderwerker, L. L., Chen, J. H., Charpentier, P., Paulk, M. E., Michalski, M., & Prigerson, H. G. (2007). Differences in risk factors for suicidality between African American and White patients vulnerable to suicide. *Suicide & Life-Threatening Behavior, 37*(1), 1–9.

Vega, W. A., Gil, A., Warheit, G., Apospori, E., & Zimmerman, R. (1993). The relationship of drug use to suicide ideation and attempts among African American, Hispanic, and white non-Hispanic male adolescents. *Suicide & Life-Threatening Behavior, 23*(2), 110–119.

Walker, R. L. (2007). Acculturation and acculturative stress as indicators for suicide risk among African Americans. *American Journal of Orthopsychiatry, 77*(3), 386–391.

Walker, R. L., Lester, D., & Sean, J. (2006). Lay theories of suicide: An examination of culturally relevant suicide beliefs and attributions among African Americans and European Americans. *Journal of Black Psychology, 32*(3), 320–334.

Williams, C. L., & Berry, J. W. (1991). Primary prevention of acculturative stress among refugees: Application of psychological theory and practice. *American Psychologist, 46,* 632–641.

Woods, E. R., Lin, Y. G., Middleman, A., Beckford, P., Chase, L., & DuRant, R. H. (1997). The associations of suicide attempts in adolescents. *Pediatrics, 99,* 791–796.

World Health Organization. (1994). *World health statistic annual: Health for all 2000 database.* Geneva: Author.

Yip, P. S. (1996). Suicides in Hong Kong, Taiwan and Beijing. *British Journal of Clinical Psychiatry, 169*(4), 495–500.

Yip, P. S., Callanan, C., & Yuen, H. P. (2000). Urban/rural and gender differentials in suicide rates: East and west. *Journal of Affective Disorders, 57*(1–3), 99–106.

Young, J. (2002). Morals, suicide, and psychiatry: A view from Japan. *Bioethics, 16*(5), 412–424.

Yuen, N. Y., Nahulu, L. B., Hishinuma, E. S., & Miyamoto, R. H. (2000). Cultural identification and attempted suicide in Native Hawaiian adolescents. *Journal of the American Academy of Child & Adolescent Psychiatry, 39*(3), 360–367.

Zayas, L. (1987). Toward an understanding of suicide risks in youth Hispanic females. *Journal of Adolescent Research, 2*(1), 1–11.

Zayas, L. H., Lester, R. J., Cabassa, L. J., & Fortuna, L. R. (2005). Why do so many Latina teens attempt suicide? A conceptual model for research. *American Journal of Orthopsychiatry, 75*(2), 275–287.

Zhang, J., Conwell, Y., Zhou, L., & Jiang, C. (2004). Culture, risk factors and suicide in rural China: A psychological autopsy case control study. *Acta Psychiatrica Scandinavica, 110*(6), 430–437.

3 Religion and Suicide

Religion impacts suicidality; an individual's degree of religiosity can potentially serve as a protective factor against suicidal behavior. In order to accurately identify and assess risk of suicide, and to determine resources to modify and enhance treatment of suicidal individuals, it is imperative to understand and not ignore the role of religion in relation to suicidality. While it is recognized that a number of factors are interrelated with one's religiosity, such as gender, age, ethnicity, and/or culture, the influence of these factors on suicide is discussed in more depth in other chapters. This chapter intentionally focuses on the key risk and protective factors of religion as it relates to suicidality. Because a discussion of all religious and/or spiritual traditions would be beyond the scope of this text, this chapter focuses on the four dominant religions in the United States. Perspectives and influences of Christianity, Islam, Hinduism, and Judaism on suicide are described and related to assessing and treating patients with suicidality.

■ Goals and Objectives of This Chapter

An understanding of:

- The influence of religion on suicidality
- The importance of assessing an individual's religiosity
- The protective role of religion against suicidal behavior
- Risk factors within religions
- Protective factors within religions

- Suicide trends and rates within religions
- Christianity and suicidality
- Hinduism and suicidality
- Islam and suicidality
- Judaism and suicidality

INTRODUCTION

Empirical evidence indicates that the rate of suicide varies across religions (Gearing & Lizardi, 2009; Lizardi & Gearing, 2010). Among the most common religious groups in the United States, Protestants have the highest suicide rate followed by Roman Catholics. Jewish individuals have the lowest rates of suicide (Maris, Berman, & Silverman, 2000). There are lower recorded rates of suicidal behavior found among Muslims when compared to other religions, such as Christianity or Hinduism (Abdel-Khalek, 2004; Ineichen, 1998). However, across religious denominations a higher degree of religiosity is associated with decreased suicide risk (Dervic et al., 2004; Martin, 1984). Research establishing a relationship between high levels of religiosity and decreased suicide risk dates back over 40 years (Kranitz, Abrahams, Spiegel, & Keith-Spiegel, 1968). Individuals who attend church more frequently are four times less likely to commit suicide than those who never attend (Martin, 1984). In addition, the relationship between religiosity and suicide appears to vary by gender. Among males, higher male suicide rates are associated with lower levels of religious belief and religious attendance. This relationship has not been demonstrated among females (Neeleman, Halpern, Leon, & Lewis, 1997).

In 1897, Emile Durkheim was the first to propose that spiritual commitment may contribute to emotional well-being because it provides a source of meaning and order in the world (Durkheim, 1951). Given the potential protective impact of religious affiliation and commitment against suicide risk, it is essential to include an evaluation of religion in any psychosocial assessment, particularly with suicidal clients. An accurate understanding of a client's religious faith and participation may indicate potential suicide risk. It may also help to identify potential areas that treatment may target to enhance life-affirming beliefs and expectations.

In addition to understanding the relationship between religion and suicide, as a clinician treating suicidal individuals from diverse religious backgrounds, it is necessary to be aware of any religious stereotypes and/

or biases. As the previous chapters have highlighted, our personal values and beliefs impact how we assess, treat, and interact with our clients. It is essential to become aware of your personal attitudes and assumptions regarding religion to fully understand how they affect your work with your clients.

▓ Individual Exercise 3.1

1. What is your religious background, if any? How would you describe your degree of religious affiliation/identification?
2. What is the belief and attitude toward suicide from your religion? Is your perspective on suicide the same as that of your religion? If it differs, how do you reconcile those differences?
3. Considering your answers to the above questions, how may these factors impact your work with suicidal individuals from diverse religious backgrounds and different degrees of religious faith?

RELIGION AS A PROTECTIVE FACTOR AGAINST SUICIDE

Religiosity has been shown to be associated with reduced risk of suicidality (Dervic et al., 2004; Lizardi et al., 2007; Stack, 1983). For example, suicide rates in religious countries are lower than suicide rates in secular countries (Breault, 1993; Dervic et al., 2004; Stack, 1983). Furthermore, intensity of religious commitment has been shown to be related to suicidal behaviors (Nelson, 1977). These findings are not specific to particular religious denominations (Dervic et al., 2004; Lizardi et al., 2007; Stack, 1983).

Moral and religious objections to suicide have a unique association with suicidal behavior. The life-saving beliefs associated with religious commitment may protect against suicide (Dervic et al., 2004; Koenig, McCullough, & Larson, 2001; Lizardi et al., 2007; Neeleman et al., 1997; Stack, 1983). Studies indicate that individuals with low moral and religious objections to suicide are more likely to have a lifetime history of suicide attempts (Dervic et al., 2004; Lizardi et al., 2007; Neeleman et al., 1997; Stack, 1983). Individuals with higher moral and religious objections to suicide perceive more reasons for living.

The protective role of religiosity includes a number of mechanisms. Most religions have strong sanctions against suicide; thus, those individuals who report stronger commitment to those religions would be less likely to resort to suicide. In addition to condoning suicide, involvement in organized religions provides the opportunity to develop an extended support network in congregation members and clergy, which has been shown to be a protective factor against suicidality (Cheng, Chen, Chen, & Jenkins, 2000; Gould, Fisher, Parides, Flory, & Shaffer, 1996; Greening & Stoppelbein, 2002; Koenig et al., 2001; Mann, 2002; Szanto, Mulsant, Houck, Dew, & Reynolds, 2003). Religiosity has also been shown to be associated with lower levels of aggression and hostility (Koenig et al., 2001; Malone, Haas, Sweeny, & Mann, 1995; Mann et al., 2005; Oquendo et al., 2000), which have been consistently shown to be related to suicidal behavior. Additionally, many religions proscribe elicit behaviors such as substance abuse (Hilton, Fellingham, & Lyon, 2002) and smoking (Martin, 1984), which have an established relationship to suicide. Thus, high levels of religiosity could have an indirect protective effect on suicide via the prohibition of substance use (Hilton et al., 2002).

Further, the motivation to commit suicide involves considerable ambivalence, and suicidal individuals often experience an internal struggle between wanting to live and wanting to die (Shneidman & Farberow, 1957). Given that the moral objections to suicide are founded in traditional religious beliefs (Linehan, Goodstein, Nielsen, & Chiles, 1983), religious values and optimism may be important considerations for many individuals contemplating suicide (Linehan et al., 1983) and may serve to positively influence the decision to live (Pinto, Whisman, & Conwell, 1998). Further studies with more comprehensive assessment of religiosity are needed to clarify the relationship between suicidality and religiosity.

▓ Role Play 3.1

Taking turns as client and practitioner, engage in a role play in which you would assess for degree of religious commitment of your client.

1. What protective factors does the client (not clinician) associate with their religion and their own personal religiosity?
2. Does the individual's religion contain any real or perceived risk factors for the client?
3. Does the individual's religion or religious community offer any supports for or obstacles against treatment?

CHRISTIANITY AND SUICIDE

The word *suicide* does not appear in the Bible; however, there are several examples of individuals committing suicide, such as Judas, King Saul, and Samson (Maris et al., 2000; Phipps, 1985). Biblical writers neither condemn nor praise those whom they recorded as having taken their own lives. The Christian perspective on suicide has remained relatively stable since the fifth century (Phipps, 1985). St. Augustine argued in the fifth century that suicide was a violation of the sixth commandment, "Thou shall not kill" (Kennedy, 2000; Maris et al., 2000; Phipps, 1985; Retterstol, 1993). He argued that this applied to one's own life as well as the lives of others and all life should be preserved (Kennedy, 2000; Phipps, 1985; Retterstol, 1993). St. Thomas Aquinas, Catholic theologian, expanded on Augustine's perspective and described suicide as a sin against self, neighbor, and God (Aquinas, 1225–1274). St. Aquinas claimed that every living organism naturally desires to preserve its life, thus, suicide is against nature. St. Aquinas also claimed that suicide is contrary to religious rights, in that only God has the right to decide when a person will live or die. Further, St. Aquinas believed that confession of sins must be made prior to departing from the world in order to enter Heaven. Consequently, suicide is one of the most serious of all sins because the individual who completes suicide is unable to confess to the act and repent (Kennedy, 2000; Phipps, 1985).

The view of suicide as a sin dominates current Christian attitudes across the various denominations (e.g., Catholics, Baptists, and Protestants). The sin of suicide is equated with other forms of taking life, such as abortion and murder (Maris et al., 2000; Wogaman, 1990). According to the Catechism of the Catholic Church (1994), one has to be mentally competent to understand that the act in which he or she partakes is a sin. Thus, if one considers suicide an act of the mentally ill, it cannot simultaneously be viewed a sin. When an individual dies, s/he faces judgment by God, and only God can decide if the individual will go to heaven, hell, or purgatory (Catholic Church, 1994). Historically, those who committed suicide were unable to be buried in Catholic cemeteries (Phipps, 1985); however, this is now a rarely practiced custom within Catholicism. During funeral services, forgiveness is asked for the deceased, and comfort for the survivors (Turner, 1998).

There are 2.1 billion Christians worldwide. Among the dominant Christian denominations (Catholics, Baptists, and Protestants), the lowest suicide rates are found among Catholics and evangelical Baptists, with higher incidence occurring among Protestant faiths (Pescosolido & Georgianna, 1989). Researchers indicate that Catholics and Baptists are more likely to be actively involved in church activities and, therefore, may benefit more from expanded social support networks (Pescosolido & Georgianna, 1989). Furthermore, Catholic countries have lower suicide rates than Protestant ones, and within Protestant countries, areas with a preponderance of Catholics have lower suicide rates (Hood-Williams, 1996). There are significantly higher suicide rates in men and in the elderly in Catholic and Christian orthodox countries compared to rates in non-Catholic and orthodox countries (Pritchard & Baldwin, 2001).

HINDUISM AND SUICIDE

There are an estimated 900,000 million Hindus in the world, predominantly in the Indian subcontinent. Unlike Muslim or Christian writings, Hindu scriptures are relatively ambivalent on the issue of suicide (Ineichen, 1998). Also, Hindu philosophies of reincarnation and karma mean, that for Hindus, life does not end at death because death leads to rebirth (Hassan, 1983; Ineichen, 1998). Thus, it has been purported by some that Hindu religion is more tolerant toward suicide (Hassan, 1983; Ineichen, 1998; Kamal & Loewenthal, 2002).

There is limited research on suicidality and Hindus. In a study examining suicide beliefs and behavior among Hindus and Muslims living in the United Kingdom, it was found that Hindus less strongly endorsed moral objections and survival-and-coping reasons for living than Muslims (Kamal & Loewenthal, 2002). Another survey study found a higher rate of suicide among Hindus than Muslims (Ineichen, 1998). Research seems to indicate that males have higher rates of suicide than females, and the majority of suicide attempters studied had a psychiatric diagnosis (Latha, Bhat, & D'Souza, 1996).

The centuries' old Hindu practice of **Sati** is a ritual act of suicide in which widows self-immolate on the funeral pyre of their husbands. Although this ritual is now illegal, it continues to be practiced in some areas of the Indian subcontinent (Kumar, 2003). Research has found little evidence that women who engage in Sati have a psychiatric disorder (Bhugra, 2005). It is important to recognize that Sati is not a religious act nor is it related to psychiatric illness; rather this form of suicide appears more related to social, gender, and cultural factors (Bhugra, 2005).

ISLAM AND SUICIDE

The impact and influence of the Islamic faith on suicidality remains difficult to determine due to the limited research in the area (Cosar, Kocal,

Arikan, & Isik, 1997; Khan & Reza, 2000). No Middle Eastern country has reported mortality data to the World Health Organization (WHO) since 1989 (Lester, 2006), and very few Islamic countries record suicide or report suicide rates (Khan & Hyder, 2006; Pritchard & Amanullah, 2007). It is important to separate the concept of suicide from martyrdom. The focus here is on suicide, the self-inflicted intentional act designed to end one's own life, not on martyrdom, which involves using one's death in a defense of one's homeland by inflicting losses on an enemy (Abdel-Khalek, 2004).

Limited research has indicated that suicide rates are lower in predominantly Islamic countries in comparison to other countries (Abdel-Khalek, 2004). Similarly, there are lower recorded rates of suicidality found among the 1.5 billion Muslims when compared to other religions, such as Christianity or Hinduism (Abdel-Khalek, 2004; Ineichen, 1998; Kamal & Loewenthal, 2002). In studies that have focused on psychological disorders and traits such as depression, anxiety, obsessive compulsion, neuroticism, pessimism, and death obsession, samples from Islamic countries have scored higher than Western samples (Abdel-Khalek, 2004, 2006; Abdel-Khalek & Lester, 1999, 2003).

Studies examining this phenomenon of low suicide rates, but higher levels of psychological distress scores, have proposed several explanations. One, higher rates of religiosity among Muslims act as a buffer to suicidality (Thorson, Powell, Abdel-Khalek, & Beshai, 1997); however, religiosity is associated with lower levels of depression and anxiety (Abdel-Khalek, 2006). Two, Islam is firmer in regard to the sinfulness of suicide as compared to other religions (Ineichen, 1998; Lester, 2006; Pritchard & Amanullah, 2007). Three, the social stigma of suicidality in predominantly Islamic countries artificially lowers the reported rates (Lester & Akande, 1994; Sarfraz & Castle, 2002). It has been suggested that the reported rareness of Muslim suicide is a myth because of the under-reporting due to social stigma (Lester & Akande, 1994; Sarfraz & Castle, 2002).

In the Holy Qu'ran, suicide is expressly forbidden in Surah 4, verses 29 and 30, which state "do not kill or destroy yourself," with eternal punishment for suicide resulting in the individual burning in hell. Similar to the Christian Bible, however, the Qu'ran is interpreted differently across various (Islamic) countries, regions, and sects (Pritchard & Amanullah, 2007). Furthermore, as many Islamic countries have incorporated the Sharia (Islamic law) into their legal system, such as in Saudi Arabia, Pakistan, or Kuwait, suicide and suicide attempts remain criminal offenses

(Al-Jahdali et al., 2004; Khan & Hyder, 2006; Sarfraz & Castle, 2002; Suleiman, Moussa, & El-Islam, 1989).

Some research, however, has indicated an increasing suicide trend in Islamic countries (Khan, 2007; Khan & Hyder, 2006). For example, the number of suicides have reportedly increased in the Sindh region in Pakistan from 90 in 1987 to 360 in 1999 (Khan & Hyder, 2006). Another study surveying suicide ideation among Pakistan college students found high overall rates equally in both men and women (Khokher & Khan, 2005). Research investigating suicide in predominantly Islamic countries has found suicidality to be both a reality and a growing concern (Al-Jahdali et al., 2004; Cosar et al., 1997; Khan & Reza, 2000). According to Pritchard and Amanullah's (2007) analysis comparing suicide and undetermined deaths in 17 Islamic countries, patterns of suicide (e.g., increased risk with age) similar to those in Western countries have been found. Suicide in Islamic countries was found to be a significant problem.

Nonetheless, there are few mental health or social services in predominantly Islamic countries for individuals who are suicidal and fewer for survivors and family members following a suicide (Khan & Hyder, 2006; Sarfraz & Castle, 2002). Often individuals who have attempted suicide and their families will avoid going to public hospitals, which will report the event as a crime to the police (Khan, 2007; Khan & Hyder, 2006). Surviving family members are stigmatized and often ostracized in traditional Muslim communities (Sarfraz & Castle, 2002). Muslim graveyards are often reluctant to bury an individual after a suicide, which is considered a *haram* or forbidden death (Sarfraz & Castle, 2002).

To date, research into Muslim suicidality remains limited not only in reported data but also across religious subgroups. Islam is not a single unified religion, rather it is made up of many competing sects (Lester, 2006). Yet, there is little investigation or empirical data across the various Islamic sects of the Sunni or Shia, or the smaller sects of the Ahmadi, Alawai, Druze, Islaili, Qadiani, Sufi, or Yezidi (Lester, 2006).

JUDAISM AND SUICIDE

Judaism strictly forbids suicide and regards suicide as a criminal act. Suicide is likened to murder. According to Jewish doctrine, an individual does not have the right to wound his/her own body, let alone to take his own life (Bailey & Stein, 1995; Schwartz & Kaplan, 1992). Jewish law does not consider the fifth commandment of "Thou shall not kill" as applying to suicide (Jacobs, 1995). However, it does value the preservation of human life above all else (Jacobs, 1995) and, thus, condemns suicide.

According to Kaplan and Schoenberg (1988), Judaic principles ascribe a great spiritual consequence to suicide. When an individual commits suicide, the soul has nowhere to go (Kaplan & Schoenberg, 1988). It cannot return to the body because the body has been destroyed. It cannot be let in to any of the soul worlds because its time has not come. Thus, it is in a state of limbo, which is very painful. A person may commit suicide because he wants to escape, but in reality, the result is a far worse situation. While problems have the opportunity to be resolved in this world, after death there are no more opportunities, only consequences. According to strict Judaic belief, individuals who commit suicide are unable to receive traditional postdeath rituals such as a proper burial and blessings (Kaplan & Schoenberg, 1988).

Across the world, 14 million people identity themselves as Jewish. Suicide rates among Jewish individuals in the United States and Israel have historically been noted to be low (Dublin, 1963; Levav & Aisenberg, 1989; Miller, 1976), with suicide rates in Israel being lower than suicide rates in the United States (Levav & Aisenberg, 1989). Overall, Jewish individuals have the lowest rate of suicide in the United States as compared to Christians and Protestants (Maris et al., 2000). Several studies have reported that suicide rates are lower among Jews as compared to the general population in predominantly Protestant communities (Danto & Danto, 1983; Goss & Reed, 1971; Levav, Magnes, Aisenberg, Rosenblum, & Gil, 1988; Williams, 1997). Additionally, in a study of the United States examining the proportion of the Jewish population and corresponding suicide rates across 50 states, a significant negative correlation was found (Bailey & Stein, 1995).

In Israel, suicide rates among the Jewish population are among the lowest in the world (Kohn, Levav, Chang, Halperin, & Zadka, 1997), yet they are higher for Jewish individuals than for Muslims (Levav & Aisenberg, 1989; Lubin, Glasser, Boyko, & Barell, 2001). Among the Jewish population, suicide rates are higher for men than for women (Lubin et al., 2001). The suicide rate increases directly with age. In addition, the suicide rate for Jewish males in Israel is increasing, particularly in the 18- to 21-year-old age group. Rates of suicide are found to differ according to marital status. The highest rates were in married individuals (Nachman et al., 2002). An increase in the use of firearms has also been cited (Lubin et al., 2001).

■ Case Example 3.1

A young woman was brought in by a friend to a local emergency department of a community hospital due to an overdose attempt. She was hysterical, broke a picture in the hospital hallway, and tried to use a shard of glass to cut her wrists. She required restraints. You, as a mental health clinician, are called to work with her family, who upon arrival have asked that she be immediately discharged. Reportedly, the patient is in love with a young man of a different religion, and her traditional family has barred her from seeing him again.

1. The young women and her family are Muslim, and her boyfriend is Hindu. How would you engage the family?
2. How would your assessment and treatment recommendations be different if religion were not a core factor in this case?
3. What personal issues may affect your professional practice?
4. Complete questions 1–3, but change the young woman and her family's religion to Christianity and her boyfriend's religion to Islam. Are your responses the same or different? Why?

■ Small Group Exercise 3.1

Considering case example 3.1, please complete the answers first individually, then discuss in group of four to six.

1. In the case of a couple of different religions, what combinations of religions would be the easiest for you to work with and why?
2. What combinations of religions would be the hardest for you to work with and why?

■ Role Play 3.2

Role play the assessment and discharge planning of case example 3.1. One person takes the role of the clinician; one of the young woman and one a member of her family. You may alternate religions (and degree of orthodoxy) of the participants.

SUMMARY

The act of suicide is condemned in most major religious sects. Research has established that degree of religiosity is directly related to degree of suicidality, with greater religiosity predicting decreased risk of suicidal behavior. Several mechanisms have been attributed to the protective role of religion, including a decrease of aggression and hostility and an increase in reasons for living. The protective role of religion can be found across major religious denominations; thus, assessing a client's degree of religious affiliation may serve as an effective indicator of suicide risk.

■ Key Points

1. Religion plays a protective role against suicide via the strict sanctions against suicide in most major religions (among other mechanisms).
2. Many religions foster extended social support networks, which are protective factors against suicide.
3. Fostering a suicidal patient's religiosity and/or spirituality may contribute to effectiveness of psychosocial interventions.
4. In Christianity, suicide is a sin, and in some denominations (e.g., Catholicism) results in the individual's inability to enter Heaven.
5. While more tolerant toward individuals who suicide, Hindu scriptures denounce suicide.
6. Islam sects traditionally hold a very strict interpretation of suicide as an unforgivable sin.
7. Sharia, Islamic law, has been incorporated into many Islamic countries' legal systems, where suicide and suicide attempt are criminal offenses.
8. Judaism equates suicide with murder and views it as unacceptable under any conditions.
9. Suicide is condemned across Christianity, Hinduism, Islam, and Judaism, but the strictness of this condemnation varies across religions and within each religion's denominations or sects.
10. Individuals with more traditional or orthodox religiosity tend to have lower rates of suicide.

FURTHER READINGS

Bailey, W. T., & Stein, L. B. (1995). Jewish affiliation in relation to suicide rates. *Psychological Reports, 76*(2), 561–562.

Burdette, A. M., Hill, T. D., & Moulton, B. E. (2005). Religion and attitudes toward physician-assisted suicide and terminal palliative care. *Journal for the Scientific Study of Religion, 44*(1), 79–93.

Durkheim, E. (1951). *Suicide: A study in sociology* (J. A. Spaulding & G. Simpson, Trans.). New York: Free Press.

Domino, G., & Miller, K. (1992). Religiosity and attitudes toward suicide. *Omega: Journal of Death and Dying, 25*(4), 271–282.

Holmes, R. M., & Holmes, S. T. (2005). *Suicide: Theory, practice, and investigation.* Thousand Oaks, CA: Sage.

Lester, D. (2006). Suicide and Islam. *Archives of Suicide Research, 10,* 77–97.

Medoff, M. H., & Skov, I. L. (1992). Religion and behavior: An empirical analysis. *The Journal of Socio-Economics, 21,* 143–151.

Pritchard, C., & Amanullah, S. (2007). An analysis of suicide and undetermined deaths in 17 predominantly Islamic countries contrasted with the UK. *Psychological Medicine, 37,* 421–430.

Siegrist, M. (1996). Church attendance, denomination, and suicide ideology. *Journal of Social Psychology, 136*(5), 559–566.

ELECTRONIC RESOURCES

General

National and World Religion Statistics—Church Statistics—World Religions: http://www.adherents.com

Religions of the Word, Minnesota State University: http://www.mnsu.edu/emuseum/cultural/religion

Religious Tolerance: http://www.religioustolerance.org

Christianity

American Baptist Churches: http://www.abc-usa.org

Campus Crusade for Christ International: http://www.ccci.org

The Presbyterian Coalition: http://www.presbycoalition.org

Roman Catholicism: http://www.catholic.org/

World Vision International: http://www.wvi.org

Youth for Christ: http://www.yfc.org

Hinduism

Hinduism Today: http://www.hinduismtoday.com

The Hindu Universe: http://www.hindunet.org

Hindu Web site: http://www.hinduwebsite.com/hinduindex.asp

Islam

Islam.com: http://www.islam.com

Islam 101: http://islam101.net

Islam World: http://islamworld.net

Judaism

B'nai B'rith International: http://www.bnaibrith.org

Jewish Coalition for Service: http://www.jewishservice.org

National Foundation for Jewish Culture: http://www2.jewishculture.org

United Jewish Communities: http://www.ujc.org

World Jewish Congress: http://www.worldjewishcongress.org

■ Knowledge Acquisition Test

True or False

1. Religiosity is associated with lower levels of aggression and hostility.
2. Strong religious commitment is not related to extent of social support networks.
3. Moral objections to suicide protect against suicidal behavior.
4. Judaism views suicide as acceptable under certain circumstances.
5. Modern Catholicism prevents individuals who committed suicide from receiving a Catholic funeral.
6. Muslims have higher rates of suicide than Christians.
7. Individuals residing in predominantly Islamic countries have higher rates of psychological distress then individuals in Western countries.
8. Hinduism fully accepts suicide as a natural form of death.
9. Suicide in old age is more tolerated in world religions.

Short Answer

10. What are two ways in which religiosity may protect against suicidal behavior?
11. Describe the predominant Judeo-Christian view of suicide.
12. On what principles did St. Thomas Aquinas determine suicide to be a sin?
13. In Judaism, what value comes before all else, and how does this relate to Judaic attitudes toward suicide?
14. What are the potential reasons for the lower suicide rates among Muslims?
15. Why is Sati considered a type of nonpsychiatric suicide?

Multiple Choice

16. Suicide and religion are associated through which of the following?
    A. Hopelessness
    B. Impulsivity
    C. Aggression
    D. All of the above
    E. None of the above

17. Religiosity may protect against suicide because:
    A. Most major religions forbid suicide
    B. Religious activities build social support networks
    C. Moral objections to suicide are related to reasons for living
    D. All of the above
    E. None of the above

18. Reported lower rates of suicide in predominantly Islamic countries may result because:
    A. Islam is an strong protective religion against suicide
    B. Islam is firmer in regard to the sinfulness of suicide

C. The social stigma of suicidality in Islam may artificially lowers rates
D. All of the above
E. None of the above

19. Suicide is acceptable in what major religion?

A. Christianity
B. Hinduism
C. Islam
D. Judaism
E. None of the above

20. In Hinduism, Sati is:

A. A purification rite
B. A religious ritual for men before marriage
C. An act where women self-immolate on the funeral pyre of their husbands
D. A religious text condemning suicide
E. None of the above

Answer key is available in the Instructor's Manual; qualified instructors may e-mail textbook@springerpub.com *to request a copy.*

REFERENCES

Abdel-Khalek, A. (2004). Neither altruistic suicide, nor terrorism but martyrdom: A Muslim perspective. *Archives of Suicide Research, 8*(1), 99–113.

Abdel-Khalek, A. (2006). Optimism and pessimism in Kuwaiti and American college students. *International Journal of Social Psychiatry, 52*(2), 110–126.

Abdel-Khalek, A., & Lester, D. (1999). Obsession-compulsion in college students in the United States and Kuwait. *Psychological Reports, 85*, 799–800.

Abdel-Khalek, A., & Lester, D. (2003). Death obsession in Kuwaiti and American college students. *Death Studies, 27*, 541–553.

Al-Jahdali, H., Al-Johani, A., Al-Hakawi, A., Arabi, Y., Ahmed, Q. A., Altowirky, J., et al. (2004). Pattern and risk factors for intentional drug overdose in Saudi Arabia. *Canadian Journal of Psychiatry, 49*(5), 331–334.

Aquinas, T. (1948). *Summa theologica*. New York: Benzinger Brothers.

Bailey, W. T., & Stein, L. B. (1995). Jewish affiliation in relation to suicide rates. *Psychological Reports, 76*(2), 561–562.

Bhugra, D. (2005). Sati: A type of nonpsychiatric suicide. *Crisis: The Journal of Crisis Intervention and Suicide Prevention, 26*(2), 73–77.

Breault, K. D. (1993). Suicide in America: A test of Durkheim's theory of religious family integration, 1933–1980. *American Journal of Sociology, 92*, 628–656.

Catholic Church. (1994). *Catechism*. United States Catholic Conference, Inc.-Libreria Editrice Vaticana.

Cheng, A., Chen, T., Chen, C., & Jenkins, R. (2000). Psychosocial and psychiatric risk factors for suicide: Case-control psychological autopsy study. *British Journal of Psychiatry, 177*, 360–365.

Cosar, B., Kocal, N., Arikan, Z., & Isik, E. (1997). Suicide attempts among Turkish psychiatric patients. *Canadian Journal of Psychiatry, 42,* 1072–1075.

Danto, B. L., & Danto, J. M. (1983). Jewish and non-Jewish suicide in Oakland County, Michigan. *Crisis, 4,* 33–60.

Dervic, K., Oquendo, M. A., Grunebaum, M. F., Ellis, S., Burke, A. K., & Mann, J. J. (2004). Religious affiliation and suicide attempt. *American Journal of Psychiatry, 161*(12), 2303–2308.

Dublin, L. I. (1963). *Suicide in Jewish history. In suicide: A sociological and statistical study.* New York: The Ronald Press Co.

Durkheim, E. (1951). *Suicide: A study in sociology* (J. A. Spaulding & G. Simpson, Trans.). New York: Free Press.

Gearing, R. E., & Lizardi, D. (2009). Religion and suicide. *The Journal Religion and Health, 48*(3), 332–341.

Goss, M., & Reed, J. (1971). Suicide and religion: A study of white adults in New York City, 1963–67. *Life Threatening Behaviour, 1,* 163–177.

Gould, M. S., Fisher, P., Parides, M., Flory, M., & Shaffer, D. (1996). Psychosocial risk factors of child and adolescent completed suicides. *Archives of General Psychiatry, 53,* 1155–1162.

Greening, L., & Stoppelbein, L. (2002). Religiosity, attributional style, and social support as psychosocial buffers for African American and white adolescents' perceived risk for suicide. *Suicide & Life-Threatening Behavior, 32,* 404–417.

Hassan, R. (1983). *A way of dying: Suicide in Singapore.* Kuala Lumpur: Oxford University Press.

Hilton, S. C., Fellingham, G. W., & Lyon, J. L. (2002). Suicide rates and religious commitment in young adult males in Utah. *Journal of Epidemiology and Community Health, 155*(5), 413–419.

Hood-Williams, J. (1996). Studying suicide. *Health & Place, 2*(3), 167–177.

Ineichen, B. (1998). The influence of religion on the suicide rate: Islam and Hinduism compared. *Mental Health, Religion and Culture, 1,* 31–36.

Jacobs, L. (1995). *The Jewish religion: A companion.* Oxford: Oxford University Press.

Kamal, Z., & Loewenthal, K. M. (2002). Suicide beliefs and behaviour among young Muslims and Hindus in the UK. *Mental Health, Religion & Culture, 5*(2), 111–118.

Kaplan, S. J., & Schoenberg, L. A. (1988). Defining suicide: Importance and implications for Judaism. *Journal of Religion & Health, 27*(2), 154–156.

Kennedy, T. D. (2000). Suicide and the silence of scripture. *Christianity Today.* Retrieved March 26, 2008, from http://www.christianitytoday.com/ct/2000/julywebonly/42.0.html?start=1

Khan, M. M. (2007). Suicide prevention in Pakistan: An impossible challenge? *Journal of Pakistan Medical Association, 57*(10), 478–480.

Khan, M. M., & Hyder, A. A. (2006). Suicides in the developing world: Case study from Pakistan. *Suicide & Life-Threatening Behavior, 36*(1), 76–81.

Khan, M. M., & Reza, H. (2000). The pattern of suicide in Pakistan. *Crisis, 21*(1), 31–35.

Khokher, S., & Khan, M. M. (2005). Suicidal ideation in Pakistani college students. *Crisis, 26*(3), 125–127.

Koenig, H. G., McCullough, M. E., & Larson, D. B. (2001). *Handbook of religion and health.* New York: Oxford University Press.

Kohn, R., Levav, I., Chang, B., Halperin, B., & Zadka, P. (1997). Epidemiology of youth in Israel. *Journal of the American Academy of Child & Adolescent Psychiatry, 36*(11), 1537–1542.

Kranitz, L., Abrahams, J., Spiegel, D., & Keith-Spiegel, P. (1968). Religious beliefs of suicidal patients. *Psychological Reports, 22,* 936.

Kumar, V. (2003). Burnt wives—A study of suicides. *Burns, 29*(1), 31–51.

Latha, K. S., Bhat, S. M., & D'Souza, P. (1996). Suicide attempters in a general hospital unit in India: Their socio-demographic and clinical profile—emphasis on cross-cultural aspects. *Acta Psychiatrica Scandinavica, 94*(1), 26–30.

Lester, D. (2006). Suicide and Islam. *Archives of Suicide Research, 10,* 77–97.

Lester, D., & Akande, A. (1994). Attitudes about suicide among the Yoruba of Nigeria. *The Journal of Social Psychology, 134,* 851–853.

Levav I., & Aisenberg, E. (1989). Suicide in Israel: crossnational comparisons. *Acta Psychiatrica Scandinavica, 79*(5), 468–473.

Levav, I., Magnes, J., Aisenberg, E., Rosenblum, I., & Gil, R. (1988). Sociodemographic correlates of suicidal ideation and reported attempts—A brief report on a community survey. *Israel Journal of Psychiatry, 25,* 38–45.

Linehan, M. M., Goodstein, J. L., Nielsen, S. L., & Chiles, J. A. (1983). Reasons for staying alive when you are thinking of killing yourself: The reasons for living inventory. *Journal of Consulting & Clinical Psychology, 51,* 276–286.

Lizardi, D., Currier, D., Galfalvy, H., Sher, L., Burke, A., Mann, J. J., et al. (2007). Perceived reasons for living at index hospitalization and future suicide attempt. *Journal of Nervous and Mental Disease, 195*(5), 451–455.

Lizardi, D., & Gearing, R. E. (2010). Religion and suicide: Buddhism, Native American and African religions, atheism, and agnosticism. *The Journal Religion and Health,* 1–8.

Lubin, G., Glasser, S., Boyko, V., & Barell, V. (2001). Epidemiology of suicide in Israel: A nationwide population study. *Social Psychiatry and Psychiatric Epidemiology, 36*(3), 123–127.

Malone, K. M., Haas, G. L., Sweeny, J. A., & Mann, J. J. (1995). Major depression and the risk of attempted suicide. *Journal of Affective Disorders, 34,* 173–185.

Mann, J. J. (2002). A current perspective of suicide and attempted suicide. *Annals of Internal Medicine, 136,* 302–311.

Mann, J. J., Bortinger, J., Oquendo, M. A., Currier, D., Li, S., & Brent, D. A. (2005). Family history of suicidal behavior and mood disorders in probands with mood disorders. *American Journal of Psychiatry, 162*(9), 1672–1679.

Maris, R. W., Berman, A. L., & Silverman, M. M. (2000). *Comprehensive textbook of suicidology.* New York: Guilford Press.

Martin, W. T. (1984). Religiosity and United States suicide rates, 1972–1978. *Journal of Clinical Psychology, 40,* 1166–1169.

Miller, L. (1976). Some data on suicide and attempted suicide of the Jewish population in Israel. *Mental Health and Society, 3,* 178–181.

Nachman, R., Yanai, O., Goldin, L., Swartz, M., Barak, Y., & Hiss, J. (2002). Suicide in Israel: 1985–1997. *Journal of Psychiatry & Neuroscience, 27*(6), 423–428.

Neeleman, J., Halpern, D., Leon, D., & Lewis, G. T. (1997). Tolerance of suicide, religion, and suicide rates: An ecological and individual study in 19 Western countries. *Psychological Medicine, 227,* 1165–1171.

Nelson, F. L. (1977). Religiosity and self-destructive crises in the institutionalized elderly. *Suicide & Life-Threatening Behavior, 7,* 67–74.

Oquendo, M., Waternaux, C., Brodsky, B., Parsons, B., Haas, G. L., Malone, K. M., et al. (2000). Suicidal behavior in bipolar mood disorder: Clinical characteristics of attempters and non-attempters. *Journal of Affective Disorders, 59,* 107–117.

Pescosolido, B. A., & Georgianna, S. (1989). Durkheim, suicide and religion: Toward a network theory of suicide. *American Sociology Review, 54,* 33–48.

Phipps, W. (1985). Christian perspectives on suicide. *The Christian Century,* 970–972.

Pinto, A., Whisman, M. A., & Conwell, Y. (1998). Reasons for living in a clinical sample of adolescents. *Journal of Adolescence, 21,* 397–405.

Pritchard, C., & Amanullah, S. (2007). An analysis of suicide and undetermined deaths in 17 predominantly Islamic countries contrasted with the UK. *Psychological Medicine, 37,* 421–430.

Pritchard, C., & Baldwin, D. (2001). Effects of age and gender on elderly suicide rates in Catholic and orthodox countries: An inadvertent neglect? *International Journal of Geriatric Psychiatry, 15*(10), 904–910.

Retterstol, N. (1993). *Suicide: A European perspective* (R. Williams, Trans.). Cambridge: Cambridge University Press.

Sarfraz, A., & Castle, D. J. (2002). A Muslim suicide. *Australasian Psychiatry, 10*(1), 48–50.

Schwartz, M., & Kaplan, K. J. (1992). Judaism, Masada, and suicide: A critical analysis. *Journal of Death and Dying, 25*(2), 127–132.

Shneidman, E. S., & Farberow, N. L. (1957). Some comparisons between genuine and simulated suicide notes in terms of Mowrer's concepts of discomfort and relief. *Journal of General Psychology, 56,* 251–256.

Stack, S. (1983). The effect of religious commitment on suicide: Across-national analysis. *Journal of Health and Social Behavior, 24,* 362–374.

Suleiman, M. A., Moussa, M. A., & El-Islam, M. F. (1989). The profile of parasuicide repeaters in Kuwait. *International Journal of Social Psychiatry, 235*(2), 146–155.

Szanto, K., Mulsant, B. H., Houck, P., Dew, M. A., & Reynolds, C. F. (2003). Occurrence and course of suicidality during short-term treatment of late-life depression. *Archives of General Psychiatry, 60,* 610–617.

Thorson, J. A., Powell, F. C., Abdel-Khalek, A., & Beshai, J. A. (1997). Constructions of religiosity and death anxiety in two cultures: The United States and Kuwait. *Journal of Psychology and Theology, 25,* 374–383.

Turner, P. (1998). Suicide funerals. Retrieved March 26, 2008, from http://www.rpinet.com/ml/2503bi1.html

Williams, M. (1997). *Cry of pain: Understanding suicide and self-harm.* Harmondsworth (UK): Penguin.

Wogaman, P. J. (1990). *Ethical perspectives for the community.* Louisville: Westminster/John Knox Press.

Evidence-Based Treatments

Effective clinical work in the field of mental health requires knowledge of suicide assessment and treatment. Although many different approaches to suicide treatment exist, Part II focuses on empirically supported, evidence-based psychosocial practices. The science of suicide assessment and treatment has improved dramatically in recent years leading to the establishment of several rigorous and efficacious evidence-based treatments. Part II presents four widely used psychosocial evidence-based treatments for suicidality.

Psychopharmacology has a unique role in the treatment of suicidality. Although there is no medication that can directly prevent suicide, psychotropic medications have been successful at treating a wide number of symptoms related to suicidality, including depressed mood, hallucinations, and, anxiety. These medications are often most effective in conjunction with psychosocial evidence-based treatments. Research has often found that the joint treatment approach of utilizing psychopharmacology and psychosocial evidence-based treatments can be more effective than using either one alone. The scope of Part II is on psychosocial evidence-based practices in the assessment and treatment of suicidality.

Part II contains five chapters. The first chapter focuses on assessment, and the following four chapters present specific psychosocial evidence-based treatments. Chapter 4, "Assessment," presents a comprehensive structure for assessing suicidality and offers important practice consideration regarding suicide assessment. Chapter 5, "Crisis Intervention and Suicide," presents the key stages and strategies of crisis intervention. Chapter 6, "Cognitive-Behavioral Therapy and Suicide," presents the core elements and techniques of cognitive-behavioral therapy (CBT) in working with suicidal clients. Chapter 7, "Dialectical Behavior Therapy and Suicide," introduces dialectical behavior therapy (DBT) as a treatment model to address suicidal individuals. Chapter 8, "Interpersonal Psychotherapy and Suicide," describes the preliminary adaptation of this emergent model of intervention with individuals experiencing suicidality.

Part II offers a comprehensive description of these four psychosocial evidence-based treatments for suicidality. The core elements of working from these approaches is presented in relation to the unique challenges of assessing and treating suicidality. Clinical practice expertise requires ongoing training and supervision.

Assessment

Assessment is the cornerstone of effective treatment for individuals with suicidality. Every individual presenting for clinical treatment should be assessed for risk of suicide. Suicide risk assessment must be individualized based on the person, presenting issues, and personal and family history. Although there is no one universal assessment format, there are a number of key components essential to every suicide assessment. This chapter provides a comprehensive structure for assessing suicide risk, including specific questions and recommendations for consideration.

■ Goals and Objectives of This Chapter

An understanding of:

- The role of sociodemographic data in relation to suicide assessment
- The importance of establishing identified problem/symptom history in relation to suicide assessment
- The influence of current suicidality in relation to suicide assessment
- The importance of determining suicide history in relation to suicide assessment
- How family/peer suicide history may impact suicide assessment
- Determining relevant risk factors in relation to suicide assessment
- Determining relevant protective factors in relation to suicide assessment
- Using suicide rating scales

■ Potential outcomes of assessment
■ Core assessment recommendations

INTRODUCTION

Suicide risk assessment should be seen as an individualized, ongoing process. Every individual presenting for treatment should be evaluated for past and present suicidality. Every contact with an individual deemed to be at some level of risk for suicide should incorporate monitoring for changes in risk status. Efficacious treatment begins with a thorough assessment. The more comprehensive and detailed the assessment, the more likely the prescribed treatment will be helpful.

Approximately 2.1% of individuals in the United States have attempted suicide, 3.1% have made suicide plans, and 9.2% have suicidal thoughts (Nock et al., 2008). Given the prevalence of suicidality in the community, it is likely that you will encounter a suicidal individual in your practice. Good clinical practice requires that all clinical evaluations include an assessment of suicidality. While there is no one "correct" approach to suicide assessment, all suicide assessments should incorporate both clinical judgment and comprehensive psychiatric evaluation (Jacobs & Brewer, 2004). In addition, knowledge on the most recent evidence-based practice in your clinical area (e.g., youth with depression, adults with HIV, elderly with cancer, etc.) is also essential to supplement the general guidelines that follow (Roberts & Jennings, 2005; Simon, 2006).

CORE SUICIDE ASSESSMENT QUESTION

Suicide assessment should be clear, unambiguous, direct, and nonjudgmental. The assessment should include initially asking the **core suicide question:** "Are you suicidal?" or "Have you ever thought of killing yourself?" The manner in which this question is asked is fundamentally important. If asked with judgment, hesitation, anxiety, or accusation, the client will be less candid in their response. However, if the question is asked with genuine neutrality and openness, the client will be more likely to honestly respond. It is important to recognize that this core suicide assessment question is not a checklist question, but rather the beginnings of a dialogue required for an effective clinical suicidal assessment.

There are three general categories of responses that often emerge from this question:

1. A clear denial of suicidal feelings, **ideations** (thoughts of suicide), and/or plans
2. A clear endorsement of suicidal feelings, ideations, and/or plans
3. A vague, nebulous response that neither endorses nor denies suicidality

The categorical response will help determine the breadth and depth of the suicide assessment dialogue. Further, it is critical to note that even a clear denial requires follow-up assessment. It is recommended that every client regardless of their presentation or diagnosis be assessed with this core suicide assessment question. Not to do so is a clinical error.

■ Role Play 4.1

Break into groups of three in which one person assumes the role of the mental health clinician, another the role of a new client in an emergency room, and the third an impartial observer. For this role play you can adopt the stance that the client is actively suicidal, passively suicidal (having suicidal thoughts without intention to act), or not suicidal in the least. Engage in a role play in which you ask the core suicide assessment question. Role play this discussion for two to four minutes. The observer should record the verbal and nonverbal presentation of the question and the verbal and nonverbal response to the question and provide feedback to the group.

■ Small Group Exercise 4.1

Based on role play 4.1, stay in your role play groups and discuss the following questions. Remember, answers are personal and there are no correct or incorrect answers.

1. What were your thoughts and feelings as a mental health professional when you asked the core suicide assessment question?
2. What were your thoughts and feelings as a client when you were asked the core suicide assessment question?
3. Did you find any surprises in the responses to the first two questions? If so, what were they, and how were you surprised?

FUNDAMENTAL SUICIDE ASSESSMENT COMPONENTS

The key components of the follow-up questions are to determine the nature and degree of the suicide risk. Beyond a traditional biopsychosocial assessment, when assessing suicide risk a number of critical areas need to be considered and investigated. According to established guidelines (Academy of Child & Adolescent Psychiatry, 2001; American Psychiatric Association [APA], 2003; Barber, Marzuk, Leon, & Portera, 2001; Jacobs, 1999; Posner, Oquendo, Gould, Stanley, & Davies, 2007; Rudd, 2006; Rudd, Cukrowicz, & Bryan, 2008; Shea, 2002; Wingate, Joiner, Walker, Rudd, & Jobes, 2004), it is important to recognize that it may not always be feasible to obtain all of the following recommended information. The APA (2003) Practice Guidelines for the Assessment and Treatment of Patients with Suicidal Behaviors is an example of a comprehensive guideline for suicide assessment, however, it focuses on psychiatry. A clinician may have to begin with an assessment of the most pertinent categories and continue with a more in-depth evaluation during later sessions. A detailed assessment results in an effective treatment plan. The more detailed the assessment, the greater the clinician's ability to plan and implement an effective intervention. Therefore, the following seven areas require detailed assessment:

1. Sociodemographic data
2. Identified problem/symptom history
3. Current suicidality
4. Suicide history
5. Family/peer suicide history
6. Risk factors
7. Protective factors

Sociodemographic Data

An assessment of demographic data is essential to any suicide assessment. Given that there is different risk attributed to specific demographic characteristics (as is discussed in various chapters of this text), this assessment provides for the ability to determine the relevant risk and **protective factors** that may be present and subsequently incorporated into an individualized treatment plan. While not exhaustive, pertinent demographic information to assess includes the following:

- Age
- Gender
- Race
- Culture
- Ethnicity

- Immigration status/experience
- Languages spoken
- Religion
- Marital status
- Domestic violence
- Substance use and/or abuse
- Past or current abuse/neglect (e.g., physical, emotional, sexual, bullying)
- Sexual orientation (coming-out process)
- Socioeconomic status (SES)
- Education level
- Academic history (current and past academic status, changes in status, type of education)
- Occupation
- Employment history (current and past employment status, changes in status, type of work)
- Social support
- Where do they live
- Who resides with them
- Recent changes, moves, births, deaths, separations, etc.
- Overall health (includes: pregnancy, medications, smoking, any changes in health status)
- Current medical conditions (thyroid problems, AIDS, HIV status, etc.)
- Past medical history (diagnoses, operations, time in hospital, etc.)
- Developmental history (birth history, health problems as a child, developmental milestones, academic and cognitive functioning)
- Referral source and information

Identified Problem/Symptom History

In this section, the focus is on issues beyond current and past suicidality, which are assessed in detail in the following sections. A detailed history of the client's presenting problem, along with a detailed symptom history, allows a clinician to further assess suicide risk and to individualize a treatment plan targeting key issues and diagnostic features. Some key questions to assess in this area include the following:

- What is the client's main/chief concern/problem?
- Does the client have a *DSM* diagnosis (e.g., depressive disorder, anxiety disorder, substance abuse, schizophrenia)?
- When did the problem start? How long has it been there?
- Is the problem constant, intermittent, episodic, and so forth?

- What makes the problem worse?
- What makes the problem better?
- How does the problem impact them? How does it impact their family and friends?
- How have they managed/coped?
- Where in their life does the problem impact them the most? Least?
- Why do they think they have the problem?
- Who first identified or diagnosed the issue? When? Where? Why? How?
- What is the treatment and treatment history? What treatments (e.g., professional, personal, alternative) have they sought out and/or received? Therapy, counseling, medication, and so forth?
- If they received counseling/therapy, where? With whom? In what ways was it helpful and/or unhelpful?
- If they are on medication, what is its name? Type? Dose? Treatment regimen? Did the medication work? Did/does the medication had side effects? Have they changed the medication(s)? Were they adherent? Why or why not?
- Have they ever been hospitalized because of to the problem? (If so, provide details)

Current Suicidality

There are several criteria that are essential to consider in assessing for current suicidality. These are: ideation, intent, plan/planning, feasibility, lethality, timing, impulsivity/aggression, and hopelessness. In considering these factors, it is important to recognize that they are not a yes/no checklist, but rather, they frequently exist along a spectrum of severity. Assessment of current suicidality should specifically focus on the following:

A. Ideation
   a. Have they ever felt life is not worth living?
   b. Are they tired of living?
   c. What things in their life make them want to go on living?
   d. Do they ever wish they were not born? Or would not wake up in the morning?
   e. Have they ever felt trapped and that there is no way out?
   f. Have they thought about death recently?
   g. How comfortable are they with these thoughts?
   h. When did they first have these thoughts?

  i. What do they think led up to the thoughts?
  j. Have they discussed these thoughts with anyone?

B. Intent

  a. How close have they come to acting on these thoughts?
  b. On a scale of 1 to 10, 1 being not at all likely and 10 being extremely likely, how likely is it that they will act on these thoughts now?
  c. On a scale of 1 to 10, how likely do they think it is that they will act on them in the future?
  d. Do they want to die, no longer want to live, or can they just not think of any other solution to their problems?
  e. If there was another solution to their problem, would they take it?

C. Plan/planning (rehearsals)

  a. Have they made a specific plan to kill themselves? Is there more than one plan?
  b. If yes, what does the plan include? How detailed is it?
  c. Have they thought of a time when they will carry out the plan?
  d. Have they researched various means to kill themselves (e.g., Internet, books, etc.)?
  e. Have they ever started to act out a plan to hurt or kill themselves but then stopped (e.g., picked up a bottle of pills, picked up a knife, walked to a bridge, etc.)?
  f. Have they made any specific preparations?
      i. Purchased items to facilitate the plan?
      ii. Written a note?
      iii. Given things away?
      iv. Stocked up on pills?

D. Feasibility

  a. Is the method readily available to them?
  b. Are they able to carry out the plan (e.g., cognitively and physically)?
  c. Do they have access to guns?
  d. Do they have access to weapons?
  e. Do they have access to pills or other drugs?
  f. Is there anything that prohibits them from carrying out the plan (e.g., supervision, environmental factors, and individual values/beliefs)?
  g. Did they invest sufficient planning so as not to be caught/interrupted?

E. Lethality
   a. What is the degree of lethality associated with the method?
   b. Is death likely?
   c. Have they researched whether the method is likely to end in death?
   d. Is it likely that they could be saved if medical intervention is sought?

F. Timing
   a. How often are the thoughts occurring?
   b. Do they occur more often when with certain individuals?
   c. Do they occur more often in certain places?
   d. Do they occur more often during certain times of the day or year?
   e. When do they not occur?

G. Impulsivity/aggression
   a. Do they have a history of acting impulsively? If yes, in what ways? Provide examples.
   b. Do they have a history of acting aggressively? If yes, in what ways? Provide examples.
   c. Do they feel they have control over their thoughts or behaviors?
   d. Have they ever acted impulsively while under the influence of a substance?

H. Hopelessness
   a. Do they feel hopeless?
   b. If yes, how long have they felt hopeless?
   c. What things in life have lead them to feel more or less hopeless about the future?

Suicide History

An assessment of suicide history should begin by ascertaining whether or not the individual has a history of past suicide attempts. Whenever a history of suicidal behavior is present, a thorough assessment of current suicide risk requires an understanding of past attempts. It is important to consider the following areas in assessing for suicide history:

A. Number of attempts
   a. Total number of attempts they have made in their lifetime
   b. Breakdown of number of attempts in the last month, year, 5 years, total

For each attempt reported, assess the following areas, beginning with the most recent attempt:

B. Nature of attempt

   a. Describe the attempt

      i. Circumstances

         1. Who else was around, if anyone?

         2. Where did the attempt take place?

         3. When did the attempt take place?

      ii. Method

         1. What did the attempt consist of?

         2. Were alcohol and/or substances used?

         3. If yes, were they used to facilitate carrying out the method or as a means to increase lethality?

      iii. Purpose of attempt

         1. Escaping their problems

         2. Reactions or manipulation of others

         3. Injury

         4. Death

         5. Unknown

      iv. Precipitants to the attempt

      v. Was the attempt completed, interrupted, or aborted?

      vi. Did they think they would be found?

C. Lethality/Severity

   a. On a scale of 1 to 10, how lethal did they think their attempt would be?

   b. Did they research the lethality of their method?

   c. Did they think their life could be saved by medical intervention if they were found?

D. Postattempt Factors

   a. Postvention

      i. Were they found by someone else? If yes, describe circumstances.

      ii. Did they bring themselves in for help? Describe the circumstances.

      iii. Did they do nothing yet the attempt passed without causing injury?

   b. What were their thoughts and feelings after the attempt (e.g., relief, regret)?

    c. Did they tell someone they made an attempt?
    d. Reflecting on the attempt, what would they have done differently?
E. Consequences
    a. Medical attention
      i. Was there an emergency room visit/treatment?
      ii. Were they hospitalized? If yes, describe.
    b. Outpatient referral
    c. Family support
    d. Nothing
F. Plan/planning (rehearsals)
    a. How long did they plan the attempt before acting on it?
    b. Was the attempt impulsive?
    c. What thoughts did they have prior to attempting?
    d. Did they leave a note?
    e. Did they tell others of their plans to attempt?
    f. Did they give personal items away?
    g. Did they create a will (e.g., on paper, electronically, or on the Internet)?

Family/Peer Suicide History

It is indicated that individuals who experience the suicide or attempted suicide of a relative or peer are at increased risk for attempting suicide themselves (Grossman, Milligan, & Deyo, 1991; Ho, Leung, Hung, Lee, & Tang, 2000; Lewinsohn, Rohde, & Seeley, 1994; Mann, 2002; Roy, 1983). Therefore, accurate assessment of suicide risk requires evaluation of the suicide history of an individual's support network. It is important to determine the nature of the relationship because the risk of suicide varies according to degree of relation. This evaluation should begin with the question: "Have any of your relatives and/or peers completed or attempted suicide?" A more detailed history should then be gathered that assesses the following:

A. If yes, what was your relationship to the individual?
B. How closely did you identify with this individual?
C. Number of attempts
    a. Total number of attempts made in the relative/peer's lifetime
    b. Recency of attempts

For each attempt reported, assess the following areas, beginning with the most recent attempt:

D. Describe the attempt
  a. Circumstances
  b. Method
  c. Did the person tell you about the attempt or did you find him/her?
  d. Consequences
E. Impact of Attempt
  a. How did the attempt/completed suicide affect you?
  b. Did you feel responsible? If yes, in what ways?

Risk Factors

There are several established **risk factors** for suicidality. It is important to recognize that having one or more risk factor(s) does not make someone suicidal, nor does the absence of risk factors negate the risk. However, the number of risk factors present often correlates with the level of suicide risk. The following list of risk factors is not a checklist but should be the basis for a dialogue regarding the factors impacting an individual's risk. It is important to assess for whether these factors are acute or chronic. (Please refer to chapters 9–11 for a comprehensive discussion of pertinent risk factors for suicide across the life span.)

A. Social
  a. Who is in their family of origin?
  b. Who is in their current family? (Note any significant recent changes, e.g., divorce, separation, birth, etc.)
  c. Is there a history of recent amorous crises?
  d. Is there a history of isolation/rejection?
  e. Is there a family history of psychiatric illness/mental health problems (include suicide/suicide attempts)?
  f. What is their family's medical history?
  g. Is there a family history of abuse, state involvement, children's services, and so forth?
  h. What is their family's economic status?
  i. What are their family's ethnic/cultural customs traditions (specifically those related to health and illness)?

j. Does their family have immigration history, issues, difficulties, current problems?

k. What are their family's religious/spiritual beliefs or customs?

l. What does their family/partner/friends/social network think of the presenting problem? Do they exacerbate the issue? Do they support treatment?

B. Environmental

  a. Poverty

  b. Poor access to health and mental health care

  c. Safety (e.g., community, housing, family, etc.)

  d. Recent or pending changes in home academic, and/or occupational status (e.g., moves, evictions, losing jobs)

  e. Involvement with the legal system

  f. Access to lethal means

C. Psychiatric

  a. Mental illness diagnosis

    i. Do they have a current *DSM* diagnosis (e.g., depressive disorder, substance abuse, schizophrenia, etc.)? If yes, how many?

    ii. Do they have a past *DSM* diagnosis? If yes, what were they?

  b. Current mental status

    i. Cognitive and emotional functioning

  c. Psychiatric treatment history

    i. Inpatient admissions

    ii. Outpatient treatment

    iii. Emergency room visits/treatment

    iv. Psychopharmacological treatments

    v. Adherence to treatment

D. Individual

  a. Poor coping skills

  b. Change in or loss of past coping strategies

  c. Limited problem-solving skills

  d. External loci of control

  e. Poor self-esteem

  f. Low self-efficacy

  g. Few reasons for living

  h. Shame

  i. Guilt

j. Worthlessness
k. Hopelessness
l. Low frustration tolerance
m. Perfectionism
n. Increased impulsivity/aggression
o. Impaired relatedness

Protective Factors

Similar to risk factors, protective factors are highly individualized, yet there are several known factors that have been shown to be associated with decreased suicide risk. While risk factors are often explored, protective factors are often minimized. Therefore, it is essential to purposefully assess for these factors. It is important to note that while the opposite of a given risk factor is not necessarily a protective factor, often this is the case (e.g., having a positive support network versus a negative support network).

The following list of protective factors should not be used as a checklist but should be the basis for a discussion regarding the factors impacting an individual's risk. Again, it is necessary to determine whether these factors are acute or chronic. Please refer to chapters 9–11 for a comprehensive review of protective factors for suicide across the life span. The following four areas should be considered:

A. Social
   a. Who is in their family of origin?
   b. Quality/quantity of support network
   c. What does their family/partner/friends/social network think of the presenting problem? Are they supportive (i.e., interest/concern for the individual), or do they exacerbate the issue/treatment?
   d. Family strengths and resources
   e. Family religion/spiritual beliefs or customs
   f. Availability and willingness of family to be involved in treatment
   g. Family involvement in self-help groups (e.g., National Alliance for the Mentally Ill [NAMI])
   h. Ethnic/cultural health treatments (practices, folk lore, remedies, alternative medication, etc.)
B. Environmental
   a. Stable SES
   b. Adequate access to health and mental health care

      c. Safety (e.g., community, housing, family, etc.)

      d. Restricted access to lethal means

C. Psychiatric

      a. Lack of a mental illness diagnosis

      b. Intact cognitive and emotional functioning

      c. Limited psychiatric history

      d. History of adherence to treatment recommendations

D. Individual

      a. Effective coping skills

      b. Comprehensive problem-solving skills

      c. Internal loci of control

      d. High self-esteem

      e. Self-efficacy

      f. Increased reasons for living

      g. Ability to relate to others

      h. Repulsion to death/attraction to life

SUICIDE RATING SCALES

There are a number of well-known psychiatric rating scales for assessing suicidality with established psychometric properties. While suicide rating scales can never replace a fundamental suicide assessment, they can enhance a clinician's determination of suicide risk. Suicide rating scales may evaluate the presence or absence of risk and protective factors, or they may focus more on specific aspects of suicidal thoughts and behaviors such as degree of intent or lethality of plan. It is recommended that, when possible, suicide assessment be supplemented by use of an established rating scale. Amongst the most well-known and widely used suicide rating scales worth considering are the following: (1) Scale for Suicidal Ideation (Beck, Kovacs, & Weissman, 1979), (2) Suicide Intent Scale (Beck, Resnick, Lettieri, & Bowie, 1974), (3) Suicide Assessment Scale (Stanley, Träskman-Bendz, & Stanley, 1986) (4) Columbia Suicide History Form (Oquendo, Halberstam, & Mann, 2003), and (5) Reasons for Living Inventory (Linehan, Goodstein, Nielsen, & Chiles, 1983).

▧ Case Example 4.1

You are a mental health clinician in an outpatient psychiatric clinic. You are scheduled to do an intake with a new client who was self-referred for services.

Selena is a currently unemployed, 24-year-old female who recently graduated from college. She has been actively seeking employment for over 6 months to no avail and has been struggling with student loan payments and other expenses throughout this time. Usually a very independent person, Selena has become increasingly dependent on others for financial support. Two weeks ago, her boyfriend of 2.5 years who had moved away for graduate school unexpectedly broke up with her via e-mail. While she has suffered from bouts of depression in the past, Selena has no formal psychiatric history of major mental illness or suicidality.

▓ Role Play 4.2

Based on case example 4.1, engage in a role play in which you conduct an assessment of suicide risk using the Fundamental Suicide Assessment Components described in this chapter. One person takes on the role of the clinician, and one takes the role of the client, Selena. As the client, improvise the data regarding Selena's family history and risk/protective factors.

RECOMMENDATIONS FOR CONDUCTING A SUICIDE ASSESSMENT

It is critical to understand that the guidelines in this chapter provide comprehensive details on working with suicidality in general. It is necessary to individualize the assessment based on evidence-based knowledge regarding suicide within specific contexts. For example, assessing a 75-year-old with stage IV prostate cancer, a 16-year-old in the coming-out process with substance abuse, a 29-year-old with anorexia nervosa, or a 35-year-old woman who recently lost her two children in a car accident requires unique and specific targeted assessment. Apart from clinical presentation, the following recommendations are offered as a framework for conducting an effective suicide risk assessment. These recommendations are designed to support and facilitate the data-gathering dialogue described previously.

1. A transparent, neutral, and nonjudgmental stance on the part of the clinician will improve engagement and facilitate more honest, open responses on the part of the client.
2. The development and maintenance of a therapeutic alliance enhances suicide risk assessment.
3. The patterning, flow, and sensitivity of questions is critical to the outcome of a suicide risk assessment. It is important to avoid an

interrogational style. If the client is talking, they may answer many of your questions out of order or sequence, but this will encourage a more natural comfortable conversation.

4. The instillation of hope that alternative solutions to suicide exist is key.

5. Conveying to the client that effective assessment is only the first step in an ongoing process of intervention is extremely important to engage and motivate their commitment to treatment.

6. A client's honest communication of his or her thoughts and feelings should be recognized and commended as a first step in the change process.

7. Knowledge of evidence-based practice in one's specific practice area, one's professional codes of ethics, and the laws regarding suicide within one's state of practice should be considered in and/or integrated into assessment as required.

8. Clinical supervision and guidance are vital in working with suicidal individuals. Professional supervision is particularly important when determining disposition based on the information gathered during the assessment.

DETERMINING OUTCOMES BASED ON ASSESSMENT

The fundamental suicide assessment informs the level of suicide risk of the client. In essence, the level of risk determines the disposition to follow. The level of risk can be seen as existing along a spectrum of risk ranging from an absence of suicide risk (where there is no suicide risk present) to acute, severe suicide risk (where the individual is actively suicidal and is unsafe to be left alone). The disposition ranges from no referral to outpatient referral with or without psychopharmacological intervention to immediate psychiatric hospitalization. Documentation of risk level and rationale for this determination is critical.

There are no absolute, scientific categories of suicide risk. However, treatment disposition can be seen across five general categories of suicide risk: (1) absences of risk, (2) low risk, (3) moderate risk, (4) high risk, and (5) severe risk. The following are broad possible dispositions based on level of risk and are not to be considered disposition recommendations, which require full suicide assessment and cannot be determined without individual client contact.

■ If the client presents with an absence of suicide risk, disposition should be based on the nature of the clinical presentation and other issues present (e.g., divorce, homelessness, depression, etc.).

■ If the client presents with low suicide risk, outpatient referral may be an acceptable disposition.

■ If the client presents with moderate suicide risk, an outpatient referral can be a reasonable disposition, and psychopharmacological treatment may be considered to supplement outpatient psychotherapy.

■ If the client presents with high suicide risk, observation in the emergency room (ER) for up to 72 hours is often recommended.

■ If the client presents with severe suicide risk, admission to a psychiatric hospital is generally required.

Clients that are not admitted to an ER or psychiatric hospital should be monitored at each contact for changes in their suicide risk level and may require safety planning and/or future crisis intervention (see chapter 5 for a full review of crisis intervention).

SUMMARY

As clinicians it is imperative that we effectively assess every client for risk of suicide. Using the core suicide assessment question and the fundamental suicide assessment components can facilitate an informative, thorough assessment of suicide risk that aids clinicians in level of suicide risk and appropriate intervention and treatment. Level of suicide risk will vary over time. Although past suicide risk assessments may be helpful, they cannot serve as present indicators of suicide risk. The most comprehensive assessment is at best an assessment of risk at that moment; therefore, clinicians should continually monitor clients for any changes in risk level.

■ Key Points

1. Assessment is an ongoing process that should be revisited during every contact with clients at risk for suicide.
2. Every client is different, therefore, suicide assessment must be individualized.
3. It is required to ask the core suicide assessment question of every client.
4. Every client with any level of suicide risk should participate in a fundamental suicide assessment.

5. Level of suicide risk exists along a continuum.
6. Suicide rating scales can enhance the evaluation of suicide risk.
7. Supervision is essential for effective suicide assessment and management.
8. Knowledge of evidence-based practice in the specific problem area of the client is essential.
9. Awareness of professional code of ethics and state laws regarding suicide are required.
10. Assessment should be followed by appropriate disposition.

FURTHER READINGS

Brown, G. S., Jones, E. R., Betts, E., & Wu, J. (2003). Improving suicide risk assessment in a managed-care environment. *Crisis: Journal of Crisis Intervention & Suicide*, *24*(2), 49–55.

Forster, P. (1994). Accurate assessment of short-term suicide risk in a crisis. *Psychiatric Annals, 24*(11), 571–578.

Galloucis, M., & Francek, H. (2002). The Juvenile Suicide Assessment: An instrument for the assessment and management of suicide risk with incarcerated juveniles. *International Journal of Emergency Mental Health, 4*(3), 181–199.

Hall, R. C., Platt, D. E., & Hall, R. C. (1999). Suicide risk assessment: A review of risk factors for suicide in 100 patients who made severe suicide attempts. Evaluation of suicide risk in a time of managed care. *Psychosomatics, 40*(1), 18–27.

Larzelere, R. E., Andersen, J. J., Ringle, J. L., & Jorgensen, D. D. (2004). The child suicide risk assessment: A screening measure of suicide risk in pre-adolescents. *Death Studies, 28*(9), 809–827.

Maris, R. W., Berman, A. L., Maltsberger, J. T., & Yufit, R. I. (1992). *Assessment and prediction of suicide*. New York: Guilford Press.

O'Connor, N., Warby, M., Raphael, B., & Vassallo, T. (2004). Changeability, confidence, common sense and corroboration: Comprehensive suicide risk assessment. *Australasian Psychiatry, 12*(4), 352–360.

Stuart, C., Waalen, J. K., & Haelstromm, E. (2003). Many helping hearts: An evaluation of peer gatekeeper training in suicide risk assessment. *Death Studies, 27*(4), 321–333.

ELECTRONIC RESOURCES

National Mental Illness Screening project: http://www.mentalhealthscreening.org
Suicide Information & Education Centre: http://www.suicideinfo.ca
Training Institute for Suicide Assessment: http://www.suicideassessment.com

KNOWLEDGE ACQUISITION TEST

In lieu of a knowledge acquisition test, test your ability to recall the questions involved in fundamental assessment components: sociodemographic data, identified problem/symptom history, current suicidality, suicide history, family/peer suicide history, risk factors, and protective factors.

REFERENCES

Academy of Child & Adolescent Psychiatry. (2001). Practice parameter for the assessment and treatment of children and adolescents with suicidal behavior. *Journal of the American Academy of Child & Adolescent Psychiatry, 40,* 24S–50S.

American Psychiatric Association. (2003). *Practice guideline for the assessment and treatment of patients with suicidal behaviors.* Washington, DC: Author.

Barber, M. E., Marzuk, P. M., Leon, A. C., & Portera, L. (2001). Gate questions in psychiatric interviewing: The case of suicide assessment. *Journal of Psychiatric Research, 35*(1), 67–69.

Beck, A. T., Kovacs, M., & Wiessman, A. (1979). Assessment of suicidal intention: The Scale for Suicide Ideation. *Journal of Consulting and Clinical Psychology, 47*(2), 343–352.

Beck, A. T., H. L. P. Resnick, D. J. Lettieri, & M. D. Bowie (Eds.) (1974). Development of suicidal intent scales. In *The prediction of suicide.* Charles Press.

Grossman, D. C., Milligan, B. C., & Deyo, R. A. (1991). Risk factors for suicide attempts among Navajo adolescents. *American Journal of Public Health, 81,* 870–874.

Ho, T P., Leung, P. W., Hung, S. F., Lee, C. C., & Tang, C. P. (2000). The mental health of peer suicide completers and attempters. *Journal of Child Psychology and Psychiatry, 41,* 301–308.

Jacobs, D. (1999). *The Harvard guide to suicide assessment and intervention.* San Francisco: Jossey-Bass.

Jacobs, D., & Brewer, M. (2004). APA Practice Guideline provides recommendations for assessing and treating patients with suicidal behaviors. *Psychiatric Annals, 34*(5), 373–380.

Lewinsohn, P. M., Rohde, P., & Seeley, J. R. (1994). Psychosocial risk factors for future adolescent suicide attempts. *Journal of Consulting and Clinical Psychology, 62,* 297–305.

Linehan, M. M., Goodstein, J. L., Nielsen, S. L.,& Chiles, J. A. (1983). Reasons for staying alive when you are thinking of killing yourself: The Reasons for Living Inventory. *Journal of Consulting and Clinical Psychology, 51*(2), 276–286.

Mann, J. J. (2002). A current perspective of suicide and attempted suicide. *Annals of Internal Medicine, 136*(4), 302–311.

Nock, M. K., Borges, G., Bromet, E. J., Alonso, J., Angermeyer, M., Beautrais, A., et al. (2008). Cross-national prevalence and risk factors for suicidal ideation, plans and attempts. *British Journal of Psychiatry, 192*(2), 98–105.

Oquendo, M., Halberstam, B., & Mann, J. J. (2003). Risk factors for suicidal behavior: Utility and limitations of research instruments. In M. First (Ed.), *Standardized assessment for the clinician.* Washington, DC: APPI.

Posner, K., Oquendo, M. A., Gould, M., Stanley, B., & Davies, M. (2007). Columbia Classification Algorithm of Suicide Assessment (C-CASA): Classification of suicidal events in the FDA's pediatric suicidal risk analysis of antidepressants. *American Journal of Psychiatry, 164*(7), 1035–1043.

Roberts, A. R., & Jennings, T. (2005). Hanging by a thread: How failure to conduct an adequate lethality assessment resulted in suicide. *Brief Treatment and Crisis Intervention, 5*(3), 251–260.

Roy, A. (1983). Family history of suicide. *Archives of General Psychiatry, 40,* 971–974.

Rudd, D. M. (2006). *Assessment and management of suicidality.* Sarasota, FL: Professional Resource Press.

Rudd, D. M., Cukrowicz, K. C., & Bryan, C. J. (2008). Core competencies in suicide risk assessment and management: Implications for supervision. *Training and Education in Professional Psychology, 2*(4), 219–228.

Shea, S. (2002). *The practical art of suicide assessment: A guide for mental health professionals and substance abuse counselors.* Hoboken, NJ: Wiley.

Simon, R. L. (2006). Suicide risk assessment: Is clinical experience enough? *Journal of the American Academy of Psychiatry and the Law, 34*(3), 276–278.

Stanley, B., Träskman-Bendz, L., & Stanley, M. (1986). The Suicide Assessment Scale: A scale evaluating change in suicidal behavior. *Psychopharmacology Bulletin, 22*(1), 200–205.

Wingate, L., Joiner, T. E., Walker, R., Rudd, D. M., & Jobes, D. A. (2004). Empirically informed approaches to topics in suicide risk assessment. *Behavior Sciences & the Law, 22*(5), 651–655.

5 Crisis Intervention and Suicide

Although most people will experience a crisis at some point or points in their lives, most of these experiences do not result in suicidality. However, when an individual is experiencing a suicidal crisis, crisis intervention may be an appropriate treatment modality. This chapter presents a model of crisis intervention for suicidal individuals. Key stages and strategies are examined. Evidence regarding the effectiveness of crisis intervention is explored. Finally, recommendations for clinical practice when implementing crisis intervention are provided.

■ Goals and Objectives of This Chapter

An understanding of:

- The definition of crisis
- The key factors of a crisis
- Crisis intervention models
- Robert's Seven-Stage Crisis Intervention Model (RSSCIM)
- Core stages of crisis intervention
- Evidence to support the use of crisis interventions
- Populations for and settings in which crisis intervention is supported
- Clinical considerations when conducting crisis interventions
- Common errors or pitfalls when conducting crisis intervention
- The opportunity for positive change during a crisis period

INTRODUCTION

A **crisis** can be defined as a time-limited response to an event or group of events that significantly disrupts and distresses an individual and overwhelms his or her coping strategies. Literature further highlights that the crisis stimuli is typically unexpected (Westefeld & Heckman-Stone, 2003). The resultant disruption or distress has been described as a loss of psychological homeostasis (Roberts & Ottens, 2005) or a severe disequilibrium (Maris, Berman, & Silverman, 2000; Westefeld & Heckman-Stone, 2003), signifying a loss of stability and possible functional impairment due to a failure of existing coping mechanisms' abilities to regulate an individual's response to the stimuli.

Interestingly, the Chinese symbol for crisis comprises two separate symbols, those of *danger* and *opportunity* (Roberts & Dziegielewski, 1995). A moment of crisis often represents a threat to the individual, yet produces a time where positive change may occur. When an individual is in crisis and experiencing suicidality, effective crisis intervention is a treatment option that can ameliorate distress and provide motivation and mechanism for productive change.

Every crisis is different and individually defined, that is, what may qualify as a crisis for one individual may not produce a crisis for another individual or even for that same individual at a different time in his or her life. In order to effectively treat an individual experiencing a crisis, it is important to recognize your preconceived ideas regarding what constitutes a crisis and how a crisis can be managed.

▨ Individual Exercise 5.1

Think of a past personal crisis. (This may evoke some distressing thoughts and feelings. If you prefer, you may consider skipping this exercise or reflecting on a historical experience in the distant rather than recent past, or a less painful experience. The intention of this exercise is one of reflection and understanding related to crisis. It is not designed or intended for you to relive a traumatic event.)

1. How do you define a crisis? Be as specific as possible.
2. List events or situations that may result in a crisis and rank in order of severity. From your personal experience, reflect on a time when you have experienced a crisis.
3. What were the key elements of the experience that made it a crisis for you?
4. Which, if any, of the elements described above was the most critical for you during this experience?

5. During the time of the crisis, did it feel like it would never end?
6. In looking back at that prior experience, what was the first sign that the crisis was abating?
7. What helped you to resolve this crisis?
8. What, if anything, made the crisis more difficult to resolve? Or did any intended help have the opposite effect?

Small Group Exercise 5.1

In a small group of two or three, please discuss, as you are comfortable, your responses to questions 1–3 in individual exercise 5.1. Remember, answers are personal, and there are no correct or incorrect answers.

1. What were the response similarities in your group?
2. What were the response differences in your group?
3. Did you find any surprises in the group discussion? If so, what were they, and how were you surprised?
4. As every crisis is unique according to the individual, discuss how you think your ranking of crisis may impact the treatment you provide to a client in crisis, both positively and negatively?

Small Group Exercise 5.2

In a small group of two or three, please discuss, as you are comfortable, your responses to questions 4–8 in individual exercise 5.1. Remember, answers are personal, and there are no correct or incorrect answers.

1. What were the response similarities in your group?
2. What were the response differences in your group?
3. Did you find any surprises in the group discussion? If so, what were they, and how were you surprised?
4. As a mental health clinician, how does hearing about others' experiences of crisis impact how you approach clients experiencing a crisis?

CRISIS INTERVENTION MODEL

There is no one universal **crisis intervention model**. Several models of crisis intervention exist in the literature. Despite differences, these models closely parallel each other in structure and composition. Some comprehensive crisis intervention models have been studied for effectiveness across populations and settings. A model that has received more detailed attention in the literature is Roberts' Seven-Stage Crisis Intervention Model (RSSCIM; Roberts, 1991; Roberts & Jennings, 2005; Roberts & Ottens, 2005) (see Figure 5.1).

Figure 5.1 Roberts' Seven-Stage Crisis Intervention Model.
Source: Copyright © Albert R. Roberts, 1991. Reprinted by permission of the author.

These stages of the RSSCIM are intended to be completed sequentially with recognition that there may be overlap across some stages. All of the stages are considered necessary and include:

Stage I: Psychosocial and Lethality Assessment—Plan and conduct a thorough biopsychosocial assessment (see chapter 4). This assessment may need to be conducted quickly and specifically target

strengths, supports, stressors, coping strategies and resources, medications, medical needs, and, substance use. This assessment should
evaluate current lethality and intent of ideation or plan and should
result in a determination of whether the client is in imminent danger (see chapter 5).

Stage II: Rapidly Establish Rapport—Make psychological contact, and rapidly establish the collaborative relationship. Empathy,
reflective listening, reframing, reinforcing strengths, supporting
existing coping strategies, and maintaining a nonjudgmental stance
are essential skills during this stage to develop a positive working
relationship with the client in a short period of time in order to address the crisis.

Stage III: Identify the Major Problems or Crisis Precipitants—
Identify the major problems, including crisis precipitants. Elicit
from the client what the current stimuli is that led to the crisis. Par-
tializing problems is critical in order to determine which problem
should be addressed first. Answering the questions "Why now?"
and "Where to start?" are the two main components of this stage.

Stage IV: Deal With Feelings and Emotions—Encourage an exploration of feelings and emotions. The two main components of this
stage include providing the opportunity for clients to express their
feelings and to tell their story about the crisis. This stage involves
employing active listening skills and supporting client statements
and also requires gently challenging client maladaptive beliefs'
or negative cognitive schemas relating to their suicidal ideation,
intent, or behavior to consider alternative viewpoints and coping
mechanisms.

Stage V: Generate and Explore Alternatives—Generate and explore
alternatives and new coping strategies. Often considered the most
difficult stage of crisis intervention, this stage requires that clients
acknowledge that suicide is not the only solution and consequently
begin to identify more appropriate and effective means of coping. It is essential that Stage IV is sufficiently addressed in order
for clients to let go of previous unhelpful and maladaptive coping
mechanisms that may have resulted in suicidality. This solution-
focused work is often more successful after some emotional
stability has been achieved through Stage IV. Alternative coping
mechanisms should be developed collaboratively between client

and practitioner. These alternatives have a greater chance of success if they are owned by the client.

Stage VI: Implement an Action Plan—Restore functioning through implementation of an action plan. The strategies developed in the previous stage are transformed into an action plan in this stage. Critical components to consider include: identifying and removing lethal means of suicide (i.e., pills, knives, guns, etc.); contracting for safety as a part of the overall plan; including family and friends in the plan to mobilize support, decrease isolation, and provide initial safety monitoring; address any outstanding mental or physical health issues (i.e., reducing anxiety or depression, improving sleep hygiene); identifying future action steps; and connecting the client to future treatment (i.e., outpatient treatment, hotlines, support groups, etc.).

Stage VII: Follow-Up—Plan follow-up and booster sessions. Following up on stage VI, this stage involves determining a plan for follow-up contact with the client to evaluate postcrisis presentation. Areas to consider during postcrisis assessment include affect regulation, comfort and mastery with new coping skills, substance use, and ongoing support.

The RSSCIM is a model of intervention that can be effectively used across mental health professions. In addition to providing a framework for intervening, it is client-centered in that it incorporates client strengths and resiliency.

A similar crisis intervention model, the 10-stage Integrated Problem-Solving Model (IPSM; Westefeld & Heckman-Stone, 2003) presents a parallel stage model but further subdivides and reorders RSSCIM and emphasizes different aspects of the crisis intervention process. Specifically, IPSM draws initial focus on establishing and maintaining rapport with the client as the first stage. In addition, The IPSM further delineates among the problem-solving model by dividing the tasks of setting goals, generating options, evaluating options, and selecting a plan of action as individual stages.

EVIDENCE FOR AND AGAINST CRISIS INTERVENTION

In general, there is a poverty of research examining the effectiveness of crisis intervention models. As far back as 1977, Auerbach and Kilmann conducted a review of outcome research regarding the effectiveness of crisis intervention and noted the dramatic lack of evidence in this area. Since that time, minimal work has been conducted. However, there is some evidence to support that RSSCIM is an effective mode of treatment for specific populations and in specific settings. Females ranging in age from 15 to 24 and 55 to 64 have been found to benefit from suicide prevention and crisis intervention programs (Roberts, 2002). Individuals presenting with psychiatric crises also demonstrated positive outcomes from crisis intervention programs (Roberts, 2002; Roberts & Ottens, 2005). In-home intensive family-based crisis intervention has been shown to be highly effective at reducing child abuse and neglect in troubled families (Roberts & Everly, 2006). Studies indicate that Roberts's model is effective for use with female domestic violence survivors and battered women (Burman, 2003; Lee, 2007). Adolescents experiencing problems with suicide, substance abuse, and loss also benefit from crisis intervention (Roberts, 2002). However, longitudinal and comparative studies are sorely needed (Roberts & Jennings, 2005), as are multicultural studies examining the impact of race, ethnicity, socioeconomic status, gender, and age in relation to the effectiveness of crisis intervention (Stone & Conley, 2004).

RECOMMENDED CLINICAL GUIDELINES FOR CRISIS INTERVENTION

Crisis intervention is a complex and delicate process. Above and beyond following a specific crisis intervention model there are other practice considerations that require recognition. The following recommendations may aid clinicians in implementing and conducting crisis intervention with suicidal clients:

1. *Psychoeducation for support networks.* When possible, it is recommended that mental health practitioners educate family members and support networks regarding means of ensuring the safety of the individuals in suicidal crisis. According to McManus and colleagues (1997), 96% of suicide attempts occur at home, and 94.4% of homes have at least one form of suicide available at the time an individual makes a suicide attempt. Among families who received psychoeducation regarding restricting access to lethal means, 86% locked up or disposed of means compared to only 32% of families who did not

receive such psychoeducation. Although it is important to keep this recommendation in mind with all clients, it is specifically important when working with adolescents.

2. *Encouraging treatment engagement.* Having plans for follow-up treatment is not sufficient. It is important to recognize that approximately 60% of individuals who present for initial treatment of suicidality attend their first scheduled follow-up outpatient treatment appointment (O'Brien, Holton, Hurren, Wyatt, & Hassanyeh, 1987). This is particularly concerning given that the 3-month period following a suicide attempt is the highest risk period for repeat suicidality (Rudd, Joiner, Jobes, & King, 1996). Consequently, it is recommended that specific attention be paid to and strategies be developed for supporting the individual's engagement in follow-up treatment. Such strategies may include: addressing barriers to psychosocial barriers to treatment; providing additional contact via telephone, writing, or in-person to support attendance at outpatient treatment; and assessing and promoting the individual's motivation for treatment.

3. *Building resources.* In addition to enlisting the support of immediate family and significant others, it is recommended that clinicians working with individuals in suicidal crisis help their clients to develop resources they can access and implement during times of stress. Two important examples of such resource development include: (1) a list of coping strategies that the client has found to be effective in managing prior stressors, and (2) a list of individuals across social settings and networks that can be contacted in times of stress, such as extended family, neighbors, occupational or academic peers, social organizations (i.e., religious organizations, sports clubs), hotline numbers, support group information, and emergency room numbers, to name a few.

4. *Supervision.* Using formal supervision or clinical consultation with colleagues is highly recommended as a means of managing one's anxieties, concerns, and stress related to working with individuals in crisis. In addition, consultation can provide feedback and input on how the crisis intervention process is being carried out.

Crisis intervention can result in clinicians intentionally or unintentionally committing a number of possible errors or mistakes. It is important for clinicians not only to be aware of positive and effective recommendations but to be mindful of potential errors or pitfalls of crisis intervention. Following are some recommendations that mental health clinicians should be guarded against during a crisis intervention:

1. *Marginalizing or dehumanizing the client.* Mental health clinicians possess unequal power in their relationship with a client. During a crisis, clinicians can adopt an expert, directing, or evaluative position that increases this power imbalance or inequity. This may distance or marginalize the client (Shenassa, Rogers, Spalding, & Roberts, 2004).
2. *Contributing to the stigma of suicide.* Clinicians can directly add to a client's stigma or shame through their interactions or responses (e.g., self-reproach, judgment). More insidiously, clinicians can increase stigma by indirectly centering on the facts of the suicide and minimizing the process. The overwhelming focus on collecting data relating to the risk and lethality (i.e., the facts) with less attention on the narrative story, including the client's context and meaning (i.e., the process) can significantly contribute to a client's sense of being stigmatized (Shenassa et al., 2004).
3. *Superficial reassurance and/or minimization of intense affect.* Clinicians may alienate their client by overly focusing on the positives, strengths, or optimistic aspects of their situation. This alienation can be further exacerbated by clinicians' avoidance or minimization of difficult, strong, and intense emotions (Neimeyer & Pfeiffer, 1994).
4. *Passivity and insufficient directiveness.* Over-reliance on empathic responses during the crisis intervention process can have a negative impact on forming a collaborative relationship with the client. The crisis intervention process requires active, direct, structured interventions (Neimeyer & Pfeiffer, 1994).

▨ Role Play 5.1

You are a mental health clinician in an outpatient mental health center. A client you treated briefly 2 years prior for depression unexpectedly presents to your office expressing suicidal ideation with intent.

Using this scenario, break into groups of three and assume the role of the mental health clinician and patient. The third member will act as a recorder and can be called upon to consult and assist the mental health clinician. Engage in a role play in which you would conduct a crisis intervention with this client.

■ Role Play 5.2

You are a mental health clinician in an outpatient mental health center. A client you treated briefly 2 years prior for depression unexpectedly presents to your office expressing suicidal ideation with intent.

Using this scenario, break into groups of three and assume the role of the mental health clinician and supervisor. The third member will act as a recorder and can be called upon to consult and assist the mental health clinician. Engage in a role play in which you would discuss this client with your supervisor. What questions might you ask? What kind of support might you try to elicit? Is the supervision for you? The client? Both?

SUMMARY

Treating individuals presenting in crisis, particularly a crisis involving suicide, can be an anxiety-provoking experience. As clinicians, it is our role to set the tone and pace of the intervention process. It is essential to respond and interact according to the client's needs and situational context and not react to our own potential anxiety or concerns. Supervision is essential for any clinician conducting crisis intervention. There are several models of crisis intervention that can inform effective practice, yet it is essential to involve the client in every stage of the process.

■ Key Points

1. Crisis is time-limited.
2. Crisis stimuli is typically unexpected.
3. A crisis significantly disrupts and distresses an individual and overwhelms his/her coping strategies.
4. Crisis results in psychological disequilibrium.
5. Crisis intervention models are structured and sequential and, at times, the stages may overlap.
6. RSSCIM has been found to be an effective model of crisis intervention.
7. Mental health practitioners should provide psychoeducation to family members and support networks regarding means of ensuring the safety of the individual in suicidal crisis.
8. Collaborative work with clients throughout the crisis intervention process is essential to a successful outcome.
9. Crisis intervention is not a one-session process. It requires follow-up treatment with an emphasis on treatment engagement.

10. Accessing clients' strengths is important for crisis intervention, such as identifying coping strategies and building support networks.

FURTHER READINGS

Ellison, J. M. (2001). *Treatment of suicidal patients in managed care*. Washington, DC: American Psychiatric Association.

Franklin, C., Harris, M. B., & Allen-Meares, P. (2008). *The school practitioner's concise companion to mental health*. New York: Oxford University Press.

Leenaars, A. A., Maltsberger, J. T., & Neimeyer, R. A. (1994). *Treatment of suicidal people*. Philadelphia: Taylor & Francis.

Lester, D. (2005). *Assessment, treatment, and prevention of suicidal behavior*. Hoboken, NJ: Wiley.

Milton, T. D. (2009). Review of *The assessment and management of suicidality*. *American Journal of Family Therapy, 37*(1), 82–84.

Roberts, A. R. (2005). *Crisis intervention handbook: Assessment, treatment, and research* (3rd ed.). New York: Oxford University Press.

Wolters, W. H. (1998). Adolescents and suicide: Recognition of signals and crisis intervention. *International Journal of Adolescent Medicine and Health, 3*(3), 217–224.

ELECTRONIC RESOURCES

All About Counseling: http://www.allaboutcounseling.com/crisis_hotlines.htm
San Pedro Youth Coalition: http://www.spyc.sanpedro.com/agency.htm
Suicide Awareness Voices of Education: http://www.save.org
Suicide Prevention: http://www.suicidepreventionlifeline.org

■ Knowledge Acquisition Test

True or False

1. Nothing good can come from a crisis.
2. Crisis is a long-term, chronic process.
3. Individuals experiencing a crisis are unable to integrate new ideas or change.
4. The stages of crisis intervention are intended to be used sequentially.
5. There is limited research support for the use of crisis intervention models.
6. Reassurance is a key stage of RSSCIM.
7. Assessment is not a requirement of crisis intervention models.
8. Good crisis intervention practice should incorporate supervision or consultation.
9. Families and extended support networks should not be included in crisis intervention.

Short Answer

10. Describe the key components of a crisis.
11. What are the seven stages of RSSCIM?
12. How may a clinician contribute to a client's feeling stigmatized through the process of crisis interventions?
13. Describe how IPSM differs from RSSCIM.
14. What behaviors and actions should a clinician avoid when conducting crisis intervention?
15. Why would a mental health clinician avoid strong emotions expressed by a client during crisis intervention, and what are the potential implications of this action?

Multiple Choice

16. What is not a component of Stage V: Generate and Explore Alternatives in the RSSCIM?
    - **A.** Clients acknowledge other solutions than suicide to their problems
    - **B.** Brainstorming alternative solutions
    - **C.** Can be completed before Stage IV
    - **D.** Develop coping strategies
    - **E.** All of the above
    - **F.** None of the above

17. How can supervision assist mental health clinicians conducting crisis intervention with a client experiencing suicidality?
    - **A.** Removes liability
    - **B.** Can diffuse authority of the clinician
    - **C.** Agency requirement
    - **D.** Assists management of clinician's anxieties or stress
    - **E.** All of the above
    - **F.** None of the above

18. According to RSSCIM, what does not belong in Stage VI: Implement an Action Plan?
    - **A.** Goal is to assist in improving the client's functioning
    - **B.** Removal of lethal means of suicide
    - **C.** Plan should try to increase client supports
    - **D.** Establish rapport
    - **E.** Identify future action steps

19. When considering ongoing treatment engagement to the plan following the initial treatment of suicidality, it is important for clinicians to remember that:
    - **A.** Encouraging treatment engagement is not recommended because 95% of clients attend all recommended follow-up appointments
    - **B.** Treatment engagement to follow-up plans should be left to the client and not unduly influenced by the clinician
    - **C.** Encouraging treatment when the client is not ready to address their barriers to treatment is unethical

    D. Client motivation develops over time and can be negative impacted by an overly involved clinician

    E. All of the above

    F. None of the above

20. Clinicians may contribute to a client's stigma or shame by:

    A. Centering on the facts of the suicide

    B. Minimizing the process of the crisis intervention

    C. Giving less attention on the client's narrative story

    D. Rushing over the client's meaning of events

    E. All of the above

    F. None of the above

Answer key is available in the Instructor's Manual; qualified instructors may e-mail textbook@springerpub.com *to request a copy.*

REFERENCES

Burman, S. (2003). Battered women: Stages of change and other treatment models that instigate and sustain leaving. *Brief Treatment and Crisis Intervention, 3*(1), 83–98.

Lee, M. (2007). Discovering strengths and competencies in female domestic violence survivors: An application of Roberts' continuum of the duration and severity of woman battering. *Brief Treatment and Crisis Intervention, 7*(2), 102.

Maris, R., Berman, A., & Silverman, M. (2000). *Comprehensive textbook of suicidology*. New York: Guilford Press.

McManus, B. L., Kruesi, M. J., Dontes, A. E., Defazio, C. R., Piotrowski, J. T., & Woodward, P. J. (1997). Child and adolescent suicide attempts: An opportunity for emergency departments to provide injury prevention education. *The American Journal of Emergency Medicine, 15*(4), 357–360.

Neimeyer, R. A., & Pfeiffer, A. M. (1994). Evaluation of suicide intervention effectiveness [review]. *Death Studies, 18*(2), 131–166.

O'Brien, G., Holton, A., Hurren, K., Wyatt, L., & Hassanyeh, F. (1987). Deliberate self-harm and predictors of outpatient attendance. *British Journal of Psychiatry, 150*, 246–247.

Roberts, A. R. (Ed.). (1991). *Conceptualizing crisis theory and the crisis intervention model*. Englewood Cliffs, NJ: Prentice-Hall.

Roberts, A. R. (2002). Assessment, crisis intervention, and trauma treatment: The Integrative ACT Intervention Model. *Brief Treatment and Crisis Intervention, 2*(1), 17–18.

Roberts, A. R., & Dziegielewski, S. F. (Eds.). (1995). *Foundation skills and applications of crisis intervention and cognitive therapy*. Thousand Oaks, CA: Sage.

Roberts, A. R., & Everly, G. S. (2006). A meta-analysis of 36 crisis intervention studies. *Brief Treatment and Crisis Intervention, 6*(1), 10–21.

Roberts, A. R., & Jennings, T. (2005). Hanging by a thread: How failure to conduct an adequate lethality assessment resulted in suicide. *Brief Treatment and Crisis Intervention, 5*(3), 251–260.

Roberts, A. R., & Ottens, A. J. (2005). The seven-stage crisis intervention model: A road map to goal attainment, problem solving, and crisis resolution. *Brief Treatment and Crisis Intervention, 5*(4), 329.

Rudd, D., Joiner, T., Jobes, D., & King, C. (1996). The outpatient treatment of suicidality: An integration of science and recognition of its limitations. *Professional Psychology: Research and Practice, 30*(5), 437–446.

Shenassa, E. D., Rogers, M. L., Spalding, K. L., & Roberts, M. B. (2004). Safer storage of firearms at home and risk of suicide: A study of protective factors in a nationally representative sample. *Journal of Epidemiology and Community Health, 58*(10), 841–848.

Stone, D. A., & Conley, J. A. (2004). A partnership between Roberts' crisis intervention model and the multicultural competencies. *Brief Treatment and Crisis Intervention, 4*(4), 367.

Westefeld, J. S., & Heckman-Stone, C. (2003). The Integrated Problem-Solving Model of Crisis Intervention: Overview and application. *Counseling Psychologist, 31*(2), 221–239.

6 Cognitive-Behavioral Therapy and Suicide

This chapter presents cognitive-behavioral therapy (CBT) as a treatment model to address suicidal individuals. CBT was originally conceived as a treatment for depression (Beck, Rush, Shaw, & Emery, 1979). In recent years, a strong evidence base has been established for the use of CBT for individuals experiencing suicidality. This chapter explores the theory behind CBT and provides a thorough description of the key components and strategies of CBT. Research examining the effectiveness of CBT across psychiatric disorders and settings is also explored. Recommendations for clinical practice when implementing CBT are also reviewed.

■ Goals and Objectives of This Chapter

An understanding of:

- The theory behind CBT
- The major components of CBT
- The goals of CBT intervention
- The major tasks of CBT
- The treatment targets of CBT
- Core strategies used in CBT
- Evidence to support the use of CBT
- Populations for and settings in which CBT is supported
- Factors that impact the effectiveness of CBT
- Clinical considerations when conducting CBT

INTRODUCTION

Cognitive-behavioral therapy (CBT) is a term used to classify a type of psychotherapy that involves several approaches, such as rational emotive behavior therapy, cognitive therapy, rational behavior therapy, and schema focused therapy, to name a few. Each approach has its own developmental history. This chapter focuses on cognitive therapy initially developed by Aaron Beck in the 1960s (Beck, 1964).

CBT grew out of cognitive theory and behavior theory. **Cognitive theory** originated in the field of psychology and the works of Alfred Adler (McMullin, 2000). Adler proposed that individuals are motivated by social drives and that behavior is shaped by beliefs regarding one's self, others, and the world (McMullin, 2000). This is known as the **cognitive triad** (Beck, 1976). Albert Ellis expanded Adler's theory by proposing that maladaptive emotions and behaviors were the result of irrational beliefs (Ellis, 1962). Ellis incorporated behavior theory into CBT by adopting the stance that a person behaves in a certain way due to events that occur before and after the behavior is performed (antecedents, behaviors, and consequences). Aaron Beck refined Ellis's notion of the importance of irrational beliefs and devised a systematic treatment process known as **cognitive therapy** (Beck, 1976), commonly referred to under the umbrella term CBT.

Although initially developed to treat depression (Beck, 1976), CBT has subsequently become a time-limited effective approach for treating suicide (Beck, 2005; Brown et al., 2005; Weinberg, Gunderson, Hennen, & Cutter, 2006). CBT suggests that there is a connection between cognition, affect, and behavior. Feelings are based on ideas, and an individual can gain control over even the most overwhelming feelings by changing his or her thoughts. The goal is to determine the cognitions that are elicited by specific behaviors and to then modify those thoughts and behaviors (Beck, 1995; Beck et al., 1979). Also, individuals can develop coping and problem-solving strategies to better manage difficult thoughts and behaviors (Beck, 1995; Beck et al., 1979). In order to practice CBT effectively, a clinician needs to (1) be able to distinguish between thoughts and feelings; (2) recognize the connection between thoughts, feelings, and behaviors; and (3) understand that the way an individual interprets a given situation directly impacts their ensuing feelings and behaviors.

▪ Individual Exercise 6.1

In this exercise we are going to ask you to think of a past situation. This may evoke some distressing thoughts and feelings. You may consider skipping this exercise or reflecting on a historical experience in the distant rather than recent past, or a strong positive emotion rather than a negative one. The intention of this exercise is one of reflection and understanding related to CBT. It is not designed or intended for you to relive a traumatic event.

1. Think of a situation in which you experienced a strong emotion (frustration, anger, joy, etc.). Describe the situation with as much detail as possible.
2. Describe the various emotions that you felt with as much detail as possible.
3. What factors do you believe contributed to experiencing these emotions?
4. Prioritize these emotions in order of the most intense through least intense.
5. For questions 5–7, focus on your top two or three emotions. Is it possible you experienced these emotions for other reasons than the situation itself? Were there other factors that may have contributed to these emotions? Brainstorm and develop a list of other factors that may have accounted for the emotions you experienced.
6. On a scale of 1 to 10, 1 being "not strongly at all" and 10 being "very strongly," how strongly do you believe these other factors may have accounted for the emotions you felt?
7. What would it take to convince you that these other factors may have played a major role in the emotions you experienced?

▪ Small Group Exercise 6.1

In a small group of two or three please discuss, as you are comfortable, your responses to individual exercise 6.1. Remember, share only what you are comfortable sharing. Answers are personal, and there are no correct or incorrect answers.

1. What were the response similarities in your group?
2. What were the response differences in your group?
3. Did you find any surprises in the group discussion? If so, what were they, and how were you surprised?

COGNITIVE-BEHAVIORAL THERAPY (CBT)

Cognitive-behavioral therapy suggests that there is a connection between thoughts, emotions, and behavior. Intervention that targets or focuses on the thought processes can promote change in affect and behavior.

Cognitive-behavioral therapy aims to identify and modify negative or maladaptive cognitions that contribute to problematic behaviors and emotions, which in turn further influences and maintains **dysfunctional thought** processes (Beck, 1995; Beck et al., 1979).

Cognitive-behavioral therapy posits that an individual's cognitions are based on attitudes or assumptions developed from earlier experiences (Beck, 1995; Beck et al., 1979). The manner in which an individual interprets and understands situations and information over time can lead to **maladaptive** or dysfunctional thought processes. Dysfunctional thoughts or beliefs can result in an individual distorting and misinterpreting experiences. Maladaptive thought processes include, but are not limited to, faulty **automatic thoughts** (thoughts that occur automatically without conscious effort or any attention; these thoughts can be true or untrue [Beck, 1976]), **overgeneralizations** (using a limited negative occurrence to make broad conclusions about a given issue), and **catastrophic thinking** (assuming or predicting the very worst possible outcome in all situations).

These cognitive deficits can impair an individual's capacity to regulate affect and manage interpersonal problems (Beck, 1995; Beck et al., 1979; Brent et al., 1997; Van der Sande, Buskens, Allart, van der Graaf, & van Engeland, 1997). For example, anxious individuals may have the maladaptive thought process of catastrophizing. This could negatively impact their ability to engage in effective, rewarding interpersonal relationships and may also negatively impact their academic and/or occupational performance.

Cognitive-behavioral therapy focuses on active identification and exploration of automatic thoughts, inferences, and assumptions (Beck, 1995; Beck et al., 1979). To understand the nature of an emotional episode or disturbance it is essential to focus on the cognitive content of an individual's reaction to the upsetting event or stream of thoughts. The goal of CBT is to change the way clients think by using their automatic thoughts to identify core schema and to achieve **cognitive restructuring**. Interventions are then aimed at decreasing negative **schemas** (Beck, 1995; Beck et al., 1979; Rotherman-Borus, Piacentini, Miller, Graae, & Castro-Blanco, 1994). The literature also suggests that treatment should focus on decreasing cognitive distortions and rigidity to help clients develop more adaptive views of themselves, others, and the world, called the cognitive triad (Beck et al., 1979), to assist them in goal attainment (Emery, 1985).

Treatment also focuses on the client's behavior, specifically enhancing problem-solving skills as a coping mechanism. Individuals attempt to identify effective strategies (e.g., problem solving, relaxation, effective communication, social skills) for managing problems they encounter in everyday life (Beck, 1995; Pollock & Williams, 1998). Modifying and enhancing behavioral and coping skills influences one's thought processes and decisions (evaluating and adopting more adaptive beliefs) and the ability to tolerate difficult affect (e.g., anxiety, frustration, anger, low self-esteem).

Strategies are taught and assignments given aimed at the acquisition of behavior and affect regulation (Blumenthal, 1990; Beck et al., 1979). Techniques include monitoring negative thoughts, countering catastrophic thinking, and identifying triggers to hopeless feelings and suicidal thoughts. Assignments include keeping a diary, completing automatic or dysfunctional thought records, setting up reinforcements for certain behaviors and activities, and physical exercise (Beck, 1995; Beck et al., 1979; Blumenthal, 1990). **Activity scheduling** is another major technique implemented in which the client schedules activities he or she enjoyed in the past in order to change emotions by changing behaviors. For example, a depressed client who has stopped meeting her friend for weekend lunches would be encouraged to plan this activity. Educating clients regarding the nature of the dysfunction and the treatment process, referred to as psychoeducation, is also a major component of CBT (Beck, 1995; Beck et al., 1979; Brent et al., 1997).

There are several characteristics specific to CBT. Treatment is focused on the present, on the here and now, based on the idea that if one can correct current problematic or negative automatic thinking than future emotional suffering will be reduced, if not eliminated. Treatment is goal-oriented and problem-focused (Beck, 1995).

Cognitive-behavioral therapy is considered a process of "guided discovery" (Beck, 1995), implying that the therapist acts as a catalyst and guide to help clients understand the connection between their thinking and ways they feel and act. The major technique used to achieve this is Socratic questioning in which the therapist asks questions of the client to help them discover for themselves the misconceptions under which they operate. When describing a situation that causes distress for a client, a clinician may ask a client the simple question, "What would it mean to you if it were true" until the underlying belief is revealed. This is discussed in further detail later in the chapter.

Cognitive-behavioral therapy is also seen as a collaborative process that requires active engagement from both the mental health clinician and the client. Homework or between session practice of skills developed in therapeutic sessions is important to the success of this approach. Mental health clinicians help frame client conclusions in the form of testable hypotheses. Clinicians are active and interactive and engage the client through all phases of treatment (Beck, 1995).

The key strategy used in CBT is cognitive restructuring (Beck, 1995; Beck et al., 1979). Cognitive restructuring suggests that people can choose to think differently and this, ultimately, will lead to more constructive behavior patterns. To change negative emotions and consequences one must dispute and restructure negative, self-defeating thoughts. The goal is to replace one's negative irrational beliefs with more rational, constructive thoughts. Clients are taught to identify their "self-talk" (Beck, 1995; McMullin, 2000), the musts, shoulds, woulds, coulds, and oughts that they tell themselves about how they, others, and the world operate (McMullin, 2000).

Cognitive-behavioral therapy is a highly structured intervention. According to Beck (1995), a CBT mental health clinician's goals for an initial session include:

1. Establishing rapport and trust
2. Socializing the patient into cognitive therapy
3. Educating the patient about his/her disorder and the process of therapy for the disorder
4. Normalizing the patient's difficulties and instilling hope
5. Eliciting (and correcting if necessary) the patient's expectations for therapy
6. Gathering additional information about the patient's difficulties
7. Using this information to develop a goal list

The recommended structure of this first session is to:

1. Set the agenda (providing a rationale for doing so)
2. Do a mood check
3. Briefly review the presenting problem and obtain an update
4. Identify problems and set goals
5. Educate the patient about the cognitive model
6. Elicit the patient's expectations for therapy
7. Educate the patient about his disorder

8. Set homework
9. Provide a summary
10. Elicit feedback

The structure of subsequent sessions is recommended as follows (Beck, 1995):

1. Setting the agenda
2. Doing a mood check (include objective scores, such as standard measures)
3. Addressing agenda items, including identifying automatic/intermediate/core thought, evaluating automatic/intermediate/core thoughts, modifying automatic/intermediate/core thoughts, sharing of the cognitive conceptualization, and modifying goals as necessary
4. Setting homework
5. Providing a summary
6. Eliciting feedback

The tasks of CBT are hierarchical in nature. They are sequential and build upon one another. While the progress through which a client progresses through CBT is individualized, every client must pass through each task, in order. The first task of CBT is centered on teaching clients the theory behind CBT, often referred to as the **ABC model** (antecedents, event, consequences) (see Figure 6.1).

Clients are initially presented with the common misperception that their emotional or behavioral responses are caused by some triggering event or stimuli. This two-step model asserts that an experienced stimulus directly leads to a response. Clients are then presented with CBT's ABC model, which posits that it is not the situation or event (event = A) that elicits a response (response = C), but rather our thoughts about the situation or event that elicits the response (thoughts = B). The same situation can be interpreted in many different ways, and it is the thoughts or interpretation, the "B," rather than the situation, which is most important.

For example, a situation may occur in which a woman is sitting in a restaurant and notices people staring at her, and she begins to feel embarrassed. The two-step model would suggest that the staring led to her embarrassment. The ABC model, on the other hand, suggests that it is the way in which the staring was interpreted that led to her embarrassment. She could have had the thought "there must be food on my face,"

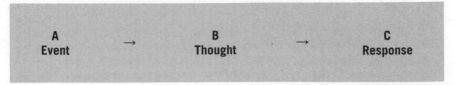

Figure 6.1 ABC model.

which led to her feeling embarrassed. Alternatively, if she had thought, "they are staring because I am beautiful," she may have felt happy or confident rather than embarrassed. If she had the thought "they are staring because I am ugly or I have been stood up," she may have felt depressed instead of embarrassed (Beck, 1995; McMullin, 2000). Consequently, CBT focuses on working with the client to understand their "B" thoughts within the ABC model.

Once clients understand the ABC theory, clients are taught to identify and modify their automatic thoughts. Automatic thoughts represent systematic negative bias in thought processes. Clients are taught to identify actual words or images that go through their minds in stressful situations. The goal of this repeated review of distressing situations is the identification of themes and patterns of automatic thoughts (Beck, 1995; McMullin, 2000).

After clients have gained some mastery over identifying and modifying their automatic thoughts, the next task focuses on identifying and modifying intermediate thoughts. Intermediate beliefs represent rules, attitudes, and assumptions clients have about themselves, others, and the world that give rise to specific automatic thoughts. The mental health practitioner stresses that there are a range of beliefs that the client could acquire and that they are learned, not innate, and, therefore, can be revised. Mental health practitioners utilize behavioral experiments, rational-emotional role plays, and a cognitive continuum to modify intermediate beliefs (Beck, 1995; McMullin, 2000). Socratic questioning, also known as the **downward arrow** technique, is also a major tool utilized. In the downward arrow method the clinician and client begin by discussing an upsetting event in which automatic thoughts occurred. The clinician then asks the client to consider about each automatic thought, "If this were true, what would it mean to you?"

This questioning continues until the underlying automatic thought is revealed (Burns, 1980; McMullin, 2000; Persons, 2008). For example, a client experienced an upsetting family reunion. After implementing the downward arrow technique, the client was able to recognize that he or she feels unlovable.

The task of identifying and modifying intermediate beliefs is followed by the task of identifying and modifying core beliefs. Core beliefs tend to be rigid, global ideas or generalizations clients hold about themselves and others. Core beliefs generally fall into two categories: helpless (e.g., I am needy, I am powerless), or unlovable (e.g., I am unwanted, I am bad). The groups or patterns of cognitions in which core beliefs occur are known as schemas. Core beliefs represent the actual content of the schemas. Most individuals maintain positive core beliefs throughout their lives. It may only be in times of stress that negative core beliefs surface. For others, negative core beliefs may pervade their lives. While clients often identify traumatic events as the root of their core beliefs, often it is actually the smaller, less significant incidents that leave a standing impression. Core beliefs develop in childhood as a result of interactions with significant others. They serve as "life themes" that guide individuals throughout their lives. The fundamental goal of CBT is to uncover core beliefs. Several key strategies are used to identify and modify core beliefs, including Socratic questioning, creating a list of critical events, developing a master list of beliefs, and cognitive maps or cognitive conceptualization diagrams (Beck, 1995; McMullin, 2000).

EVIDENCE FOR AND AGAINST CBT

Cognitive-behavioral therapy was initially developed for depression and has been found to be efficacious in its treatment (Beck et al., 1979). CBT's treatment of depression has been found to be effective across various age groups, including adolescents (Brent et al., 1997) and older adults (Wilson, Mottram, & Vassilas, 2008).

Similarly, CBT has demonstrated efficacy with the treatment of bipolar disorder (Scott et al., 2006), but recent research has not found it to be an effective treatment strategy for prevention of relapse in bipolar disorder (Lynch, Laws, & McKenna, 2009). In addition, CBT has demonstrated efficacy for treating depression in individuals following a stroke (Lincoln & Flannaghan, 2003) and after quitting smoking (Kahler et al., 2002).

In regards to anxiety, CBT has been demonstrated effective in the treatment of phobias and generalized anxiety disorder in children (Walkup et al., 2008), adolescents (James, Soler, & Weatherall, 2005), and adults (Hunot, Churchill, Silva de Lima, & Teixeira, 2007). CBT has also shown some effectiveness in the treatment of bulimia nervosa (Fairburn et al., 1991) and posttraumatic stress disorder (Cohen, Mannarino, & Knudsen, 2005).

The versatility of CBT techniques has allowed for the model to be effectively adapted and applied to help individuals managing a number of health conditions, including severe functional bowel disorders (Drossman et al., 2003), rheumatoid arthritis (Sharpe et al., 2001), breast cancer (Edelman, Bell, & Kidman, 1999), and insomnia (Morgan, Dixon, Mathers, Thompson, & Tomeny, 2004).

However, CBT has not demonstrated efficacy in the treatment of schizophrenia (Lynch et al., 2009) or for bereaved individuals experiencing complicated grief (de Groot et al., 2007).

CBT AND SUICIDE

CBT describes suicidal behavior as due to vulnerabilities that result from certain cognitive characteristics, such as rigidity and poor problem-solving and coping skills (Brown et al., 2005; Coleman & Casey, 2007; Freeman & Reinecke, 1994; Joiner, 2006; Pollock & Williams, 1998). Suicidal individuals, therefore, have difficulty generating solutions when faced with emotional problems (Brown et al., 2005; Freeman & Reinecke, 1994; Joiner, 2006; Pollock & Williams, 1998). They tend to have a negative attributional style, including negative views of themselves and of their future. Suicidal individuals will typically have experiences based on distortions, irrational beliefs, or pathological ways of viewing oneself and the world leading to hopelessness and a lack of positive expectations. Suicidal behavior is the result of erroneous or faulty logic (Beck et al., 1979). Such behavior is seen as an ineffective effort to resolve a problem (Rotherman-Borus et al., 1994).

CBT has been adapted as a treatment for suicidality (e.g., Stanley et al., 2009). Tarrier and colleagues conducted a meta-analysis that compared 28 studies treating suicidal behavior with CBT (Tarrier, Haddock, Lewis, Drake, & Gregg, 2006). Overall, findings indicated that CBT can reduce suicidal behavior in the immediate, short term and maintains significant, albeit less, reduction in suicidal behavior for the medium term. This review also found that CBT was highly significantly effective in the treatment of adults with suicidality but was nonsignificant for adolescents (Tarrier et al., 2006). However, the authors recognize that there were limited studies focusing solely on adolescents, which may have contributed to this finding. In addition, CBT treatment is more effective when it directly focuses on some aspect or component of suicidal behavior, rather than when focused on other symptoms (e.g., depression) with a secondary focus on suicidality (Tarrier et al., 2006).

Two specific areas relating to the treatment of suicidality that CBT has demonstrated some promise in working with include changing negative schemas or automatic thoughts and improving problem-solving and coping skills.

Adapting CBT to suicidality (ideation or behavior) has lead to the specific tailoring of certain aspects of the approach, specifically, the maladaptive thoughts or core schemas of hopelessness, worthlessness or self-criticism, and perfectionism (Coleman & Casey, 2007). Preliminary research has found that decreasing maladaptive automatic thoughts was associated with decreased suicidal ideation (Coleman & Casey, 2007).

CBT that focuses on building and developing problem-solving skills, such as cognitive behavioral problem solving therapy, has also yielded some encouraging findings relating to reduced suicidality (Eskin, Ertekin, & Demir, 2008; Salkovskis, Atha, & Storer, 1990). Specifically, the targeting, development, and improvement of problem-solving skills may reduce levels of depression and suicide potential, while increasing levels of protective factors, such as self-esteem and assertiveness (Eskin et al., 2008). Cognitive-behavioral therapy's focus on problem solving has also been adapted and applied to clients presenting with suicidal crisis in psychiatric emergency services by helping clients and their families to develop problem-solving strategies and to enhance their ability to cope with immediate difficulties (Asarnow, Berk, & Baraff, 2009; Bilsker & Forster, 2003).

RECOMMENDED CLINICAL GUIDELINES FOR CBT

CBT is an effective treatment approach for addressing suicidality. It is a structured approach that requires active participation of both the client and the therapist. As a mental health professional working with suicidal clients and practicing CBT, several recommended clinical guidelines to consider include:

1. *Automatic thoughts.* Just like clients, therapists, too, are subject to automatic thoughts that can interfere with the treatment process. Therapists may have automatic thoughts about their ability to manage a session, client, or issue, or they may automatic thoughts about the responses their clients will have to an intervention they suggest or even them as individuals. When working from a CBT approach, it is essential for therapists to monitor their own automatic thoughts and how they may be interfering with the treatment process (Beck, 1995).
2. *Summarize.* Providing a summary and seeking feedback throughout sessions and at the closing of sessions is critical. A clinician practicing CBT should never assume that a patient understands what the therapist intends or that the therapist understand what the patients intends. It is important to clarify the understanding of both parties to ensure that the treatment process stays on track. Even if an issue seems very clear, it is recommended to always summarize the issue at hand for the client and seek the client's feedback regarding their understanding of the issue. As the client acclimates to the CBT process, he or she may take over the responsibility of making summarizations (Beck, 1995; Haarhoff, 2006).
3. *Homework.* For CBT to be effective, clients need to practice strategies and techniques outside of session. Homework plays a major role in this treatment approach. If homework is to be successful, it must be reinforced by the therapist. It is recommended that homework assignments always be reviewed. Even if there is a big issue that has arisen in between sessions or during a session that requires a change in the set agenda, it should never compromise the homework review. It may be that a client's distress necessitates the delay of the homework review until later in the session, but it should not be forsaken altogether (Beck, 1995; Neimeyer & Feixas, 1990).
4. *CBT treatment for suicide needs to directly target suicidality.* If suicidality is the focus of treatment, CBT needs to target it directly and not indirectly or as a secondary symptom related to another presenting problem (e.g., depression). For treatment to be most effective, CBT suicide treatment needs to be designed, planned, tailored, and implemented around the client's suicidality (Tarrier et al., 2006). Areas of

focus may include improving or changing maladaptive thoughts and enhancing the client's coping and problem-solving abilities (Coleman & Casey, 2007; Eskin et al., 2008).

■ Role Play 6.1

You are a mental health clinician in an outpatient mental health center. A client you treated briefly 2 years prior for depression unexpectedly presents to your office expressing suicidal ideation with intent.

Using this scenario, break into groups of three and assume the role of the mental health clinician and patient. The third member will act as a recorder and can be called upon to consult and assist the mental health clinician. Engage in a role play in which you would implement CBT with this client.

■ Role Play 6.2

You are a mental health clinician in an outpatient mental health center. A client you treated briefly 2 years prior for depression unexpectedly presents to your office expressing suicidal ideation with intent.

Using this scenario, break into groups of three and assume the role of the mental health clinician and supervisor. The third member will act as a recorder and can be called upon to consult and assist the mental health clinician. Engage in a role play in which you would discuss this client with your supervisor. What questions might you ask? What kind of support might you try to elicit? Is the supervision for you? The client? Both?

SUMMARY

Cognitive-behavioral therapy (CBT) is a short-term, goal-oriented, evidence-based treatment approach for addressing suicidality. Initially developed for the treatment of depression, CBT has demonstrated wide applicability to a number of diagnoses and presenting problems, including suicidality. CBT focuses on the connection between thoughts, behaviors, and emotions. The goal is to identify and address maladaptive thought processes triggered by stressful events that results in clients experiencing difficult emotional and behavioral responses. CBT has demonstrated some promise in working with suicidal clients to change negative schemas or automatic thoughts as well as to improve problem-solving and coping skills.

■ Key Points

1. CBT stresses the connection between cognition, affect, and behavior.
2. CBT focus on active exploration of automatic thoughts, inferences, and assumptions.
3. Even the most overwhelming feelings can be modified by modifying ones thoughts.
4. The goal of CBT is to change the way clients think by using their automatic thoughts to identify core schema and to achieve cognitive restructuring.
5. Suicidality from a CBT perspective is the result of cognitive deficits, such as rigidity, poor problem-solving skills, and poor coping skills.
6. CBT follows the ABC model of understanding the connection between events, thoughts, and resulting responses (emotions and behaviors).
7. CBT has been found to be efficacious in the treatment of a number of mental disorders (e.g., depression, anxiety, and eating disorders) and other presenting problems (e.g., arthritis and insomnia).
8. CBT has been demonstrated to reduce suicidal behavior in the immediate, short term and maintains reduction in suicidal behavior for the medium term.
9. CBT is significantly effective in the treatment of adults with suicidality but was found to be nonsignificant for the treatment of adolescents with suicidality.
10. For the treatment of suicidality, CBT should focus directly on the client's suicidality.

FURTHER READINGS

Beck, A. T. (Ed.). (1976). *Cognitive therapy and the emotional disorders.* New York: International Universities Press.

Beck, J. S. (Ed.). (1995). *Cognitive therapy: Basics and beyond.* New York: Guilford Press.

Chadwick, P., Williams, C., & Mackenzie, J. (2003). Impact of case formulation in cognitive behaviour therapy for psychosis. *Behaviour Research and Therapy, 41*(6) 671–680.

Freeman, A., & Reinecke, M. (Eds.). (1994). *Cognitive therapy of suicidal behavior.* New York: Springer Publishing.

Joiner, T. (Ed.). (2006). *Why people die by suicide.* Cambridge, MA: Harvard University Press.

Persons, J. B. (2005). Empiricism, mechanism, and the practice of cognitive-behavior therapy. *Behavior Therapy, 36*(2), 107–118.

Rudd, M. D., Joiner, T. E., & Rajab, M. S. (Eds.). (2001). *Treating suicidal behavior: An effective, time-limited approach (Treatment manuals For practitioners).* New York: Guilford Press.

Tarrier, N., Haddock, G., Lewis, S., Drake, R., & Gregg, L. (2006). Suicide behaviour over 18 months in recent onset schizophrenic patients: The effects of CBT. *Schizophrenia Research, 83*(1), 15–27.

ELECTRONIC RESOURCES

Academy of Cognitive Therapy: http://www.academyofct.org/Library/InfoManage/Guide.asp?FolderID=1001&SessionID={F9A6CC95-0F63-47B0-8BBE-D4A3B6032A0E}

The American Institute of Cognitive Therapy: http://www.cognitivetherapynyc.com

Behavioral Associates: Cognitive Behavioral Therapy: http://www.behavioralassociates.com/treatment_mot_cog.asp

Cognitive Behavioral Therapy Arena: http://www.cbtarena.com

The International Association for Cognitive Psychotherapy: http://www.the-iacp.com/

National Association of Cognitive-Behavioral Therapists: http://www.nacbt.org

University of Pennsylvania: http://www.med.upenn.edu/cct

Knowledge Acquisition Test

True or False

1. CBT is a long-term treatment approach.
2. CBT focuses on personality development.
3. The connection between cognitions, affect, and behavior is central to CBT.
4. CBT believes that specific situations lead directly to emotions.
5. Cognitive restructuring is a key strategy in CBT.
6. CBT has been found to effectively treat depression.
7. CBT has been found to effectively treat complicated grief.
8. CBT has been demonstrated to reduce suicidal behavior in the long term.
9. CBT has been shown to significantly treat adolescent suicide.
10. CBT can be used with suicidal clients in emergency departments.

Short Answer

11. Describe how CBT accounts for suicidality.
12. What are intermediate beliefs, and what strategies are used to modify them?
13. What are core beliefs, and what are the strategies used to modify them?
14. Describe the ABC model, and provide an example.
15. For what conditions and diagnoses has CBT been demonstrated effective?
16. Under what conditions and diagnoses does CBT not have demonstrated efficacy?

Multiple Choice

17. Which of the following is a key characteristic of CBT?

  A. Time-limited
  B. Highly structured
  C. Involves homework
  D. Monitors activities
  E. None of the above
  F. All of the above

18. Which of the following comes second in the ABC model?

  A. The event or situation
  B. The emotion experienced by the individual
  C. The thought the individual has about the event or situation
  D. None of the above
  E. All of the above

19. For which diagnoses has CBT not demonstrated treatment efficacy?

  A. Depression
  B. Schizophrenia
  C. Generalized anxiety disorder
  D. Posttraumatic stress disorder
  E. All of the above

20. CBT treatment for suicide is effective when it directly focuses on:

  A. Cognitive distortions
  B. Problem solving
  C. Coping strategies
  D. None of the above
  E. All of the above

Answer key is available in the Instructor's Manual; qualified instructors may e-mail textbook@springerpub.com *to request a copy.*

REFERENCES

Asarnow, J. R., Berk, M. S., & Baraff, L. J. (2009). Family intervention for suicide prevention: A specialized emergency department intervention for suicidal youths. *Professional Psychology: Research and Practice, 40*(2), 118–125.

Beck, A. T. (1964). Thinking and depression II: Theory and therapy. *Archives of General Psychiatry, 10,* 561–571.

Beck, A. T. (Ed.). (1976). *Cognitive therapy and the emotional disorders.* New York: International Universities Press.

Beck, A. T. (2005). The current state of cognitive therapy: A 40-year retrospective. *Archives of General Psychiatry, 62,* 953–959.

Beck, A. T., Rush, A. J., Shaw, B. F., & Emery, G. (Eds.). (1979). *Cognitive therapy of depression.* New York: Guilford Press.

Beck, J. S. (Ed.). (1995). *Cognitive therapy: Basics and beyond.* New York: Guilford Press.

Bilsker, D., & Forster, P. (2003). Problem-solving intervention for suicidal crises in the psychiatric emergency service. *Crisis: The Journal of Crisis Intervention and Suicide Prevention, 24*(3), 134–136.

Blumenthal, S. J. (1990). Youth suicide: Risk factors, assessment, and treatment of adolescent and young adult suicidal patients. *Psychiatric Clinic of North America, 13*(3), 511–551.

Brent, D. A., Holder, D., Kolko, D., Birmaher, B., Baugher, M., Roth, C., et al. (1997). A clinical psychotherapy trial for adolescent depression comparing cognitive, family, and supportive therapy. *Archives of General Psychiatry, 54*, 877–885.

Brown, G. K., Have, T. T., Henriques, G. R., Xie, S. X., Hollander, J. E., & Beck, A. T. (2005). Cognitive therapy for the prevention of suicide attempts: A randomized controlled trial. *Journal of the American Medical Association, 294*, 563–570.

Burns, D. D. (1980). *Feeling good: The new mood therapy.* New York: Marrow.

Cohen, J. A., Mannarino, A. P., and Knudsen, K. (2004). Treating childhood traumatic grief: A pilot study. *Journal of the American Academy of Child & Adolescent Psychiatry, 43*, 1225-1233.

Coleman, D., & Casey, J. T. (2007). Therapeutic mechanisms of suicidal ideation: The influence of changes in automatic thoughts and immature defenses. *Crisis: Journal of Crisis Intervention & Suicide, 28*(4), 198–203.

Drossman, D. A., Toner, B. B., Whitehead, W. E., Diamant, N. E., Dalton, C. B., Duncan, S., et al. (2003). Cognitive-behavioral therapy versus education and desipramine versus placebo for moderate to severe functional bowel disorders. *Gastroenterology, 125*(1), 19–31.

Edelman, S., Bell, D. R., & Kidman, A. D. (1999). A group cognitive behaviour therapy programme with metastatic breast cancer patients. *Psycho-Oncology, 8*(4), 295–305.

Ellis, A. (Ed.). (1962). *Reason and emotion in psychotherapy.* New York: Lyle Stuart.

Emery, G. (1985). Cognitive therapy: Techniques and applications. In A. T. Beck & G. Emery (Eds.), *Anxiety disorders and phobias: A cognitive perspective* (pp. 167–313). New York: Basic Books.

Eskin, M., Ertekin, K., & Demir, H. (2008). Efficacy of a problem-solving therapy for depression and suicide potential in adolescents and young adults. *Cognitive Therapy and Research, 32*(2), 227–245.

Fairburn, C. G., Jones, R., Peveler, R. C., Carr, S. J., Solomon, R. A., O'Connor, M. E., et al. (1991). Three psychological treatments for bulimia nervosa: A comparative trial. *Archives of General Psychiatry, 57*(2), 463–469.

Freeman, A., & Reinecke, M. (Eds.). (1994). *Cognitive therapy of suicidal behavior.* New York: Springer Publishing.

de Groot, M., de Keijser, Neeleman, J., Kerkhof, A., Nolen, W., & Burger, H. (2007). Cognitive behaviour therapy to prevent complicated grief among relatives and spouses bereaved by suicide: cluster randomised controlled trial. *BMJ, 334*(7601), 994.

Haarhoff, B. A. (2006). The importance of identifying and understanding therapist schema in cognitive therapy training and supervision. *New Zealand Journal of Psychology, 35*(3), 126–131.

Hunot, V., Churchill, R., Silva de Lima, M., & Teixeira, V. (2007). Psychological therapies for generalised anxiety disorder. *Cochrane Database of Systematic Reviews, 1,* CD001848.

James, A., Soler, A., & Weatherall, R. (2005). Cognitive behavioural therapy for anxiety disorders in children and adolescents. *Cochrane Database of Systematic Reviews, 4,* CD004690.

Joiner, T. (Ed.). (2006). *Why people die by suicide.* Cambridge, MA: Harvard University Press.

Kahler, C. W., Brown, R. A., Ramsey, S. E., Niaura, R., Abrams, D. B., Goldstein, M. G., et al. (2002). Negative mood, depressive symptoms, and major depression after smoking cessation treatment in smokers with a history of major depressive disorder. *Journal of Abnormal Psychology, 111*(4), 670–675.

Lincoln, N. B., & Flannaghan, T. (2003). Cognitive behavioral psychotherapy for depression following stroke: A randomized controlled trial. *Stroke, 34*(1), 111–115.

Lynch, D., Laws, K. R., & McKenna, P. J. (2009). Cognitive behavioural therapy for major psychiatric disorder: Does it really work? A meta-analytical review of well-controlled trials. *Psychological Medicine, 40*(1), 1–16.

McMullin, R. (Ed.). (2000). *A new handbook of cognitive therapy techniques.* New York: W.W. Norton & Company.

Morgan, K., Dixon, S., Mathers, N., Thompson, J., & Tomeny, M. (2004). Psychological treatment for insomnia in the regulation of long-term hypnotic drug use. *Health Technology Assessment, 8*(8), 1–68.

Neimeyer, R. A., & Feixas, G. (1990). The role of homework and skill acquisition in the outcome of cognitive therapy for depression. *Behavior Therapy, 21*(3), 281–292.

Persons, J. B. (2008). *The case formulation approach to cognitive behavior therapy.* New York: Guilford Press.

Pollock, L. R., & Williams, M. G. (1998). Problem solving and suicidal behavior. *Suicide & Life-Threatening Behavior, 28*(4), 375–387.

Rotherman-Borus, M. J., Piacentini, J., Miller, S., Graae, F., & Castro-Blanco, D. (1994). Brief cognitive-behavioral treatment for adolescent suicide attempters and their families. *Journal of the American Academy of Child and Adolescent Psychiatry, 33*(4), 508–517.

Salkovskis, P. M., Atha, C., & Storer, D. (1990). Cognitive-behavioural problem solving in the treatment of patients who repeatedly attempt suicide: A controlled trial. *British Journal of Psychiatry, 157,* 871–876.

Scott, J., Paykel, E., Morriss, R., Bentall, R., Kinderman, P., Johnson, T., et al. (2006). Cognitive-behavioural therapy for severe and recurrent bipolar disorders: Randomised controlled trial. *British Journal of Psychiatry, 188,* 313–320.

Sharpe, L., Sensky, T., Timberlake, N., Ryan, B., Brewin, C. R., & Allard, S. (2001). A blind, randomized, controlled trial of cognitive-behavioural intervention for patients with recent onset rheumatoid arthritis: Preventing psychological and physical morbidity. *Pain, 89*(2-3), 275–283.

Stanley, B. H., Brown, G., Brent, D., Wells, K., Poling, K., Curry, J., et al. (2009). Cognitive-Behavioral Therapy for Suicide Prevention (CBT-SP): Treatment model, feasibility, and acceptability. *Journal of the American Academy of Child & Adolescent Psychiatry, 48*(10), 1005–1013.

Tarrier, N., Haddock, G., Lewis, S., Drake, R., & Gregg, L. (2006). Suicide behaviour over 18 months in recent onset schizophrenic patients: The effects of CBT. *Schizophrenia Research, 83*(1), 15–27.

Van der Sande, R., Buskens, E., Allart, E., van der Graaf, Y., & van Engeland, H. (1997). Psychosocial intervention following suicide attempt: A systematic review of treatment interventions. *Acta Psychiatrica Scandinavica, 96,* 43–50.

Walkup, J. T. M., A. A., Piacentini, J., Birmaher, B., Compton, S. N., Sherrill, J. T., et al. (2008). Cognitive behavioral therapy, sertraline, or a combination in childhood anxiety. *New England Journal of Medicine, 359*(26), 2753–2766.

Weinberg, I., Gunderson, J. G., Hennen, J., & Cutter, C. J. (2006). Manual assisted cognitive treatment for deliberate self-harm in borderline personality disorder patients. *Journal of Personality Disorders, 20,* 482–492.

Wilson, K. C. M., Mottram, P. G., & Vassilas, C. A. (2008). Psychotherapeutic treatments for older depressed people. *Cochrane Database of Systematic Reviews, 1,* CD004853.

Dialectical Behavior Therapy and Suicide

This chapter presents **dialectical behavior therapy** (DBT) as a treatment model to address suicidal individuals. DBT was originally developed by Marsha Linehan in 1987 as a treatment for **borderline personality disorder** (Linehan, 1987). In recent years a strong evidence base has been established for the use of DBT for individuals experiencing suicidality. The theory behind DBT is explored in this chapter. Additionally, a thorough description of the key components and strategies of DBT is presented. Research examining the effectiveness of DBT across psychiatric disorders and settings also is explored. Lastly, recommendations for clinical practice when implementing DBT are provided.

■ Goals and Objectives of This Chapter

An understanding of:

- The theory behind DBT
- The major components of DBT
- The hierarchy of DBT goals
- The stages of DBT
- The treatment targets of DBT
- Core strategies used in DBT
- Evidence to support the use of DBT
- Populations for and settings in which DBT is supported
- Factors that impact the effectiveness of DBT
- Clinical considerations when conducting DBT

INTRODUCTION

Borderline personality disorder (BPD), characterized by a pattern of instability in interpersonal relationships, self-image, affect, and marked impulsivity (American Psychiatric Association [APA], 2000), is highly associated with suicide attempts and completions (Pompili, Girardi, Ruberto, & Tatrelli, 2005). Individuals with BPD also engage in nonsuicidal self-injury at an alarmingly high rate (Gunderson, 2001; Linehan, 1993b). It is estimated that approximately 75% of individuals suffering from BPD engage in nonsuicidal self-injury (Gunderson, 2001; Linehan, 1993a). In an effort to address the high rate of suicide and deliberate self-harm in this group, Marsha Linehan (1987) developed a new treatment approach, dialectical behavior therapy (DBT). DBT is based on the principle that individuals struggle with the dialect of change and acceptance. Rather than emphasizing a purely change-oriented approach, Linehan recognized the importance of helping clients accept themselves as they are. Given the difficulties that individuals with BPD have in tolerating distress and regulating affect and interpersonal relationships, DBT aims to help patients develop distress-tolerance and coping as well as acceptance-oriented skills thereby helping clients to strike a balance between change and acceptance (Linehan, 1987).

DBT draws upon several theoretical and philosophical perspectives. Acceptance-oriented strategies are based on Zen principles, the client-oriented and emotion-focused treatment approaches. Change strategies stem from a combination of dialectical philosophy; psychodynamic, cognitive, and behavioral treatment approaches; and biopsychosocial theory (Linehan, 1993a).

Mental health practitioners generally adhere to a particular or favored theoretical approach to clinical work. DBT is unique in that it represents a blending together of multiple treatment approaches and philosophies. In order to effectively implement DBT, it is important to explore one's openness to alternative treatment approaches that are different from those to which one proscribes. If DBT is to be effective, the clinician, as well as the client, needs to accept the theoretical approach behind the evidence-based practice intervention.

▨ Individual Exercise 7.1

1. From which perspective do you approach clinical work (i.e., psychodynamic, cognitive-behavioral therapy (CBT), interpersonal psychotherapy (IPT), dia-

lectical behavior therapy (DBT), etc.)? Be as specific as possible. (If you are not currently in clinical practice, describe which approach you anticipate using, or which approach resonates most strongly with you.)

2. What about this approach resonates with you as a mental health clinician?
3. What are the pros to using this approach?
4. What are the cons to using this approach?
5. List the major theoretical approach(es) that you do not adhere or ascribe to. (If you are not currently in clinical practice, describe which approaches you do not anticipate using, or which do not resonate with you.)
6. What about this/these approaches do/does not resonate with you?
7. Are you able to identify any pros to these methods? Explain.
8. Under what circumstances do you feel this/these approaches might be useful?

◼ Small Group Exercise 7.1

In a small group of two or three please discuss, as you are comfortable, your responses to the questions in individual exercise 7.1. Remember, answers are personal, and there are no correct or incorrect answers.

1. What were the response similarities in your group?
2. What were the response differences in your group?
3. Explore with group members who adhere to different treatment approaches than your own the pros and cons they identify regarding their approach.
4. Did you find any surprises in the group discussion? If so, what were they, and how were you surprised?

DIALECTICAL BEHAVIOR THERAPY (DBT)

DBT serves four main functions in an attempt to reduce self-harm behaviors. It is designed to: (1) help the patient develop new skills, (2) address the motivational obstacles that impede skill use, (3) help patients generalize the skills they learn in treatment to their daily lives, and (4) provide therapists with the support and supervision they need to remain motivated and skilled in treatment (Linehan, 1987, 1993a).

The guiding principle of DBT is the **biosocial theory of borderline personality disorder** (BPD). Proposed by Linehan (1987), the biosocial theory of BPD suggests that the emotional and behavioral dysregulation experienced by clients with BPD is both a byproduct of and reinforced by the transaction between an invalidating early childhood home environment and an inherent biological emotional vulnerability (Ivanoff, Linehan, & Brown, 2001; Linehan, 1993a; Shearin & Linehan,

1994). In other words, the emotional and behavioral dysregulation of a client is considered a natural reaction to environmental reinforcers (Linehan, 1993a).

This biosocial theory of BPD directly informs DBT because it provides the foundation for the four stages of DBT (Linehan, 1993a; Shearin & Linehan, 1994).

The goal of stage 1 is to address the severe behavioral dysregulation of clients by helping clients to develop greater behavioral control. The goal of stage 2 treatment is to develop emotional regulation, or to increase the client's ability to experience an appropriate range of emotions. Stage 3 treatment goals are to facilitate the client's experience of happiness, to improve interpersonal relationships and self-esteem, and to improve problems in daily living. Stage 4 treatment emphasizes the development of an increased sense of connectedness and freedom and reducing feelings of emptiness and loneliness (Ivanoff et al., 2001; Lynch, Trost, Salsman, & Linehan, 2007; Robins & Chapman, 2004).

Unlike other treatment models, a client can begin treatment at any one of the stages depending on his or her presentation and symptomatology. For example, a client experiencing extreme behavioral dysregulation (i.e., suicidal behaviors) would enter treatment at stage 1, whereas a client struggling with emotional dysregulation without engaging in dangerous behaviors might enter treatment at stage 2.

In addition to the biosocial theory of BPD, DBT is organized around the following hierarchy of goals: (1) eliminating life-threatening behaviors, including suicide attempts and deliberate self-harm; (2) eliminating therapy-interfering behavior, such as treatment nonadherence or not completing homework assignments; and (3) ameliorating behaviors and factors associated with poor quality of life, such as substance abuse (Linehan, 1993a; Shearin & Linehan, 1994).

DBT also emphasizes skills training or teaching clients more adaptive ways of responding to stressors rather than engaging in self-harm behaviors. Four main sets of skills are the focus of this mode of treatment, including: (1) **mindfulness,** (2) **distress tolerance,** (3) **emotional regulation,** and (4) **interpersonal effectiveness** (Ivanoff et al., 2001; Robins & Chapman, 2004; Robins, Ivanoff, & Linehan, 2001). *Mindfulness* has to do with the quality of awareness that a client brings to what he or she is doing and experiencing. It encourages individuals to live in the here and now, to focus on the present, and to pay attention to what is happening in the moment. Clients learn to control their attention and to limit distracting thoughts, images, and feelings associated with negative mood and anxiety. *Distress tolerance* involves helping clients to endure adverse situations, feelings, and/or thoughts. Both mindfulness and distress tolerance are acceptance-oriented skills (Robins et al., 2001). *Emotional regulation* involves helping clients to manage recent as well as long-standing difficult feelings. Clients are taught to observe their emotions and accept their emotions rather than to push them away. They are also taught not to judge their emotions, not to hang on to them, and not to intensify them. In addition, clients are taught to recognize where their emotions come from and how to describe their emotions. Emotional regulation skills also teach clients how to modulate their emotions should they desire to do so (Ivanoff et al., 2001; Robins et al., 2001). Lastly, *interpersonal effectiveness* seeks to improve the client's communication skills and the way in which they manage interpersonal relationships. Both emotional regulation and interpersonal effectiveness skills are change-oriented (Ivanoff et al., 2001; Robins et al., 2001).

The next mode of DBT focuses on helping clients to generalize the skills that they have learned in the previous mode and apply them to real-life situations. Typically via brief telephone sessions, sometimes referred to as "coaching calls" (Lynch et al., 2007; Robins & Chapman, 2004), clinicians help clients to apply the four skills to here and now situations.

The last mode of treatment is clinician-centered. Given that DBT requires active participation of the clinician and 24-hour availability to clients, clinicians are highly susceptible to burn-out. Furthermore, due to the nature of BPD, clinicians practicing DBT frequently encounter difficult and challenging cases. Thus, supervision and consultation is a major aspect of treatment. Clinicians are part of consultation teams where difficult cases can be discussed and feedback on treatment issues is provided (Linehan, 1993a; Robins et al., 2001).

DBT involves once-weekly psychotherapy sessions during which a specific problematic behavior or event from the past week is examined in detail via a **behavioral chain analysis** (BCA). The BCA begins with identifying a specific situation or event and examining the chain of events leading up to the situation or event and how they may be related. The BCA continues by then exploring alternative solutions and adaptive responses (Linehan, 1993a). Weekly individual sessions are supplemented with weekly two-and-a-half-hour group therapy sessions during which interpersonal skills, mindfulness skills, distress tolerance skills, and emotional regulation skills are taught (Linehan, 1993a).

EVIDENCE FOR AND AGAINST DBT

Several randomized controlled trials (RCTs) have examined the efficacy of DBT for the treatment of BPD (Koons et al., 2001; Linehan, 1993b; Linehan, Armstrong, Suarez, Allmon, & Heard, 1991; Linehan, Tutek, Heard, & Armstrong, 1994; Linehan et al., 1999, 2002, 2006; Turner, 2000; van den Bosch, Koeter, Stijnen, Verheul, & van den Brink, 2005; van den Bosch, Verheul, Schippers, & van den Brink, 2002; Verheul et al., 2003). In 1991, Linehan and colleagues conducted the first study examining the efficacy of DBT and compared 1 year of DBT to 1 year of **treatment as usual** (standard care received in the agency where treatment is occurring) in a group of 44 woman diagnosed with BPD who experienced parasuicide. Participants who received DBT exhibited greater decreases in the frequency and severity of parasuicide as compared to participants who received treatment as usual. DBT participants also experienced greater reduction in the frequency and length of inpatient hospitalization and demonstrated higher rates of treatment adherence (Linehan et al., 1991).

Also important to recognize is the first RCT of a briefer form of DBT. Koons and colleagues (2001) conducted a randomized control trial of a 6-month version of DBT compared to 6 months of treatment as usual among a group of 20 female veterans, 40% of whom experienced suicidality. Again, DBT participants experienced greater reductions in suicidal ideation and parasuicidal behavior. They also experienced greater improvements in levels of hopelessness, depression, and anger (Koons et al., 2001).

Stanley, Brodsky, Nelson, and Dulit (2007) also examined a brief 6-month course of dialectical behavior therapy—brief (DBT-B) to determine its effectiveness in improving rates of retention in treatment and reducing nondeliberate self-harm among 20 clients with BPD. Results indicated that DBT-B lead to vast improvement in treatment retention and a significant reduction in target behaviors.

In an attempt to isolate the factors that may contribute to the efficacy of DBT, Linehan and colleagues (2002) conducted an RCT to determine the impact of the training, supervision, and monitoring of treatment fidelity associated with DBT versus treatment as usual. In this study, DBT was compared to "treatment by experts" who received training from leaders in the field rather than to comparing it to treatment as usual. Results indicated that participants in the DBT group had a significantly lower rate of suicide attempts and severity of attempts. DBT participants also experienced lower rates of emergency room and inpatient hospitalization and higher rates of treatment adherence than those who received treatment by experts.

Harned and colleagues (2008) conducted a similar study and evaluated the efficacy of DBT versus treatment by experts in psychotherapies other than behavioral treatment. This study also concluded that the efficacy of DBT cannot be attributed to general factors associated with therapist characteristics.

There are also several uncontrolled trials and nonrandomized control trials of DBT and studies of modified courses of DBT based on setting and population. Overall, DBT has been shown to be effective at reducing suicidality with adolescents, adults, and the elderly, particularly within the context of BPD (Linehan, Heard, & Armstrong, 1993; Linehan et al., 1994, 2006) but also for depression (Lynch, Morse, Mendelson, & Robins, 2003), attention-deficit hyperactivity disorder (ADHD; Hesslinger et al., 2002), substance abuse (Linehan et al., 1999, 2002; Verheul et al., 2003), and eating disorders (Chen, Matthews, Allen, Kuo, & Linehan, 2008; Safer, Telch, & Agras, 2001; Telch, Agras, & Linehan, 2000, 2001). In addition, DBT also has evidence to support its use in inpatient settings (Barlcy et al., 1993; Bohus et al., 2004; Katz, Cox, Gunasekara, & Miller, 2004; McCann, Ball, & Ivanoff, 2000; Rathus & Miller, 2002; Rusch et al., 2008; Swenson, 2000; Trupin, Stewart, Beach, & Boesky, 2002). The efficacy of DBT is generally examined in the context of a year-long course of treatment. It is important to note that the greatest treatment effects have been found to occur during the first 4 months of treatment. The remaining 8 months, considered a period of skills consolidation (Linehan et al., 1991), requires further examination.

RECOMMENDED CLINICAL GUIDELINES FOR DBT

DBT is an effective treatment approach for addressing suicidality that is flexible based on the level of pathology of the client (Comtois & Linehan, 2006; Lynch et al., 2007; Robins et al., 2001). Nonetheless, it is an intensive treatment modality for both clients and clinicians. Several important aspects have been emphasized in the literature examining DBT that require specific attention (Linehan, 1993a; Robins et al., 2001). The following recommendations should be kept in mind when utilizing DBT with suicidal clients:

1. *Training.* DBT is a highly complex intervention. It is recommended that no clinician utilize DBT without proper training and that no modified or adapted versions be utilized until the full model has been mastered.
2. *Supervision.* DBT builds into the treatment process a supervision component. It is important that clinicians adhere to this component as it is critical for effective DBT. Proper supervision and consultation reduces risk of clinician burn-out and provides the opportunity to receive feedback and direction with difficult cases.
3. *Maintaining perspective on client functioning.* DBT operates from a clear perspective regarding clients. DBT approaches practice from the perspective that clients are doing the best they can, that they desire to do better, and that they can learn the skills they need to improve. It is essential for clinicians practicing DBT to maintain this perspective. If clinicians take the stance that clients already have the skills they need and choose not to use them or that clients are not interested in changing then the DBT process will fail.
4. *Maintaining boundaries.* DBT requires intense therapist involvement in terms of time and active participation in treatment. That said, it is critical to set and maintain appropriate boundaries with clients in order to avoid burn-out and to allow clients to enjoy the maximum benefit of treatment. For example, coaching calls are a standard part of DBT, however, clients should be provided with clear instructions as to under what circumstances it is appropriate/acceptable to page their therapist. Clients need the opportunity to retrieve and implement skills on their own, and therapists need to know that they will not be receiving phone calls every hour.

▓ Role Play 7.1

You are a mental health clinician in an outpatient mental health center. A client you treated briefly 2 years prior for depression unexpectedly presents to your office expressing suicidal ideation with intent.

Using this scenario, break into groups of three and assume the role of the mental health clinician and patient. The third member will act as a recorder and can be called upon to consult and assist the mental health clinician. Engage in a role play in which you would implement DBT with this client.

▓ Role Play 7.2

You are a mental health clinician in an outpatient mental health center. A client you treated briefly 2 years prior for depression unexpectedly presents to your office expressing suicidal ideation with intent.

Using this scenario, break into groups of three and assume the role of the mental health clinician and supervisor. The third member will act as a recorder and can be called upon to consult and assist the mental health clinician. Engage in a role play in which you discuss this client with your supervisor. What questions might you ask? What kind of support might you try to elicit? Is the supervision for you? The client? Both?

SUMMARY

Dialectical behavior therapy (DBT) is an evidence-based practice for the treatment of deliberate and nondeliberate self-harm. Initially introduced to target these behaviors in women with borderline personality disorder, DBT now has evidence to support its use across a number of major diagnostic categories. DBT emphasizes the dialect of change and acceptance and provides clients with skills that target both of these poles. DBT is successful at reducing self-harm via teaching clients adaptive ways to experience their emotions, modulate affect and emotion, improve interpersonal relationships, and manage stressful life experiences. Supervision, training, and consultation are essential for any clinician practicing DBT.

■ Key Points

1. DBT is based on a biosocial theory of borderline personality disorder.
2. DBT represents a blending together of multiple theoretical orientations and philosophies.
3. There are four stages of DBT.
4. There is an overarching hierarchical order of goals associated with DBT.
5. DBT is skills focused.
6. DBT seeks to improve the behavioral and emotional dysregulation of clients.
7. DBT relies on active involvement of clinicians.
8. Supervision and consultation are essential to the practice of DBT.
9. DBT is typically delivered in a year-long period, and the greatest improvements are experienced in the first 4 months of treatment.
10. DBT has a strong evidence base for the treatment of suicidality.

FURTHER READINGS

Ben-Porath, D. D., & Koons, C. R. (2005). Telephone coaching in dialectical behavior therapy: A decision-tree model for managing inter-session contact with clients. *Cognitive and Behavioral Practice, 12*(4), 448–460.

Brown, M. Z. (2006). *Linehan's theory of suicidal behavior: Theory, research, and dialectical behavior therapy*. Washington, DC: American Psychological Association.

Gould, M. S., Greenberg, T., Velting, D. M., & Shaffer, D. (2003). Youth suicide risk and preventive interventions: A review of the past 10 years. *Journal of the American Academy of Child & Adolescent Psychiatry, 42*(4), 386–405.

Koerner, K., & Linehan, M. M. (2000). Research on dialectical behavior therapy for patients with borderline personality disorder. *Psychiatric Clinics of North America, 23*(1), 151–167.

Koons, C. R. (2008). Dialectical behavior therapy. *Social Work in Mental Health, 6*(1–2), 109–132.

Linehan, M. M., Goodstein, J. L., Nielsen, S. L., & Chiles, J. A. (1983). Reasons for staying alive when you are thinking of killing yourself: The reasons for living inventory. *Journal of Consulting & Clinical Psychology, 51*, 276–286.

Miller, A. L., Rathus, J. H., & Linehan, M. M. (2007). *Dialectical behavior therapy with suicidal adolescents*. New York: Guilford Press.

ELECTRONIC RESOURCES

BPD Resource Center: http://bpdresourcecenter.org/
DBT Self Help: http://www.dbtselfhelp.com/
International Society for the Improvement and Teaching of Dialectical Behavior Therapy: http://www.isitdbt.org/
Middle Path: http://www.middle-path.org/DBT/dbtr-index.html
University of Washington: http://depts.washington.edu/brtc/about/dbt

■ Knowledge Acquisition Test

True or False

1. DBT requires active participation of the clinician.
2. DBT has evidence to support its efficacy with individuals with borderline personality disorder only.
3. Distress-tolerance strategies are change-oriented skills.
4. DBT is based on a biosocial theory of borderline personality disorder.
5. Individuals treated with DBT rather than treatment as usual do not experience greater reduction in inpatient hospitalizations.
6. A behavior chain analysis focuses strictly on precipitating events.
7. DBT represents a blend of theoretical orientations, philosophies, and perspectives.
8. Individuals experiencing emotional dysregulation typically enter DBT at stage 1.
9. Interpersonal effectiveness strategies are change-oriented skills.

Short Answer

10. What are the four main functions of DBT?
11. What are the four main skill sets taught in DBT?

12. Why is the last mode of DBT clinician-centered?
13. Describe the skill of mindfulness.
14. What is the hierarchy of goals around which DBT is organized?
15. How are the individual and weekly sessions organized in DBT?

Multiple Choice

16. DBT has been shown to be effective at treating individuals with which of the following disorders?

    A. Eating disorders
    B. Depression
    C. Substance abuse
    D. Borderline personality disorder
    E. All of the above
    F. None of the above

17. Emotional regulation skills do not include:

    A. Helping clients to manage recent as well as longstanding difficult feelings
    B. Observing emotions
    C. Pushing away emotions
    D. Learning not judge their emotions
    E. Recognizing where their emotions come from and how to describe them

18. Which of the following is not part of the hierarchy of goals of DBT?

    A. Eliminating life-threatening behaviors
    B. Eliminating therapy-interfering behavior
    D. Ameliorating behaviors and factors associated with poor quality of life
    E. All of the above
    F. None of the above

19. The four main skill sets of DBT include:

    A. Mindfulness
    B. Distress tolerance
    C. Emotional regulation
    D. Medication management
    E. Interpersonal effectiveness

20. Which of the following is not a goal of stage 3 of DBT?

    A. Provide psychoeducation regarding diagnosis
    B. Facilitate the client's experience of happiness
    C. Improve interpersonal relationships
    D. Improve self-esteem
    E. Improve problems in daily living

Answer key is available in the Instructor's Manual; qualified instructors may e-mail textbook@springerpub.com *to request a copy.*

REFERENCES

American Psychiatric Association (APA). (2000). *Diagnostic and statistical manual of mental disorders* (4th ed., text revision). Arlington, VA: Author.

Barley, W. D., Buie, S. E., Peterson, E. W., Hollingsworth, A. S., Griva, M., Hickerson, S. C., et al. (1993). Development of an inpatient cognitive-behavioral treatment program for borderline personality disorder. *Journal of Personality Disorders, 7,* 232–240.

Bohus, M., Haaf, B., Simms, T., Limberger, M., Schmahl, C., Unckel, C., et al. (2004). Effectiveness of inpatient dialectical behavioral therapy for borderline personality disorder: A controlled trial. *Behaviour Research and Therapy, 42,* 487–499.

Chen, E. Y., Matthews, L., Allen, C., Kuo, J. R., & Linehan, M. M. (2008). Dialectical behavior therapy for clients with binge-eating disorder or bulimia nervosa and borderline personality disorder. *International Journal of Eating Disorders, 41*(6), 505–512.

Comtois, K. A., & Linehan, M. M. (2006). Psychosocial treatments for suicidal behaviors: A practice-friendly review. *Journal of Clinical Psychology, 62*(2), 161–170.

Gunderson, J. G. (2001). *Borderline personality disorder: A clinical guide.* Washington, DC: American Psychiatric Publishing.

Harned, M. S., Chapman, A. L., Dexter-Mazza, E. T., Murray, A., Comtois, K. A., & Linehan, M. M. (2008). Treating co-occurring Axis I disorders in recurrently suicidal women with borderline personality disorder: A 2-year randomized trial of dialectical behavior therapy versus community treatment by experts. *Journal of Consulting & Clinical Psychology, 76*(6), 1068–1075.

Hesslinger, B., Tebartz van Elst, L., Nyberg, E., Dykierek, P., Richter, H., Berner, M., et al. (2002). Psychotherapy of attention deficit hyperactivity disorder in adults: A pilot study using a structured skills training program. *European Archives of Psychiatry and Clinical Neuroscience, 252,* 117–184.

Ivanoff, A., Linehan, M. M., & Brown, M. (Eds.). (2001). *Dialectical behavior therapy for impulsive self-injurious behaviors.* Washington, DC: American Psychiatric Publishing.

Katz, L. Y., Cox, B. J., Gunasekara, S., & Miller, A. L. (2004). Feasibility of dialectical behavior therapy for suicidal adolescent inpatients. *Journal of the American Academy of Child & Adolescent Psychiatry, 43,* 276–282.

Koons, C., Robins, C. J., Tweed, J. L., Lynch, T. R., Gonzelez, A. M., Morse, J. Q., et al. (2001). Efficacy of dialectical behavior therapy in women veterans with borderline personality disorder. *Behavior Therapy, 32,* 371–390.

Linehan, M. M. (1987). Dialectical behavior therapy: A cognitive-behavioral approach to parasuicide. *Journal of Personality Disorders, 1,* 328–333.

Linehan, M. (1993a). *Cognitive behavioral treatment of borderline personality disorder.* New York: Guilford Press.

Linehan, M. M. (1993b). *Skills training manual for treating borderline personality disorder.* New York: Guilford Press.

Linehan, M., Armstrong, H. E., Suarez, A., Allmon, D., & Heard, H. L. (1991). Cognitive-behavioral treatment of chronically parasuicidal borderline patients. *Archives of General Psychiatry, 48,* 1060–1064.

Linehan, M. M., Comtois, K. A., Murray, A. M., Brown, M. Z., Gallop, R. J., Heard, H. L., et al. (2006). Two year randomized controlled trial and follow-up of dialectical behavior therapy vs therapy by experts for suicidal behaviors and borderline personality disorder. *Archives of General Psychiatry, 62,* 1–10.

Linehan, M. M., Dimeff, L. A., Reynolds, S. K., Comtois, K. A., Welch, S. S., Heagerty, P., et al. (2002). Dialectical behavior therapy versus comprehensive validation therapy plus 12-step for the treatment of opioid dependent women meeting criteria for borderline personality disorder. *Drug and Alcohol Dependence, 67,* 13–26.

Linehan, M. M., Heard, H. L., & Armstrong, H. E. (1993). Naturalistic follow-up of a behavioral treatment for chronically parasuicidal borderline patients. *Archives of General Psychiatry, 50*(12), 971–974.

Linehan, M. M., Schmidt, H. I., Dimeff, L. A., Craft, J. C., Kanter, J., & Comtois, K. A. (1999). Dialectical behavior therapy for patients with borderline personality disorder and drug-dependence. *American Journal on Addictions, 8,* 279–292.

Linehan, M. M., Tutek, D. A., Heard, H. L., & Armstrong, H. E. (1994). Interpersonal outcome of cognitive behavioral treatment for chronically suicidal borderline patients. *American Journal of Psychiatry, 151,* 1771–1776.

Lynch, T. R., Morse, J. Q., Mendelson, T., & Robins, C. J. (2003). Dialectical behavior therapy for depressed older adults: A randomized pilot study. *The American Journal of Geriatric Psychiatry, 11,* 33–45.

Lynch, T. R., Trost, W. T., Salsman, N., & Linehan, M. M. (2007). Dialectical behavior therapy for borderline personality disorder. *Annual Review of Clinical Psychology, 3,* 181–205.

McCann, R. A., Ball, E. M., & Ivanoff, A. (2000). DBT with an inpatient forensic population: The CMHIP forensic model. *Cognitive and Behavioral Practice, 7,* 447–456.

Pompili, M., Girardi, P., Ruberto, A., & Tatarelli, R.(2005). Suicide in borderline personality disorder: A meta-analysis. *Norwegian Journal of Psychiatry, 59,* 319–324.

Rathus, J. H., & Miller, A. L. (2002). Dialectical behavior therapy adapted for suicidal adolescents. *Suicide & Life-Threatening Behavior, 32,* 146–157.

Robins, C. J., & Chapman, A. L. (2004). Dialectical behavior therapy: Current status, recent developments, and future directions. *Journal of Personality Disorders, 18,* 73–89.

Robins, C. J., Ivanoff, A. M., & Linehan, M. M. (2001). *Dialectical behavior therapy.* New York: Guilford Press.

Rusch, N., Schiel, S., Corrigan, P. W., Leihener, F., Jacob, G. A., Olschewski, M., et al. (2008). Predictors of dropout from inpatient dialectical behavior therapy among women with borderline personality disorder. *Journal of Behavior Therapy & Experimental Psychiatry, 39*(4), 497–503.

Safer, D. L., Telch, C. F., & Agras, W. (2001). Dialectical behavior therapy for bulimia nervosa. *American Journal of Psychiatry, 158,* 632–634.

Shearin, E. N., & Linehan, M. M. (1994). Dialectical behavior therapy for borderline personality disorder: Theoretical and empirical foundations. *Acta Psychiatrica Scandinavica, 379*(Suppl), 61–68.

Stanley, B. H., Brodsky, B. S., Nelson, J. D., & Dulit, R. (2007). Brief dialectical behavior therapy (DBT_B) for suicidal behavior and non-suicidal self injury. *Archives of Suicide research, 11*(4), 337–341.

Swenson, C. R. (2000). How can we account for DBT's widespread popularity? *Clinical Psychology Science and Practice, 7,* 87–91.

Telch, C. F., Agras, W., & Linehan, M. M. (2000). Group dialectical behavior therapy for binge eating disorder: A preliminary uncontrolled trial. *Behavior Therapy, 31,* 569–582.

Telch, C. F., Agras, W., & Linehan, M. M. (2001). Dialectical behavior therapy for binge eating disorder. *Journal of Consulting and Clinical Psychology, 69,* 1061–1065.

Trupin, E. W., Stewart, D. G., Beach, B., & Boesky, L. (2002). Effectiveness of dialectical behavior therapy program for incarcerated female juvenile offenders. *Child and Adolescent Mental Health, 7,* 121–127.

Turner, R. M. (2000). Naturalistic evaluation of dialectical behavior therapy-oriented treatment for borderline personality disorder. *Cognitive and Behavioral Practice, 7,* 413–419.

van den Bosch, L.M.C., Koeter, M.W.J., Stijnen, T., Verheul, R., & van den Brink, W. (2005). Sustained efficacy of dialectical behavior therapy for borderline personality disorder. *Behaviour Research and Therapy, 43,* 1231–1241.

van den Bosch, L.M.C., Verheul, R., Schippers, G. M., & van den Brink, W. (2002). Dialectical behavior therapy of borderline patients with and without substance use problems: Implementation and long-term effects. *Addictive Behaviors, 27,* 911–923.

Verheul, R., van den Bosch, L. M., Koeter, M. W., De Ridder, M. A., Stijnen, T., & van den Brink, W. (2003). Dialectical behavior therapy for women with borderline personality disorder: 12-month, randomised clinical trial in The Netherlands. *British Journal of Psychiatry, 182,* 135–140.

8 Interpersonal Psychotherapy and Suicide

Interpersonal psychotherapy (IPT) has been demonstrated an effective evidence-based practice (EBP) for depression in randomized controlled and open trials. The efficacy of IPT has further been demonstrated as superior to **treatment as usual** (standard treatment provided by an organization) or **waitlist controls** (a comparison group of individuals not currently receiving treatment but awaiting service provision). The empirical support for IPT has been found in a number of populations, but it is only beginning to emerge as a potential EBP for individuals experiencing suicidality. This chapter presents the IPT approach and its adaptation as an emergent model of intervention with individuals experiencing suicidality. The core elements and strategies of IPT are examined, as well as evidence on the effectiveness of this EBP. Finally, recommendations for clinical practice with IPT are provided (Mufson & Sills, 2006).

■ Goals and Objectives of this Chapter

An understanding of:

- Background and key theories underlying IPT
- The description of IPT
- Core goals of IPT
- Key strategies, skills, and techniques of IPT
- The three phases of IPT
- Diverse applications of IPT
- Evidence that supports the use of IPT

- Evidence that is not supportive of the use of IPT
- Emergent adaptation of IPT with older adults
- IPT and suicidality

INTRODUCTION

Interpersonal psychotherapy (IPT) is a psychosocial treatment that was developed for adults with depression (Klerman & Weissman, 1993; Klerman, Weissman, Rounsaville, & Chevron, 1984) and is a brief outpatient evidence-based practice (EBP; Klerman et al., 1984). IPT emerged out of **interpersonal theory**, originating under Harry Stack Sullivan, which hypothesized that interpersonal experiences help in the formation of personality (Sullivan, 1953). In addition, IPT draws from Adolf Meyer's theory that postulates an individual's psychological disorder comes from his or her adaptations to interpersonal relationships and the larger environment (Mufson & Sills, 2006). Difficulties in or loss of relationships occur through an individual's interpersonal interactions and can contribute to depression. IPT's psychological treatment of depression emphasizes current, not past, interpersonal relations of the client with specific focus on the individual's immediate social context (Klerman et al., 1984; Weissman & Markowitz, 1994). Further, IPT seeks to intervene in symptom formation and the social dysfunction associated with depression, but it does not target aspects of an individual's personality (de Mello, de Jesus Mari, Bacaltchuk, Verdeli, & Neugebauer, 2005; Weissman & Markowitz, 1994).

Since its emergence in the 1970s, IPT has developed from an intervention that focused on adults with depression to an effective intervention that can be applied to a number of different populations and diagnoses. Recently, IPT has begun to focus directly on older adults experiencing suicidality.

■ Small Group Exercise 8.1

Discuss the following questions in small groups of three or four.

1. How can a client's current interpersonal difficulties contribute to his/her suicidal risk factors?
2. By working with a client's current interpersonal difficulties, how can a mental health clinician positively contribute to their client's protective factors against suicidality?

INTERPERSONAL PSYCHOTHERAPY

IPT was designed to treat adults with depression and was originally conceptualized as having three treatment phases (de Mello et al., 2005; Klerman et al., 1984; Weissman & Markowitz, 1994, 1998). Specifically, IPT strived to treat depression through two central goals: (1) to reduce depressive symptoms, and (2) to improve and restore interpersonal functioning (Mufson & Sills, 2006). The achievement of these goals revolves around three main overarching strategies: (1) identification of the problem area(s), which are identified in the first phase of treatment; (2) identification of effective communication and problem-solving skills for the client's problems, which occurs in the second phase of treatment; and (3) practicing these skills and techniques both in and out of treatment sessions. Such practicing occurs in the second and third phase of treatment (Mufson & Sills, 2006).

Phase 1

The initial assessment phase centers on an evaluation of the client's psychiatric history, diagnoses and symptoms, current social functioning, existing social relationships, relational patterns, and any recent changes. This phase may also assess for the need for medication. The client is given the "sick role" during this phase. This assessment provides the clinician a base understanding of the client's social and interpersonal context of his/her depressive symptoms and assists in setting the framework for treatment. The client's depressive symptoms are subsequently connected to his or her current situation with specific focus on the following four main problem area(s): grief, interpersonal role disputes, role transitions, and interpersonal deficits (de Mello et al., 2005; Weissman & Markowitz, 1994, 1998).

Phase 2

The middle or treatment phase centers on development of specific strategies for the client's current interpersonal problem areas (grief, interpersonal role disputes, role transitions, and interpersonal deficits) as determined in phase 1. Grief strategies facilitate mourning and assist in the development of new activities and relationships to compensate for the client's loss. Interpersonal role dispute strategies target the management and resolution of conflicts with significant others. Role transition strategies seek to help the client deal with change of life status (e.g., career changes, new diagnoses, new or ending relationships) by recognizing the positives and negatives of his/her new role. Finally, interpersonal deficit strategies recognize the client's social skills limitations and seek to develop, maintain, and/or expand his/her social relationships (Weissman & Markowitz, 1994, 1998).

Phase 3

The final phase is one of consolidation and ending. The client is provided support and encouragement to recognize and consolidate their therapeutic gains as a method to reassert their independence, efficacy, and competence. In addition, clinicians work with clients to be able to identify and counter depressive symptoms that may emerge or reemerge in the future (Weissman & Markowitz, 1994, 1998).

EVIDENCE FOR AND AGAINST IPT

Initially, IPT was developed for the treatment of adult depression, and investigations soon demonstrated its efficacy in the treatment approach of depression (de Mello et al., 2005; Ryan, 2005; Weissman & Markowitz, 1994). The proven effectiveness of IPT and its time-limited, manualized approach readily lent this EBP to be adapted to diverse populations and diagnostic disorders (de Mello et al., 2005).

Interpersonal psychotherapy for adolescents (IPT-A) has been adapted from the original approach to treat depressed adolescents (Brunstein-Klomek, Zalsman, & Mufson, 2007; Klomek & Mufson, 2006; Moreau, Mufson, Weissman, & Klerman, 1991; Mufson & Sills, 2006). IPT-A has now been demonstrated effective for treating depression with adolescents, including White, African American, and Latina youth (Mufson & Fairbanks, 1996; Mufson, Weissman, Moreau, & Garfinkel, 1999; Mufson et al., 1994, 2004). Research has similarly found that IPT is effective in treating older adults with late-life depression in general practice, uptake, and satisfaction by patients, therapists, and physicians (van Schaik, van Marwijk, Beekman, de Haan, & van Dyck, 2007; van Schaik et al., 2006).

IPT has yielded empirical support for treatment of postpartum depression (O'Hara, Stuart, Gorman, & Wenzel, 2000). Interpersonal and social rhythm therapy (IPSRT), an adaptation of IPT, has demonstrated early evidence to support the treatment of bipolar 1 disorders (Frank et al., 2005). Also, IPT has been found to be efficacious in the treatment of **dysthymia** (Markowitz, 1994) and for individuals with dysthymia and secondary alcohol abuse; however, only a small effect was found in increasing the percentage of days abstinent (Markowitz, Kocsis, Christos, Bleiberg, & Carlin, 2008).

IPT has also been successfully adapted to eating disorders (Fairburn, Jones, Peveler, Hope, & O'Connor, 1993; Wilfley et al., 2002). Emerging research has also found preliminary data that supports the effectiveness of IPT in treating posttraumatic stress disorder (PTSD; Bleiberg & Markowitz, 2005; Krupnick et al., 2008; Markowitz, Milrod, Bleiberg, & Marshall, 2009) and **borderline personality disorder** (BPD; Markowitz, Bleiberg, Pessin, & Skodol, 2007).

Although IPT has increasingly been applied effectively across a number of populations, it has not been efficacious in every application. For example, IPT has not demonstrated effectiveness in the treatment of substance disorders (Markowitz et al., 2008, 2009). In addition, IPT has not been found to be efficacious in the treatment of anxiety (adults), although a small open pilot study seemed promising (Lipsitz et al., 2008).

IPT AND SUICIDE

IPT has not yet been demonstrated as an effective EBP for the treatment of suicidality. However, IPT has recently been adapted and investigated as a *potential* treatment of suicidality (Heisel, Duberstein, Talbot, Tu, & King, 2009). In addition, since its inception IPT has focused on depression, a major underlying risk factor for suicidality. Depression is the most common psychiatric disorder associated with suicide. Further, research has found that more than 90% of individuals who suicide fulfill the criteria for one or more psychiatric disorders (American Psychiatric Association, 2003), of which 60% of all suicides occur in persons with a mood disorder (Malone & Lartey, 2004). Although IPT was not developed to treat suicide, its approach and efficacious treatment of depression may position this EBP as a potential, promising, and emerging treatment that may provide a basis that can be adapted more directly for the treatment of suicidality. Future research into IPT will indicate the potential of this intervention as a treatment for suicidality.

Currently there is some very limited research investigating the adaptation of IPT as a treatment for suicidality, but this preliminary evidence is promising. Research has found that IPT adaptation to the treatment of depression in older adults is efficacious (Bruce et al., 2004; Heisel & Duberstein, 2005). Because older adults have high rates of suicidality (Bruce et al., 2004; Heisel & Duberstein, 2005), researchers have started to recommend that IPT may be adaptable to the treatment of suicidality in older adults (Szanto, Mulsant, Houck, Dew, & Reynolds, 2003). A recent pilot study investigated a modified IPT treatment for older outpatients at elevated risk for suicide and found a substantial reduction in participant suicide ideation (Heisel et al., 2009). Although this study investigated 12 participants enrolled in this open trail of a modified 16-week IPT intervention, results found participants reported a robust reduction in suicide ideation and death ideation (Heisel et al., 2009).

Researchers adapted existing IPT treatment manuals and incorporated safety precautions to treat older persons experiencing suicidality (Heisel et al., 2009). Specifically, study IPT therapists were instructed to focus on suicidal risk factors (past and current suicide ideation, death ideation, suicide plan, intent, and self-injurious behaviors) and to educate participants to the potential connection of interpersonal difficulties and suicidal ideation and behaviors during the assessment sessions (Heisel et al., 2009). In particular, attention was given to associations between suicide ideation and four main problem areas: grief, interpersonal role disputes, role transitions, and interpersonal deficits.

During treatment, IPT therapists monitored suicidal thoughts and linked these symptoms to identified interpersonal problems. In addition, IPT therapists helped participants to clarify and improve their interpersonal needs and identified opportunities to enhance their positive social networks by encouraging more engagement in pleasant activities with others, while decreasing the participants exposure to painful or self-defeating interpersonal interactions (Heisel et al., 2009).

The termination phase focused on participants continuing to develop positive interpersonal relationships and to utilize their social supports and professionals when feeling suicidal in the future. Throughout the intervention, safety precautions were also added to the IPT protocols, including routine monitoring of suicidal ideation, in-session focus on validation of their feelings and problem-solving strategies to alleviate ideation, and the provision of the study therapist's 24-hour cellular phone number to access in the event of imminent risk (Heisel et al., 2009).

▇ Small Group Exercise 8.2

In small groups of four to six discuss the following:

1. As a practitioner, consider what strengths a researcher may consider important for future adaptations of IPT for suicidality.
2. What are some potential interesting or concerning elements of the emergent application of IPT for suicidal older adults?

RECOMMENDED CLINICAL GUIDELINES FOR IPT

Research has not established recommended clinical guidelines for the use of IPT in the treatment of suicidality. However, ongoing research with this approach may shortly produce such guidelines. Currently, there exists very little research to support the use of IPT for suicidality, and this preliminary investigation focuses only on older adults. Consequently, IPT is not yet recommended for the treatment of suicidality.

Considering the nature of IPT, its manualized and established strategies, adaptations across numerous populations and issues, and very early findings in the treatment of suicidal older adults, this approach has considerable, albeit unexplored potential for working with suicidality. IPT with such strong empirical support for the treatment of depression is an EBP mental health clinicians may want to follow in the research.

SUMMARY

Treating individuals is best achieved through the use of EBP that has been demonstrated to be effective in research with similar populations. It is important for mental health clinicians to be aware of and use EBPs in their work with clients. IPT is an empirically supported treatment for individuals experiencing depression. The core elements and strategies of IPT have been adapted and effectively applied to the treatment of a number of populations and presenting issues. Recently, IPT has been modified to treat suicidal older adults, but this emergent research is too limited and not yet sufficient to support its application to suicidality. However, current and future research may yield this EBP as an effective future EBP in the area of suicidality, and clinicians are encouraged to keep up to date on this intervention's progress.

▒ Key Points

1. IPT has been demonstrated an effective time-limited, EBP treatment for depression.
2. IPT treatment of depression seeks the reduction of depressive symptoms and improvement and restoration of interpersonal functioning.
3. IPT uses three main overarching strategies to achieve treatment goals.
4. There are three main phases in IPT treatment.
5. IPT has been effectively adapted to the treatment of depression in adolescent, adults, and older adults.
6. Empirical research has supported the efficacious use of IPT in the treatment of several diagnoses and presenting problems including; postpartum depression, dysthymia, bipolar disorder, borderline personality disorder, eating disorders, and posttraumatic stress disorder.
7. IPT has not demonstrated effectiveness in the treatment of some disorders or presenting problems (e.g., substance disorders).
8. A recent pilot study that investigated a modified IPT treatment for older outpatients at elevated risk for suicide found a substantial reduction in suicide ideation.
9. Adaptation to IPT for the treatment of suicidal older adults has been developed.
10. Although promising, IPT has not yet been sufficiently investigated to support its application to suicidality.

FURTHER READINGS

Heisel, M. J., Duberstein, P. R., Talbot, N. L., Tu, X. M., & King, D. A. (2009). Adapting interpersonal psychotherapy for older adults at risk for suicide: Preliminary findings. *Professional Psychology: Research and Practice, 40*(2), 156–164.

Klerman, G. L., & Weissman, M. M. (1993). *New applications of interpersonal psychotherapy*. Washington, DC: American Psychiatric Press.

Klerman, G. L., Weissman, M. M., Rounsaville, B. J., & Chevron, E. S. (1984). *Interpersonal psychotherapy of depression*. New York: Basic Books.

Markowitz, J. C. (1998). *Interpersonal psychotherapy*. Washington, DC: American Psychiatric Press.

Mufson, L., Moreau, D., Dorta, K. P., & Weissman, M. M. (2004). *Interpersonal psychotherapy for depressed adolescents* (2nd ed.). New York: Guilford Press.

Mufson, L., & Sills, R. (2006). Interpersonal psychotherapy for depressed adolescents (IPT-A): An overview. *Nordic Journal of Psychiatry, 60*(6), 431–437.

Weissman, M. M,. Markowitz, J. C., & Klerman, G. L. (2000). *Comprehensive guide to interpersonal psychotherapy.* New York: Basic Books.

Weissman, M. M, Markowitz, J. C., & Klerman, G. L. (2007). *Clinician's quick guide to interpersonal psychotherapy.* New York: Oxford University Press.

ELECTRONIC RESOURCES

Depression Center: http://www.depressioncenter.org/treatments/ipt.asp

Interpersonal Psychotherapy: http://www.interpersonalpsychotherapy.org

Interpersonal Psychotherapy Institute: http://www.ipt-institute.com

University of Wisconsin: http://www.psychiatry.wisc.edu/mridepressionstudy/briefhistory IPT.pdf

▧ Knowledge Acquisition Test

True or False

1. IPT is a long-term intervention.
2. IPT is an effective intervention for anxiety.
3. Youth, adults, and older adults can be effectively treated with IPT.
4. IPT is a well-developed, manualized EBP intervention.
5. IPT has found limited success as an intervention outside of mood disorders.
6. IPT was initially developed in the 1970s.
7. The treatment of IPT comprises 8 discrete phases.
8. IPT focuses on an individual's personality.
9. Currently, IPT is an established empirically supported EBP intervention for all individuals experiencing suicidality.

Short Answer

10. Name two theories that IPT uses.
11. What are the four main interpersonal problem areas that IPT focuses on?
12. IPT was originally conceptualized as having three treatment phases. Describe Phase 1.
13. IPT was originally conceptualized as having three treatment phases. Describe Phase 2.
14. IPT was originally conceptualized as having three treatment phases. Describe Phase 3.
15. Describe how researchers have adapted IPT to the treatment of suicidal older adults.

Multiple Choice

16. IPT uses what following strategy(ies)?

A. Identification of the problem area(s)

B. Identification of effective communication and problem-solving skills for the client's problems

C. Practicing these skills and techniques both in and out of treatment sessions

D. All of the above

E. None of the above

17. IPT has been demonstrated as an effective treatment for which of the following depressive disorder(s)?

A. Major depressive disorder

B. Bipolar 1 disorder

C. Dysthymia disorder

D. Postpartum depression

E. All of the above

F. None of the above

18. IPT has not been demonstrated as effective in the treatment for which of the following disorder(s)?

A. Posttraumatic stress disorder

B. Substance disorders

C. Eating disorders

D. Personality disorders

E. All of the above

F. None of the above

19. Very preliminary investigations into adapting IPT to suicidality have demonstrated positive findings in which of the following areas?

A. Children

B. Adolescents

C. Adults

D. Older adults

E. All of the above

F. None of the above

20. The use of IPT as an EBP for the treatment of suicidality is currently:

A. Recommended

B. Tentatively recommended

C. Recommended only for mild suicidal ideation

D. Recommended only for older adults

E. Not recommended

Answer key is available in the Instructor's Manual; qualified instructors may e-mail textbook@springerpub.com *to request a copy.*

REFERENCES

American Psychiatric Association. (2003). Assessing and treating suicidal behaviors: A quick reference guide. Retrieved July 5, 2008, from http://www.psychiatryonline.com/pracGuide/loadPracQuickRefPdf.aspx?file=Suibehavs_QRG

Bleiberg, K. L., & Markowitz, J. C. (2005). Interpersonal psychotherapy for posttraumatic stress disorder. *American Journal of Psychiatry, 162,* 181–183.

Bruce, M. L., Ten Have, T. R., Reynolds III, C. F., Katz, I. I., Schulberg, H. C., Mulsant, B. H., et al. (2004). Reducing suicidal ideation and depressive symptoms in depressed older primary care patients: A randomized controlled trial. *Journal of the American Medical Association, 291*(9), 1081–1091.

Brunstein-Klomek, A., Zalsman, G., & Mufson, L. (2007). Interpersonal psychotherapy for depressed adolescents (IPT-A). *Israel Journal of Psychiatry & Related Sciences, 44*(1), 40–46.

de Mello, M. F., de Jesus Mari, J., Bacaltchuk, J., Verdeli, H., & Neugebauer, R. (2005). A systematic review of research findings on the efficacy of interpersonal therapy for depressive disorders. *European Archives of Psychiatry and Clinical Neuroscience, 255,* 75–82.

Fairburn, C. G., Jones, R., Peveler, R. C., Hope, R. A., & O'Connor, M. (1993). Psychotherapy and bulimia nervosa: Longer-term effects of interpersonal psychotherapy, behavior therapy and cognitive behavior therapy. *Archives of General Psychiatry, 50,* 419–428.

Frank, E., Kupfer, D. J., Thase, M. E., Mallinger, A. G., Swartz, H., Fagiolini, A. M., et al. (2005). Two year outcomes for interpersonal and social rhythm therapy in individuals with bipolar I disorder. *Archives of General Psychiatry, 62,* 996–1004.

Heisel, M. J., & Duberstein, P. R. (2005). Suicide prevention in older adults. *Clinical Psychology: Science and Practice, 12*(3), 242–259.

Heisel, M. J., Duberstein, P. R., Talbot, N. L., Tu, X. M., & King, D. A. (2009). Adapting interpersonal psychotherapy for older adults at risk for suicide: Preliminary findings. *Professional Psychology: Research and Practice, 40*(2), 156–164.

Klerman, G. L., & Weissman, M. M. (1993). *New applications of interpersonal psychotherapy.* Washington, DC: American Psychiatric Press.

Klerman, G. L., Weissman, M. M., Rounsaville, B. J., & Chevron, E. S. (1984). *Interpersonal psychotherapy of depression.* New York: Basic Books.

Klomek, A. B., & Mufson, L. (2006). Interpersonal psychotherapy for depressed adolescents. *Child & Adolescent Psychiatric Clinics of North America, 15*(4), 959–975.

Krupnick, J. L., Green, B. L., Stockton, P., Miranda, J., Krause, E., & Mete, M. (2008). Group interpersonal psychotherapy with low-income women with post-traumatic stress disorder. *Psychotherapy Research, 18,* 497–507.

Lipsitz, J. D., Gur, M., Vermes, D., Petkova, E., Cheng, J., Miller, N., et al. (2008). A randomized trial of interpersonal therapy versus supportive therapy for social anxiety disorder. *Depression & Anxiety, 25*(6), 542–553.

Malone, D. A., & Lartey, P. (2004). *Depression and suicide-recognition and early intervention* (2nd ed.). Washington, DC: American Medical Association.

Markowitz, J. C. (1994). Psychotherapy of dysthymia. *American Journal of Psychiatry, 151*(8), 1114–1121.

Markowitz, J. C., Bleiberg, K., Pessin, H., & Skodol, A. E. (2007). Adapting interpersonal psychotherapy for borderline personality disorder. *Journal of Mental Health, 16*(1), 103–116

Markowitz, J. C., Kocsis, J. H., Christos, P., Bleiberg, K., & Carlin, A. (2008). Pilot study of interpersonal psychotherapy versus supportive psychotherapy for dysthymic patients with secondary alcohol abuse or dependence. *Journal of Nervous & Mental Disease, 196*(6), 468–474.

Markowitz, J. C., Milrod, B., Bleiberg, K., & Marshall, R. D. (2009). Interpersonal factors in understanding and treating posttraumatic stress disorder. *Journal of Psychiatric Practice, 15*(2), 133–140.

Moreau, D., Mufson, L., Weissman, M. M., & Klerman, G. L. (1991). Interpersonal psychotherapy for adolescent depression: Description of modification and preliminary application. *Journal of the American Academy of Child & Adolescent Psychiatry, 30*(4), 642–651.

Mufson, L., Dorta, K. P., Wickramaratne, P., Nomura, Y., Olfson, M., & Weissman, M. M. (2004). A randomized effectiveness trial of interpersonal psychotherapy for depressed adolescents. *Archives of General Psychiatry, 61*(6), 577–584.

Mufson, L., & Fairbanks, J. (1996). Interpersonal psychotherapy for depressed adolescents: A one-year naturalistic follow-up study. *Journal of the American Academy of Child & Adolescent Psychiatry, 35*(9), 1145–1155.

Mufson, L., Moreau, D., Weissman, M. M., Wickramaratne, P., Martin, J., & Samoilov, A. (1994). Modification of interpersonal psychotherapy with depressed adolescents (IPT-A): Phase I and II studies. *Journal of the American Academy of Child & Adolescent Psychiatry, 33*(5), 695–705.

Mufson, L., & Sills, R. (2006). Interpersonal psychotherapy for depressed adolescents (IPT-A): An overview. *Nordic Journal of Psychiatry, 60*(6), 431–437.

Mufson, L., Weissman, M. M., Moreau, D., & Garfinkel, R. (1999). Efficacy of interpersonal psychotherapy for depressed adolescents. *Archives of General Psychiatry, 56,* 573–579.

O'Hara, M. W., Stuart, S., Gorman, L. L., & Wenzel, A. (2000). Efficacy of interpersonal psychotherapy for postpartum depression. *Archives of General Psychiatry, 57,* 1039–1045.

Ryan, N. (2005). Treatment of depression in children and adolescents. *The Lancet, 366*(9489), 933–940.

Sullivan, H. S. (Ed.). (1953). *The interpersonal theory of psychiatry.* New York: W.W. Norton & Company.

Szanto, K., Mulsant, H. B., Houck, P., Dew, M. A., & Reynolds III, C. F. (2003). Occurrence and course of suicidality during short-term treatment of late-life depression. *Archives of General Psychiatry, 60,* 610–617.

van Schaik, A., van Marwijk, H., Adèr, H., van Dyck, R., de Haan, M., Penninx, B., et al. (2006). Interpersonal psychotherapy for elderly patients in primary care. *American Journal of Geriatric Psychiatry, 14*(9), 777–786.

van Schaik, D. J., van Marwijk, H. W., Beekman, A. T., de Haan, M., & van Dyck, R. (2007). Interpersonal psychotherapy (IPT) for late-life depression in general practice: Uptake and satisfaction by patients, therapists and physicians. *BMC Family Practice, 8,* 52.

Weissman, M. M., & Markowitz, J. C. (1994). Interpersonal psychotherapy: Current status. *Archives of General Psychiatry, 51,* 599–606.

Weissman, M. M., & Markowitz, J. C. (1998). An overview of interpersonal psychotherapy. In J. Markowitz (Ed.), *Interpersonal psychotherapy* (pp. 1–33). Washington, DC: American Psychiatric Press.

Wilfley, D. E., Welch, R. R., Stein, R. I., Spurrell, E. B., Cohen, L. R., Saelens, B. E., et al. (2002). A randomized comparison of group cognitive-behavioral therapy and group interpersonal psychotherapy for the treatment of overweight individuals with binge-eating disorder. *Archives of General Psychiatry, 59,* 713–721.

Suicidality Across the Life Span

Suicidality is experienced across the life span. The nature, risk, and protective factors of suicidality differ among the various stages of life. The assessment and treatment of suicidality is directly related to the age, developmental stage, and experiences of the client. Part III consists of three chapters that explore suicidality among children and adolescents, adults, and older adults.

Chapter 9, "Child and Adolescent Suicide," explores the identification of unique and common risk and protective factors for suicide among youth. Chapter 10, "Adult Suicide," examines the epidemiological trends, prevalence, and incident rates of adult suicidality as well as unique risk and protective factors for suicide in this age group. Chapter 11, "Older Adult Suicide," focuses on the identification of risk and protective factors unique to the aging population, which has the highest rate of suicide. Each chapter also deconstructs myths and misconceptions related to suicide within that age group.

The importance of age should not be underestimated. Age not only impacts the risk and protective factors related to a client's suicidality, but it can positively or negatively influence mental health professionals in their approach to and treatment of suicidal clients.

9 Child and Adolescent Suicide

The rising rates of suicide attempts and completions in children and adolescents are a significant and growing concern. In order to work with this population, it is important to understand the epidemiological trends, prevalence, and incident rates of child and adolescent suicidality. Identification of unique and common risk and protective factors to this population are investigated. In addition, this chapter deconstructs myths and misconceptions related to suicide among children and adolescents, and it highlights the importance of developmental issues with this population. An overview of empirically grounded strategies for effective assessment and treatment of this population is also provided.

■ Goals and Objectives of This Chapter

An understanding of:

- Epidemiology of child and adolescent suicidality
- The rates of completed suicide, attempted suicide, and suicidal ideation
- The impact of age and gender on suicidality
- Risk factors for child and adolescent suicide
- Protective factors against child and adolescent suicide
- The influence of family systems in child and adolescent suicide
- Social learning theory of transmission of suicidal behavior
- Parental psychiatric illness and its impact on offspring suicide
- Deconstructing the dominant myths and misconceptions of child and adolescent suicidality

- The importance and impact of child and adolescent development on the risk of suicide
- A review of the major evidence-based interventions for working with this population

---

INTRODUCTION

The death of any individual due to suicide is tragic. The terrible impact of such an event seems to exponentially increase when the individual is a child. Despite the rareness of the event, child and adolescent suicide exerts considerable impact on families, society, and the treating clinician(s). Although completed suicides in this population may be rare, attempts and ideation are far more common in children and adolescents. Approximately 2 million U.S. adolescents attempt suicide annually, with almost 700,000 receiving medical attention for their attempt (American Academy of Child and Adolescent Psychiatry [AACAP], 2001).

It is clinically beneficial for mental health professionals to understand suicidality across the life span for two fundamental reasons. One, professional awareness of the epidemiology, risk and protective factors, misconceptions, developmental issues, and interventions that are unique to the specific age group can guide clinicians in their practice. Two, personal awareness to your response, thoughts, and beliefs connected to suicidality and age equally impact your clinical assessment, interaction, and treatment of clients.

■ Individual Exercise 9.1

The suicide of a patient in which demographic below would be the hardest for you to accept? Please rank in order of impact (1 representing the most impactful to 8 the least impactful):

_____ 39-year-old female	_____ 78-year-old male
_____ 17-year-old male	_____ 23-year-old male
_____ 13-year-old male	_____ 57-year-old female
_____ 64-year-old female	_____ 15-year-old female

■ Individual Exercise 9.2

Describe at least three reasons for your following answers based on individual exercise 9.1:

1. What are your reasons for selecting number 1 (most impactful)?
2. What are your reasons for selecting number 2 (the second most impactful)?
3. What are your reasons for selecting number 8 (the least impactful of the group)?
4. Was this exercise more difficult or less difficult than you anticipated? Explain your rationale.
5. What lessons did you learn from this exercise?

■ Small Group Exercise 9.1

In small groups of two or three, please discuss, as you are comfortable, your responses to individual exercises 9.1 and 9.2. Remember, answers are personal, and there are no correct or incorrect answers.

1. What were the response similarities in your group?
2. What were the response differences in your group?
3. Did you find any surprises in the group discussion? If so, what were they, and how were you surprised?

STATISTICS, EPIDEMIOLOGY, AND TRENDS IN CHILD AND ADOLESCENT SUICIDE

Completed Suicide

As individuals grow from childhood into adolescence and then into adulthood and their senior years, so, too, does the risk of suicide grow with them. In 2004, the general rate of suicide deaths in the United States was approximately 10.9 per 100,000 people (Centers for Disease Control and Prevention [CDC], 2006). Suicide is the third highest cause of death in youth (Wintersteen, Diamond, & Fein, 2007). According to epidemiological research, it is estimated that each year approximately 2,000 U.S. adolescents aged 13–19 years complete suicide (Martin, Kochanek, Strobino, Guyer, & MacDorman, 2005; National Center for Health Statistics, 2000). In 2001, the number of suicide deaths among young people between 15 to 24 years of age was 3,971 (Anderson & Smith, 2003).

Completed suicides in children under the age of 10 years are exceptionally rare. For example in 1992, there were no reported suicides for children under 4 years of age, and there were only 10 completed suicides in children 5 through 9 years of age (Maris, Berman, & Silverman, 2000).

For children between the ages of 10 to 14 years of age the rates of suicide increase marginally to 1.3 per 100,000. In 1997, 330 children age 10 to 14 years completed suicide, with most of those deaths occurring between 12 to 14 years of age. This age group accounts for 7% of the total population but only 1% of all U.S. suicides (National Center for Health Statistics, 2000). However, the rate of completed suicide in children (10 to 14 year of age) has doubled since 1979 (National Center for Health Statistics, 2000).

This rate of completed suicide continues to climb with age. Among adolescents 15 through 19 years of age the suicide rate is 8.2 per 100,000 suicides (National Center for Health Statistics, 2000). This age group comprises approximately 6% of the overall U.S. population but accounts for 6.6% of all completed suicides (National Center for Health Statistics, 2000). In this age range, the completed suicide rate among males was 15.2 per 100,000, and among females it was 3.4 per 100,000 (National Center for Health Statistics, 2000). Since the 1960s, the suicide rate among all adolescents 15 to 19 years of age has tripled, but the female rate has changed little (Peters, Kochanek, & Murphy, 1998) (National Center for Health Statistics, 2000). Reportedly in 2001, 86% of all U.S. youth (15 to 24 years of age) suicide deaths were male, while only 14% were female (Anderson & Smith, 2003). In young adults ages 20 to 24 years of age, the suicide rate continues to increase to 12.5 suicides per 100,000 (CDC, 2006).

In general, males are typically four to six times more likely than females to complete suicide (CDC, 2006). A number of theories and studies have investigated this distinct gender disparity in completed suicide, including: (1) males use more lethal means (e.g., firearms); (2) females have higher rates of depression for which they receive treatment, while males have higher rates of substance use/abuse and do not receive the same levels of mental health treatment; and (3) socialization of genders, where suicide is viewed as more masculine and attempting is seen as more feminine (Canetto & Sakinofsky, 1998; Moscicki, 1994). Additionally, differences in help-seeking behaviors of males and females may partially explain the higher rate of suicide attempts among females and completed suicides among males. Women more often seek help for psychosocial distress and emotional difficulties (Galdas, Cheater, & Marshall, 2005; Möller-Leimkühler, 2002), whereas men more often seek treatment when physical symptoms are present (Corney, 1990; Galdas et al., 2005; Möller-Leimkühler, 2002; NHS Executive, 1998). Furthermore, men have more difficulty than females expressing emotions (Good & Sherrod, 2001; Taylor, Ryan, & Bagby, 1985), fearing the appearance of being weak and lacking masculinity (Chapple, Ziebland, & McPherson, 2004; Davies et al., 2000; Gascoigne & Whitear, 1999; Good & Mintz, 1990; Good, Dell, & Mintz, 1989; Pleck, 1995; Richardson, 2001; Wisch, Mahalik, Hayes, & Nutt, 1995).

Research into methods of suicide indicates that younger people are more likely to use firearms, suffocation, and poisoning than other methods. However, while adolescents and young adults are more likely to use firearms than suffocation, children are dramatically more likely to use suffocation (CDC, 2006).

Suicide Attempt and Ideation

Suicide attempts across all age groups have a higher prevalence rate than completed suicide. In the general population, men and the elderly are more likely to have fatal attempts than are women and youth (Moscicki, 2001). For every completed suicide, approximately 8–25 nonfatal suicide attempts occur (CDC, 2006; Moscicki, 2001).

According to a systematic review of population-based studies by Evans, Hawton, Rodham, and Deeks (2005), 9.7% of adolescents had reported attempting suicide, and 29.9% reported that they had thought about suicide at some point. The ratio of nonfatal attempts to completed suicides in children and adolescents has been found to be significantly greater than among adults and older persons (Moscicki, 1995). In adolescents, males are more likely to complete suicide than females (Canetto & Sakinofsky, 1998); however, adolescent females are more likely to attempt suicide (Schmidtke, Bille-Brahe, DeLeo, & Kerkhof, 1996). Across studies, research has found that females have a 1.25 times higher prevalence of suicidal ideation than males and attempt suicide at least twice as often as males (Evans et al., 2005).

RISK FACTORS

Over the past 30 years, research has extensively investigated characteristics associated with child and adolescent suicide. Three major categories of risk have been identified: (1) psychiatric, (2) demographic, and (3) relational (Hollis, 1996).

Psychiatric Risk Factors

Among children and adolescents, psychiatric illness, particularly depression, is the greatest known risk factor for suicide (Brent, Perper, & Moritz, 1993; Garrison, Jackson, Addy, McKeown, & Waller, 1991; Harrington et al., 1994; Hollis, 1996; Kovacs, Goldston, & Catsonis, 1993; Pfeffer, 1991; Pfeffer et al., 1993). Other psychiatric disorders associated with an increased risk of suicide among youth include substance abuse, conduct disorders, anxiety disorders, and schizophrenia (Andrews & Lewinsohn, 1992; Beautrais, Joyce, & Mulder, 1998b; D. Brent et al., 1988, 1993; Fergusson & Lynskey, 1995b; Fombonne, 1998; Joffe, Offord, & Boyle, 1988; Lesage et al., 1994; Patton et al., 1997; Shaffer et al., 1996; Shafi, Steltz-Lenarsky, Derrick, Beckner, & Whittinghill, 1988). Please refer to Part IV for a detailed discussion of psychiatric disorders and suicide.

Parental psychiatric illness is also a risk factor for suicide in children and adolescents (Brent & Mann, 2005; Brent et al., 2002, 2004; Egeland & Sussex, 1985; Garfinkel, Froese, & Hood, 1982; Linkowski, de Maertelaer, & Mendlewicz, 1985; Roy, Segal, Centerwall, & Robinette, 1991; Roy, Segal, & Sarchiapone, 1995; Runeson, 1998; Sorenson & Rutter, 1991; Tsuang, 1983). This issue is discussed later in this chapter.

Relational Risk Factors

Family conflict is a significant risk factor for suicide among children and adolescents (Adams, Overholser, & Lehnert, 1994; Asarnow, Carlson, & Mintz, 1988; de Wilde, Kienhorst, Diekstra, & Wolters, 1992; Hollis, 1996; Kosky, Silburn, & Zubrick, 1990; Randell, Wang, Herting, & Eggert, 2006; Taylor & Stansfeld, 1984; Zalsman & Mann, 2005). In particular, a negative mother–child relationship and lack of family warmth are highly associated with increased suicide risk (Hollis, 1996). Furthermore, research has indicated that suicidal youth are more likely to have increased family instability and chaos (Adam, Bouckoms, & Streiner, 1982; de Jong, 1992). In addition, exposure to physical and sexual abuse (Beautrais et al., 1996; Brodsky & Stanley, 2008; de Wilde et al., 1992; Evans et al., 2005; Fergusson, Woodward, & Harwood, 2000; Gould, Fisher, Parides, Flory, & Shaffer, 1996; Salzinger, Rosario, Feldman, & Ng-Mak, 2007; Shaunessey, Cohen, Plummer, & Berman, 1993; Zalsman & Mann, 2005) and to family violence (Hawton, O'Grady, Osborn, & Cole, 1982; Kosky, 1983) is associated with increased suicide risk among children and adolescents. Parental divorce is another significant risk factor for suicide among youth (Fergusson et al., 2000; Gould & Kramer, 2001; Rubenstein, Halton, Kasten, Rubin, & Stechler, 1998).

Sociodemographic Risk Factors

Several demographic characteristics are significantly associated with child and adolescent suicide. Low socioeconomic status (SES) and low educational achievement have been found to increase the risk of suicidal behavior among youth (Andrews & Lewinsohn, 1992; Beautrais, Joyce, & Mulder, 1998a; Bucca et al., 1994; Dubow, Kausch, Blum, Reed, & Bush, 1989; Fergusson & Lynskey, 1995a; Gould et al., 1996; Lesage et al., 1994). However, research in this area has been inconsistent; some studies have failed to find any association between low SES and youth suicidality (Brent et al., 1988; Pelkonen, Marttunen, Pulkkinen, Laippala, & Aro, 1997).

Additionally, research has consistently demonstrated that sexual orientation, specifically identifying as gay, lesbian, and bisexual, may result in an increased risk for suicidal behavior among adolescents (Bagley & Tremblay, 2000; Borowsky, Ireland, & Resnick, 2001; Eisenberg & Resnick, 2006; Gould & Kramer, 2001; Stronski-Huwiler & Remafedi, 1998; Saewyc, Heinz, Bearinger, Blum, & Resnick, 1998). Research indicates that the rate of suicide attempts among gay, lesbian, and bisexual adolescents is as much as four times higher than the rate of suicide attempts among heterosexual adolescents (Bagley & Tremblay, 2000; Eisenberg & Resnick, 2006; Gould & Kramer, 2001; Saewyc et al., 1998; Stronski-Huwiler & Remafedi, 1998). This is discussed in more detail in Chapter 15, "At-Risk Groups."

Lastly, gender is another major risk factor for suicide among adolescents. Among older adolescents (15 years and older) females have been consistently shown to be at greater risk for suicide than males (Evans et al., 2005). Chapter 3 reviews ethnic/cultural risk and protective factors among adolescents.

PROTECTIVE FACTORS

Research examining protective factors against youth suicide is much more limited in comparison to the literature examining risk factors. Having a strong social support network, particularly family cohesion, is the strongest protective factor against suicide in children and adolescents

(Armstrong & Manion, 2006; Borowsky et al., 2001; Eisenberg, Ackard, & Rsenick, 2007; Eisenberg & Resnick, 2006; Hall-Lande, Eisenberg, Christenson, & Neumark-Sztainer, 2007; Rubenstein, Heeren, Housman, Rubin, & Stechler, 1989). Researchers have specified the importance of perceived social support in particular as compared to just family cohesion as a protective factor against suicide among youth (Chioqueta & Stiles, 2007). Peer relationships have been demonstrated to have an indirect protective effect against suicidality among adolescents (Rubenstein et al., 1989).

The presence of a caring adult has also been shown to be a protective factor against youth suicide (Borowsky et al., 2001; Eisenberg & Resnick, 2006; Eisenberg et al., 2007; Resnick et al., 1997). Additionally, a safe school environment, including teacher caring, has been shown to be protective against suicidal behavior in youth (Borowsky et al., 2001; Eisenberg & Resnick, 2006; Eisenberg et al., 2007).

■ Case Example 9.1

You are a mental health clinician in an outpatient child and adolescent psychiatric clinic. You are scheduled to do an intake with a new client who was referred for services following a visit to the local hospital's emergency department for an attempted suicide.

Your client, Robert, a 17-year-old high school junior, attempted suicide a week earlier by ingesting his mother's prescribed medication for arthritis. Upon intake you learn that Robert has been experiencing a slow decline in functioning over the past 2 years since the divorce of his parents. Robert explained that the divorce did not come as a surprise because his parents never got along and always argued. He said he could not think of one time when the family was together without his parents verbally fighting.

Robert reacted strongly to their divorce. He mainly attributed his reaction to the fact that his older brother, Jonathan, chose to go and live with their father. He described Jonathan's moving away as a greater loss than his father's leaving the household. Jonathan was his idolized older brother, the person Robert turned to for advice and support, and he feared their relationship would change once Jonathan left home. Although Robert did not want to live with his father, he considered leaving his mother's house to be able to stay with his brother. Robert explained that when he mentioned the idea to his mother she looked so devastated that he did not have the heart to go through with it. He grew to feel responsible for his mother and guilty for contributing any further to her emotional pain.

Robert described feeling disconnected from and pressured by the people he cared about, and in response, he became increasingly withdrawn. A year prior to his suicide attempt he had a discussion with his mother during which she asked him about being depressed. He reported feeling unable to tell her the truth because he was afraid that it would further hurt her. He unsuccessfully attempted to talk to his father about his feelings; however, he responded by saying that Robert's grandfather had suffered from depression and had attempted suicide. Consequently, his father reported that he "had no room in his life for any more sadness or stress." Feeling unsupported and alone, Robert withdrew from his friends, and his grades started slipping. He described feeling irritable and losing pleasure in most activities. Later, he spoke to his school guidance counselor about his depression and was subsequently referred to a mental health clinic; however, Robert never followed up on this referral. He reported feeling comfortable talking to the guidance counselor that knew him for years, but he was worried that a stranger might think he "was crazy."

Robert explained that the week he attempted suicide he felt almost a "sense of relief" because he knew "it would all be over soon." Although his mother may be hurt by his suicide, she would not have to face constant disappointment and frustration with him alive. He hid a few of his mother's pills every day for 5 days until he had stored up what he believed to be enough pills to end his life. He stayed home from school, feigning ill. After he kissed his mother goodbye and she left for work, he wrote letters to his mother, brother, and father, and then took all the pills. Unknowingly, his mother left her briefcase at home and shortly returned to find him unconscious in his bed.

1. What risk factors are present in the case example?
2. What other risk factors would you assess for?
3. What protective factors are present in the case example?
4. What other protective factors would you assess for?
5. What issues are important to focus on in establishing a treatment plan?

▨ Role Play 9.1

Using case example 9.1, engage in a role play in which you would assess for familial transmission of suicidal behavior. Have one person take the role of the clinician and another take the role of Robert.

MYTHS AND MISCONCEPTIONS

There are a number of myths and misconceptions that have developed and evolved in the field of suicidality in relation to children and adolescents. The following list highlights some of these key myths and misconceptions. The first six items are derived from Moskos, Achilles, and Gray (2004).

1. *Suicide attempters and completers are similar.* According to research, males are four times more likely to die due to a suicide attempt, but females are more likely to attempt. The ratio between youth suicide attempters and youth suicide completers is estimated at 100–200:1. Attempting suicide is a recognized risk factor; however, the majority of suicide completers have no prior attempts.

2. *Current prevention programs work.* Adolescent prevention programs (school education programs, teen suicide hotlines, media campaigns, efforts to limit firearm access to teens) have not had a significant impact on lowering the teen suicide rate. Several reasons have been proposed as to why these programs have failed to effectively reduce teen suicide, including: they are not rigorously investigated, programs are used more by females than males, they have little impact on **cluster suicides** (suicides by unrelated groups of individuals), and they do not address access to means.

3. *Teenagers have the highest rate of suicide.* Statistically, senior adults, specifically older White males, are at the highest risk for suicide.

4. *Suicide is caused by family and social stress.* Research has found that adolescent completers may have experienced some social difficulty (disciplinary, shame, or amorous crisis event) prior to a suicide, but these events are not uncommon for adolescents, most of whom do not suicide. Research has clearly found that approximately 90% of teen completers have a psychiatric diagnosis.

5. *Suicidality is not inherited.* Genetics appears to have a strong association with mental health and suicide, including a risk of inheriting mental illnesses and/or increased impulsivity or aggression.

6. *Teen suicide represents treatment failure.* Research has found that few adolescent suicide completers were in treatment at the time of their death (1% in public mental health treatment; 3% had detectable levels of psychotropic medications in the blood sample).

7. *Most suicides do not occur at home.* The majority of adolescent suicides occur in the home, with most households having at least one lethal means available at the time of the attempt (McManus et al., 1997). It is recommended that parents/caregivers of suicidal youth be provided with injury prevention education in emergency departments. However, many parents do not receive or do not act on injury prevention education, such as education regarding restricting access to lethal means of suicide (e.g., disposing or locking up of medications or guns) or monitoring/supervising the youth (Brent, Baugher, Birmaher, Kolko, & Bridge, 2000; McManus et al., 1997).

CHILD AND ADOLESCENT DEVELOPMENT

Suicide is extremely rare before puberty (AACAP, 2001). As noted earlier, epidemiologically, suicide prior to 12 to 13 years of age is extraordinary infrequent. There are many potential theories as to why children do not suicide, including lack of cognitive ability or formal operational thinking, low rates of substance use, lack of opportunity due to near constant parent/teacher/adult supervision, children's developmentally-based reliance on parent/family support during stressful times or events, and fewer tumultuous social difficulties with peers.

Adolescence is a period of rapid developmental change that may exert increasing risk of suicide on youths as they transition from childhood. In addition, adolescents experience significant social, emotional, and cognitive transitions (Everall, Bostik, & Paulson, 2005). Research indicates that there are three major developmental processes that may influence adolescent suicidality, specifically: (1) cognitive development, (2) **identity formation**, and (3) the search for autonomy (Everall et al., 2005).

Cognitive development in adolescence is characterized by increased hypothetical and abstract reasoning abilities, viewing themselves as unique and different from others and becoming more introspective and vulnerable to feelings of hopelessness, while having "limited decision making skills, poor problem-solving abilities, and irrational decision making when overcome by stress, intense affect, or inescapable conflict" (Everall et al., 2005, p. 696).

Adolescence is a period of identity formation. According to Arnett (1999), during the process of developing their personal identities, adolescents will experience a range of difficulties, concerns, stresses, problems, and anxieties as they explore their individual thoughts, feelings, abilities, skills, and values (Arnett, 1999). Research has indicated that difficulties in developing an identity can result in maladaptive coping and ultimately become a suicide risk factor (Everall et al., 2005; Stillion & McDowell, 1991).

During adolescence, youth seek a balance between striving for autonomy and a renegotiated attachment with their parents (Allen, Aber, & Leadbeater, 1990; Allen & Land, 1999). This is a critical stage-salient task (Allen, Hauser, Bell, & O'Connor, 1994). Fundamental to successful youth development of this balance between autonomy and relatedness are skills to manage conflict, learning new coping and problem-solving strategies, and parents' abilities to provide security and negotiate their adolescent's increasing independence. Inadequate negotiation of autonomy and attachment systems may limit an adolescent's social and psychological well-being, resulting in increased suicide risk (Kaplan & Worth, 1993).

FAMILY SYSTEM

Current literature focusing on the **familial transmission** of suicide largely examines suicide attempters with a family history of suicide compared to nonattempters with a family history of suicide (Birmaher et al., 1996; Egeland & Sussex, 1985; Gould et al., 1996; Johnson, Brent, Bridge, & Connolly, 1998; Malone, Haas, Sweeny, & Mann, 1995; Powell, Geddes, Deeks, Goldacre, & Hawton, 2000; Roy, 2002a, 2002b, 2003; Runeson & Asberg, 2003; Sorenson & Rutter, 1991; Tsai, Kuo, Chen, & Lee, 2002; Tsuang, 1983). Additionally, several high-risk studies have been conducted examining offspring of parents with and without a family history of suicide attempt (Brent et al., 2002, 2003; Fergusson, Beautrais, & Harwood, 2003).

Overall, this research has clearly established an association between family history of suicidal behavior and increased suicide attempt risk in study participants (Birmaher et al., 1996; Cheng, Chen, Chen, & Jenkins, 2000; Fu et al., 2002; Glowinski et al., 2001; Gould et al., 1996; Hawton, Haw, Houston, & Townsend, 2002; Mann et al., 2005; Roy, 1993; Roy, Rylander, & Sarchiapone, 1997; Roy et al., 1995; Sorenson & Rutter, 1991). For example, Brent et al. (2002) found that the risk of suicide attempt was six times greater among offspring of depressed suicide attempters as compared to offspring of depressed non–suicide attempters. Others have found that as many as 24% of suicide attempters report a history of completed suicide among first- and second-degree relatives (Brodie & Leff, 1971; Linkowski et al., 1985; Mann et al., 2005; Pitts & Winokur, 1964; Roy, 1983, 1985).

No one mechanism has been determined that fully accounts for the familial transmission of suicide risk. Rather, several mechanisms have been posited to explain the increased risk of suicidality among family members. The two areas that have gained the most support are: (1) parental psychiatric illness as a moderator of suicide risk in offspring, and (2) **social learning models** of suicide.

Parental Psychiatric Illness

Several studies indicate that parental psychiatric illness confers the risk of suicidal behavior in offspring, including completed suicide, attempted suicide, and suicidal ideation (Brent et al., 2002, 2004; Brent & Mann, 2005; Egeland & Sussex, 1985; Fergusson et al., 2000; Garfinkel et al., 1982; Linkowski et al., 1985; Roy et al., 1991, 1995; Runeson, 1998; Sorenson & Rutter, 1991; Tsuang, 1983). It has clearly been established that parental psychiatric illness leads to an increased risk of psychiatric illness in offspring (Beardslee, Versage, & Gladstone, 1998; Del Bello & Geller, 2001; Downey & Coyne, 1990; Nomura, Warner, & Wickramaratne, 2001; Rutter & Quinton, 1984; Rutter, Silberg, O'Connor, & Simonoff, 1999). Furthermore, psychiatric illness is among the greatest risk factors for suicidality (Antikainen, Hintikka, Lehtonen, Koponen, & Arstila, 1995; Kaplan & Harrow, 1996; Mehlum, Friis, Vaglum, & Karterud, 1994; Sabo, Gunderson, Najavits, Chauncey, & Kisiel, 1995; Schneider, Philipp, & Muller, 2001; Scocco, Marietta, Tonietto, & Buono, 2000; Statham et al., 1998). Thus, offspring suicide risk may be moderated through the presence of psychiatric illness transmitted from parents to their offspring. Parental mood disorder (specifically depression and bipolar disorder), panic disorder, schizophrenia, and alcohol abuse are most often associated with increased risk for offspring suicide (Mann et al., 2005; Sorenson & Rutter, 1991).

Research in this area, however, is inconclusive. While familial transmission of suicide may be partly accounted for by the transmission of psychiatric illness, several studies have also demonstrated that even after controlling for psychopathology, vulnerability toward suicidal behavior continues to appear to run in families (Agerbo, Nordentoft, & Mortenson, 2002; Brent, Bridge, Johnson, & Connolly, 1996; Bridge, Brent, Johnson, & Connolly, 1997; Cheng et al., 2000; Fu et al., 2002; Garfinkel et al., 1982; Glowinski et al., 2001; Gould et al., 1996; Johnson et al., 1998; Linkowski et al., 1985; Malone et al., 1995; Powell et al., 2000; Runeson & Asberg, 2003; Statham et al., 1998; Tsuang, 1983). Some researchers have associated the familial transmission of risk with a genetic inheritance or predisposition to suicidality, for example, twin studies have found a higher rate of suicide monozygotic compared to dizygotic twins (Roy et al., 1991, 1997). Further research is needed to understand the role of parental psychiatric illness and the impact it has on offspring suicide risk.

Social Learning Model of Familial Suicide Risk

Another explanation for the high rate of suicidality among offspring of individuals who attempt and/or complete suicide is that parents model such behavior for their offspring (Lester, 1987; Runeson, 1998; Stack & Kposowa, 2008). According to social learning theory, when parents complete or attempt suicide, a message is sent to their offspring regarding acceptability of such behavior as a means for coping with distress.

The social learning model of suicide extends beyond the micro level of family transmission and also has been applied to the societal level (Stack & Kposowa, 2008). It is suggested that the degree to which a community or society has positive attitudes toward suicide can have an impact on the overall societal suicide rate. Communities in which there is a strong positive attitude toward suicide may represent a "subculture of suicide" and may have elevated rates of suicide (Cutright & Fernquist, 2004; Stack & Kposowa, 2008). This has severe consequences. It has been suggested that being exposed to elevated suicide rates increases the likelihood that individuals will develop more accepting attitudes toward suicidal behavior (Baller, Shin, & Richardson, 2005). Agnew (1998) further suggests when a community or society has a positive attitude toward suicide individuals may not feel compelled to deter others from engaging in suicidal behaviors. Furthermore, according to social learning theory, individuals who complete suicide in such communities serve as models for how to cope with problems (Stack & Kposowa, 2008), thereby potentially increasing suicide risk even further. Adolescents may have a lower attraction to life and a lower repulsion of death, which may make suicide a more acceptable option during times of heightened distress (Orbach, 1997).

Conversely, in communities with low suicide rates, individuals are more likely to have negative attitudes toward suicide. Given that fewer individuals are engaging in suicidal acts in these communities, there are fewer individuals modeling suicidal behavior as an acceptable option for dealing with stress. Individuals who do not engage in suicidal behavior serve as role models for alternative coping mechanisms and further support the message of suicide as an unacceptable act (Stack & Kposowa, 2008). On a micro level, parents who cope with distress by seeking support from friends and family or by seeking psychosocial treatment serve as role models for positive coping mechanisms and model the unacceptability of suicide for their children. Although limited, the research that exists supports a social learning model of suicide (Agnew, 1998; Baller et al., 2005; Stack, 2002; Stack & Kposowa, 2008).

INTERVENTIONS WITH CHILDREN AND ADOLESCENTS

There are three general but essential intervention approaches for children and adolescents at risk of suicide, specifically crisis management, psychosocial evidence-based practice (EBP) interventions, and psychopharmacology.

A child or adolescent who has attempted suicide or is at risk of suicide and in need of crisis management should be brought to a hospital emergency department for a complete assessment. According to AACAP (2001) practice guidelines, crisis staff and emergency room health professionals should attempt to establish a relationship and convey the importance of treatment to the youth and their family. If the youth remains at risk and either continues to express a desire to die or has an evident abnormal mental state, inpatient admission may be warranted.

Whether the youth is discharged home, is not admitted, or is a suicidal risk but does not require a hospital assessment, research has found several EBPs to be effective in working with suicidal children and adolescents. The specific EBP treatment should meet the needs of the youth and the family. Evidence-based practices found to be effective in working with children and adolescents at risk of suicide are **cognitive-behavioral therapy** (CBT), **dialectical behavior therapy (DBT)**, **interpersonal psychotherapy for adolescents (IPT-A)**, psychodynamic therapy, and family therapy (AACAP, 2001). For further information on these EBP interventions see Part II of this text.

Finally, psychopharmacology interventions may occur independently or in conjunction with psychotherapeutic EBP treatments. Depending on the psychiatric presentation, symptoms, or disorder, several psychopharmacology treatments have been found to be effective with youth at risk of suicide, including, but not limited to, antidepressants to target symptoms of depression, mood stabilizers to target symptoms of mania, and antipsychotics to target symptoms of psychosis.

SUMMARY

Completed suicide by children and adolescents is rare; however, attempts and ideation are more common. Across the life span, suicide risk increases with age. Developmentally, adolescents may be exposed to an increased risk of suicide. In youth, females are more likely to attempt, while males are more likely to complete suicide. Families can serve as a protective or risk factor for suicidality among children and adolescents. Identification and thorough assessment of risk and protective factors for suicide among youth is critical for suicide prevention and effective intervention.

■ Key Points

1. The suicide risk of prepubertal children is very rare, but the risk grows with each year of adolescence.
2. Female youth report higher suicide ideation and have more attempted suicide than males; however, adolescent males completed suicide 4 to 6 times more than females.
3. Although suicide in young children is rare, it does occur.
4. Suicide in children is often related to a stressful home environment.
5. Adolescent suicide is often associated with mood disorders, substance abuse, and gender identity issues.
6. Offspring of parents who have a history of suicidal behavior are at increased risk for completed suicide, suicide attempt, and suicidal ideation.
7. Family transmission of suicide can be explained by genetic factors as well as social learning models.
8. It is important to separate fact from fiction because there are a number of myths and misconceptions that surround children and adolescents at risk of suicide.
9. Three important developmental processes that may influence adolescent suicidality are cognitive development, identity formation, and autonomy.
10. The three intervention approaches in working with children and adolescents at risk of suicide are crisis management, psychosocial evidence-based practice (EBP) interventions, and psychopharmacology.

FURTHER READINGS

Adams, G. R., & Berzonsky, M. D. (2006). *Blackwell handbook of adolescence.* Malden, MA: Blackwell Publishing.

American Academy of Child and Adolescent Psychiatry [AACAP]. (2001). Practice parameter for the assessment and treatment of children and adolescents with suicidal behavior. *Journal of the American Academy of Child & Adolescent Psychiatry, 40*(7), 24S–51S.

Byrne, M., Agerbo, E., & Mortensen, P. B. (2002). Family history of psychiatric disorders and age at first contact in schizophrenia: An epidemiological study. *British Journal of Psychiatry—Supplementum, 43,* s19–s25.

Cerel, J., Jordan, J. R., & Duberstein, P. R. (2008). The impact of suicide on the family. *Crisis: The Journal of Crisis Intervention & Suicide Prevention, 29*(1), 38–44.

Eisenberg, N. (2006). *Handbook of child psychology: Social, emotional, and personality development* (Vol. 3, 6th ed.). Hoboken, NJ: John Wiley & Sons, Inc.

Egeland, J. A., & Sussex, J. N. (1985). Suicide and family loading for affective disorders. *Journal of the American Medical Association, 254,* 915–918.

Evens, D. L., Foa, E. B., Gur, R. E., Hendin, H., O'Brien, C. P., Seligman, M.E.P., et al. (2005). *Treating and preventing adolescent mental health disorders.* Oxford: Oxford University Press.

Gould, M. S., Greenberg, T., Velting, D., & Shafer, D. (2003). Youth suicide risk and preventive interventions: A review of the past 10 years. *Journal of the American Academy of Child and Adolescent Psychiatry, 42,* 386–405.

Jeglic, E. L., Sharp, I. R., Chapman, J. E., Brown, G. K., & Beck, A. T. (2005). History of family suicide behaviors and negative problem solving in multiple suicide attempters. *Archives of Suicide Research, 9*(2), 135–146.

Koplin, B., & Agathen, J. (2002). Suicidality in children and adolescents: A review. *Current Opinion in Pediatrics, 14*(6), 713–717.

Lohan, J. A. (2002). Family functioning and family typology after an adolescent or young adult's sudden violent death. *Journal of Family Nursing, 8,* 49.

Roche, A. M., Giner, L., & Zalsman, G. (2005). Suicide in early childhood: A brief review. *International Journal of Adolescent Medicine & Health, 17*(3), 221–224.

Roy, A. (2006). Family history of suicide and impulsivity. *Archives of Suicide Research, 10*(4), 347–352.

Roy, A., & Janal, M. (2005). Family history of suicide, female sex, and childhood trauma: Separate or interacting risk factors for attempts at suicide? *Acta Psychiatrica Scandinavica, 112*(5), 367–371.

Sameroff, A., Lewis, M., & Miller, S. M. (2000). *Handbook of developmental psychology* (2nd ed.). New York: Kluwer Academic/Plenum Press.

Scheftner, W. A., Young, M. A., Endicott, J., Coryell, W., Fogg, L., Clark, D. C., et al. (1988). Family history and five-year suicide risk. *British Journal of Psychiatry, 153,* 805–809.

ELECTRONIC RESOURCES

General

About Pediatrics: http://pediatrics.about.com/od/suicide/Suicide_in_Children_and_Teens.htm

American Academy of Child and Adolescent Psychiatry: http://www.aacap.org/cs/root/facts_for_families/teen_suicide

Healthy Minds: http://www.healthyminds.org/multimedia/teensuicide.pdf

Healthy Place: http://www.healthyplace.com/communities/depression/children_9.asp

Mental Health Matters: http://www.mental-health-matters.com/articles/article.php?artID=122

National Alliance on Mentally Illness: http://www.nami.org/Content/ContentGroups/Helpline1/Teenage_Suicide.htm

Surgeon General: http://www.surgeongeneral.gov/library/mentalhealth/chapter3/sec5.html

Teen Suicide: http://www.teensuicide.us

Support for Parents

Bereaved Parents: http://www.bereavedparentsusa.org
Greif Net: http://www.griefnet.org
Kids Aid: http://www.kidsaid.com
Suicide and Mental Health Association International: http://www.suicideandmental
    healthassociationinternational.org/osg.html
Support Line: http://www.supportline.org.uk
Yellow Ribbon: http://www.yellowribbon.org/Msg-to-Parents.htm

Support Groups and Other Resources for Children and Adolescents

The Dougy Center: http://www.dougy.org
Kids Aid: http://www.kidsaid.com/k2k_support.html
Kids Help: http://www.kidshelp.sympatico.ca
Suicide Awareness Voices of Education: http://www.save.org
Support Line: http://www.supportline.org.uk
Yellow Ribbon: http://www.yellowribbon.org
Youth violence and suicide prevention: http://www.cdc.gov/ncipc/dvp/bestpractices.htm

■ Knowledge Acquisition Test

True or False

1. Children do not commit suicide.
2. There are no warning signs that children and adolescents may be considering suicide.
3. Suicide risk is familial.
4. Parental modeling of suicide is not a possible cause of offspring suicide.
5. Substance abuse is a risk factor for adolescent suicide.
6. Females attempt suicide more than males.
7. Males tend to use more lethal methods of suicide than females.
8. Children under 10 years of age have a higher suicide rate than children over
   10 years of age.
9. Younger males (10 to 14 years) complete suicide more than older males
   (14–19 years).

Short Answer

10. What are the main mechanisms presumed to explain family transmission of
    suicide?
11. Explain the social learning theory of family transmission of suicide.
12. What are the main risk factors against suicide among adolescents?
13. What are some key theories that may explain why suicide completion is
    higher in males than females?
14. Why are younger prepubertal children less likely to complete suicide than
    older adolescents?
15. Describe the key developmental issues that may increase the risk of sui-
    cidality in adolescents.

Multiple Choice

16. What age group is at the highest risk of suicide?
    A. 0 to 9 years of age
    B. 10 to 14 years of age
    C. 15 to 19 years of age
    D. All of the above are at equal risk
    E. None of the above

17. What item is untrue in the following list of myths or misconceptions related to suicidality and youth?
    A. Current prevention programs work
    B. Suicide is caused by family and social stress
    C. Most suicides occur at home
    D. All of the above
    E. None of the above

18. Which of the following is a protective factor against adolescent suicide?
    A. Family cohesion
    B. Musical ability
    C. Employment
    D. None of the above
    E. All of the above

19. Which of the following parental psychiatric illnesses is associated with an increased risk of suicidality in offspring?
    A. Depression
    B. Bipolar disorder
    C. Panic disorder
    D. Schizophrenia
    E. None of the above
    F. All of the above

20. Which of the following is NOT a risk factor for child suicide?
    A. Parental divorce
    B. Depression
    C. Parental psychiatric illness
    D. Unsafe school environment
    E. None of the above
    F. All of the above

Answer key is available in the Instructor's Manual; qualified instructors may e-mail textbook@springerpub.com *to request a copy.*

REFERENCES

American Academy of Child and Adolescent Psychiatry [AACAP]. (2001). Practice parameter for the assessment and treatment of children and adolescents with suicidal behavior. *Journal of the American Academy of Child & Adolescent Psychiatry, 40*(7), 24S–51S.

Adam, K. S., Bouckoms, A., & Streiner, D. (1982). Parental loss and family stability in attempted suicide. *Archives of General Psychiatry, 39,* 1081–1085.

Adams, D. M., Overholser, J. C., & Lehnert, K. L. (1994). Perceived family functioning and adolescent suicidal behavior. *Journal of the American Academy of Child and Adolescent Psychiatry, 33*(4), 498–507.

Agerbo, E., Nordentoft, M., & Mortenson, P. B. (2002). Familial, psychiatric, and socio-economic risk factors for suicide in young people: Nested case-control study. *British Medical Journal, 325,* 74.

Agnew, R. (1998). The approval of suicide: A social psychological model. *Suicide & Life-Threatening Behavior, 28*(2), 205–225.

Allen, J. P., Aber, J. L., & Leadbeater, B. J. (1990). Adolescent problem behaviors: The influence of attachment and autonomy. *Psychiatric Clinics of North America, 13*(3), 455–467.

Allen, J. P., Hauser, S. T., Bell, K. B., & O'Connor, T. G. (1994). Longitudinal assessment of autonomy and relatedness in adolescent–family interactions as predictors of adolescent ego development and self-esteem. *Child Development, 65,* 179–194.

Allen, J. P., & Land, D. (1999). Attachment in adolescent. In J. Cassidy & P. R. Shaver (Eds.), *Handbook of attachment: Theory, research, and clinical applications* (pp. 319–335). New York: Guilford Press.

Anderson, R. N., & Smith, B. L. (2003). Deaths: Leading causes for 2001. *National Vital Statistics Report, 52*(9), 1–86.

Andrews, J. A., & Lewinsohn, P. M. (1992). Suicidal attempts among older adolescents: Prevalence and co-occurrence with psychiatric disorders. *Journal of the American Academy of Child and Adolescent Psychiatry, 31,* 655–662.

Antikainen, R., Hintikka, J., Lehtonen, J., Koponen, H., & Arstila, A. (1995). A prospective three-year follow-up study of borderline personality disorder inpatients. *Acta Psychiatrica Scandinavica, 92,* 327–335.

Armstrong, L. L., & Manion, I. G. (2006). Suicidal ideation in young males living in rural communities: Distance from school as a risk factor, youth engagement as a protective factor. *Vulnerable Children and Youth Studies, 1*(1), 102–113.

Arnett, J. J. (1999). Adolescent storm and stress, reconsidered. *American Psychologist, 54,* 317–326.

Asarnow, J. R., Carlson, G., & Mintz, J. (1988). Suicide attempts in preadolescent child psychiatry inpatients. *Suicide & Life-Threatening Behavior, 18,* 129–136.

Bagley, C., & Tremblay, P. (2000). Elevated rates of suicidal behavior in gay, lesbian, and bisexual youth. *Crisis: The Journal of Crisis Intervention & Suicide Prevention, 21,* 111–117.

Baller, R. D., Shin, D. J., & Richardson, K. (2005). An extension and test of Sutherland's concept of differential social organization: The geographic clustering of Japanese suicide and homicide rates. *Suicide & Life-Threatening Behavior, 35*(3), 343–355.

Beardslee, W. R., Versage, E. M., & Gladstone, T. (1998). Children of affectively ill parents: a review of the past ten years. *Journal of the American Academy of Child and Adolescent Psychiatry, 37,* 1134–1141.

Beautrais, A. L., Joyce, P. R., & Mulder, R. T. (1998a). Psychiatric illness in a New Zealand sample of young people making serious suicide attempts. *New Zealand Medical Journal, 111,* 44–48.

Beautrais, A. L., Joyce, P. R., & Mulder, R. T. (1998b). Youth suicide attempts: A social and demographic profile. *Australian and New Zealand Journal of Psychiatry, 32,* 349–357.

Beautrais, A., Joyce, P., Mulder, R., Fergusson, D., Deavoll, B., & Nightingale, S. (1996). Prevalence and comorbidity of mental disorders in persons making serious suicide attempts: A case-control study. *American Journal of Psychiatry, 153,* 1009–1014.

Birmaher, B., Ryan, N. D., Williamson, D. E., Brent, D. A., Kaufman, J., Dahl, R. E., et al. (1996). Childhood and adolescent depression: a review of the past 10 years. Part I. *Journal of the American Academy of Child & Adolescent Psychiatry, 35,* 1427–1439.

Borowsky, I. W., Ireland, M., & Resnick, M. D. (2001). Adolescent suicide attempts: Risks and protectors. *Pediatrics, 107,* 485–493.

Brent, D., & Mann, J. (2005). Family genetic studies, suicide, and suicidal behavior. *American Journal of Medical Genetics Part C: Seminars in Medical Genetics, 133*(1), 13–24.

Brent, D. A., Baugher, M., Birmaher, B., Kolko, D. J., & Bridge, J. (2000). Compliance with recommendations to remove firearms in families participating in a clinical trial for adolescent depression. *Journal of the American Academy of Child & Adolescent Psychiatry, 39*(10), 1220–1226.

Brent, D., Bridge, J., Johnson, B. A., & Connolly, J. (1996). Suicidal behavior runs in families: A controlled family study of adolescent suicide victims. *Archives of General Psychiatry, 53*(12), 1145–1152.

Brent, D. A., Oquendo, M., Birmaher, B., Greenhill, L., Kolko, D., Stanley, B., et al. (2002). Familial pathways to early-onset suicide attempt: Risk for suicidal behavior in offspring of mood-disordered suicide attempters. *Archives of General Psychiatry, 59,* 801–807.

Brent, D., Oquendo, M., Birmaher, B., Greenhill, L., Kolko, D., Stanley, B., et al. (2003). Peripubertal suicide attempts in offspring of suicide attempters with siblings concordant for suicidal behavior. *American Journal of Psychiatry, 160*(8), 1486–1493.

Brent, D., Oquendo, M., Birmaher, B., Greenhill, L., Kolko, D., Stanley, B., et al. (2004). Familial transmission of mood disorders: Convergence and divergence with transmission of suicidal behavior. *Journal of the American Academy of Child & Adolescent Psychiatry 43*(10), 1259–1266.

Brent, D., Perper, J., Goldstein, C., Kolko, D., Allan, M., Allman, C., et al. (1988). Risk factors for adolescent suicide: A comparison of adolescent suicide victims with suicidal inpatients. *Archives of General Psychiatry, 45,* 581–588.

Brent, D. A., Perper, J. A., & Moritz, G. (1993). Psychiatric sequelae to the loss of an adolescent peer to suicide. *Journal of the American Academy of Child & Adolescent Psychiatry, 32,* 509–517.

Bridge, J. A., Brent, D. A., Johnson, B. A., & Connolly, J. (1997). Familial aggregation of psychiatric disorders in a community sample of adolescents. *Journal of the American Academy of Child & Adolescent Psychiatry, 36,* 628–636.

Brodie, H. K., & Leff, M. J. (1971). Bipolar depression—A comparative study of patient characteristics. *American Journal of Psychiatry, 127,* 1086–1090.

Brodsky, B., & Stanley, B. H. (2008). Adverse childhood experiences and suicidal behavior. *Psychiatric Clinics of North America, 31*(2), 223–235.

Bucca, M., Ceppi, M., Pelosa, P., Archellaschi, M., Mussi, D., & Fele, P. (1994). Social variables and suicide in the population of Genoa, Italy. *Comprehensive Psychiatry, 35,* 64–69.

Canetto, S. S., & Sakinofsky, I. (1998). The gender paradox in suicide. *Suicide & Life-Threatening Behavior, 28*(1), 1–23.

Centers for Disease Control and Prevention [CDC]. (2006). National Center for Injury Prevention and Control. Retrieved June 13, 2008, from http://www.cdc.gov/ncipc/wisqars

Chapple, A., Ziebland, S., & McPherson, A. (2004). Qualitative study of men's perceptions of why treatment delays occur in the UK for those with testicular cancer. *British Journal of General Practice, 54*, 25–32.

Cheng, A., Chen, T., Chen, C., & Jenkins, R. (2000). Psychosocial and psychiatric risk factors for suicide: Case-control psychological autopsy study. *British Journal of Psychiatry, 177*, 360–365.

Chioqueta, A. P., & Stiles, T. C. (2007). The relationship between psychological buffers, hopelessness, and suicidal ideation: Identification of protective factors. *Crisis, 28*(2), 67–73.

Corney, R. (1990). Sex differences in general practice attendance and help seeking for minor illness. *Journal of Psychosomatic Research, 34*(5), 525–534.

Cutright, P., & Fernquist, R. (2004). The culture of suicide through societal integration and regulation: 1996–1998: Gender-specific suicide rates in 50 American states. *Archives of Suicide Research, 8*, 271–285.

Davies, J., McCrae, B. P., Frank, J., Dochnahl, A., Pickering, T., Harrison, B., et al. (2000). Identifying male college students' perceived health needs, barriers to seeking help, and recommendations to help men adopt healthier lifestyles. *Journal of American College Health, 48*, 259–267.

de Jong, M. L. (1992). Attachment, individuation and risk of suicide in late adolescence. *Journal of Youth and Adolescence, 21*, 357–373.

Del Bello, M. P., & Geller, B. (2001). Review of studies of child & adolescent offspring of bipolar parents. *Bipolar Disorders, 3*, 325–334.

de Wilde, E. J., Kienhorst, I., Diekstra, R., & Wolters, W. (1992). The relationship between adolescent suicidal behavior and life events in childhood and adolescence. *American Journal of Psychiatry, 149*, 45–51.

Downey, G., & Coyne, J. C. (1990). Children of depressed parents an integrative review. *Psychological Bulletin, 108*, 50–76.

Dubow, E. F., Kausch, D. F., Blum, M. C., Reed, J., & Bush, E. (1989). Correlates of suicidal ideation and attempts in a community sample of junior high and high school students. *Journal of Clinical Child Psychology, 18*, 158–166.

Egeland, J. A., & Sussex, J. N. (1985). Suicide and family loading for affective disorders. *Journal of the American Medical Association, 254*, 915–918.

Eisenberg, M. E., Ackard, D. M., & Resnick, M. D. (2007). Protective factors and suicide risk in adolescents with a history of sexual abuse. *Journal of Pediatrics, 151*(5), 482–487.

Eisenberg, M. E., & Resnick, M. D. (2006). Suicidality among gay, lesbian and bisexual youth: The role of protective factors. *Journal of Adolescent Health, 39*(5), 662–668.

Evans, E., Hawton, K., Rodham, K., & Deeks, J. (2005). The prevalence of suicidal phenomena in adolescents: A systematic review of population-based studies. *Suicide & Life-Threatening Behavior, 35*(3), 239–250.

Everall, R. D., Bostik, K. E., & Paulson, B. L. (2005). I'm sick of being me: Developmental themes in a suicidal adolescent. *Adolescence, 40*(160), 693–708.

Fergusson, D. M., & Lynskey, M. T. (1995a). Childhood circumstances, adolescent adjustment, and suicide attempts in a New Zealand birth cohort. *Journal of the American Academy of Child and Adolescent Psychiatry, 34,* 612–622.

Fergusson, D. M., & Lynskey, M. T. (1995b). Suicide among female adolescents: Characteristics and comparison with males in the age group 13 to 22 years. *Journal of the American Academy of Child & Adolescent Psychiatry, 34*(10), 1297–1307.

Fergusson, D. M., Beautrais, A. L., & Harwood, L. J. (2003). Vulnerability and resiliency to suicidal behaviours in young people. *Psychological Medicine, 33,* 61–73.

Fergusson, D. M., Woodward, L. J., & Harwood, L. J. (2000). Risk factors and life processes associated with the onset of suicidal behaviour during adolescence and early adulthood. *Psychological Medicine, 30,* 23–39.

Fombonne, E. (1998). Suicidal behaviours in vulnerable adolescents. Time trends and their correlates. *British Journal of Psychiatry, 173,* 154–159.

Fu, Q., Heath, A. C., Bucholz, K. K., Nelson, E. C., Glowinski, A. L., Goldberg, J. F., et al. (2002). A twin stud of genetic and environmental influences on suicidality in men. *Psychological Medicine, 32,* 11–24.

Galdas, P., Cheater, F., & Marshall, P. (2005). Men and health help-seeking behaviour: Literature review. *Journal of Advanced Nursing, 49*(6), 616–623.

Garfinkel, B. D., Froese, A., & Hood, J. (1982). Suicide attempts in children and adolescents. *American Journal of Psychiatry, 139,* 1257–1261.

Garrison, C. Z., Jackson, K. L., Addy, C. L., McKeown, R. E., & Waller, J. L. (1991). Suicidal behaviors in young adolescents. *American Journal of Epidemiology, 133*(10), 1005–1014.

Gascoigne, P., & Whitear, B. (1999). Making sense of testicular cancer symptoms: A qualitative study of the way in which men sought help from the health care services. *European Journal of Oncology Nursing, 3*(2), 62–69.

Glowinski, A., Bucholz, K. K., Nelson, E. C., Fu, Q., Madden, P., Reich, W., et al. (2001). Suicide attempt in an adolescent female twin sample. *Journal of the American Academy of Child & Adolescent Psychiatry, 40,* 1300–1307.

Good, G., & Sherrod, N. (2001). *Men's problems and effective treatments: Theory and empirical support* (Vols. 1 & 2). San Francisco: Jossey-Bass.

Good, G. E., Dell, D. M., & Mintz, L. B. (1989). Male role and gender role conflict: Relations to help seeking in men. *Journal of Counseling Psychology, 36,* 295–300.

Good, G. E., & Mintz, L. B. (1990). Gender role conflict and depression in college men: Evidence for compounded risk. *Journal of Counseling and Development, 69,* 17–21.

Gould, M. S., Fisher, P., Parides, M., Flory, M., & Shaffer, D. (1996). Psychosocial risk factors of child and adolescent completed suicides. *Archives of General Psychiatry, 53,* 1155–1162.

Gould, M. S., & Kramer, R. A. (2001). Youth suicide prevention. *Suicide & Life-Threatening Behavior, 31*(Suppl), 6–31.

Hall-Lande, J. A., Eisenberg, M. E., Christenson, S. L., & Neumark-Sztainer, D. (2007). Social isolation, psychological health, and protective factors in adolescence. *Adolescence, 42*(166), 265–286.

Harrington, R., Bredenkamp, D., Groothues, C., Rutter, M., Fudge, H., & Pickles, A. (1994). Adult outcomes of childhood and adolescent depression. III links with suicidal behaviours. *Journal of Child Psychology and Psychiatry, 35*(7), 1309–1319.

Hawton, K., Haw, C., Houston, K., & Townsend, E. (2002). Family history of suicidal behavior: Prevalence and significance in deliberate self-harm patients. *Acta Psychiatrica Scandinavica, 106,* 387–393.

Hawton, K., O'Grady, J., Osborn, M., & Cole, D. (1982). Adolescents who take overdoses: Their characteristics, problems and contacts with helping agencies. *British Journal of Psychiatry, 140,* 118–123.

Hollis, C. (1996). Depression, family environment, and adolescent suicidal behavior. *Journal of the American Academy of Child & Adolescent Psychiatry, 35,* 622–630.

Joffe, R. T., Offord, D. R., & Boyle, M. H. (1988). Ontario Child Health Study: Suicidal behaviour in youth age 12–16 years. *American Journal of Psychiatry, 145,* 1420–1423.

Johnson, B. A., Brent, D. A., Bridge, J., & Connolly, J. (1998). The familial aggregation of adolescent suicide attempts. *Acta Psychiatrica Scandinavica, 97,* 18–24.

Kaplan, K. J., & Harrow, M. (1996). Positive and negative symptoms as risk factors for later suicidal activity in schizophrenics versus depressives. *Suicide & Life-Threatening Behavior, 26*(2), 105–120.

Kaplan, K. J., & Worth, S. A. (1993). Individuation-attachment and suicide trajectory: A developmental guide for the clinician. *Omega, 27,* 207–237.

Kosky, R. (1983). Childhood suicidal behavior. *Journal of Child Psychology and Psychiatry, 24,* 457–468.

Kosky, R., Silburn, S., & Zubrick, S. R. (1990). Are children and adolescents who have suicidal thoughts different from those who attempt suicide? *Journal of Nervous and Mental Disease, 178,* 38–43.

Kovacs, M., Goldston, D., & Catsonis, C. (1993). Suicidal behaviors and child and adolescent depressive disorders: A longitudinal investigation. *Journal of the American Academy of Child and Adolescent Psychiatry, 32,* 8–20.

Lesage, A. D., Boyer, R., Grunberg, F., Vanier, C., Morisette, R., Menard-Buteau, C., et al. (1994). Suicide and mental disorders: A case-control study of young men. *American Journal of Psychiatry, 151,* 1063–1068.

Lester, D. (1987). *Suicide as a learned behavior.* Springfield, MA: Charles C. Thomas.

Linkowski, P., de Maertelaer, V., & Mendlewicz, J. (1985). Suicidal behaviour in major depressive illness. *Acta Psychiatrica Scandinavica, 72*(3), 233–238.

Malone, K. M., Haas, G. L., Sweeny, J. A., & Mann, J. J. (1995). Major depression and the risk of attempted suicide. *Journal of Affective Disorders, 34,* 173–185.

Mann, J. J., Bortinger, J., Oquendo, M. A., Currier, D., Li, S., & Brent, D. A. (2005). Family history of suicidal behavior and mood disorders in probands with mood disorders. *American Journal of Psychiatry, 162*(9), 1672–1679.

Maris, R. W., Berman, A. L., & Silverman, M. M. (2000). *Comprehensive textbook of suicidology.* New York: Guilford Press.

Martin, J. A., Kochanek, K. D., Strobino, D. M., Guyer, B., & MacDorman, M. F. (2005). Annual summary of vital statistics—2003. *Pediatrics, 115*(3), 619–634.

McManus, B. L., Kruesi, M. J., Dontes, A. E., Defazio, C. R., Piotrowski, J. T., & Woodward, P. J. (1997). Child and adolescent suicide attempts: An opportunity for emergency departments to provide injury prevention education. *The American Journal of Emergency Medicine, 15*(4), 357–360.

Mehlum, L., Friis, S., Vaglum, P., & Karterud, S. (1994). The longitudinal pattern of suicidal behaviour in borderline personality disorder: A prospective follow-up study. *Acta Psychiatrica Scandinavica, 90*(2), 124–130.

Möller-Leimkühler, A. M. (2002). Barriers to help seeking by men: a review of sociocultural and clinical literature with particular reference to depression. *Journal of Affective Disorders, 71*, 1–9.

Moscicki, E. K. (1994). Gender differences in completed and attempted suicides. *Annals of Epidemiology, 4*, 152–158.

Moscicki, E. K. (1995). Epidemiology of suicidal behavior. *Suicide & Life-Threatening Behavior, 25*(1), 22–35.

Moscicki, E. K. (2001). Epidemiology of completed and attempted suicide: Toward a framework for prevention. *Clinical Neuroscience Research, 1*, 310–323.

Moskos, M. A., Achilles, J., & Gray, D. (2004). Adolescent suicide myths in the United States. *Crisis, 25*(4), 176–182.

National Center for Health Statistics. (2000). *Death rates for 72 selected causes, by 5-year age groups, race, and sex: United States, 1979–1997*. Atlanta, GA: Centers for Disease Control and Prevention.

NHS Executive. (1998). *National survey of NHS patients, general practice*. London: TSO.

Nomura, Y., Warner, U., & Wickramaratne, P. (2001). Parents concordant for major depressive disorder and the effect of psychopathology in offspring. *Psychological Medicine, 31*, 1211–1222.

Orbach, I. (1997). A taxonomy of factors related to suicidal behavior. *Clinical Psychology: Science and Practice, 4*, 208–224.

Patton, G. C., Harris, R., Carlin, J. B., Hibbert, M. E., Coffey, C., Scwartz, M., et al. (1997). Adolescent suicidal behaviours: A population-based study of risk. *Psychological Medicine, 27*, 715–724.

Pelkonen, M., Marttunen, M., Pulkkinen, E., Laippala, P., & Aro, H. (1997). Characteristics of out-patient adolescents with suicidal tendencies. *Acta Psychiatrica Scandinavica, 95*, 100–107.

Peters, K. D., Kochanek, K. D., & Murphy, S. L. (1998). Deaths: Final data for 1996. *National Vital Statistics Reports, 49*(9).

Pfeffer, C. R. (1991). Suicide in Japan. *Journal of the American Academy of Child & Adolescent Psychiatry, 30*(5), 847–848.

Pfeffer, C. R., Klerman, G. L., Hurt, S. W., Kakuma, T., Peskin, J. R., & Siefker, C. A. (1993). Suicidal children grow up: Rates and psychosocial risk factors for suicide attempts during follow-up. *Journal of the American Academy of Child & Adolescent Psychiatry, 32*(1), 106–113.

Pitts, F. N., & Winokur, G. (1964). Affective disorder, III: Diagnostic correlates and incidence of suicide. *Journal of Nervous & Mental Disease, 139*, 176–181.

Pleck, J. H. (1995). *The gender role strain paradigm: An update*. New York: Basic Books.

Powell, J. M., Geddes, J., Deeks, J., Goldacre, M., & Hawton, K. (2000). Suicide in psychiatric hospital in-patients: Risk factors and their predictive powers. *British Journal of Psychiatry, 176*, 266–272.

Randell, B. P., Wang, W., Herting, J. R., & Eggert, L. L. (2006). Family factors predicting categories of suicide risk. *Journal of Family and Child Studies, 15*(3), 255–270.

Resnick, M. D., Bearman, P. S., Blum, R. W., Bauman, K. E., Harris, K. M., Jones, J., et al. (1997). Protecting adolescents from harm: Findings from the National Longitudinal Study on Adolescent Health. *Journal of the American Medical Association, 278*, 823–832.

Richardson, L. A. (2001). Seeking and obtaining mental health services: What do parents expect? *Archives of Psychiatric Nursing, 15,* 223–231.

Roy, A. (1983). Family history of suicide. *Archives of General Psychiatry, 40,* 971–974.

Roy, A. (1985). Family history of suicide in manic-depressive patients. *Journal of Affect Disorders, 8,* 187–189.

Roy, A. (1993). Genetic and biological risk factors for suicide in depressive disorders. *Psychiatric Quarterly, 64,* 345–358.

Roy, A. (2002a). Characteristics of opiate dependent patients who attempt suicide. *Journal of Clinical Psychiatry, 63,* 403–407.

Roy, A. (2002b). Family history of suicide and neuroticism: A preliminary study. *Psychiatry Research, 110,* 87–90.

Roy, A. (2003). Characteristics of drug addicts who attempt suicide. *Psychiatry Research, 121,* 99–103.

Roy, A., Rylander, G., & Sarchiapone, M. (1997). Genetics of suicides. Family studies and molecular genetics. *Annals of the New York Academy of Sciences, 836,* 135–157.

Roy, A., Segal, N. L., & Sarchiapone, M. (1995). Attempted suicide among living co-twins of twin suicide victims. *American Journal of Psychiatry, 152,* 1075–1076.

Roy, A., Segal, N. L., Centerwall, B. S., & Robinette, C. D. (1991). Suicide in twins. *Archives of General Psychiatry, 48,* 29–32.

Rubenstein, J. L., Halton, A., Kasten, L., Rubin, C., & Stechler, G. (1998). Suicidal behavior in adolescents: Stress and protection in different family contexts. *American Journal of Orthopsychiatry, 68*(2), 274–284.

Rubenstein, J. L., Heeren, T., Housman, D., Rubin, C., & Stechler, G. (1989). Suicidal behavior in "normal" adolescents: Risk and protective factors. *American Journal of Orthopsychiatry, 1,* 59–71.

Runeson, B. S. (1998). History of suicidal behaviour in the families of young suicides. *Acta Psychiatrica Scandinavica, 98,* 497–501.

Runeson, B., & Asberg, M. (2003). Family history of suicide among suicide victims. *American Journal of Psychiatry, 160,* 1525–1526.

Rutter, M., & Quinton, D. (1984). Parental psychiatric disorder: Effects on children. *Psychological Medicine, 14,* 853–880.

Rutter, M., Silberg, J., O'Connor, T., & Simonoff, E. (1999). Genetics and child psychiatry: 1. Advances in quantitative and molecular genetics. *Journal of Child Psychology and Psychiatry, 40,* 3–18.

Sabo, A. N., Gunderson, J. G., Najavits, L. M., Chauncey, D., & Kisiel, C. (1995). Changes in self-destructiveness of borderline patients in psychotherapy: A prospective follow-up. *Journal of Nervous and Mental Disease, 183*(6), 337–376.

Salzinger, S., Rosario, M., Feldman, R. S., & Ng-Mak, D. S. (2007). Adolescent suicidal behavior: Associations with preadolescent physical abuse and selected risk and protective factors. *Journal of the American Academy of Child and Adolescent Psychiatry, 46*(7), 859–866.

Saewyc, E. M., Heinz, P. A., Bearinger, L. H., Blum, R. W., & Resnick, M. D. (1998). Gender differences in health and risky behaviors among bisexual and homosexual adolescents. *Journal of Adolescent Health, 23,* 181–188.

Schmidtke, A., Bille-Brahe, U., DeLeo, D., & Kerkhof, A. (1996). Attempted suicide in Europe: Rates, trends and sociodemographic characteristics of suicide attempters during the period 1989–1992. *Acta Psychiatrica Scandinavica, 93*(5), 327–338.

Schneider, B., Philipp, M., & Muller, M. J. (2001). Psychopathological predictors of suicide in patients with major depression during a 5-year follow-up. *European Psychiatry, 16*, 283–288.

Scocco, P., Marietta, P., Tonietto, M., & Buono, M. D. (2000). The role of psychopathology and suicidal intention in predicting suicide risk: A longitudinal study. *Psychopathology, 33*, 143–150.

Shaffer, D., Gould, M., Fisher, P., Trautman, P., Moreau, D., & Kleinman, M. (1996). Psychiatric diagnosis in child and adolescent suicide. *Archives of General Psychiatry, 53*, 339–348.

Shafi, M., Steltz-Lenarsky, J., Derrick, A. M., Beckner, C., & Whittinghill, R. (1988). Comorbidity of mental disorders in the post-mortem diagnosis of completed suicide in children and adolescents. *Journal of Affective Disorders, 14*, 227–233.

Shaunessey, K., Cohen, J. L., Plummer, B., & Berman, A. (1993). Suicidality in hospitalized adolescents: Relationship to prior abuse. *American Journal of Orthopsychiatry, 63*, 113–119.

Sorenson, S. B., & Rutter, C. M. (1991). Transgenerational patterns of suicide attempt. *Journal of Consulting & Clinical Psychology, 59*(6), 861–866.

Stack, S. (2002). Opera subculture and suicide for honor. *Death Studies, 26*, 431–437.

Stack, S., & Kposowa, A. J. (2008). The association of suicide rates with individual-level suicide attitudes: A cross-national analysis. *Social Science Quarterly, 89*(1), 39–59.

Statham, D. J., Heath, A. C., Madden, P. A., Bucholz, K. K., Bierut, L., Dinwiddie, S. H., et al. (1998). Suicidal behaviour: An epidemiological and genetic study. *Psychological Medicine, 28*, 839–855. Stillion, J. M., & McDowell, E. E. (1991). Examining suicide from a life-span perspective. *Death Studies, 15*, 327–354.

Stronski-Huwiler, S. M., & Remafedi, G. (1998). Adolescent homosexuality. *Advances in Pediatrics, 45*, 107–144.

Taylor, G. J., Ryan, D., & Bagby, R. M. (1985). Toward the development of a new self-report alexithymia scale. *Psychotherapy and Psychosomatics, 44*, 191–199.

Taylor, E., & Stansfeld, S. (1984). Children who poison themselves: II. Prediction of attendance for treatment. *British Journal of Psychiatry, 145*, 132–135.

Tsai, S.-Y. M., Kuo, C.-J., Chen, C.-C., & Lee, H.-C. (2002). Risk factors for completed suicide in bipolar disorder. *Journal of Clinical Psychiatry, 63*(6), 469–476.

Tsuang, M. T. (1983). Risk of suicide in relative of schizophrenics, manics, depressives, and controls. *Journal of Clinical Psychiatry, 44*, 396–400.

Wintersteen, M. B., Diamond, G. S., & Fein, J. A. (2007). Screening for suicide risk in the pediatric emergency and acute care setting. *Current Opinion in Pediatrics, 19*(4), 398–404.

Wisch, A. F., Mahalik, J. R., Hayes, J. A., & Nutt, E. A. (1995). The impact of gender role conflict and counseling technique on psychological help seeking in men. *Sex Roles, 33*, 77–88.

Zalsman, G., & Mann, J. J. (2005). Editorial: The neurobiology of suicide in adolescents: An emerging field of research. *International Journal of Adolescent Medicine and Health, 17*(3), 195–196.

10 Adult Suicide

Despite increased federal spending on suicide prevention, the overall number of suicides in the United States has remained consistent for several years. Furthermore, rates of suicide attempts and completions among adults continue to rise. It is important to understand the epidemiological trends, prevalence, and incident rates of adult suicidality. In order to improve existing prevention and intervention efforts, identification of risk and protective factors among adults is essential. These factors are highlighted in this chapter. In addition, this chapter deconstructs myths and misconceptions related to suicide among adults. An overview of empirically grounded strategies for effective assessment and treatment of this population also is provided.

■ Goals and Objectives of This Chapter

An understanding of:

- The impact of aging on suicidality
- The influence of gender on adult suicidality
- Epidemiology of adult suicidality
- Adult rates of completed suicide and attempted suicide
- Deconstructing the dominant myths and misconceptions of adult suicidality
- Psychiatric risk and protective factors for adult suicide
- Sociodemographic risk and protective factors for adult suicide
- Help-seeking behavior in relation to adult suicide

■ Mental health service utilization and adult suicide
■ A review of the major evidence-based interventions for working with this population

---

INTRODUCTION

Suicide is a leading cause of death worldwide (Nock et al., 2008). Studies have tended to find an association between age and suicide risk. The older an individual, the greater the suicide risk (Shah & De, 1998). Nearly 90 Americans complete suicide every day with hundreds more attempting. The majority of suicide attempts and completions are by adults (U.S. Department of Health and Human Services, 2001).

Suicide at any age is a tragedy. Although we often associate suicide with adolescents, adults are more at risk. A question that emerges is how does the age of a suicidal client impact the clinician? More specifically, does the age of the individual at risk of suicide impact our ability to engage, assess, and treat them? Is the suicide of a younger person a greater tragedy than an older individual? As a mental health clinician, do you hold one age more vulnerable than another? Should older individuals know better, be wiser, or be more able make decisions? How does the age of a client impact you? In clinically working with individuals experiencing suicidality it is important to assess and treat every individual with professional rigor, ethics, compassion, and empathy. To assume that the age of a client does not impact you professionally may be a disservice to both you and your clients.

■ Individual Exercise 10.1

1. Would working with a suicidal client who was an adult, rather than an adolescent suicidal client, be more problematic for you as a mental health clinician? Why or why not?
2. Would working with a suicidal client who was an adult, rather than an adolescent suicidal client, be easier for you as a mental health clinician? Why or why not?
3. What lessons do you learn from this exercise?

■ Small Group Exercise 10.1

In a small group of two to three, please discuss, as you are comfortable, your responses to individual exercise 10.1. Remember, answers are personal, and there are no correct or incorrect answers.

1. What were the response similarities in your group?
2. What were the response differences in your group?
3. Did you find any surprises in the group discussion? If so, what were they, and how were you surprised?

EPIDEMIOLOGY OF ADULT SUICIDE

In a crossnational study of 17 countries, Nock and colleagues (2008) estimated the lifetime prevalence of suicidal ideation (9.2%), plans (3.1%), and attempts (2.1%). In addition, an estimated 60% of ideators transition into planners or attempters within the first year of having suicidal ideation (Nock et al., 2008). Research frequently finds that on average suicide rates increase with age (Shah & De, 1998). However, Shah's (2007) study using World Health Organization (WHO) suicide data from 62 countries found a significant increase in suicide rates with increasing age in many countries, but no significant increase in other countries. Findings suggest regional and crossnational variations influence this relationship between increased suicide rates and aging (Shah, 2007).

In the United States, aging remains associated with an increased suicide risk. U.S. suicide rates by age group (15–24 years, 25–44 years, 45–64 years, and 65+ years) indicate two unique trends (McKeown, Cuffe, & Schulz, 2006). One, each of these age groups has experienced a decline, excluding a slight increase among the 15 to 24 age group. Two, the older the age group the higher the suicide risk. Nonetheless, it is important to recognize that trends do not account for age, gender, geographical, race, or ethnic differences. For example, the highest U.S. suicide rates have consistently been among older White males (Keppel, Pearcy, & Wagener, 2002). However, the suicide risk for White females and Blacks in the United States tends to peak at midlife (Maris & Nisbet, 2000; Woodbury, Manton, & Blazer, 1988). In regards to attempted suicide, it is difficult to determine prevalence rates because many suicide attempts remain unreported. However, Doshi, Boudreaux, Wang, Pelletier, and Camargo (2005) investigated U.S. emergency department (ED) visits from 1997 to 2001 for attempted suicide and self-inflicted injury. Their research found that the average age of patients presenting in an ED due to attempted suicide and self-inflicted injury was 31 years but that ED visits were more common in younger than older patients (Doshi et al., 2005).

RISK AND PROTECTIVE FACTORS

Risk Factors for Adult Suicide

Research has extensively examined risk factors for future suicide. Several factors have been identified as predictive of future suicide attempts and completions.

A history of suicide attempts has been found to increase the likelihood of a future attempt as much as four times (Bradvik & Berglund, 1993; Duggan, Sham, Lee, & Murray, 1991; Fawcett et al., 1990; Goldstein, Black, Nasrallah, & Winokur, 1991; Nordstrom, Asberg, Aber-Wistedt, & Nordin, 1995; Bille-Brahe et al., 1997; Wasserman & Cullberg, 1989; Sidley, Calam, Wells, Hughes, & Whitaker, 1999; Schneider, Philipp, & Muller, 2001). The presence of a psychiatric disorder, such as depression, has also been shown to double the risk of future suicide attempt (Antikainen, Hintikka, Lehtonen, Koponen, & Arstila, 1995; Mehlum, Friis, Vaglum, & Karterud, 1994; Sabo, Gunderson, Najavits, Chauncey, & Kisiel, 1995; Statham et al., 1998); Scocco, Marietta, Tonietto, & Buono, 2000; Schneider et al., 2001; Kaplan & Harrow, 1996). For a further analysis and discussion of the impact of psychiatric disorders on suicide, see Part IV of this text.

A relationship between loss or separation and suicidality has also been established (Borg & Stahl, 1982). Interestingly, Duggan et al. (1991) found that experience of loss by either death or separation was more common among suicide attempters than nonattempters (59% vs. 37.5%). However, further analysis revealed that loss by separation, rather than loss by death, is more associated with increased suicide risk. This may indicate that the family instability and conflict associated with separation is associated with suicidal behavior.

Impulsivity and aggression have been shown to be risk factors for suicide (Angst & Clayton, 1998; Brent et al., 2003; Goldney, Winefiwld, Saebel, Winefield, & Tiggeman, 1997; Malone, Haas, Sweeny, & Mann, 1995; Mann et al., 2005). Several studies comparing suicide attempters and nonattempters with a family history of suicidal behavior have found that impulsivity and aggression mediate the familial transmission of suicide (Brent, Bridge, Johnson, & Connolly, 1996; Carballo et al., 2008; Forman, Berk, Henriques, Brown, & Beck, 2004; Galfalvy et al., 2006; Garfinkel, Froese, & Hood, 1982; Hawton, Haw, Houston, & Townsend, 2002; Jeglic, Sharp, Chapman, Brown, & Beck, 2005; Linkowski, de Maertelaer, & Mendlewicz, 1985; Roy, 1993). A family history of suicidality is associated with increased risk of suicidal behavior (Mann et al., 2005). See chapter 9 for a more detailed review of family impact on suicide risk.

In addition to psychiatric and personality variables, numerous sociodemographic characteristics have been shown to increase suicide risk. Gender is a main risk factor for suicidality among adults. Females attempt suicide three to four times more often than males, and males complete suicide more often than females (Houle, Mishara, & Chagnon, 2008; Suominen, Isometsa, Haukka, & Lonnqvist, 2004; Skogman, Alsen, & Ojehagen, 2004; Pirkis, Burgess, & Dunt, 2000; Lefebvre, Lesage, Cyr, & Toupin, 1998; Moscicki et al., 1988; Schmidtke et al., 1996). Several explanations have been posited for this gender differential. For example, alcohol use disorders occur more frequently in males (Kessler et al., 1994; Robins & Regier, 1991), and such disorders are associated with increased suicide risk (Blair-West, Cantor, Mellsop, & Eyeson, 1999; Buckley, 2006; Mukamal, Kawachi, Miller, & Rimm, 2007; Tidemalm, Elofsson, Stefansson, Waern, & Runeson, 2005). Additionally, males have easier access to lethal means of suicide, such as guns (Chuang & Huang, 2004; Fischer, Comstock, Monk, & Sencer, 1993; Helmkamp, 1996; Lester, 2000; Mahon, Tobin, Cusack, Kelleher, & Malone, 2005; Stark et al., 2006). Males are also more likely to employ highly lethal methods of suicide as compared to females (Denning, Conwell, King, & Cox, 2000; Gibb, Beautrais, & Fergusson, 2005; Klerman, 1987; Suokas & Lonnqvist, 1991).

Low education and low income have been demonstrated to be associated with increased suicide rates (Abel & Kruger, 2005). Unemployment has also been shown to increase the risk of suicide attempt (Kposowa, 2001). This relationship is particularly strong among women (Kposowa, 2001). Age is also a risk factor for suicide among adults. The suicide rate among elderly males is higher than that of any other age group (Joe, Baser, Breeden, Neighbors, & Jackson, 2006). This is discussed in detail in chapter 11.

Interestingly, cigarette smoking has been found to be a strong indicator of suicide risk (Donald, Dower, Correa-Velez, & Jones, 2006; Oquendo et al., 2007). This relationship between cigarette smoking and increased suicide risk has been found for both men and women (Oquendo et al., 2007).

Adult Risk Factors for Suicide

- History of suicide attempts
- History of psychiatric illness

- Impulsivity
- Aggression
- Loss and separation
- Family history of psychiatric illness
- Family history of suicide attempts and/or completions
- Gender
- Unemployment
- Fewer years of education
- Low income
- Cigarette smoking

Protective Factors Against Adult Suicide

Protective factors against adult suicidal behavior have received less scientific scrutiny than risk factors for suicide. Reasons for living, as measured by the Reasons for Living Inventory (Linehan, Goodstein, Nielsen, & Chiles, 1983), are said to reflect adaptive beliefs and expectations that help individuals resist suicidal urges. Recently, research has begun to prospectively examine the role of reasons for living as a protective factor against suicidality. This research indicates that reasons for living serve as a protective factor against suicide attempt for females but not for males (Lizardi et al., 2007; Oquendo et al., 2007).

Social support and connectedness have consistently been shown to be protective factors against suicidality (Donald et al., 2006; Duberstein et al., 2004). Marital status, in particular, is associated with suicide risk. Divorced and separated individuals are more likely to commit suicide than married individuals (Kposowa, 2000). The relationship between marital status and gender is especially strong. The suicide rate among divorced males is twice the rate among married males (Hawton, 2000; Kposowa, 2000; Moller-Leimkuhler, 2003). Among females, the protective effect of marriage seems to be mediated by the effect of being a parent (Agerbo, 2005; Oquendo et al., 2007).

Consistently, restricted access to firearms has been shown to be a protective factor against suicidality (Agerbo, Gunnell, Bonde, Mortensen, & Nordentoft, 2007; Dahlberg, Ikeda, & Kresnow, 2004; Ilgen, Zivin, McMannon, & Valenstein, 2008; Miller, Lippmann, Azrael, & Hemenway, 2007; Shenassa, Rogers, Spalding, & Roberts, 2004). Limited access to firearms is associated with decreased suicide attempts and completions. The protective effects of ethnicity and religion are discussed in detail in chapters 3 and 4.

Adult Protective Factors Against Suicide

- Reasons for living
- Social support and connectedness
- Limited access to firearms
- Marital status
- Religious affiliation
- Ethnicity

▓ Individual Exercise 10.2

You are a mental health clinician on an inpatient adult psychiatry unit. You are scheduled to do an intake with a new patient who was transferred from a medical unit where she was being treated for the past week for medical consequences due to an attempted suicide. The patient is known to the unit from two prior admissions, once for a major depressive episode and the other for an attempted suicide. Consider the following questions:

1. What risk factors will you assess for during your interview with the client?
2. What protective factors will you assess for during your interview with the client?
3. What factors need to be considered in order to establish a treatment plan?

▓ Role Play 10.1

Using the scenario from individual exercise 10.2, break into groups of three and assume the role of the mental health clinician and the new patient on the psychiatry unit. The third member will act as a recorder and can be called upon to consult and assist the mental health clinician. Engage in a role play in which you would assess for risk and protective factors for a repeat suicide attempt.

MYTHS AND MISCONCEPTIONS ABOUT ADULT SUICIDE

A number of unfounded perceptions and beliefs exist among lay individuals and clinical professionals relating to suicide. While many of these accepted misconceptions or myths are ill-informed but harmless, some erroneous thoughts can negatively influence clinical assessments and treatment. The following are six commonly held fallacies related to suicide.

1. *Using the word "suicide" increases the likelihood that at-risk people may view suicide as an option.* A widespread, but unfounded, belief

is that when assessing or talking to someone who is at-risk of suicide the use of the word *suicide* should be avoided lest it provide the individual with a previously unconsidered option. There is no evidence that using the word *suicide* increases risk (Thobaben, 2000). Rather, it will frequently option a dialogue that can aid an individual in opening up and discussing a taboo topic, resulting in a fuller, more detailed assessment and effective treatment.

2. *People who want to end their lives will not talk about their suicidal thoughts.* A common myth is that individuals intending to suicide do not talk about their suicidal thoughts or plans. The overwhelming majority of individuals who are seriously considering suicide have clearly described their thoughts on the issue or provided hints (Barrero, 2008).

3. *Suicide-prevention or no-harm contracts work.* There has existed for some time a common practice to use suicide-prevention or no-harm contracts in working with individuals who express suicidal ideation. There is no empirical support for the effectiveness of suicide-prevention contracts in clinical practice (Rudd, Mandrusiak, & Joiner, 2006). Furthermore, the belief that such contracts can work may result in some clinicians substituting contracting for a thorough clinical assessment and treatment (Goin, 2003; Lee & Bartlett, 2005; Rudd et al., 2006).

4. *"Birthday blues" lead to an increase in suicide.* It is often believed that people are more likely to suicide near or on their birthday. Reulbach and colleagues' population-based research study found no evidence of a birthday blues effect on suicide (Reulbach, Biermann, Markovic, Kornhuber, & Bleich, 2007).

5. *Seasonal influences of suicide increase the risk in the late fall and early winter.* There does exist a distinct suicide seasonal pattern. There is a peak of suicides in spring and early summer and a decline in suicides during the late fall and early winter seasons (Jamison & Hawton, 2005; Voracek, Tran, & Sonneck, 2007). However, people commonly believe the direct opposite. It is important for mental health clinicians to distinguish fact from fiction and to be aware of the documented seasonal influence of suicides.

6. *Lunar phases influence suicide.* A commonly held unsubstantiated misconnection is that there is a relationship between lunar phases and suicide. There is no evidence to support this perceived association (Biermann et al., 2005; Gutierrez-Garcia & Tusell, 1997).

SERVICE UTILIZATION

Research finds that between 11% and 50% of suicide attempters who present to emergency rooms refuse outpatient referrals or drop out of outpatient therapy very early on in treatment (Kurz & Moller, 1984). Some studies have noted rates of up to 60% of suicide attempters failing to attend outpatient psychosocial treatment one week post discharge from the emergency room (O'Brien, Holton, Hurren, Wyatt, & Hassanyeh, 1987). Of those who do attend treatment, after 3 months postdischarge from a psychiatric hospitalization for a suicide attempt, 38% of attempters will not be attending outpatient treatment (Monti, Cedereke, & Ojehagen, 2003), and after a year, 73% of attempters will no longer be in treatment (Krulee & Hayes, 1988). This is particularly concerning given that the risk of a repeat suicide attempt is highest within the first 3 months following an initial attempt (Appleby et al., 1999; Kerkhof et al., 1998).

Research examining characteristics of suicide attempters associated with a lack of engagement with treatment has been inconclusive. Some studies have identified marital status (Cremniter, Payanb, Meidingera, Batistaa, & Fermanian, 2001; Jauregui, Martinez, Rubio, & Santo-Domingo, 1999), history of suicide attempts (Goethe, Dornelas, & Gruman, 1999), and previous psychiatric history (Cremniter et al., 2001; Goethe et al., 1999; Krulee & Hayes, 1988) as predictors of poor treatment engagement, with being married and having a history of previous suicide attempt and hospitalizations predicting greater rates of treatment attendance. Yet, other studies have not been able to identify any sociodemographic or clinical characteristics that distinguish between those who do and do not attend outpatient treatment (Cedereke, Monti, & Ojehagen, 2002).

Research indicates that among suicidal individuals, the main barriers to service, in addition to stigma regarding mental illness, include limited awareness of mental disorders, limited understanding of the mental health system, lack of information, language barriers, and lack of insurance (Fiscella, Franks, Doescher, & Saver, 2002; Sadavoy, Meier, Ong, & Yuk, 2004; Snowden, Masland, & Guerrero, 2003; Strug & Mason, 2001; Vega & Rumbaut, 1999; Wells, Golding, Hough, Burnam, & Karno, 1988). Furthermore, when help is sought by suicide attempters, research demonstrates that it is generally done so at the recommendation of friends and family (Barnes, Ikeda, & Kresnow, 2001; Owens, Lambert,

Donovan, & Lloyd, 2005). This may factor in to the protective role that having a strong support network plays against suicidal behavior.

HELP-SEEKING BEHAVIOR

Research indicates that females are more willing to seek help than males (Corney, 1990; Gijsbers Van Wijk, Kolk, Van den Bosch, & Van den Hoogen, 1992; Hibbard & Pope, 1983, 1986).

■ Individual Exercise 10.3

1. List the main reasons for which you believe women seek help.
2. List the main reasons for which you believe men seek help.
3. Was this exercise more difficult or less difficult than you anticipated? Explain your rationale.

Research demonstrates that females and males seek help for problems that are seen as gender related, for example, women are more likely to seek help for depression (Jorm et al., 2000), whereas men are more likely to seek help for alcohol problems (Substance Abuse and Mental Health Services Administration [SAMHSA], 2002). Women more often seek consultation for psychosocial distress and emotional difficulties (Galdas, Cheater, & Marshall, 2005; Möller-Leimkühler, 2002). Men more often seek treatment when physical symptoms are present (Corney, 1990; Galdas et al., 2005; Möller-Leimkühler, 2002; NHS Executive, 1998), and they have more difficulty expressing emotions (Good & Sherrod; 2001; Taylor, Ryan, & Bagby, 1985).

It is important to note that the differences seen in help-seeking behavior are not merely due to men needing help less often, but rather to differences in how help is sought and in the perception of need for treatment. For example, it has been suggested that the higher rate of depression in women (nearly two times the rate of men) actually reflects underreporting of depressive symptoms by males rather than a lower rate of depression among males (Cochran, 2001). Furthermore, research indicates that men do not consider mental health treatment as a solution to problems, and they tend to rationalize any pain experienced (Sanden, Larsson, & Eriksson, 2000; Sharpe & Arnold; 1998).

▓ Small Group Exercise 10.2

In a small group of two or three, please discuss, as you are comfortable, your responses to the individual exercise 10.3. Remember, answers are personal, and there are no correct or incorrect answers.

1. What were the response similarities in your group?
2. What were the response differences in your group?
3. Did you find any surprises in the group discussion? If so, what were they, and how were you surprised?
4. What lessons did you learn from this exercise?

INTERVENTIONS WITH ADULT SUICIDAL CLIENTS

In working with individuals with suicidal ideation, intention, plans, or after a suicide attempt a number of interventions have been developed. The three most common approaches include crisis management, psychosocial evidence-based practice (EBP) interventions, and psychopharmacology. These approaches are reviewed in Part II of this text.

As with children, any adult who is at risk of suicide, has attempted suicide, or is in need of crisis management should be brought to a hospital emergency department for complete psychiatric assessment. According to the American Psychiatric Association (APA) practice guidelines (2003b), after an assessment, management of an at-risk individual requires establishing and maintaining a therapeutic alliance, attending to the patient's safety, determining a treatment setting, developing a plan of treatment, and coordinating care and collaborating with other clinicians.

Research has found several EBPs to be effective in treating adults experiencing suicidality. The specific EBP treatment should meet the needs of the client, with the input of their family when possible or advisable. Evidence-based practices found to be effective in working with adults at risk of suicide are **cognitive-behavioral therapy (CBT)**, **dialectical behavior therapy (DBT)**, **interpersonal psychotherapy (IPT)**, and family therapy. These treatments are often combined with psychopharmacology. Although there is inconclusive evidence that antidepressants lower suicide rates, they are effective in treating the anxiety and depression that may contribute to individuals at higher risk of suicide (American Psychiatric Association, 2003a, 2003b). For further information on these interventions see Part II of this text.

SUMMARY

Generally aging increases the suicide risk in individuals. As clinicians we cannot assume that an individual is not at risk without conducting a comprehensive assessment. Consequently, it is critical to be aware of current research when working with at-risk adults to effectively assess for suicidal ideation and plans. Sociodemographic and psychiatric risk and protective factors should be assessed to aid in determining suicide risk.

▦ Key Points

1. The suicide risk generally increases with age.
2. While females' and Black adults' suicide risk peaks at midlife, White males' risk continues into old age.
3. Talk openly and directly about suicide when working with clients at risk.
4. Suicide contracts do not work and do not replace rigorous assessment or effective evidence-based treatments.
5. There is not empirical support to the belief that lunar phases or birthdays increase suicidal risk.
6. A history of suicide attempt is the strongest known predictor of future suicide risk.
7. Social connectedness is a major protective factor against suicide.
8. The majority of suicide attempters do not engage in outpatient psychosocial treatment.
9. Differences seen in help-seeking behavior are not explained by men needing help less often but rather by differences in how help is sought and in the perception of need for treatment.
10. Family and friends are very influential regarding the decision to seek help.

FURTHER READINGS

American Psychiatric Association. (2003). Practice guidelines for the assessment and treatment of patients with suicidal behaviors. Retrieved July 5, 2008, from http://www.psychiatryonline.com/pracGuide/pracGuideTopic_14.aspx

Barrero, S.A.P. (2008). Preventing suicide: A resource for the family. *Annals of General Psychiatry, 7*(1), e1–e8.

Beautrais, A. (2002). A case control study of suicide and attempted suicide in older adults. *Suicide & Life-Threatening Behavior, 32,* 1–9.

Neeleman, J., de Graaf, R., & Vollebergh, W. (2004). The suicidal process; prospective comparison between early and later stages. *Journal of Affective Disorders, 82*(1), 43–52.

Nojomi, M., Malakouti, S.-K., Bolhari, J., & Poshtmashhadi, M. (2007). A predictor model for suicide attempt: Evidence from a population-based study. *Archives of Iranian Medicine, 10*(4), 452–458.

Tremeau, F., Staner, L., Duval, F., Correa, H., Crocq, M. A., Darreye, A., et al. (2005). Suicide attempts and family history of suicide in three psychiatric populations. *Suicide & Life-Threatening Behavior, 35*(6), 702–713.

Ungemack, J. A., & Guarnaccia, P. J. (1998). Suicidal ideation and suicide attempts among Mexican Americans, Puerto Ricans and Cuban Americans. *Transcultural Psychiatry, 35*, 307–327.

U.S. Department of Health and Human Services. (2001). Summary of national strategy for suicide prevention: goals and objectives for action [National Strategy for Suicide Prevention Web site]. Retrieved June 10, 2008, from http://mentalhealth.samhsa.gov/SuicidePrevention/

ELECTRONIC RESOURCES

APA Guideline

Psychiatry Online: Suicide: http://www.psychiatryonline.com/content.aspx?aid=111622
General: http://www.psychiatryonline.com/pracGuide/pracGuideHome.aspx

Myths and Misconceptions About Suicide

Annals of General Psychiatry: http://www.annals-general-psychiatry.com/content/7/1/1
Family Resource: http://www.familyresource.com/health/mental-health/suicide-myth-versus-reality
National Alliance on Mental Illness: http://www.nami.org/Content/ContentGroups/Helpline1/Suicide_-_Learn_more,_learn_to_help.htm
Nevada Department of Health and Human Services: http://dhhs.nv.gov/Suicide-Adult-TruthMyth.htm
University of Oregon: http://www.uoregon.edu/~counsel/newpage5.htm
World Health organization: http://www.searo.who.int/en/Section1174/Section1199/Section1567/Section1824_8077.htm

Support

American Foundation for Suicide Prevention: http://www.afsp.org
National Alliance on Mental Illness: http://www.nami.org
Samaritans: http://www.samaritans.org
ULifeline: http://www.ulifeline.org

Education and Resources

American Foundation for Suicide Prevention: http://www.afsp.ord
Mental Health Association of New York City: http://www.mhaofnyc.org
National Alliance for Research on Schizophrenia and Depression: http://www.nasrad.org

National Health Information Center: http://www.mentalhealth.org
Northwestern Memorial Hospital: http://www.nmh.org
Suicide Prevention Action Network USA: http://www.spanusa.org
Suicide Prevention Resource Center: http://www.sprc.org

■ Knowledge Acquisition Test

True or False

1. Generally, age increases suicide risk.
2. A woman's suicide risk continues to increase with age.
3. Suicide contracts are effective at reducing suicidal risk.
4. Individuals who complete suicide talk about suicide before their attempt.
5. Research has comprehensively found that antidepressants lower suicide rates.
6. The majority of suicide attempters seek treatment.
7. Males and females do not seek professional help for the same reasons.
8. Being divorced is a greater risk factor for suicide for males than for females.
9. Impulsivity is associated with decreased risk for suicide attempt.

Short Answer

10. Discuss how age is a risk factor for all adults but impacts gender and race differently.
11. What does research inform us about suicide contracts? As a mental health clinician, why can such contracts be a concern?
12. How does using the word *suicide* generally impact clients?
13. Explain two possible reasons for the differences in help-seeking behavior among males and females as they relate to suicidal behavior.
14. List the main barriers to service utilization among suicidal individuals.
15. Describe the gender difference in the protective role of marital status against suicidal behavior.

Multiple Choice

16. What group is at the highest risk of suicide?
    A. White adult males
    B. White adult females
    C. Black adult males
    D. Black adult females
    E. All of the above are at equal risk
    F. None of the above

17. What item is untrue in the following list of myths or misconceptions related to suicidality and adults?
    A. Suicide contracts do not work
    B. Adults who complete suicide talk about suicide before attempting

C. Most suicides occur in winter
D. An approaching birthday does not increase the risk of suicide
E. All of the above
F. None of the above

18. Which of the following is NOT a risk factor for suicide among adults?
    A. Prior suicide attempt
    B. Gender
    C. Cigarette smoking
    D. Age
    E. Height

19. Which of the following is NOT a protective factor for males?
    A. Social support
    B. Marriage
    C. Restricted access to firearms
    D. Reasons for Living
    E. All of the above
    F. None of the above

20. Which of the following is a barrier to accessing mental health treatment?
    A. Perceived stigma
    B. Lack of insurance
    C. Limited understanding of the mental health system
    D. Language barriers
    E. All of the above
    F. None of the above

Answer key is available in the Instructor's Manual; qualified instructors may e-mail textbook@springerpub.com *to request a copy.*

REFERENCES

Abel, E. L., & Kruger, M. L. (2005). Educational attainment and suicide rates in the United States. *Psychological Reports, 91*(1), 25–28.

Agerbo, E. (2005). Midlife suicide risk, partner's psychiatric illness, spouse and child bereavement by suicide or other modes of death: A gender-specific study. *Journal of Epidemiology and Community Health, 59*(5), 407–412.

Agerbo, E., Gunnell, D., Bonde, J., Mortensen, P., & Nordentoft, M. (2007). Suicide and occupation: The impact of socio-economic, demographic and psychiatric differences. *Psychological Medicine, 37*(8), 1131–1140.

American Psychiatric Association. (2003a). Assessing and treating suicidal behaviors: A quick reference guide. Retrieved July 5, 2008, from http://www.psychiatryonline.com/pracGuide/loadPracQuickRefPdf.aspx?file=Suibehavs_QRG

American Psychiatric Association. (2003b). Practice guidelines for the assessment and treatment of patients with suicidal behaviors. Retrieved July 5, 2008, from http://www.psychiatryonline.com/pracGuide/pracGuideTopic_14.aspx.

Angst, J., & Clayton, P. J. (1998). Personality, smoking and suicide: A prospective study. *Journal of Affective Disorders, 51*, 55–62.

Antikainen, R., Hintikka, J., Lehtonen, J., Koponen, H., & Arstila, A. (1995). A prospective three-year follow-up study of borderline personality disorder inpatients. *Acta Psychiatrica Scandinavica, 92*, 327–335.

Appleby, L., Shaw, A., Amos, T., McDonnell, R., Harris, C., McCann, K., et al. (1999). Suicide within 12 months of contact with mental health services: National clinical survey. *BMJ, 318*(7193), 1235–1239.

Barnes, L. S., Ikeda, R. M., & Kresnow, M. J. (2001). Help-seeking behavior prior to nearly lethal suicide attempts. *Suicide & Life-Threatening Behavior, 32*(Suppl 1), 68–75.

Barrero, S.A.P. (2008). Preventing suicide: A resource for the family. *Annals of General Psychiatry, 7*(1), e1–e8.

Biermann, T., Estel, D., Sperling, W., Bleich, S., Kornhuber, J., & Reulbach, U. (2005). Influence of lunar phases on suicide: The end of a myth? A population-based study. *Chronobiology International, 22*(6), 1137–1143.

Bille-Brahe, U., Kerkhof, A., DeLeo, D., Schmidke, A., Crepet, P., Lonngvist, J., et al. (1997). A repetition-prediction study on European parasuicide populations: A summary of the first report from Part II of the WHO/EURO Multicentre Study on Parasuicide in co-operation with the EC Concerted Action on Attempted Suicide. *Acta Psychiatrica Scandinavica, Supplementum, 95*, 81–86.

Blair-West, G.W., Cantor, C.H., Mellsop, G.W., & Eyeson, M.L. (1999). Lifetime suicide risk in major depression: Sex and age determinants. *Journal of Affective Disorders, 55*(3), 171–178.

Borg, S.E., & Stahl, M. (1982). A prospective study of suicides and controls among psychiatric patients. *Acta Psychiatrica Scandinavica, 65*, 221–232.

Bradvik, L., & Berglund, M. (1993). Risk factors for suicide in melancholia: A case-record evaluation of 89 suicides and their controls. *Acta Psychiatrics Scandinavica, 87*, 306–311.

Brent, D., Bridge, J., Johnson, B.A., & Connolly, J. (1996). Suicidal behavior runs in families: A controlled family study of adolescent suicide victims. *Archives of General Psychiatry, 53*(12), 1145–1152.

Brent, D., Oquendo, M., Birmaher, B., Greenhill, L., Kolko, D., Stanley, B., et al. (2003). Peripubertal suicide attempts in offspring of suicide attempters with siblings concordant for suicidal behavior. *American Journal of Psychiatry, 160*(8), 1486–1493.

Buckley, P.F. (2006). Prevalence and consequences of the dual diagnosis of substance abuse and severe mental illness. *Journal of Clinical Psychiatry, 67*(Suppl 7), 5–9.

Carballo, J.J., Harkavy-Friedman, J., Burke, A.K., Sher, L., Baca-Garcia, E., Sullivan, G.M., et al. (2008). Family history of suicidal behavior and early traumatic experiences: Additive effect on suicidality and course of bipolar illness? *Journal of Affective Disorders, 109*(1), 57–63.

Cedereke, M., Monti, K., & Ojehagen, A. (2002). Telephone contact with patients in the year after a suicide attempt: Does if affect treatment attendance and outcome? A randomized controlled study. *European Psychiatry, 17*, 82–91.

Chuang, H.L., & Huang, W.C. (2004). A multinomial logit analysis of methods used by persons who completed suicide. *Suicide & Life-Threatening Behavior, 34*, 298–310.

Cochran, S. (2001). *Assessing and treating depression in men* (Vols. 1 & 2). San Francisco, CA: Jossey-Bass.

Corney, R. (1990). Sex differences in general practice attendance and help seeking for minor illness. *Journal of Psychosomatic Research, 34*(5), 525–534.

Cremniter, D., Payanb, C., Meidingera, A., Batistaa, G., & Fermanian, J. (2001). Predictors of short-term deterioration and compliance in psychiatric emergency room patients: A prospective study of 457 patients referred to the emergency room of a general hospital. *Psychiatry Research, 104*(1), 49–59.

Dahlberg, L. L., Ikeda, R. M., & Kresnow, M. J. (2004). Guns in the home and risk of a violent death in the home: Findings from a national study. *American Journal of Epidemiology, 160*(10), 929–936.

Denning, D., Conwell, Y., King, D., & Cox, C. (2000). Method choice, intent, and gender in completed suicide. *Suicide & Life-Threatening Behavior, 30*(3), 282–288.

Donald, M., Dower, J., Correa-Velez, I., & Jones, M. (2006). Risk and protective factors for medically serious suicide attempts: A comparison of hospital-based with population-based samples of young adults. *The Australian and New Zealand Journal of Psychiatry, 40*(1), 87–96.

Doshi, A., Boudreaux, E. D., Wang, N., Pelletier, A. J., & Camargo, C. A. J. (2005). National study of U.S. emergency department visits for attempted suicide and self-inflicted injury, 1997–2001. *Annals of Emergency Medicine, 46*(4), 369–375.

Duberstein, P. R., Conwell, Y., Conner, K. R., Eberly, S., Evinger, J. S., & Caine, E. D. (2004). Poor social integration and suicide: Fact or artifact? A case-control study. *Psychological Medicine, 34,* 1331–1337.

Duggan, C. F., Sham, P., Lee, A. S., & Murray, R. M. (1991). Can future suicidal behaviour in depressed patients be predicted? *Journal of Affective Disorders, 22,* 111–118.

Fawcett, J., Scheftner, W. A., Fogg, L., Clark, D. C., Young, M. A., Hedeker, D., et al. (1990). Time-related predictors of suicide in major affective disorder. *American Journal of Psychiatry, 147,* 1189–1194.

Fiscella, K., Franks, P., Doescher, M., & Saver, B. (2002). Disparities in health care by race, ethnicity, and language among the insured: Findings from a national sample. *Medical Care, 40,* 52–59.

Fischer, E. P., Comstock, G. W., Monk, M. A., & Sencer, D. J. (1993). Characteristics of completed suicides: Implications of differences among methods. *Suicide & Life-Threatening Behavior, 23*(2), 91–100.

Forman, E. M., Berk, M. S., Henriques, G. R., Brown, G. K., & Beck, A. T. (2004). History of multiple suicide attempts as a behavioral marker of severe psychopathology. *American Journal of Psychiatry, 161*(3), 437–443.

Galdas, P., Cheater, F., & Marshall, P. (2005). Men and health help-seeking behaviour: Literature review. *Journal of Advanced Nursing, 49*(6), 616–623.

Galfalvy, H., Oquendo, M. A., Carballo, J. J., Sher, L., Grunebaum, M. F., Burke, A., et al. (2006). Clinical predictors of suicidal acts after major depression in bipolar disorder: A prospective study. *Bipolar Disorders, 8*(5, Pt 2), 586–595.

Garfinkel, B. D., Froese, A., & Hood, J. (1982). Suicide attempts in children and adolescents. *American Journal of Psychiatry, 139,* 1257–1261.

Gibb, S. J., Beautrais, A. L., & Fergusson, D. M. (2005). Mortality and further suicidal behaviour after an index suicide attempt: A 10-year study. *Australian & New Zealand Journal of Psychiatry, 39*(1–2), 95–100.

Gijsbers Van Wijk, C. M., Kolk, A. M., Van den Bosch, W., & Van den Hoogen, H.J.M. (1992). Male and female morbidity in general practice: The nature of sex differences. *Social Science & Medicine, 35,* 665–678.

Goethe, J., Dornelas, E., & Gruman, C. (1999). Predicting service utilization after psychiatric hospitalization. *Comprehensive Psychiatry, 40*(3), 192–197.

Goldney, R. D., Winefiwld, A., Saebel, J., Winefield, H., & Tiggeman, M. (1997). Anger, suicidal ideation, and attempted suicide: a prospective study. *Comprehensive Psychiatry, 38*(5), 264–268.

Goin, M. (2003). The "Suicide-Prevention Contract": A dangerous myth. *Psychiatric News, 38*(14), 3.

Goldstein, R. B., Black, D. W., Nasrallah, A., & Winokur, G. (1991). The prediction of suicide: Sensitivity, specificity, and predictive value of a multivartiate model applied to suicide among 1906 patients with affective disorders. *Archives of General Psychiatry, 48,* 418–422.

Good, G., & Sherrod, N. (2001). *Men's problems and effective treatments: Theory and empirical support* (Vols. 1 & 2). San Francisco, CA: Jossey-Bass.

Gutierrez-Garcia, J. M., & Tusell, F. (1997). Suicides and the lunar cycle. *Psychological Reports, 80*(1), 243–250.

Hawton, K. (2000). Sex and suicide: Gender differences in suicidal behaviour. *British Journal of Psychiatry, 177,* 484–485.

Hawton, K., Haw, C., Houston, K., & Townsend, E. (2002). Family history of suicidal behavior: Prevalence and significance in deliberate self-harm patients. *Acta Psychiatrica Scandinavica, 106,* 387–393.

Helmkamp, J. C. (1996). Occupation and suicide among males in the US Armed Forces. *Annals of Epidemiology, 6*(1), 83–88.

Hibbard, J., & Pope, C. (1983). Gender roles, illness orientation and use of medical services. *Social Science & Medicine, 17*(3), 129–137.

Hibbard, J. J., & Pope, C. R. (1986). Another look at sex differences in the use of medical care: Illness orientation and the types of morbidities for which services are used. *Women's Health, 11,* 21–36.

Houle, J., Mishara, B. L., & Chagnon, F. (2008). An empirical test of a mediation model of the impact of the traditional male gender role on suicidal behavior in men. *Journal of Affective Disorders, 107*(1–3), 37–43.

Ilgen, M. A., Zivin, M. A., McMannon, R. J., & Valenstein, M. (2008). Mental illness, previous suicidality, and access to guns in the United States. *Psychiatric Services, 59*(2), 198–200.

Jamison, K. R., & Hawton, K. (2005). The burden of suicide and clinical suggestions for prevention. In K. Hawton (Ed.), *Prevention and treatment of suicidal behaviour: From science to practice* (pp. 183–196). Oxford: Oxford University Press.

Jauregui, J., Martinez, M., Rubio, G., & Santo-Domingo, J. (1999). Patients who attended suicide and failed to attend mental health centres. *European Psychiatry, 14*(4), 205–209.

Jeglic, E. L., Sharp, I. R., Chapman, J. E., Brown, G. K., & Beck, A. T. (2005). History of family suicide behaviors and negative problem solving in multiple suicide attempters. *Archives of Suicide Research, 9*(2), 135–146.

Joe, S., Baser, R. E., Breeden, G., Neighbors, H. W., & Jackson, J. S. (2006). Prevalence of and risk factors for lifetime suicide attempts among blacks in the United States. *Journal of the American Medical Academy, 296,* 2112–2123.

Jorm, A. F., Medway, J., Christensen, H., Korten, A. E., Jacomb, P. A., & Rodgers, B. (2000). Attitudes towards people with depression: Effects on the public's help-seeking and outcome when experiencing common psychiatric symptoms. *Australia and New Zealand Journal of Psychiatry, 34*, 612–618.

Kaplan, K. J., & Harrow, M. (1996). Positive and negative symptoms as risk factors for later suicidal activity in schizophrenics versus depressives. *Suicide & Life-Threatening Behavior, 26*(2), 105–120.

Keppel, K., Pearcy, J., & Wagener, D. (2002). Trends in racial and ethnic-specific rates for the health status indicators: United States, 1990–1998. *Healthy People 2000 Stat Notes, 23*, 1–16.

Kerkhof, A., Arms, E., Bille-Brahe, U., Crepet, P., De Leo, D., Hjelmeland, H., et al. (1998). *Repetition of attempted suicide: Results from the WHO/EU Multicentre Study on Parasuicide, repetition-prediction part.* Ghent: University Press.

Kessler, R. C., McGonagle, K. A., Zhao, S., Nelson, C. B., Hughes, M., Eshleman, S., et al. (1994). Lifetime and 12-month prevalence of DSM-III-R psychiatric disorders in the United States. Results from the National Comorbidity Survey. *Archives of General Psychiatry, 5*, 8–19.

Klerman, G. L. (1987). Clinical epidemiology of suicide. *Journal of Clinical Psychiatry, 48*(Suppl), 33–38.

Kposowa, A. J. (2000). Marital status and suicide in the National Longitudinal Mortality Study. *Journal of Epidemiology and Community Health, 54*(4), 254–261.

Kposowa, A. J. (2001). Unemployment and suicide: A cohort analysis of social factors predicting suicide in the U.S. National Longitudinal Mortality Study. *Psychological Medicine, 31*, 127–138.

Krulee, D., & Hayes, R. (1988). Compliance with psychiatric referrals from a general hospital psychiatry outpatient clinic. *General hospital Psychiatry, 10*, 399–345.

Kurz, A., & Moller, H. (1984). Help-seeking behavior and compliance of suicidal patients. *Psychiatrische Praxis, 11*, 6–13.

Lee, J. B., & Bartlett, M. L. (2005). Suicide prevention: Critical elements for managing suicidal clients and counselor liability without the use of a no-suicide contract. *Death Studies, 29*(9), 847–865.

Lefebvre, F., Lesage, A., Cyr, M., & Toupin, J. (1998). Factors related to utilization of services for mental health reasons in Montreal, Canada. *Social Psychiatry and Psychiatric Epidemiology, 33*, 291–208.

Lester, D. (2000). *Why people kill themselves* (4th. ed.). Springfield, IL: Charles Thomas.

Linehan, M. M., Goodstein, J. L., Nielsen, S. L., & Chiles, J. A. (1983). Reasons for staying alive when you are thinking of killing yourself: The reasons for living inventory. *Journal of Consulting & Clinical Psychology, 51*, 276–286.

Linkowski, P., de Maertelaer, V., & Mendlewicz, J. (1985). Suicidal behaviour in major depressive illness. *Acta Psychiatrica Scandinavica, 72*(3), 233–238.

Lizardi, D., Currier, D., Galfalvy, H., Sher, L., Burke, A., Mann, J. J., et al. (2007). Perceived reasons for living ant index hospitalization and future suicide attempt. *Journal of Nervous and Mental Disease, 195*(5), 451–455.

Mahon, M. J., Tobin, J. P., Cusack, D. A., Kelleher, C., & Malone, K. M. (2005). Suicide among regular-duty military personnel: A retrospective case-control study of occupation-specific risk factors for workplace suicide. *American Journal of Psychiatry, 162*(9), 1688–1696.

Malone, K. M., Haas, G. L., Sweeny, J. A., & Mann, J. J. (1995). Major depression and the risk of attempted suicide. *Journal of Affective Disorders, 34*, 173–185.

Mann, J. J., Bortinger, J., Oquendo, M. A., Currier, D., Li, S., & Brent, D. A. (2005). Family history of suicidal behavior and mood disorders in probands with mood disorders. *American Journal of Psychiatry, 162*(9), 1672–1679.

Maris, R. W., & Nisbet, P. (2000). Age and the lifespan. In R. W. Maris, A. L. Berman & M. M. Silverman (Eds.), *Comprehensive textbook of suicidology* (pp. 127–144). New York: Guilford Press.

McKeown, R. E., Cuffe, S. P., & Schulz, R. M. (2006). US suicide rates by age group, 1970–2002: An examination of recent trends. *American Journal of Public Health, 96*(10), 1744–1751.

Mehlum, L., Friis, S., Vaglum, P., & Karterud, S. (1994). The longitudinal pattern of suicidal behaviour in borderline personality disorder: A prospective follow-up study. *Acta Psychiatrica Scandinavica, 90*(2), 124–130.

Miller, M., Lippmann, S. J., Azrael, D., & Hemenway, D. (2007). Household firearm ownership and rates of suicide across the 50 United States. *The Journal of Trauma, 62*(4), 1034–1035.

Möller-Leimkühler, A. M. (2003). The gender gap in suicide and premature death or: Why are men so vulnerable? *European Archives of Psychiatry & Clinical Neuroscience, 253*(1), 1–8.

Möller-Leimkühler, A. M. (2002). Barriers to help seeking by men: A review of sociocultural and clinical literature with particular reference to depression. *Journal of Affective Disorders, 71*, 1–9.

Monti, K., Cedereke, M., & Ojehagen, A. (2003). Treatment attendance and suicidal behavior 1 month and 3 months after a suicide attempt: A comparison between two samples. *Archives of Suicide Research, 7*(2), 167–174.

Moscicki, E. K., O'Carroll, P., Rae, D. S., Locke, B. Z., Roy, A., & Regier, D. A. (1988). Suicide attempts in the Epidemiologic Catchment Area Study. *Yale Journal of Biology & Medicine, 61*, 259–268.

Mukamal, K. J., Kawachi, I., Miller, M., & Rimm, E. B. (2007). Drinking frequency and quantity and risk of suicide among men. *Social Psychiatry & Psychiatric Epidemiology, 42*(2), 153–160.

NHS Executive. (1998). *National survey of NHS patients, general practice.* London: TSO.

Nock, M. K., Borges, G., Bromet, E. J., Alonso, J., Angermeyer, M., Beautrais, A., et al. (2008). Cross-national prevalence and risk factors for suicidal ideation, plans and attempts. *British Journal of Psychiatry, 192*(2), 98–105.

Nordstrom, P., Asberg, M., Aber-Wistedt, A., & Nordin, C. (1995). Attempted suicide predicts suicide risk in mood disorders. *Acta Psychiatrica Scandinavica, 92*, 345–350.

O'Brien, G., Holton, A., Hurren, K., Wyatt, L., & Hassanyeh, F. (1987). Deliberate self-harm and predictors of outpatient attendance. *British Journal of Psychiatry, 150*, 246–247.

Oquendo, M. A., Bongiovi-Garcia, M. E., Galfalvy, H., Goldberg, P. H., Grunebaum, M. F., Burke, A. K., et al. (2007). Sex differences in clinical predictors of suicidal acts after major depression: A prospective study. *American Journal of Psychiatry, 164*(1), 134–141.

Owens, C., Lambert, H., Donovan, J., & Lloyd, K. R. (2005). A qualitative study of help-seeking and primary care consultation prior to suicide. *The British Journal of*

General Practice: The Journal of the Royal College of General Practitioners, 55(516), 503–509.

Pirkis, J., Burgess, P., & Dunt, D. (2000). Suicidal ideation and suicide attempts among Australian adults. *Crisis: The Journal of Crisis Intervention & Suicide Prevention, 21*(1), 16–25.

Reulbach, U., Biermann, T., Markovic, K., Kornhuber, J., & Bleich, S. (2007). The myth of the birthday blues: A population-based study about the association between birthday and suicide. *Comprehensive Psychiatry, 48*(6), 554–557.

Robins, L. N., & Regier, D. A. (1991). *Psychiatric disorders in America: The epidemiologic catchment area study*. New York: Free Press.

Roy, A. (1993). Genetic and biological risk factors for suicide in depressive disorders. *Psychiatric Quarterly, 64,* 345–358.

Rudd, M. D., Mandrusiak, M., & Joiner, T. E. (2006). The case against no-suicide contracts: The commitment to treatment statement as a practice alternative. *Journal of Clinical Psychology, 62*(2), 243–251.

Sabo, A. N., Gunderson, J. G., Najavits, L. M., Chauncey, D., & Kisiel, C. (1995). Changes in self-destructiveness of borderline patients in psychotherapy. A prospective follow-up. *Journal of Nervous and Mental Disease, 183*(6), 337–376.

Sadavoy, J., Meier, R., Ong, A., & Yuk, M. (2004). Barriers to access to mental health services for ethnic seniors: The Toronto study. *Canadian Journal of Psychiatry, 49*(3), 192–199.

Sanden, I., Larsson, U. S., & Eriksson, C. (2000). An interview study of men discovering testicular cancer. *Cancer Nursing, 23*(4), 304–309.

Schmidtke, A., Bille-Brahe, U., Deleo, D., Kerkhof, A., Bjerke, T., Crepef, P., et al. (1996). Attempted suicide in Europe: Rates, trends and sociodemographic characteristics of suicide attempters during the period 1989–1992. Results of the WHO/EURO Multicentre Study on Parasuicide. *Acta Psychiatrica Scandinavica, 93*(5), 327–338.

Schneider, B., Philipp, M., & Muller, M. J. (2001). Psychopathological predictors of suicide in patients with major depression during a 5-year follow-up. *European Psychiatry, 16,* 283–288.

Scocco, P., Marietta, P., Tonietto, M., & Buono, M. D. (2000). The role of psychopathology and suicidal intention in predicting suicide risk: A longitudinal study. *Psychopathology, 33,* 143–150.

Shah, A. (2007). The relationship between suicide rates and age: an analysis of multinational data from the World Health Organization. *International Psychogeriatrics, 19*(6), 1141–1152.

Shah, A. J., & De, T. (1998). Suicide and the elderly. *International Journal of Psychiatry in Clinical Practice, 2,* 3–17.

Sharpe, S., & Arnold, S. (1998). *Men, lifestyle and health: A study of health beliefs and practices.* Swindon, UK: ESRC.

Shenassa, E. D., Rogers, M. L., Spalding, K. L., & Roberts, M. B. (2004). Safer storage of firearms at home and risk of suicide: A study of protective factors in a nationally representative sample. *Journal of Epidemiology and Community Health, 58*(10), 841–848.

Sidley, G. L., Calam, R., Wells, A., Hughes, T., & Whitaker, K. (1999). The prediction of parasuicide repetition in a high-risk group. *British Journal of Clinical Psychology, 38,* 375–386.

Skogman, K., Alsen, M., & Ojehagen, A. (2004). Sex differences in risk factors for suicide after attempted suicide-a follow-up study of 1052 suicide attempters. *Social Psychiatry & Psychiatric Epidemiology, 39*(2), 113–120.

Snowden, L., Masland, M., & Guerrero, R. (2003). *Ethnic access to public mental health services in California.* Berkeley: University of California, California Policy Research Center, Program on Access to Care.

Stark, C., Belbin, A., Hopkins, P., Gibbs, D., Hay, A., & Gunnell, D. (2006). Male suicide and occupation in Scotland. *Health Statistics Quarterly, 29,* 26–29.

Statham, D. J., Heath, A. C., Madden, P. A., Bucholz, K. K., Bierut, L., Dinwiddie, S. H., et al. (1998). Suicidal behaviour: An epidemiological and genetic study. *Psychological Medicine, 28,* 839–855.

Strug, D., & Mason, S. (2001). Social service needs of Hispanic immigrants: An exploratory study of the Washington Heights community. *Journal of Ethnic & Cultural Diversity in Social Work, 10*(3), 69–88.

Substance Abuse and Mental Health Services Administration [SAMHSA]. (2007). Preliminary Results from the 1997 National Household Survey on Drug Abuse. Retrieved April 10 2007, from http://www.oas.samhsa.gov/nhsda/nhsda97/toc.htm

Suokas, J., & Lonnqvist, J. (1991). Outcome of attempted suicide and psychiatric consultation: Risk factors and suicide mortality during a five-year follow-up. *Acta Psychiatrica Scandinavica, 84*(6), 545–549.

Suominen, K., Isometsa, E., Haukka, J., & Lonnqvist, J. (2004). Substance use and male gender as risk factors for deaths and suicide—a 5-year follow-up study after deliberate self-harm. *Social Psychiatry & Psychiatric Epidemiology, 39*(9), 720–724.

Taylor, G. J., Ryan, D., & Bagby, R. M. (1985). Toward the development of a new self-report alexithymia scale. *Psychotherapy and Psychosomatics, 44,* 191–199.

Thobaben, M. (2000). Myths & facts . . . about suicide. *Nursing, 30*(10), 73.

Tidemalm, D., Elofsson, S., Stefansson, C., Waern, M., & Runeson, B. (2005). Predictors of suicide in a community-based cohort of individuals with severe mental disorder. *Social Psychiatry & Psychiatric Epidemiology, 40*(8), 595–600.

U.S. Department of Health and Human Services. (2001). Summary of national strategy for suicide prevention: goals and objectives for action [National Strategy for Suicide Prevention Web site]. Retrieved June 10, 2008, from http://mentalhealth.samhsa.gov/suicideprevention/strategy.asp

Vega, W., & Rumbaut, R. G. (1991). Ethnic minorities and mental health. *Annual Review of Sociology, 17,* 351–383.

Voracek, M., Tran, U. S., & Sonneck, G. (2007). Facts and myths about seasonal variation in suicide. *Psychological Reports, 100*(3, Pt 1), 810–814.

Wasserman, D., & Cullberg, J. (1989). Early separation and suicidal behaviors in the parental homes of 40 consecutive suicide attempters. *Acta Psychiatrica Scandinavica, 79,* 296–302.

Wells, K. B., Golding, J. M., Hough, R. L., Burnam, M. A., & Karno, M. (1988). Factors affecting the probability of use of general and medical health and social/community services for Mexican Americans and non-Hispanic Whites. *Medical Care, 26,* 441–452.

Woodbury, M. A., Manton, K. G., & Blazer, D. (1988). Trends in US suicide mortality rates 1968 to 1982: Race and sex differences in age, period and cohort components. *International Journal of Epidemiology, 17*(2), 356–362.

11　Older Adult Suicide

Currently, older adults (those age 65 and older), often referred to as the elderly, have the highest rate of suicide in the United States. It is important to understand the epidemiological trends, prevalence, and incident rates of elderly suicidality. In order to improve existing prevention and intervention efforts, identification of risk and protective factors unique to the aging population is essential. These factors are highlighted in this chapter. In addition, this chapter deconstructs myths and misconceptions related to suicide among the elderly. A brief overview of empirically grounded strategies for effective assessment and treatment of this population also is provided.

■ Goals and Objectives of This Chapter

An understanding of:

- Older adult suicide risk
- Epidemiology of older adult suicidality
- Older adult rates of completed suicide and attempted suicide
- Deconstructing the dominant myths and misconceptions of older adult suicidality
- Professional bias in working with older adults
- Psychiatric risk factors for elderly suicide
- Sociodemographic risk factors for elderly suicide
- Psychiatric protective factors for elderly suicide

■ Sociodemographic protective factors for elderly suicide
■ The relationship between physical health and suicide among the aging

---

INTRODUCTION

Elderly people in the United States account for 13% of the population but 18% of suicides (Arias, Anderson, Kung, Murphy, & Kochanek, 2003). Of all age groups, the elderly are the most likely to die from a suicide attempt (Pearson & Conwell, 1995). The elderly have a higher rate of suicide, most probably because life circumstances such as living alone and poor health status leads to more fatal outcomes (Szanto et al., 2002). Additionally, attempts among the elderly are well-planned and generally involve highly lethal methods, leading to a high rate of success (Szanto et al., 2002).

Despite the high success rate and high lethality associated with suicide among the elderly, 40% to 70% of adults aged 65 and over communicated a wish to die to a health professional in the year prior to suicide (Conwell & Duberstein, 2001; Juurlink, Herrmann, Szalai, Kopp, & Redelmeier, 2004; Krach, 1998; Luoma & Pearson, 2002; Waern, Beskow, Runeson, & Skoog, 1999). Approximately 75% communicated suicidal ideation to a family member or acquaintance in the year prior to death (Waern et al., 1999). Only 8% denied suicidal ideation when asked (Waern et al., 1999).

It is alarming that even though the majority of elderly individuals who are considering suicide express such ideation, the completion rate of suicide among the elderly remains the highest of all age groups. What accounts for this discrepancy? Are elderly individuals not taken seriously when they express such ideation? Some have noted that thoughts of death are expected of older adults, and therefore, when they communicate thoughts of dying they go unrecognized as suicidal ideation and are inaccurately characterized as "typical of an old person." It is essential to be aware of the biases, stereotypes, and misconceptions that one may hold that may interfere with the accurate identification of an elderly adult at risk for suicidal behavior.

■ **Individual Exercise 11.1**

1. Do you believe that thoughts of death are common among the elderly? Why or why not?

2. Is it a natural part of the aging process to contemplate one's own death? In what way?
3. How may your responses to questions 1 and 2 impact your ability to accurately identify risk of suicide in elderly clients with whom you may work?

■ Small Group Exercise 11.1

In a small group of two or three, please discuss, as you are comfortable, your responses to individual exercise 11.1. Remember, answers are personal, and there are no correct or incorrect answers.

1. What were the response similarities in your group?
2. What were the response differences in your group?
3. Did you find any surprises in the group discussion? If so, what were they, and how were you surprised?

STATISTICS, EPIDEMIOLOGY, AND TRENDS IN OLDER ADULTS SUICIDE

Approximately every 90 minutes, an older adult (anyone 65 years of age and older) completes suicide (Hart-Hester, 2003). The highest at-risk group for suicide is older adults. In general, suicide rates in the United States are 10.9 per 100,000 people (Centers for Disease Control and Prevention, 2006). Suicide rates for older adults have been declining in the past 15 years, from a peak in 1987 of 21.7 per 100,000 to 15.6 per 100,000 in 2002 (McKeown, Cuffe, & Schulz, 2006). Despite a slight closing in the gap across age groups, older adults have consistently recorded the highest suicide rate. As mentioned earlier in the chapter, adults older than 65 years of age were 13% of the U.S. population in 1998 but accounted for 18% of all suicide deaths (Arias et al., 2003).

Older males, more than older females, and older Whites, more than older Blacks, are at higher risk. White male suicide risk continues to rise with age; however, female and Black adult suicide risk peaks around midlife and gradually lessens in older age. In addition, persons over the age of 85 have a higher suicide risk than those 65 to 85 years of age (Holkup, 2003; McKeown et al., 2006).

In contrast to the higher suicide completion rates in older adults, suicide attempts are lower in comparison to other demographic age groups. Rates of suicide attempts decline with age, and older adults have the lowest rates of attempted suicide (Doshi, Boudreaux, Wang, Pelletier, & Camargo, 2005) and nonfatal injuries (Hempstead, 2006).

In older adults violent methods are the most prevalent from of suicide (Conwell, Rotenberg, & Caine, 1990). Although methods of suicide vary depending on the country and culture, in the United States firearms are most common for both older males and females (Ojima, Nakamura, & Detels, 2004). Following firearms, males are next most likely to suicide by hanging. Females most often suicide using drugs (Ojima et al., 2004).

RISK AND PROTECTIVE FACTORS AMONG THE ELDERLY

Risk Factors For Suicide

Assessing for suicide risk among the elderly population is complicated by several factors:

1. Communications of possible suicidal intent or ideation are often unheard or misunderstood. It is assumed that the elderly are preoccupied with death and dying, so statements of passive suicidal ideation, such as "I have nothing to look forward to," are often not interpreted as suicidal statements (Conwell et al., 1998).
2. The elderly have greater intent and are more likely to take precautions against discovery (Conwell et al., 1998).
3. It is difficult to detect depression in this age group because vegetative symptoms of depression can overlap with many physical illnesses prevalent among the elderly and because the elderly tend to make somatic complaints and minimize their psychological distress (Conwell et al., 1998).

However, although a history of suicide attempts is the strongest predictor of suicidality among adults, it is noteworthy that only 20% of elderly who commit suicide have a prior history of suicide attempts (Rubenowtiz, Waern, Wilhelmmson, & Allebeck, 2001). This indicates that 80% of the elderly will not meet the criteria for suicide risk based on the strongest known risk factor for adults. Furthermore, it is estimated that, on average, 85% of elderly suicide completers have at least one diagnosed mental disorder, most frequently depression (Beautrais, 2002; Conwell, 1996; Harwood, Hawton, Hope, & Jacoby, 2001; Quan, Arboleda-Florez, Fick, Stuart, & Love, 2002; Suominen, Isometsa, & Lonnqvist, 2004; Waern, et al., 2002). This indicates that approximately 15% of suicide completers in this age group have no diagnosable disorder. Therefore, it is imperative to consider the other factors that play a role in conferring suicide risk in this age group.

Bereavement is a major risk factor for suicide among the elderly (Carney, Rich, Burke, & Fowler, 1994; Conwell et al., 1990; Isometsa et al., 1995). Within the elderly, the group with the highest rate of suicide is bereaved men. The suicide risk is highest within the first year postloss but remains elevated for as long as five years. Furthermore, the risk is higher among those experiencing complicated or traumatic grief (Szanto et al., 2002).

Other risk factors for suicide among the elderly include difficulty adjusting to physical, emotional, and social change (Clark, 1995a). Financial and legal difficulties as well as changes in employment status also confer risk (Beautrais, 2002; Carney et al., 1994; Isometsa et al., 1995; Rubenowtiz et al., 2001).

Social isolation has been demonstrated to be a risk factor for suicide among the elderly. Social isolation in this case refers to more than just living alone but also includes having limited contact with extended family members and peers (Barraclough, 1971; Beautrais, 2002; Duberstein, Conwell, Conner, Eberly, & Caine, 2004; Miller, 1978; Rubenowtiz et al., 2001; Turvey et al., 2002). Functional impairment in regard to the ability to complete activities of daily living is also associated with increased suicide risk (Conwell et al., 2000; Rubenowtiz et al., 2001).

Several sociodemographic characteristics are associated with increased suicide risk among the elderly. Male gender, Caucasian ethnicity, and being a widower are the strongest known sociodemographic risk factors (Conwell, 2001).

Elderly Risk Factors For Suicide

- Difficulty adjusting to health status
- Recent emotional and/or social change
- Financial difficulties
- Legal difficulties
- Change in employment status
- Social isolation
- Functional impairment
- Bereavement
- Complicated or traumatic grief
- Male gender
- Older age
- Caucasian ethnicity

Protective Factors Against Suicide

Several protective factors against suicidal behavior among the elderly have been identified. Being more extroverted and open to new experiences (Kelly et al., 1998) is among the leading protective factors against suicide. Higher levels of self-care functioning are also associated with decreased suicide risk (Ross, Bernstein, Trent, Henderson, & Paganini-Hill, 1990).

Having children (Rubenowtiz et al., 2001; Waern et al., 2002) and having positive social support networks are other strong protective factors against suicide (Turvey et al., 2002). Elderly individuals who are engaged in hobbies and social organizations are at decreased risk for suicidal behavior (Rubenowtiz et al., 2001; Waern et al., 2002). Overall, perceived meaning in life, life satisfaction, adaptive coping, and a lack of hopelessness have been identified as protective factors against the elderly.

Lastly, degree of religious commitment appears to protect against suicide in the elderly (Heisel, 2006), as does female gender and a non-Caucasian ethnicity (Conwell, 2001). See chapters 2 and 3 for an in-depth review of the relationship between religion, culture, and suicide.

Elderly Protective Factors Against Suicide

- Being extroverted and open to new experiences
- Self-health care
- Having children
- Positive social support networks
- Engaged in activities (hobbies, organizations)
- Religious commitment
- Gender
- Perceived meaning in life
- Life satisfaction
- Adaptive coping
- Lack of hopelessness

▣ Individual Exercise 11.2

You are a mental health clinician in a family practice clinic. Your next client has been referred by one of the medical doctors in the clinic. Henry is a 73-year-old man who presented to the MD with complaints of body aches, exhaustion, and "just not feeling like he used to." After a brief screening, the MD concluded that a mental health evaluation to assess for depression may be appropriate.

During your meeting you learn that Henry has recently been widowed. His wife of 52 years was his best friend. She died after a complicated medical illness. Consider the following questions:

1. Is this man at risk of engaging in suicidal behavior? On what do you base your answer?
2. What risk factors will you assess for during your interview with the client?
3. What protective factors will you assess for during your interview with the client?
4. What factors need to be considered in order to establish an effective treatment plan?

■ Role Play 11.1

Using the scenario from individual exercise 11.1, break into pairs and assume the role of the mental health clinician and the client. Engage in a role play in which you would assess for risk and protective factors for suicide.

MYTHS AND MISCONCEPTIONS ABOUT ELDERLY SUICIDE

Similar to other age groups, there are a number of myths and misconceptions associated with older adults and suicidality. Unfortunately, misconceptions held by mental health professionals may exert unfortunate clinical implications when assessing and treating individuals within this demographic population. Five myths and misconceptions related to older adults and suicide include:

1. *Older adults rarely suicide.* Although many individuals may believe that older adults are not as likely to complete suicide as younger demographic groups, the reality is that older adults are statistically at the highest risk of completing suicide (McKeown et al., 2006). Individuals over 65 years of age have the highest suicide rate.
2. *Deliberate self-harm is as common in older adults as in younger adults.* Research has found that older adults are less likely to attempt suicide than other age groups (Doshi et al., 2005). In addition, rates of nonfatal injury decline with age (Hempstead, 2006). Although attempts and self-harm rates are lower, suicidal intent is often high (Hawton, 2005). Consequently, mental health professionals need to be extra vigilant regarding assessing for and treating suicidality in older adults who present following a self-harming episode.

3. *Suicide and depression is harder to recognize in older patients result-ing in less treatment.* In a study that investigated detection of suicide and depression in adults versus elderly adults, physicians overwhelm-ingly were able to detect both the depression and suicidal ideation (Uncapher & Arean, 2000). However, findings indicated that primary care physicians were willing to treat geriatric suicidal ideation but not to the extent that they are willing to treat suicide ideation in younger adults (Uncapher & Arean, 2000). It has been suggested that health care professionals may be more likely to accept suicidal thoughts, ideations, and ideas in older adults than in other age groups and, therefore, be less likely to promote treatment of underlying problems (Barnow & Linden, 2000).

4. *Health care and mental health professionals cannot help older adults who are suicidal.* A common belief is that older adults do not access health care and mental health professionals. It is estimated that be-tween 40% to 70% of elderly people who completed suicide had seen a health professional in the month before their suicide (Conwell & Duberstein, 2001; Juurlink et al., 2004; Krach, 1998; Luoma & Pear-son, 2002; Waern et al., 1999).

5. *Older adults are likely to receive the same health and mental health care as everyone else.* There appears to be a recognized bias among health care and mental health professionals in treating older individ-uals. Specifically, in comparison to younger patients, older patients were less likely to be referred for psychiatric consultation, and past psychiatric history and suicidal ideation were assessed less (Grant, 1996; Harwood, Hawton, Hope, & Jacoby, 2000; Hillerbrand & Shaw, 1990). In addition, mental health clinicians reportedly hold negative views toward working with older patients, such as the belief that it may be a waste of time, energy, and money (Lagana & Shanks, 2002).

PHYSICAL ILLNESS AND SUICIDE AMONG THE ELDERLY

Physical illness, particularly visual impairment, seizure disorders, can-cer, arthritis, chronic pulmonary disease, and moderate to severe pain, increases suicide risk in the elderly (Juurlink et al., 2004; Quan et al., 2002; Waern et al., 2002). Waern and colleagues (2002) examined the association between suicidality in later life and physical illness and found that suicide risk among physically ill elderly was elevated only among men, yet not among women.

In addition to actual physical health status, perceived physical health is a major risk factor for suicide among the elderly (Duberstein et al., 2004; Turvey et al., 2002). Furthermore, among older adults, depression and comorbid medical conditions are highly associated (Alexopoulos, Bruce, Hull, Sirey, & Kakuma, 1999; Conner, Duberstein, Conwell, Seidlitz, & Caine, 2001; Conwell, Duberstein, & Caine, 2002; Miles, 1977; Pearson & Brown, 2000; Turvey et al., 2002). Conwell et al. (2000) found that once depression was controlled for, the effect of physical illness burden and functional impairment on suicide risk among the elderly was dramatically reduced.

However, it is important to note that most elderly who commit suicide are not terminally ill at time of death (Barraclough, 1971; Clark, 1995b; Filiberti et al., 2001). In fact, studies have found that serious medical illness is present in rates as low as 2% to 4% of elderly suicides (Szanto et al., 2002).

INTERVENTIONS WITH THE ELDERLY

Research and clinical practice have demonstrated effective methods in intervening successfully with older adults. Someone's age should not be a criterion for a mental health clinician's willingness to effectively assess and treat an individual presenting with suicidality. Like other age groups, older adults manage a number of risk factors that can increase the risk of suicide. Each individual, specifically those in the most at-risk group—older adults—requires the same professionalism and dedication to mental health care.

Any older adult who is at risk of suicide, has attempted suicide, or is in need of crisis management should be brought to a hospital emergency department for complete psychiatric assessment. For all at-risk adults, effective assessment and management requires mental health clinicians to establish and maintain a therapeutic alliance, attend to the individual's safety, determine a treatment setting, develop a plan of treatment, and coordinate and collaborate care with other professionals (American Psychiatric Association, 2003). The most common approaches to intervention in working with older adults include crisis management, psychosocial evidence-based practice (EBP) interventions, **cognitive-behavioral therapy (CBT), dialectical behavior therapy (DBT), interpersonal psychotherapy (IPT),** and psychopharmacology. These approaches are reviewed in Part II of this text.

SUMMARY

The older the adult, the greater the suicide risk. However, it is not uncommon for professionals to provide a lower standard of care and service to this older population. If prevention of suicide is a goal of mental health clinical work, than the age of the client should not influence our—your—effectiveness. Like children, adolescents, or adults, older adults at risk require evidence-based interventions that have been proven effective to address their suicidality. It is critical to be aware of the factors that contribute to suicide in this group in order to design effective suicide prevention and intervention programs and to effectively assess for suicide risk in the elderly. It is equally important to be aware of the factors that protect against suicide in this group in order to support and enhance these qualities in an effort to reduce suicide rates.

■ Key Points

1. Older adults are at highest suicide risk of any age group.
2. Male gender, Caucasian ethnicity, and being a widower are the strongest known sociodemographic risk factors for suicide in later life.
3. Professionals tend to be less willing to treat older adults, even when effectively assessing for risk.
4. Older adults are less likely to attempt suicide than other age groups.
5. Generally older adults do not have the same access to and receive the same level of mental health care.
6. Of all age groups, the elderly are the most likely to die from a suicide attempt.
7. Having a positive social support network is a protective factor against suicide in later life.
8. Elderly individuals who are engaged in activities such as hobbies and/or social organizations are at decreased risk for suicidal behavior.
9. Bereavement is a major risk factor for suicide among the elderly.
10. Social support is a protective factor against suicide in later life.

FURTHER READINGS

Baker, F. M. (1994). Suicide among ethnic minority elderly: A statistical and psychosocial perspective. *Journal of Geriatric Psychiatry, 27*(2), 241–264.

Barnow, S., & Linden, M. (2000). Epidemiology and psychiatric morbidity of suicidal ideation among the elderly. *The Journal of Crisis Intervention and Suicide Prevention, 21*(4), 171–180.

Beautrais, A. (2002). A case control study of suicide and attempted suicide in older adults. *Suicide & Life-Threatening Behavior, 32*, 1–9.

Cattell, H., & Jolley, D. J. (1995). One hundred cases of suicide in elderly people. *British Journal of Psychiatry—Supplementum, 166*, 451–457.

Chima, F. O. (2002). Elderly suicidality: Human behavior and social environment perspective. *Journal of Human Behavior in the Social Environment, 6*(4), 21–46.

Chong, A. M. (2007). Promoting the psychosocial health of the elderly—The role of social workers. *Social Work in Health Care, 44*(1–2), 91–109.

Conwell, Y. (1995). Suicide among the elderly people. *Psychiatric Services, 46*, 563–564.

Conwell, Y., & Duberstein, P. R. (2001). Suicide in elders. In H. Hendin & J. J. Mann (Eds.), *The clinical science of suicide prevention* (pp. 132–150). New York: New York Academy of Sciences.

Duberstein, P. R., Conwell, Y., & Cox, C. (1998). Suicide in widowed persons: A psychological autopsy comparison of recently and remotely bereaved older subjects. *American Journal of Geriatric Psychiatry, 6*, 328–334.

Goldney, R. D., & Harrison, J. (1998). Suicide in the elderly: Some good news. *Australian Journal of Aging, 17*, 54–55.

Hawton, K., & Harriss, L. (2006). Deliberate self-harm in people aged 60 years and over: Characteristics and outcome of a 20-year cohort. *International Journal of Geriatric Psychiatry, 21*(6), 572–581.

Holkup, P. A. (2003). Evidence-based protocol elderly suicide—secondary prevention. *Journal of Gerontological Nursing, 29*(6), 6–17.

Kalichman, S. C., Heckman, T., Kochman, A., Sikkema, K., & Bergholte, J. (2000). Depression and thoughts of suicide among middle-aged and older persons living with HIV-AIDS. *Psychiatric Services, 51*, 903–907.

Prosser, J. M., Perrone, J., & Pines, J. M. (2007). The epidemiology of intentional non-fatal self-harm poisoning in the United States: 2001–2004. *Journal of Medical Toxicology: Official Journal of the American College of Medical Toxicology, 3*(1), 20–24.

Rubenowtiz, E., Waern, M., Wilhelmmson, K., & Allebeck, P. (2001). Life events and psychosocial factors in elderly suicides—A case control study. *Psychological Medicine, 31*, 1193–1202.

Shah, A. (2007). The relationship between suicide rates and age: An analysis of multinational data from the World Health Organization. *International Psychogeriatrics, 19*(6), 1141–1152.

Tueth, M. J., & Zuberi, P. (1999). Life-threatening psychiatric emergencies in the elderly: Overview. *Journal of Geriatric Psychiatry and Neurology, 12*(2), 60–66.

ELECTRONIC RESOURCES

American Foundation for Suicide Prevention: http://www.afsp.org
National Alliance on Mental Illness: http://www.nami.org
National Strategy for Suicide Prevention: http://www.mentalhealth.org/suicideprevention/elderly.asp
Samaritans: http://www.samaritans.org
Suicide Prevention Action Network USA: http://www.span.org
Suicide Prevention, Awareness, and Support: http://www.suicide.org
ULifeline: http://www.ulifeline.org

■ Knowledge Acquisition Test

True or False

1. Generally, older adults' risk of suicide decreases after age 65.
2. Older adults receive more access to mental health care than younger populations.
3. There appears to be a recognized bias in health care and mental health professionals in treating older individuals.
4. The majority of older adults experiencing suicidality do not seek out professional help.
5. The percentage of older adult suicides is lower than their population percentage.
6. Suicide attempt is a leading risk factor for suicide among the elderly.
7. Being male is a risk factor for suicidal behavior later in life.
8. Most elderly who commit suicide are seriously medically ill at the time of death.
9. More often than not, the elderly communicate suicidal ideations.

Short Answer

10. What are the clinical implications of the differences between higher rates of completed suicide and lower rates of suicide attempts for older adults?
11. Describe the common bias of health and mental health professionals in working with older adults.
12. Why is assessing for suicide risk among the elderly difficult?
13. What is the main difference in risk factors for suicide between adults and the elderly?
14. What are the main protective factors against suicidality among the elderly?
15. Describe the relationship between physical illness, depression, and suicide among the elderly.

Multiple Choice

16. Every _____ hours an older adult (65+ years of age) completes suicide.
    A. 24 hours
    B. 18 hours
    C. 12 hours
    D. 6 hours
    E. 1.5 hours
    F. None of the above
17. Common method(s) of suicide for older adults include:
    A. Firearms
    B. Hanging
    C. Overdose
    D. All of the above
    E. None of the above

18. When seeing older adults, health and mental health professionals are:
    A. More likely to be offer treatment
    B. More willing to treat geriatric suicidal ideation
    C. More likely to accept suicidal thoughts, ideations, and ideas in older adults than in other age groups
    D. All of the above
    E. None of the above

19. Which of the following is a major risk factor for late-life suicide?
    A. Social isolation
    B. Functional impairment
    C. Recent social changes
    D. Bereavement
    E. All of the above
    F. None of the above

20. Which of the following is not a protective factor against suicide among the elderly?
    A. Having children
    B. Having an extroverted personality
    C. Being engaged in hobbies
    D. High levels of education
    E. All of the above
    F. None of the above

Answer key is available in the Instructor's Manual; qualified instructors may e-mail textbook@springerpub.com *to request a copy.*

REFERENCES

Alexopoulos, G. S., Bruce, M. L., Hull, J., Sirey, J. A., & Kakuma, T. (1999). Clinical determinants of suicidal ideation and behavior in geriatric depression. *Archives of General Psychiatry, 56*(11), 1048–1053.

American Psychiatric Association. (2003). Assessing and treating suicidal behaviors: A quick reference guide. Retrieved July 5, 2008, from http://www.psychiatryonline.com/pracGuide/loadPracQuickRefPdf.aspx?file=Suibehavs_QRG

Arias, E., Anderson, R. N., Kung, H. C., Murphy, S. L., & Kochanek, K. D. (2003). Deaths: Final data for 2001. *National Vital Statistics Reports, 52*(3), 1–115.

Barnow, S., & Linden, M. (2000). Epidemiology and psychiatric morbidity of suicidal ideation among the elderly. *The Journal of Crisis Intervention and Suicide Prevention, 21*(4), 171–180.

Barraclough, B. M. (1971). Suicide in the elderly: Recent developments in psychogeriatrics. *British Journal of Psychiatry, 6*(Suppl), 87–97.

Beautrais, A. (2002). A case control study of suicide and attempted suicide in older adults. *Suicide & Life-Threatening Behavior, 32*, 1–9.

Carney, S. S., Rich, C. L., Burke, P. A., & Fowler, R. C. (1994). Suicide over 60: The San Diego study. *Journal of Geriatric Psychiatry, 3*, 251–261.

Centers for Disease Control and Prevention. (2006). National center for injury prevention and control. Retrieved July 18, 2008, from http://www.cdc.gov/ncipc/wisqars

Clark, S. (1995a). *After suicide: Help for the bereaved*. Melbourne: Hill of Content Publishing Company.

Clark, S. (1995b). Grief reactions and recovery in a support group for people bereaved by suicide. *Crisis: The Journal of Crisis Intervention & Suicide Prevention, 16*(1), 27–33.

Conner, K. R., Duberstein, P. R., Conwell, Y., Seidlitz, L., & Caine, E. D. (2001). Psychological vulnerability to completed suicide: A review of empirical studies. *Suicide & Life-Threatening Behavior, 31,* 367–385.

Conwell, Y. (1996). *Diagnosis and treatment of depression in late life*. Washington, DC: American Psychiatric Press.

Conwell, Y. (2001). Suicide in later life: A review and recommendations for prevention. *Suicide & Life-Threatening Behavior, 31*(Suppl), 32–47.

Conwell, Y., & Duberstein, P. R. (2001). Suicide in elders. In H. Hendin & J. J. Mann (Eds.), *The clinical science of suicide prevention* (pp. 132–150). New York: New York Academy of Sciences.

Conwell, Y., Duberstein, P. R., & Caine, E. D. (2002). Risk factors for suicide in later life. *Biological Psychiatry, 52,* 193–204.

Conwell, Y., Duberstein, P. R., Cox, C., Hermann, J. M., Forbes, N., & Caine, E. D. (1998). Age differences in behaviors leading to completed suicide. *American Journal of Geriatric Psychiatry, 6*(2), 122–126.

Conwell, Y., Lyness, J. M., Duberstein, P., Cox, C., Seidlitz, L., DiGiorgio, A., et al. (2000). Completed suicide among older patients in primary care practices: A controlled study. *Journal of the American Geriatrics Society, 48,* 23–29.

Conwell, Y., Rotenberg, M., & Caine, E. D. (1990). Completed suicide at age 50 and over. *Journal of the American Geriatric Society, 38*(6), 640–644.

Doshi, A., Boudreaux, E. D., Wang, N., Pelletier, A. J., & Camargo, C. A. J. (2005). National study of US emergency department visits for attempted suicide and self-inflicted injury, 1997–2001. *Annals of Emergency Medicine, 46*(4), 369–375.

Duberstein, P. R., Conwell, Y., Conner, K. R., Eberly, S., & Caine, E. D. (2004). Suicide at 50 years of age and older: Perceived physical illness, family discord and financial strain. *Psychological Medicine, 34*(1), 137–146.

Filiberti, A., Ripamonti, C., Totis, A., Ventafridda, V., De Conno, F., Contiero, P., et al. (2001). Characteristics of terminal cancer patients who committed suicide during a home palliative care program. *Journal of Pain & Symptom Management, 22*(1), 544–553.

Grant, L. D. (1996). Effects of ageism on individual and health care providers' responses to healthy aging. *Health & Social Work, 21*(1), 9–15.

Hart-Hester, S. (2003). Elderly suicides: A need for prevention. *Journal of the Mississippi State Medical Association, 44*(6), 167–172.

Harwood, D. M., Hawton, K., Hope, T., & Jacoby, R. (2000). Suicide in older people: Mode of death, demographic factors, and medical contact before death. *International Journal of Geriatric Psychiatry, 15*(8), 736–743.

Harwood, D., Hawton, K., Hope, T., & Jacoby, R. (2001). Psychiatric disorder and personality factors associated with suicide in older people. *International Journal of Geriatric Psychiatry, 16*(2), 155–165.

Hawton, K. (2005). Psychosocial treatments following attempted suicide: Evidence to inform clinical practice. In K. Hawton (Ed.), *Prevention and treatment of suicidal behaviour* (pp. 197–220). Oxford: Oxford University Press.

Hempstead, K. (2006). The geography of self-injury: Spatial patterns in attempted and completed suicide. *Social Science & Medicine, 62*(12), 3186–3196.

Heisel, M. J. (2006). Suicide and its prevention among older adults. *Canadian Journal of Psychiatry—Revue Canadienne de Psychiatrie, 51*(3), 143–154.

Hillerbrand, E. T., & Shaw, D. (1990). Age bias in a general hospital: Is there ageism in psychiatric consultation? *Clinical Gerontologist, 2*(2), 3–13.

Holkup, P. A. (2003). Evidence-based protocol elderly suicide—secondary prevention. *Journal of Gerontological Nursing, 29*(6), 6–17.

Isometsa, E., Henrikksson, M., Marttunen, M., Heikkinen, M., Aro, H., Kuoppasalmi, K., et al. (1995). Mental disorders in young and middle aged men who commit suicide. *British Medical Journal, 310,* 1366–1367.

Juurlink, D. N., Herrmann, N., Szalai, J. P., Kopp, A., & Redelmeier, D. A. (2004). Medical illness and the risk of suicide in the elderly. *Archives of Internal Medicine, 164*(11), 1179–1184.

Kelly, B., Raphael, B., Judd, F., Perdices, M., Kernutt, G., Burnett, P., et al. (1998). Suicidal ideation, suicide attempts, and HIV infection. *Psychosomatics, 39*(5), 405–415.

Krach, P. (1998). Myths & facts . . . about suicide in the elderly. *Nursing, 28*(5), 17.

Lagana, L., & Shanks, S. (2002). Mutual biases underlying the problematic relationship between older adults and mental health providers: Any solution in sight? *International Journal of Aging & Human Development, 55*(3), 271–295.

Luoma, J. B., & Pearson, J. L. (2002). Suicide and marital status in the United States, 1991–1996: Is widowhood a risk factor? *American Journal of Public Health, 92,* 1518–1522.

McKeown, R. E., Cuffe, S. P., & Schulz, R. M. (2006). US suicide rates by age group, 1970–2002: An examination of recent trends. *American Journal of Public Health, 96*(10), 1744–1751.

Miles, C. P. (1977). Conditions predisposing to suicide: A review. *Journal of Nervous and Mental Disease, 164*(4), 231–246.

Miller, M. (1978). Geriatric suicide: The Arizona study. *Gerontologist, 18*(5 Pt 1), 488–495.

Ojima, T., Nakamura, Y., & Detels, R. (2004). Comparative study about methods of suicide between Japan and the United States. *Journal of Epidemiology, 14*(6), 187–192.

Pearson, J. L., & Brown, G. K. (2000). Suicide prevention in late life: Directions for science and practice. *Clinical Psychology Review, 20*(6), 685–705.

Pearson, J. L., & Conwell, Y. (1995). Suicide in late life: Challenges and opportunities for research. *International Psychogeriatrics, 7*(2), 131–136.

Quan, H., Arboleda-Florez, J., Fick, G. H., Stuart, H. L., & Love, E. J. (2002). Association between physical illness and suicide among the elderly. *Social Psychiatry & Psychiatric Epidemiology, 37*(4), 190–197.

Ross, R. K., Bernstein, L., Trent, L., Henderson, B. E., & Paganini-Hill, A. (1990). A prospective study of risk factors for traumatic death in the retirement community. *Preventive Medicine, 19*(3), 323–334.

Rubenowtiz, E., Waern, M., Wilhelmmson, K., & Allebeck, P. (2001). Life events and psychosocial factors in elderly suicides—A case control study. *Psychological Medicine, 31,* 1193–1202.

Suominen, K., Isometsa, E., & Lonnqvist, J. (2004). Elderly suicide attempters with depression are often diagnosed only after the attempt. *International Journal of Geriatric Psychiatry, 19*(1), 35–40.

Szanto, K., Gildengerrs, A., Mulsant, B. H., Brown, G., Alexopoulos, G. S., & Reynolds, C. F. (2002). Identification of suicide ideation and prevention of suicidal behaviour in the elderly. *Drugs & Aging, 19*(1), 11–24.

Turvey, C. L., Conwell, Y., Jones, M. P., Phillips, C., Simonsick, E., Pearson, J. L., et al. (2002). Risk factors for late-life suicide: A prospective, community based study. *American Journal of Geriatric Psychiatry, 10,* 398–406.

Uncapher, H., & Arean, P. A. (2000). Physicians are less willing to treat suicidal ideation in older patients. *Journal of the American Geriatrics Society, 48*(2), 188–192.

Waern, M., Beskow, J., Runeson, B., & Skoog, I. (1999). Suicidal feelings in the last year of life in elderly people who commit suicide. *Lancet, 354*(9182), 917–918.

Waern, M., Runeson, B. S., Allebeck, P., Beskow, J., Rubenowitz, E., Skoog, I., et al. (2002). Mental disorder in elderly suicides: A case-control study. *American Journal of Psychiatry, 159,* 450–455.

Suicide and Mental Illness

It is important to recognize that not everyone with a psychiatric illness is going to experience suicidality. However, 90% of individuals who complete suicide have a psychiatric diagnosis. Consequently, Part IV centers on suicide across three high-risk diagnostic categories. Although many psychiatric disorders are associated with an elevated risk of suicide attempts and completions, Part IV focuses specifically on psychotic disorders, mood disorders, and substance disorders.

Chapter 12, "Schizophrenia and Suicide," provides a focused presentation of the suicide risk associated with schizophrenia. Chapter 13, "Depression and Suicide," examines the relationship between depression and suicide, the most common psychiatric disorder associated with suicide. Chapter 14, "Substance Disorders and Suicide," explores the relationship between substance-related disorders and risk of suicidality.

Knowledge of the influence of psychiatric disorders is a critical component in the assessment of suicide risk and is fundamentally related to the treatment of suicidality. Mental health practitioners need to be aware of the interaction between psychiatric symptomatology, treatment, and adherence issues when working with a suicidal client.

12 Schizophrenia and Suicide

In this chapter, a focused review of the suicide risk associated with **schizophrenia** is provided. Special attention to suicide within schizophrenia is critical because the rate of suicide among individuals with schizophrenia is among the highest of all psychiatric illness, with 10%–15% of individuals with schizophrenia dying by suicide (Cohen, Test, & Brown, 1990; Siris, 2001), a rate 20 to 50 times higher than that in the general population (Pinikahana, Happell, & Keks, 2003). Furthermore, the rate of suicide with schizophrenia is increasing (Maris, Berman, & Silverman, 2000).

■ Goals and Objectives of This Chapter

An understanding of:

- *DSM* criteria for schizophrenia
- The course of illness of schizophrenia
- The etiology and epidemiology of schizophrenia
- The relationship between schizophrenia and suicide
- Risk factors for suicide unique to individuals with schizophrenia
- Protective factors for suicide unique to individuals with schizophrenia
- Evidence-based practices for schizophrenia

INTRODUCTION

Schizophrenia is a major public health issue that has devastating consequences for individuals, families, and society (Buchanan & Carpenter, 2000; Dyck, Hendryx, Short, Voss, & McFarlane, 2002; Foldemo, Gullberg, Ek, & Bogren, 2005; Wu et al., 2005). Characterized by grossly impaired reality testing, which may manifest as delusions, hallucinations, negative symptoms, highly disorganized behavior or disorganized speech, and impaired interpersonal relationships, schizophrenia has an approximate lifetime risk of 1% (Nylander & Gillberg, 2001). The onset of illness is earlier for males than for females, and approximately 90% of all individuals with schizophrenia are between the ages of 15 and 55. Schizophrenics represent about 16% of all psychiatric patients who receive treatment; however, less than 50% of individuals with schizophrenia will receive treatment. Unfortunately, among those who do receive treatment, the probability of relapse within the first 2 years following a hospitalization is estimated to be as high as 60%.

Stereotypes regarding individuals with schizophrenia pervade our society. Individuals with schizophrenia are often and unfairly portrayed as violent, scary, and dangerous. Research indicates that individuals with serious and persistent mental illness such as schizophrenia are no more likely to become violent than individuals in the general community who are not abusing alcohol or substances (Angermeyer, 2002), yet there remains extreme stigma associated with the diagnosis of schizophrenia. Clinicians need to become aware of their personal and professional beliefs and assumptions regarding schizophrenia. Without such awareness, it will be impossible to engage in a positive, effective therapeutic relationship with individuals with schizophrenia.

■ Individual Exercise 12.1

1. When you hear the word *schizophrenia,* what are the first words or thoughts that come to your mind? Write them down.
2. Are your listed words or thoughts generally positive or negative? Did they surprise you in any way? If so, how?
3. What personal *and* professional considerations and assumptions may make it hard for you to work with this population?
4. What personal *and* professional considerations may make it easy for you to work with this population?

DSM-IV-TR DIAGNOSIS

Currently, there are no physical or lab tests that can diagnose schizophrenia. However, physical testing can rule out other conditions that may have some overlapping symptomatology (i.e., seizure disorders, metabolic disorders, thyroid disease, brain tumors, drug abuse, etc.) as a means of narrowing down potential diagnoses. Diagnosis is generally established via psychiatric assessment using the *Diagnostic and Statistical Manual of Mental Disorders*, fourth edition, text revision (*DSM-IV-TR*; American Psychiatric Association [APA], 2000).

Schizophrenia and other psychotic disorders are serious and persistent mental illnesses (SPMI). These conditions comprise a number of specific criteria or psychotic symptoms, across a fixed timeframe, that are not accountable for other reasons. Psychotic symptoms are clustered as positive (e.g., hallucinations, delusions, disorganized speech) or negative (e.g., affective flattening, avolition, or lack of motivation).

According to the *DSM-IV-TR*, the diagnostic criteria for schizophrenia include two or more of the following symptoms (APA, 2000, p. 312):

- Delusions
- Hallucinations
- Disorganized speech
- Grossly disorganized or catatonic behavior
- Negative symptoms

In addition, these symptoms need to have led to social and/or occupational dysfunction in one or more areas of functioning (e.g., work, interpersonal relations, self-care). Signs of disturbance must be present for a minimum of 6 months, with at least 1 month of active symptoms. Finally, these symptoms or disturbances must not be a result of a **schizoaffective** or **mood disorder** diagnosis, substance-induced, due to a general medical condition, or related to a pervasive developmental disorder (APA, 2000).

Related conditions include **schizophreniform disorder** (which is the same as schizophrenia except that its duration is under 6 months, and it may result in less impairment in social/occupational functioning) and **brief psychotic disorder** (symptoms include positive psychotic symptoms with a duration under 1 month). Other psychotic conditions are schizoaffective disorder (similar symptoms as schizophrenia, plus either a major depressive, mixed, or manic episode during the same period of time), **delusional disorder** (nonbizarre fixed false beliefs, without any of the main diagnostic criteria for schizophrenia), **substance-induced psychosis** (predominant hallucinations or delusions resulting from the use of substances), and **psychosis not otherwise specified** (NOS; includes psychotic symptoms but lacks adequate information to make a specific diagnosis).

EPIDEMIOLOGY AND PROGNOSIS

The average age of onset for schizophrenia is between 15 and 25 years for males and 25 and 35 years for females (Hafner et al., 1994). The prevalence of schizophrenia for adults over the age of 18 years is 0.5% to 1.5%, and the annual incidence is 5 to 50 per 100,000 (APA, 2000). Although onset of psychotic conditions can emerge in youth, their presence in children is noticeably rarer. Schizophrenia in children under 15 years of age is less than 0.14 per 1,000 (Beitchman, 1985), with some general population studies estimating prevalence in onset before age 15 years to be between 1.6 and 1.9 per 100,000 (Burd & Kerbeshian, 1987; Gillberg, 1984; Gillberg & Steffenburg, 1987; Nylander & Gillberg, 2001). However, prevalence rates increase in adolescents, from 0.23% in 15 to 18 year olds (Nylander & Gillberg, 2001) to approximately 1% of the general population by the age of 18 years of age.

Although the nature of schizophrenia and other psychotic conditions is episodic, these disorders are generally chronic due to frequent episodic symptom relapses, readmission to hospital, and impaired social functioning (Eaton et al., 1992; Lay, Blanz, Hartmann, & Schmidt, 2000; Schmidt, Blanz, Dippe, Koppe, & Lay, 1995). The relapse rate for individuals with psychotic disorders ranges from 34% in 6 months to over 80% within 5 years (Geddes et al., 1994; Robinson et al., 1999a) and is a major challenge in the care and prognosis of patients (Geller et al., 2002; Robinson et al., 1999b; Rosenfarb et al., 2001). Consequently, individuals managing these conditions experience poor prognostic outcomes throughout their lives (Fleischhaker et al., 2005; Gillberg, Hellgren, & Gillberg, 1993; Remschmidt, Schulz, Martin, Warnke, & Trott, 1994; Ropcke & Eggers, 2005; Werry, McClellan, & Chard, 1991).

Prognosis is complicated by poor adherence to treatment recommendations (medication and psychosocial interventions), substance use, and negative family environment. Nonadherence rates among individuals diagnosed with schizophrenia range from 33% to 60% (Bergen, Hunt, Armitage, & Bashir, 1998; Gearing et al., 2009; Gerlach & Larsen, 1999; Lacro, Dunn, Dolder, Leckband, & Jeste, 2002; Perkins, 2002; Svedberg, Mesterton, & Cullberg, 2001). Nonadherence to medications in individuals with psychosis may result in greater symptom relapses with a six times increase of hospital readmission (Verdoux, Liraud, Assens, Abalan, & van Os, 2002; Verdoux et al., 2000). Use or abuse of substances can further result in poor adherence or trigger another psychotic episode (Bergen et al., 1998; Olfson et al., 2000; Perkins et al., 2008; Sullivan, Wells, Morgenstern, & Leake, 1995). Finally, family support has been generally associated with improved treatment compliance (Olfson et al., 2000; Prentice-Dunn, Wilson, & Lyman, 1981; Ran et al., 2003), and negative family environment, characterized by expressed emotion (EE; emotional over involvement and/or criticism and dissatisfaction), has been associated with relapse (Doane & Becker, 1993; Giron & Gomez-Beneyto, 1995; Lenior, Dingemans, Schene, Hart, & Linszen, 2002).

EE embodies family attitudes, usually negative, toward the illness and/or the individual (Lenior et al., 2002) and is generally operationalized as emotional overinvolvement and/or criticism and dissatisfaction (Lenior et al., 2002). This variable has been frequently attributed as a predictor of poor outcomes (Bebbington & Kuipers, 1994; Birchwood, Todd, & Jackson, 1998; Heinrichs, Bertram, Kuschel, & Hahlweg, 2005; Jackson, Smith, & McGorry, 1990; Lenior et al., 2002; Loebel et al., 1992; Wyatt, Damiani, & Henter, 1998) and is associated with relapse (Doane & Becker, 1993; Giron & Gomez-Beneyto, 1995). Parents are impacted by the illness, which in turn affects their interaction with the patient, thereby influencing outcomes positively or negatively. Consequently, to be effective, interventions need to strengthen positive family support and minimize negative family interaction.

SCHIZOPHRENIA AND SUICIDE

On average, individuals with schizophrenia and psychotic disorders are twice as likely to die prematurely (Allebeck, 1989). Research has traditionally tended to report that approximately 10% of all individuals diagnosed with schizophrenia will complete suicide (Caldwell & Gottesman, 1990). However, a recent meta-analysis has found the lifetime suicide rate for individuals with schizophrenia to be nearer to 5% (Palmer, Pankratz, & Bostwick, 2005). Research has also indicated a heightened risk of attempted suicide, with one study finding that 18% of first-episode psychosis patients attempt suicide in the 4 years after onset of illness (Clarke et al., 2006).

In examining the suicide mortality of patients with schizophrenia, over 50% of deaths that occur in the first year of illness and 30% within 10 years were due to suicide (Limosin, Loze, Philippe, Casadebaig, & Rouillon, 2007). Study results found a 16 times higher rate of suicide among individuals with schizophrenia compared to the general population (Limosin et al., 2007).

RISK AND PROTECTIVE FACTORS

A number of key predictors of suicide for individuals diagnosed with a psychotic condition include: male gender, drug use/abuse, prior attempts, shorter duration of illness, comorbid disorders (e.g., mood disorders, personality disorders), social isolation, and poor adherence to treatment (Gut-Fayand et al., 2001; Hawton, Sutton, Haw, Sinclair, & Deeks, 2005; Limosin et al., 2007; Montross, Zisook, & Kasckow, 2005; Moran et al., 2003; Radomsky, Haas, Mann, & Sweeney, 1999; Sinclair, Mullee, King, & Baldwin, 2004). Research further indicates that individuals diagnosed with schizophrenia are more likely to complete suicide near illness onset (Palmer et al., 2005). Another risk factor is hospitalization, with an increase risk of suicide within the first week of admission and the first week after discharge (Qin & Nordentoft, 2005).

Conversely, supportive family environments are linked to positive outcomes, including reduced relapse rates, whereas negative, poor, or minimal family support and family stigma are associated with poorer outcomes (Beiser, Erickson, Fleming, & Iacono, 1993; Birchwood et al., 1998; Janssen et al., 2004; Johnstone, Macmillan, Frith, Benn, & Crow, 1990; Kavanagh, 1992; Linszen et al., 1994; Ran, Leff, Hou, Xiang, & Chan, 2003; Wyatt et al., 1998).

▇ Case Example 12.1

Adam is a 19-year-old single, White, Jewish male. He is a high school graduate and has completed 1 year of college. He was raised in an upper-middle-class family where academic and career success was extremely important, as was their Orthodox faith. Adam was the last of five children. Seven years apart from the next youngest of his siblings, Adam was an unplanned child. He was a good student but had to work hard to earn his grades. He had several friends and dated occasionally throughout high school but never had a serious girlfriend or a best friend.

After graduation from high school Adam went away to college. He did well his first semester and passed all of his classes with above average grades, but the adjustment to living away from home and college life was not easy. During the spring semester Adam began to act in bizarre ways. He became more withdrawn and suspicious of the people he befriended in the fall semester. When he came home for the summer after his first year, his parents noted that he talked to himself all the time. When they asked him about it, he indicated that he might be hearing voices. Confused and afraid, his parents agreed they would "wait and see if he got any worse" before they "jumped to any conclusions that Adam was crazy and needed help." Adam returned to school that fall but was unable to concentrate in class and began to experience increased paranoia toward his classmates, and after only a few weeks he dropped out and returned home. Over the next year, Adam continued to isolate himself socially. He would not go out with any of his friends or family members and eventually refused to even speak on the phone to anyone. When Adam refused to leave his house for over three weeks, insisting that someone was "waiting to take (him)," his parents finally insisted that he see a psychiatrist.

On mental status exam, Adam is alert and oriented times three (meaning that he was oriented to time, person, and place). His clothes are appropriate. He has full range of affect, although often it is inappropriate (laughing while discussing his beliefs that the world is ending and that he is being followed by the CIA who wants to kill him for this secret knowledge he has). He denies feeling depressed, although he reports feeling saddened by the idea that he will die so young. He reports feeling as though "people can tell what I am thinking" and that he "knows that I am being watched because the CIA wants to keep him from telling everyone what I know." Adam does not deny that he hears voices that "warn me about the CIA outside of his house" and feels as though the voices are telling him the truth and he must do as they say. Sometimes the voices tell him to kill himself before the CIA gets to him. He has a plan of how he will "do it just in case the CIA is able to infiltrate his home."

▣ Role Play 12.1

Using case example 12.1, in groups of three (clinician, client, and observer), engage the client and conduct an assessment for schizophrenia and suicide risk. What specific risk and protective factors should you consider? Be aware of your personal and professional attitudes in working with this client. What other information would you need to know?

CURRENT PRACTICE GUIDELINES
AND EVIDENCE-BASED PRACTICE

Research into the treatment of schizophrenia has highlighted the efficacy of psychopharmacological treatment, specifically atypical antipsychotic medications. There is a substantial and growing body of empirical
evidence that supports their effectiveness as a necessary treatment for
positive symptoms (e.g., hallucinations, delusions, thought disorder)
and to a lesser extent for negative symptoms (e.g., withdrawal, apa-
thy; Gearing, Mian, & Charach, 2008; Robinson, Woerner, Delman, &
Kane, 2005). Specific psychopharmacological treatments, such as Clozapine, have demonstrated effectiveness in reducing the risk of suicide in individuals with schizophrenia (Meltzer, 2005; Meltzer et al.,
2003).

The APA in 2004 and the American Academy of Child and Adolescent Psychiatry (AACAP) in 2000 released practice parameters that
recommend a comprehensive multimodal treatment approach to reduce symptoms, morbidity, and relapse rates while aiming to maintain
the individual at home and in the community (Lehman et al., 2004).
Specifically, the first line treatments include atypical antipsychotics or
traditional antipsychotic medications and a number of adjunctive psychosocial and psychoeducational interventions, which include: information about the illness, treatment options, social skills training, relapse
prevention, life skills training, and coping and problem-solving strategies. In working with individuals with schizophrenia a number of adjunctive psychosocial evidence-based practice (EBP) interventions have
been developed. EBPs found to be effective in working with adults at
risk of suicide include **cognitive-behavioral therapy (CBT)** and psychoeducational family treatment. See Part II of this text for more on
effective treatments.

SUMMARY

The majority of individuals diagnosed with a psychotic disorder do
not complete suicide. However, those with a psychotic diagnosis are
at elevated risk for both suicide attempts and completions. It is important to recognize the unique risk and protective factors associated
with suicide among those with schizophrenia or psychotic disorders. It
is also important to be vigilant regarding the potential impact of per-

sonal assumptions and bias in working with this population. Individuals managing these serious and persistent mental illnesses have a wide range of strengths and abilities that can effectively be supported and enhanced.

■ Key Points

1. Schizophrenia is characterized by the presence of positive and negative symptoms that lead to grossly impaired functioning.
2. The average age of onset for schizophrenia is between 15 and 25 years for males and 25 and 35 years for females.
3. Prognosis is complicated by poor adherence to treatment recommendations (medication and psychosocial interventions), substance use, and family environment.
4. Approximately 10% of individuals with schizophrenia will die by suicide.
5. The rate of suicide among schizophrenics is 20 times higher than among the general population.
6. Key predictors of suicide for individuals diagnosed with a psychotic condition include: male gender, drug use/abuse, prior attempts, shorter duration of illness, comorbid disorders (e.g., mood disorders, personality disorders), social isolation, and poor adherence to treatment.
7. Practice parameters recommend a comprehensive multimodal treatment approach.

FURTHER READINGS

American Academy of Child and Adolescent Psychiatry [AACAP]. (2000). Summary of the practice parameters for the assessment and treatment of children and adolescents with schizophrenia. *Journal of the American Academy of Child & Adolescent Psychiatry, 39*(12), 1580–1582.

Bassett, A. S., Chow, E. W., Waterworth, D. M., & Brzustowicz, L. (2001). Genetic insights into schizophrenia. *Canadian Journal of Psychiatry—Revue Canadienne de Psychiatrie, 46*(2), 131–137.

Bergen, J., Hunt, G., Armitage, P., & Bashir, M. (1998). Six-month outcome following a relapse of schizophrenia. *Australian & New Zealand Journal of Psychiatry, 32*(6), 815–822.

Birchwood, M., McGorry, P., & Jackson, H. (1997). Early intervention in schizophrenia. *British Journal of Psychiatry, 170,* 2–5.

Gaebel, W., Janner, M., Frommann, N., Pietzcker, A., Kopcke, W., Linden, M., et al. (2000). Prodromal states in schizophrenia. *Comprehensive Psychiatry, 41*(2 Suppl 1), 76–85.

Geddes, J., Mercer, G., Frith, C. D., MacMillan, F., Owens, D. G., & Johnstone, E. C. (1994). Prediction of outcome following a first episode of schizophrenia. A follow-up study of Northwick Park first episode study subjects. *British Journal of Psychiatry, 165*(5), 664–668.

Gerlach, J., & Larsen, E. B. (1999). Subjective experience and mental side-effects of antipsychotic treatment. *Acta Psychiatrica Scandinavica, Supplementum, 395*, 113–117.

Hafner, H. (2003). Gender differences in schizophrenia. *Psychoneuroendocrinology, 28*(Suppl 2), 17–54.

Harrison, G. (1990). Searching for the causes of schizophrenia: The role of migrant studies. *Schizophrenia Bulletin, 16*(4), 663–671.

Haw, C., Hawton, K., Sutton, L., Sinclair, J., & Deeks, J. (2005). Schizophrenia and deliberate self-harm: A systematic review of risk factors. *Suicide & Life-Threatening Behavior, 35*(1), 50–62.

Hultman, C. M., Wieselgren, I. M., & Ohman, A. (1997). Relationships between social support, social coping and life events in the relapse of schizophrenic patients. *Scandinavian Journal of Psychology, 38*(1), 3–13.

Johns, C. A., Stanley, M., & Stanley, B. (1986). Suicide in schizophrenia. *Annals of the New York Academy of Science, 487*, 294–300.

Lee, C., McGlashan, T. H., & Woods, S. W. (2005). Prevention of schizophrenia: Can it be achieved? *CNS Drugs, 19*(3), 193–206.

Lehman, A. F., Lieberman, J. A., Dixon, L. B., Lehman, A. F., Lieberman, J. A., Dixon, L. B., et al. (2004). Practice guideline for the treatment of patients with schizophrenia, second edition. *American Journal of Psychiatry, 161*, 1–56.

Linszen, D., Lenior, M., De Haan, L., Dingemans, P., & Gersons, B. (1998). Early intervention, untreated psychosis and the course of early schizophrenia. *British Journal of Psychiatry—Supplementum, 172*(33), 84–89.

Loffler, W., Kilian, R., Toumi, M., & Angermeyer, M. C. (2003). Schizophrenic patients' subjective reasons for compliance and noncompliance with neuroleptic treatment. *Pharmacopsychiatry, 36*(3), 105–112.

Muller, N. (2004). Mechanisms of relapse prevention in schizophrenia. *Pharmacopsychiatry, 37*,(Suppl 2), S141–S147.

Phelan, J. C., Bromet, E. J., & Link, B. G. (1998). Psychiatric illness and family stigma. *Schizophrenia Bulletin, 24*(1), 115–126.

Roy, A., Mazonson, A., & Pickar, D. (1984). Attempted suicide in chronic schizophrenia. *British Journal of Psychiatry, 144*, 303–306.

Sham, P. C., MacLean, C. J., & Kendler, K. S. (1994). A typological model of schizophrenia based on age at onset, sex and familial morbidity. *Acta Psychiatrica Scandinavica, 89*(2), 135–141.

ELECTRONIC RESOURCES

National Alliance for the Mentally Ill: http://www.nami.org

National Institute of Mental Health: http://www.nimh.nih.gov/health/topics/schizophrenia/index.shtml

National Schizophrenia Foundation: http://www.NSFoundation.org

▇ Knowledge Acquisition Test

True or False

1. Males with schizophrenia have a better prognosis than females.
2. Females have a later age of onset of schizophrenia than males.
3. The rate of suicide among individuals with schizophrenia is the same as that of the general population.
4. Substance abuse is not a risk factor for suicide among individuals with schizophrenia.
5. Expressed emotion reduces the risk of suicide among individuals with schizophrenia.

Short Answer

6. List the key risk and protective factors for suicide among individuals with schizophrenia.
7. Describe the recommended practice guidelines for treatment of individuals with schizophrenia.

Multiple Choice

8. What item in the following list is not a *DSM-IV-TR* criteria for schizophrenia?

   A. Auditory hallucinations
   B. Disorganized speech
   C. Loss of appetite
   D. Delusions
   E. All of the above
   F. None of the above

9. Which of the following is not a psychotic spectrum diagnosis?

   A. Schizophrenia
   B. Schizophreniform
   C. Schizoaffective
   D. Brief Psychotic
   E. All of the above
   F. None of the above

10. Which of the following items is a risk factor among individuals with schizo-phrenia?

    A. Delusions
    B. Comorbid depression
    C. Hallucinations
    D. Confused thinking
    E. All of the above
    F. None of the above

Answer key is available in the Instructor's Manual; qualified instructors may e-mail textbook@springerpub.com *to request a copy.*

REFERENCES

American Academy of Child and Adolescent Psychiatry [AACAP]. (2000). Summary of the practice parameters for the assessment and treatment of children and adolescents with schizophrenia. *Journal of the American Academy of Child & Adolescent Psychiatry, 39*(12), 1580–1582.

Allebeck, P. (1989). Schizophrenia: A life-shortening disease. *Schizophrenia Bulletin, 15,* 81–89.

Angermeyer, M. C. (2002). Schizophrenia and violence. *Acta Psychiatrica Scandinavica, 102*(407), 63–67.

American Psychiatric Association. (2000). *Diagnostic and statistical manual of mental disorders* (4th ed., text revision). Washington, DC: Author.

Bebbington, P., & Kuipers, L. (1994). The predictive utility of expressed emotion in schizophrenia: An aggregate analysis. *Psychological Medicine, 24*(3), 707–718.

Beiser, M., Erickson, D., Fleming, J. A., & Iacono, W. G. (1993). Establishing the onset of psychotic illness. *American Journal of Psychiatry, 150*(9), 1349–1354.

Beitchman, J. H. (1985). Childhood schizophrenia: A review and comparison with adult-onset schizophrenia. *Psychiatric Clinics of North America, 8*(4), 793–814.

Bergen, J., Hunt, G., Armitage, P., & Bashir, M. (1998). Six-month outcome following a relapse of schizophrenia. *Australian & New Zealand Journal of Psychiatry, 32*(6), 815–822.

Birchwood, M., Todd, P., & Jackson, C. (1998). Early intervention in psychosis: The critical period hypothesis. *British Journal of Psychiatry—Supplementum, 172*(33), 53–59.

Buchanan, R. W., & Carpenter, W. T. (2000). Schizophrenia. In B. J. Saddock & V. A. Saddock (Eds.), *Comprehensive textbook of psychiatry* (7th ed., pp. 1096–1110). Philadelphia: Lippincott.

Burd, L., & Kerbeshian, J. (1987). A North Dakota prevalence study of schizophrenia presenting in childhood. *Journal of the American Academy of Child & Adolescent Psychiatry, 26*(3), 347–350.

Caldwell, C. B., & Gottesman, I. (1990). Schizophrenics kill themselves too: A review of risk factors for suicide. *Schizophrenia Bulletin, 16,* 571–589.

Clarke, M., Whitty, P., Browne, S., Mc Tigue, O., Kinsella, A., Waddington, J. L., et al. (2006). Suicidality in first episode psychosis. *Schizophrenia Research, 86*(1–3), 221–225.

Cohen, L. J., Test, M. A., & Brown, R. L. (1990). Suicide and schizophrenia: Data from a prospective community treatment study. *American Journal of Psychiatry, 147,* 602–607.

Doane, J. A., & Becker, D. F. (1993). Changes in family emotional climate and course of psychiatric illness in hospitalized young adults and adolescents. *New Trends in Experimental & Clinical Psychiatry, 9*(3), 63–77.

Dyck, D. G., Hendryx, M. S., Short, R. A., Voss, W. D., & McFarlane, W. R. (2002). Service use among patients with schizophrenia in psychoeducational multiple-family group treatment. *Psychiatric Services, 53*(6), 749–754.

Eaton, W. W., Mortensen, P. B., Herrman, H., Freeman, H., Bilker, W., Burgess, P., et al. (1992). Long-term course of hospitalization for schizophrenia: Part I. Risk for rehospitalization. *Schizophrenia Bulletin, 18*(2), 217–228.

Fleischhaker, C., Schulz, E., Tepper, K., Martin, M., Hennighausen, K., & Remschmidt, H. (2005). Long-term course of adolescent schizophrenia. *Schizophrenia Bulletin, 31*(3), 769–780.

Foldemo, A., Gullberg, M., Ek, A. C., & Bogren, L. (2005). Quality of life and burden in parents of outpatients with schizophrenia. *Social Psychiatry & Psychiatric Epidemiology, 40*(2), 133–138.

Gearing, R. E., Mian, I., & Charach, A. (2008). Promoting adherence with children and adolescents with psychosis. *Child and Adolescent Psychopharmacology News, 13,* 5–11.

Gearing, R. E., Mian, I. A., Sholonsky, A., Barber, J., Nicholas, D., Lewis, R., et al. (2009). Developing a risk-model of time to first-relapse for children and adolescents diagnosed with psychotic disorders or mood disorders with psychotic features. *Journal of Nervous and Mental Disease, 197,* 6–14.

Geddes, J., Mercer, G., Frith, C. D., MacMillan, F., Owens, D. G., & Johnstone, E. C. (1994). Prediction of outcome following a first episode of schizophrenia: A follow-up study of Northwick Park first episode study subjects. *British Journal of Psychiatry, 165*(5), 664–668.

Geller, B., Craney, J. L., Bolhofner, K., Nickelsburg, M. J., Williams, M., & Zimerman, B. (2002). Two-year prospective follow-up of children with a prepubertal and early adolescent bipolar disorder phenotype. *American Journal of Psychiatry, 159*(6), 927–933.

Gerlach, J., & Larsen, E. B. (1999). Subjective experience and mental side-effects of antipsychotic treatment. *Acta Psychiatrica Scandinavica, Supplementum, 395,* 113–117.

Gillberg, C. (1984). Infantile autism and other childhood psychoses in a Swedish urban region: Epidemiological aspects. *Journal of Child Psychology and Psychiatry, 25*(1), 35–43.

Gillberg, C., Hellgren, L., & Gillberg, C. (1993). Psychotic disorders diagnosed in adolescence: Outcome at age 30 years. *Journal of Child Psychology & Psychiatry & Allied Disciplines, 34,* 1173–1185.

Gillberg, C., & Steffenburg, S. (1987). Outcome and prognostic factors in infantile autism and similar conditions: A population-based study of 46 cases followed through puberty. *Journal of Autism & Developmental Disorders, 17*(2), 273–287.

Giron, M., & Gomez-Beneyto, M. (1995). Relationship between family attitudes measured by the Semantic Differential and relapse in schizophrenia: A 2 year follow-up prospective study. *Psychological Medicine, 25*(2), 365–371.

Gut-Fayand, A., Dervaux, A., Olie, J. P., Loo, H., Poirier, M. F., & Krebs, M. O. (2001). Substance abuse and suicidality in schizophrenia: A common risk factor linked to impulsivity. *Psychiatry Research, 102*(1), 65–72.

Hafner, H., Maurer, K., Loffler, W., Fatkenheuer, B., an der Heiden, W., Riecher-Rossler, A., et al. (1994). The epidemiology of early schizophrenia: Influence of age and gender on onset and early course. *British Journal of Psychiatry, 164,*(23), 29–38.

Hawton, K., Sutton, L., Haw, C., Sinclair, J., & Deeks, J.J. (2005). Schizophrenia and suicide: Systematic review of risk factors. *British Journal of Psychiatry, 187,* 9–20.

Heinrichs, N., Bertram, H., Kuschel, A., & Hahlweg, K. (2005). Parent recruitment and retention in a universal prevention program for child behavior and emotional problems: Barriers to research and program participation. *Prevention Science, 6*(4), 275–286.

Jackson, H.J., Smith, N., & McGorry, P. (1990). Relationship between expressed emotion and family burden in psychotic disorders: An exploratory study. *Acta Psychiatrica Scandinavica, 82*(3), 243–249.

Janssen, I., Krabbendam, L., Bak, M., Hanssen, M., Vollebergh, W., de Graaf, R., et al. (2004). Childhood abuse as a risk factor for psychotic experiences. *Acta Psychiatrica Scandinavica, 109*(1), 38–45.

Johnstone, E.C., Macmillan, J.F., Frith, C.D., Benn, D.K., & Crow, T.J. (1990). Further investigation of the predictors of outcome following first schizophrenic episodes. *British Journal of Psychiatry, 157,* 182–189.

Kavanagh, D.J. (1992). Recent developments in expressed emotion and schizophrenia. *British Journal of Psychiatry, 160,* 601–620.

Lacro, J.P., Dunn, L.B., Dolder, C.R., Leckband, S.G., & Jeste, D.V. (2002). Prevalence of and risk factors for medication nonadherence in patients with schizophrenia: A comprehensive review of recent literature. *Journal of Clinical Psychiatry, 63*(10), 892–909.

Lay, B., Blanz, B., Hartmann, M., & Schmidt, M.H. (2000). The psychosocial outcome of adolescent-onset schizophrenia: A 12-year followup. *Schizophrenia Bulletin, 26*(4), 801–816.

Lehman, A.F., Lieberman, J.A., Dixon, L.B., Lehman, A.F., Lieberman, J.A., Dixon, L.B., et al. (2004). Practice guideline for the treatment of patients with schizophrenia, second edition. *American Journal of Psychiatry, 161,* 1–56.

Lenior, M.E., Dingemans, P.M., Schene, A.H., Hart, A.A., & Linszen, D.H. (2002). The course of parental expressed emotion and psychotic episodes after family intervention in recent-onset schizophrenia. A longitudinal study. *Schizophrenia Research, 57*(2–3), 183–190.

Limosin, F., Loze, J.Y., Philippe, A., Casadebaig, F., & Rouillon, F. (2007). Ten-year prospective follow-up study of the mortality by suicide in schizophrenic patients. *Schizophrenia Research, 94*(1–3), 23–28.

Linszen, D.H., Dingemans, P.M., Lenior, M.E., Nugter, M.. A., Scholte, W. F., & Van der Does, A. J. (1994). Relapse criteria in schizophrenic disorders: Different perspectives. *Psychiatry Research, 54*(3), 273–281.

Loebel, A.D., Lieberman, J.A., Alvir, J.M., Mayerhoff, D.I., Geisler, S.H., & Szymanski, S.R. (1992). Duration of psychosis and outcome in first-episode schizophrenia. *American Journal of Psychiatry, 149*(9), 1183–1188.

Maris, R., Berman, A., & Silverman, M. (2000). *Comprehensive textbook of suicidology.* New York: Guilford.

Meltzer, H. (2005). Suicide in schizophrenia, clozapine, and adoption of evidence-based medicine. *Journal of Clinical Psychiatry, 66*(4), 530–533.

Meltzer, H., Alphs, L., Green, A.I., Altamura, A.C., Anand, R., Bertoldi, A., et al. (2003). Clozapine treatment for suicide in schizophrenia. *Archives of General Psychiatry, 60*(1), 82–91.

Montross, L. P., Zisook, S., & Kasckow, J. (2005). Suicide among patients with schizophrenia: A consideration of risk and protective factors. *Annals of Clinical Psychiatry, 17*(3), 173–182.

Moran, P., Walsh, E., Tyrer, P., Burns, T., Creed, F., & Fahy, T. (2003). Does co-morbid personality disorder increase the risk of suicidal behaviour in psychosis? *Acta Psychiatrica Scandinavica, 107*(6), 441–448.

Nylander, L., & Gillberg, C. (2001). Screening for autism spectrum disorders in adult psychiatric out-patients: A preliminary report. *Acta Psychiatrica Scandinavica, 103*(6), 428–434.

Olfson, M., Mechanic, D., Hansell, S., Boyer, C. A., Walkup, J., & Weiden, P. J. (2000). Predicting medication noncompliance after hospital discharge among patients with schizophrenia. *Psychiatric Services, 51*(2), 216–222.

Palmer, B. A., Pankratz, V. S., & Bostwick, J. M. (2005). The lifetime risk of suicide in schizophrenia: A reexamination. *Archives of General Psychiatry, 62*(3), 247–253.

Perkins, D. O. (2002). Predictors of noncompliance in patients with schizophrenia. *Journal of Clinical Psychiatry, 63*(12), 1121–1128.

Perkins, D. O., Gu, H., Weiden, P. J., McEvoy, J. P., Hamer, R. M., & Lieberman, J. A. (2008). Predictors of treatment discontinuation and medication nonadherence in patients recovering from a first episode of schizophrenia, schizophreniform disorder, or schizoaffective disorder: A randomized, double-blind, flexible-dose, multicenter study. *Journal of Clinical Psychiatry, 69*(1), 106–113.

Pinikahana, J., Happell, B., & Keks, N. A. (2003). Suicide and schizophrenia: A review of literature for the decade (1990–1999) and implications for mental health nursing. *Issues in Mental Health Nursing, 24*(1), 27–43.

Prentice-Dunn, S., Wilson, D. R., & Lyman, R. D. (1981). Client factors related to outcome in a residential and day treatment program for children. *Journal of Clinical Child Psychiatry, 21*, 189–196.

Qin, P., & Nordentoft, M. (2005). Suicide risk in relation to psychiatric hospitalization: Evidence based on longitudinal registers. *Archives of General Psychiatry, 62*(4), 427–432.

Radomsky, E. D., Haas, G. L., Mann, J. J., & Sweeney, J. A. (1999). Suicidal behavior in patients with schizophrenia and other psychotic disorders. *American Journal of Psychiatry, 156*, 1590–1595.

Ran, M. S., Leff, J., Hou, Z. J., Xiang, M. Z., & Chan, C. L. (2003). The characteristics of expressed emotion among relatives of patients with schizophrenia in Chengdu, China. *Culture, Medicine & Psychiatry, 27*(1), 95–106.

Ran, M. S., Xiang, M. Z., Li, S. X., Shan, Y. H., Huang, M. S., Li, et al. (2003). Prevalence and course of schizophrenia in a Chinese rural area. *Australian & New Zealand Journal of Psychiatry, 37*(4), 452–457.

Remschmidt, H. E., Schulz, E., Martin, M., Warnke, A., & Trott, G. E. (1994). Childhood-onset schizophrenia: History of the concept and recent studies. *Schizophrenia Bulletin, 20*(4), 727–745.

Robinson, D., Woerner, M. G., Alvir, J. M., Bilder, R., Goldman, R., Geisler, S., et al. (1999a). Predictors of relapse following response from a first episode of schizophrenia or schizoaffective disorder. *Archives of General Psychiatry, 56*(3), 241–247.

Robinson, D. G., Woerner, M. G., Alvir, J. M., Geisler, S., Koreen, A., Sheitman, B., et al. (1999b). Predictors of treatment response from a first episode of schizophrenia or schizoaffective disorder. *American Journal of Psychiatry, 156*(4), 544–549.

Robinson, D. G., Woerner, M. G., Delman, H. M., & Kane, J. M. (2005). Pharmacological treatments for first-episode schizophrenia. *Schizophrenia Bulletin, 31*(3), 705–722.

Ropcke, B., & Eggers, C. (2005). Early-onset schizophrenia: A 15-year follow-up. *European Child & Adolescent Psychiatry, 14*(6), 341–350.

Rosenfarb, I. S., Miklowitz, D. J., Goldstein, M. J., Harmon, L., Nuechterlein, K. H., & Rea, M. M. (2001). Family transactions and relapse in bipolar disorder. *Family Process, 40*(1), 5–14.

Schmidt, M., Blanz, B., Dippe, A., Koppe, T., & Lay, B. (1995). Course of patients diagnosed as having schizophrenia during first episode occurring under age 18 years. *European Archives of Psychiatry & Clinical Neuroscience, 245*(2), 93–100.

Sinclair, J. M., Mullee, M. A., King, E. A., & Baldwin, D. S. (2004). Suicide in schizophrenia: A retrospective case-control study of 51 suicides. *Schizophrenia Bulletin, 30*(4), 803–811.

Siris, S. G. (2001). Suicide and schizophrenia. *Journal of Psychopharmacology, 15*(2), 127–135.

Sullivan, G., Wells, K. B., Morgenstern, H., & Leake, B. (1995). Identifying modifiable risk factors for rehospitalization: A case-control study of seriously mentally ill persons in Mississippi. *American Journal of Psychiatry, 152*(12), 1749–1756.

Svedberg, B., Mesterton, A., & Cullberg, J. (2001). First-episode non-affective psychosis in a total urban population: A 5-year follow-up. *Social Psychiatry & Psychiatric Epidemiology, 36*(7), 332–337.

Verdoux, H., Lengronne, J., Liraud, F., Gonzales, B., Assens, F., Abalan, F., et al. (2000). Medication adherence in psychosis: predictors and impact on outcome. A 2-year follow-up of first-admitted subjects. *Acta Psychiatrica Scandinavica, 102*(3), 203–210.

Verdoux, H., Liraud, F., Assens, F., Abalan, F., & van Os, J. (2002). Social and clinical consequences of cognitive deficits in early psychosis: A two-year follow-up study of first-admitted patients. *Schizophrenia Research, 56*(1–2), 149–159.

Werry, J. S., McClellan, J. M., & Chard, L. (1991). Childhood and adolescent schizophrenic, bipolar, and schizoaffective disorders: A clinical and outcome study. *Journal of the American Academy of Child & Adolescent Psychiatry, 30*(3), 457–465.

Wu, E. Q., Birnbaum, H. G., Shi, L., Ball, D. E., Kessler, R. C., Moulis, M., et al. (2005). The economic burden of schizophrenia in the United States in 2002. *Journal of Clinical Psychiatry, 66*(9), 1122–1129.

Wyatt, R. J., Damiani, L. M., & Henter, I. D. (1998). First-episode schizophrenia. Early intervention and medication discontinuation in the context of course and treatment. *British Journal of Psychiatry—Supplementum, 172*(33), 77–83.

13 Depression and Suicide

This chapter continues to examine the relationship between psychiatric illness and risk of suicidality. Mood disorders are the most common psychiatric disorders associated with suicide. This chapter focuses on depression in relation to suicidality. Prevalence rates indicate that, on average, 4% of males and 8% of females have diagnosable depressive disorders (Lehtinen & Joukamaa, 1994). Research demonstrates that more than 90% of individuals who suicide fulfill the criteria for one or more psychiatric disorders (American Psychiatric Association [APA], 2003), and 60% of all suicides occur in persons with a mood disorder (Malone & Lartey, 2004).

■ Goals and Objectives of This Chapter

An understanding of:

- *DSM* criteria for mood disorders
- The course of illness of depression
- The etiology and epidemiology of depression
- The relationship between depression and suicide
- Risk factors for suicide unique to individuals with depression
- Protective factors for suicide unique to individuals with depression
- Evidence-based practices for depression

INTRODUCTION

The most common psychiatric disorders impacting millions of individuals, their families, and larger society are **mood disorders**. Mood disorders are the most common psychiatric conditions associated with suicide attempts and completed suicide (Bostwick & Pankratz, 2000). Mood disorders are characterized by irritability or depressed mood; loss of interest or pleasure; changes in appetite, weight, and/or sleep; loss of energy; feelings of hopelessness and worthlessness; inappropriate guilt; difficulty making decisions; and mania (American Psychiatric Association [APA], 2000).

According to the National Health and Nutrition Examination Survey, in 2005–2006, 5.4% of Americans, that is 1 in 20 individuals 12 years of age and older, had depression (Pratt & Brody, 2008). It is estimated that diagnosable depression affects approximately 17.6 million Americans every year (National Institute of Mental Health D/ART Online Public Information, 1998). Research has suggested that the lifetime rate of mortality secondary to suicide is 2% to 15% for individuals with mood disorders (Bostwick & Pankratz, 2000).

Although there exist a number of supported evidence-based practices (EBPs; e.g., **cognitive-behavioral therapy, interpersonal psychotherapy,** and psychopharmacology) that have been found to successfully treat depression, stigma, discrimination, and unsupported stereotypes can become barriers to treatments. Mood disorders, including depression, are biological conditions that are not caused by laziness, lack of motivation, poor work ethic, improper values, and so forth. Individuals suffering from these conditions need efficacious treatment and cannot simply "pull themselves up by their bootstraps" or "just snap out of it." It is essential for clinicians working with individuals managing depression to become aware of not only the beliefs of others, but their personal and professional values and assumptions regarding depression. Lacking professional and personal awareness may pose a barrier to effectively engaging and treating individuals with depression.

■ Individual Exercise 13.1

1. When you hear the word *depression*, what are the first words or thoughts that come to your mind?
2. Are your listed words or thoughts generally positive or negative? Did they surprise you in any way? If so, how?

3. What personal *and* professional considerations and assumptions may make it hard for you to work with a depressed client?
4. What personal *and* professional considerations may make it easy for you to work with a depressed client?

DSM-IV-TR DIAGNOSIS

A diagnosis of depression can be complicated by comorbid illnesses or medications that mimic depressive symptoms. **Major depressive disorder** (MDD), or major depression, is generally diagnosed via psychiatric assessment using the *Diagnostic and Statistical Manual of Mental Disorders,* fourth edition, text revision (*DSM-IV-TR;* APA, 2000). According to the *DSM-IV-TR,* major depression is diagnosed when five or more of the following symptoms of depression are present for at least 2 weeks nearly every day for most of the day. In addition, at least one of the symptoms must be either depressed mood or loss of interest or pleasure in activities (APA, 2000). Symptoms include:

- Depressed or irritable mood
- Loss of interest or pleasure in activities (such as hobbies, work, sex, or being with friends)
- A sudden change in weight (weight loss without dieting, gaining more than 5% of body weight in 1 month) or a change in appetite
- Inability to sleep or sleeping too much
- Agitation or restlessness (observed by others)
- Constant fatigue or loss of energy
- Frequent feelings of worthlessness or inappropriate guilt
- Difficulty concentrating or making decisions
- Frequent thoughts of death or suicide (or a suicide attempt or plan)

These symptoms must represent a change from the way the individual previously functioned. Also, symptoms must cause significant distress to the individual or significant impairment in the individual's ability to function and cannot be due to the direct physiological effects of a substance (e.g., drug abuse, a medication) or a general medical condition (e.g., hypothyroidism). They symptoms also cannot be better accounted for by bereavement (i.e., after the loss of a loved one, the symptoms persist for longer than 2 months or are characterized by marked functional impairment, morbid preoccupation with worthlessness, suicidal ideation, psychotic symptoms, or psychomotor retardation).

Related conditions include **dysthymia** (which features fewer symptoms than major depression and is a chronic illness lasting at least 2 years in adults or 1 year in adolescents), **double-depression** (dysthymia with a current major depressive episode), **bipolar I** (consisting of fluctuating episodes of depression and mania), and **bipolar II** (represented by symptoms of depression and milder symptoms of mania, or hypomania), and finally, **depression not otherwise specified,** or depression NOS (which includes conditions that display fewer than five symptoms or are of insufficient duration to be considered major depression).

EPIDEMIOLOGY AND PROGNOSIS

Depression is considered the most common psychiatric illness (Lehtinen & Joukamaa, 1994). In addition, major depressive disorders were estimated to be the leading cause of disability in the United States (Ustun, Ayuso-Mateos, Chatterji, Mathers, & Murray, 2004). The annual economic consequences of depression have been estimated at $83 billion in the United States (Coyne, Fechner-Bates, & Schwenk, 1994).

At any given time, 4% of men and 8% of women suffer from a clinically significant depressive disorder, and depressive symptoms are even more common (Lehtinen & Joukamaa, 1994). Females have a lifetime rate of major depression 1.7 to 2.7 times greater than that for men (Burt & Stein, 2002). Lifetime prevalence of depression is estimated at 5%–12% in men and 12%–20% in women. In terms of the general youth population, 3% of preschoolers, 2% of school-aged children, and 9% of adolescents suffer from depression (Birmaher & Brent, 1998; Wolraich, Felice, & Drotar, 1996).

In terms of the course of illness, 50% of individuals who have a major depressive episode experience a reoccurrence in the year following an index episode; 20% will develop chronic depression; 15% to 20% suffer from lingering symptoms, considered partial remission; and 10% to 15% experience the "bipolarization" of an illness, meaning their major depressive episode is followed by a manic episode and a shift in diagnosis to bipolar disorder (Dawson, Lavori, Coryell, Endicott, & Keller, 1998).

The following factors are associated with an increased risk of depression:

- Family history of depression (Ivanova & Israel, 2005; Kendler, Gardner, & Prescott, 1999)
- Early childhood trauma (i.e., the loss of a parent before adolescence; child neglect; physical, emotional, or sexual abuse; and parental divorce)
- Negative life events (i.e., the loss of a loved one or loss of employment)
- Chronic stresses (i.e., illness, lack of social support)
- Comorbid alcohol abuse
- Residence (i.e., urban vs. rural settings; Ivanova & Israel, 2005)
- Marital status (being unmarried; Ivanova & Israel, 2005; Ohayon, 2007)
- Work status (i.e., being unemployed; Ivanova & Israel, 2005; Ohayon, 2007)
- Lower levels of education (Ohayon, 2007)
- Physical illness
- Female gender (Ivanova & Israel, 2005; Ohayon, 2007)
- Middle age (Ivanova & Israel, 2005)

Poor health status and smoking are also strongly correlated with a major depressive disorder (Ohayon, 2007). Conversely, spiritual well-being, a sense of personal value in society, social support, and family stability may serve as protective factors against depression (Ivanova & Israel, 2005).

DEPRESSION AND SUICIDE

Over 90% of individuals who successfully suicide have a psychiatric disorder (APA, 2003; Isometsa et al., 1995; Kaplan & Harrow, 1996; Strakowski, McElroy, Keck, & West, 1996). Mood disorders are the most common psychiatric conditions associated with suicide or serious suicide attempt. Approximately 60% of all suicides occur in persons with a mood disorder (Bostwick & Pankratz, 2000). Lifetime rate of mortality secondary to suicide has been estimated to be 2% to 15% for individuals with mood disorders and 15% to 20% for those psychiatric patients who have a history of one hospitalization for their disorder. Estimates of the rate of completed suicide among individuals with bipolar disorder are approximately 15%, and it is estimated that between 25% and 50% attempt suicide at least once (Bostwick & Pankratz, 2000).

There is a vast difference in the lifetime risk of suicide in depression among males and females. Where risk for males is estimated at 7%, it is estimated at only 1% for females (Blair-West, Cantor, Mellsop, & Eyeson, 1999). The risk of suicide among those depressed individuals not receiving antidepressants is 1.8 times higher than the risk of suicide among those treated with antidepressants. However, only approximately 1 out of every 5 depressed individuals is treated with antidepressants (Isacssona, Bergamn, & Rich, 1996).

RISK AND PROTECTIVE FACTORS

There are a number of established risk factors for suicidal acts among individuals with major depression. These include:

- previous suicide attempts (Malone et al., 2000; Rihmer, 2007)
- family history of psychiatric illness
- family history of suicidal behavior (Brent et al., 2002; Kendler, Gardner, & Prescott, 1999; Malone et al., 2000; Melhem et al., 2007)
- impulsive behavior (Melhem et al., 2007; Oquendo et al., 2000)
- aggressive behavior (Malone et al., 2000; Melhem et al., 2007)
- loss or separation (Malone et al., 2000)
- hopelessness (Malone et al., 2000; Valtonen et al., 2007)
- severity of depression (Malone et al., 2000; Rihmer, 2007)
- comorbidity with anxiety or substance abuse (Rihmer, 2007)
- suicidal ideation (Malone et al., 2000)

Within bipolar I and II disorders, suicide risk increases with proximity to onset of illness (Tondo, Isacsson, & Baldessarini, 2003), mixed episodes, and depressed episode (Oquendo et al., 2000; Tondo et al., 2003). Interestingly, neither objective, severity of depression nor quantity of recent life events, has been found to differentiate between depressed suicide attempters and nonattempters (Malone et al., 2000).

Conversely, having greater feelings of responsibility toward family, more fear of social disapproval, more moral objections to suicide, greater survival and coping skills, and greater fear of suicide have been found to have a protective effect against suicide among depressed individuals (Malone et al., 2000). These protective factors are considered or referred to as reasons for living. Additionally, having a strong social support network has been found to be a protective factor against suicidal acts among depressed individuals (Conwell, Duberstein, & Caine, 2002).

■ Case Example 13.1

Adam is a 19-year-old, single, White, Jewish male. He is a high school graduate and completed 1 year of college. He was raised in an upper-middle-class family where academic and career success was extremely important, as was their Orthodox faith. Adam was the last of five children. Seven years apart from the next youngest of his siblings, Adam was an unplanned child. He was a good student but had to work hard to earn his grades. He had several friends and dated occasionally throughout high school but never had a serious girlfriend or a best friend.

After graduation from high school Adam went away to college. He did well his first semester and passed all of his classes with above average grades, but the adjustment to living away from home and college life was not easy. By the spring semester Adam began to become increasingly despondent. He became more withdrawn and isolated from the people he befriended in fall semester. When he came home for the summer after his first year, his parents noted that he did not engage with his old friends and spent most of his time watching TV or in his room. Adam frequently was up very late at night and took naps during the day. His appetite dropped off, as did his general hygiene. His mother started to recognize that he was often wearing the same clothes and had very little laundry at the end of each week. When his father encouraged Adam to wake up early and go fishing with him, an old pastime they had engaged in for years, Adam responded with "why bother."

Adam returned to school that fall but was unable to concentrate in class and began to experience increased isolation and deterioration in personal hygiene, and after only a few weeks he just stopped attending classes. During the winter break he returned home and did not return to school for the spring semester. Over the next year, Adam continued to hang around the house and isolate himself socially. He would rarely go out with any of his friends from high school or his family members, and he eventually stopped speaking to anyone on the phone. One day his mother overheard Adam state, "I wish I had a gun, that's a way to end it all," while he was watching a police TV show in which a police officer suicided. His parents finally insisted that he see a psychiatrist.

On mental status exam, Adam is alert and oriented times three (meaning that he was oriented to time, person, and place); but he keeps his head down and rarely makes eye contact. His clothes are unclean and mismatched. He is unshaven and has noticeable body odor. He displays limited range of affect and frequently answers in monosyllabic monotones. Adam denies that he hears voices. In the past few months, Adam has lost 23 pounds and describes a very minimal appetite. He cannot not recall the last time he laughed, and he is not concerned by his inability to smile. He sees life as a never-ending burden. He admits long-standing suicide ideation. Although he denies any prior suicide attempts, he noted collecting pills.

Case Vignette 13.2

Using case example 13.1, change the following details:
    Gender: From Adam (male) to Anne (female)
    Religion: From Judaism to Christianity

Case Vignette 13.3

Using case example 13.1, change the following:
    Sexual Orientation: From heterosexual to homosexual
    Religion: From Judaism to Muslim

Case Vignette 13.4

Using case example 13.1, change the following:
    Immigration Status: From born in the United States to immigrated from Algeria
    Family History: Mother has a long history of MDD

■ Role Play 13.1

Using case example 13.1 and case vignette 13.2, in groups of three (clinician, client, and observer), engage the client and conduct an assessment for depression and suicide risk. What specific risk and protective factors should you consider? Be aware of your personal and professional attitudes in working with this client. What other information would you need to know? How do the changes in the vignette impact your answers to the above questions? (You may need to refer to previous chapters to consider the impacts of gender, religious affiliation, sexual orientation, etc.)

CURRENT PRACTICE GUIDELINES AND EVIDENCE-BASED PRACTICE

Several treatment approaches have been shown to be effective for the treatment of depression. Specifically, cognitive-behavioral therapy (CBT), interpersonal psychotherapy (IPT) for depression (Jackson & Lurie, 2006), and psychopharmacological approaches (especially when dealing with bipolar disorder; Frank et al., 1990; Grunze, 2005; Klerman & Weissman, 1993; Klerman, Weissman, Rounsaville, & Chevron, 1984; Thase, 1996, 2008; Thase et al., 2007; Young & Hammond, 2007) have gained wide support through randomized control trials as effective treatments for depression across age groups, gender, and ethnicity.

CBT focuses on the nature of an individual's dysfunctional beliefs (i.e., cognitive distortions based on catastrophizing; jumping to false conclusions; and maladaptive views of oneself, others, and the world; Beck, Rush, Shaw, & Emery, 1979; Thase, 1996). CBT aimed at reducing depression and risk of suicidality focuses on: (1) identifying symptoms and diagnosis of depression; (2) assessing for the presence of dysfunctional beliefs and behaviors; (3) identifying context and life events that might be triggering dysfunctional responses; (4) looking for developmental, family antecedents of automatic thoughts and beliefs and learned behaviors; (5) linking changes in mood to occurrence of self-disparaging or other negative beliefs, possibly related to early learning; and (6) treatment targets changing dysfunctional beliefs, thoughts, and behaviors (Beck et al., 1979; Thase, 1996). CBT has repeatedly been shown to be as effective as medication in the treatment of depression (Appleby, Warner, Whitton, & Faragher, 1997; Thase, 2008; Thase et al., 2007).

IPT views depression as having a dynamic relationship with interpersonal problems. Depression leads to interpersonal problems, and interpersonal problems lead to depressed mood. Interpersonal problems are categorized into four areas, including (1) grief, (2) role transition, (3) interpersonal disputes, and (4) interpersonal deficits. According to IPT, the improvement or resolution of the interpersonal problem(s) linked to the depression onset can bring about the improvement or remission of depressive symptoms (Frank et al., 1990; Klerman & Weissman, 1993; Klerman et al., 1984).

Monoamines and neurotransmitters have been identified as biological markers of depression, specifically, monoamine oxidase, serotonin, norepinephrine, and dopamine (Preston & Johnson, 2004). Medications targeting these areas, such as selective serotonin reuptake inhibitors and tricyclic antidepressants, have been shown to be effective for treating depression. However, despite their efficacy, most types of antidepressants do lead to negative side effects (Preston & Johnson, 2004; Rosse, Fanous, Gaskins, & Deutsch, 2007). Lithium, the gold standard psychopharmacological treatment for bipolar disorders, has been found to reduce the suicide rate approximately 80% for an average of 18 months (Baldessarini et al., 2006). In addition, practice guidelines recommend community intervention following a suicide, efforts to reduce suicide contagion, and training of primary care physicians and mental health professions in recognizing suicide risk and making appropriate referrals (Shaffer & Pfeffer, 2001).

SUMMARY

Although a significant number of individuals diagnosed with depression attempt and complete suicide, a majority do not. However, those with a mood disorder remain at elevated risk for both suicide attempt and completion. To engage, develop a therapeutic alliance, and effectively treat individuals with depression at risk of suicide, clinicians need to become informed of not only the risk and protective factors, but also their own personal and professional beliefs. A lack of awareness may minimize your ability to recognize, assess, and treat, as well as potentially limit your clients' abilities to openly access and work with you. Individuals with mood disorders may have an elevated risk of suicidality, but they also have a number of strengths and abilities that can effectively be supported and drawn upon in their treatment.

■ Key Points

1. Mood disorders are characterized by depressed mood or loss of interest/pleasure in activities that impairs functioning and causes significant distress.
2. Approximately 60% of all suicides occur in persons with a mood disorder.
3. Lifetime prevalence of depression is estimated at 5% to 12% in males and 12% to 20% in females.
4. Diagnoses of mood disorders are complicated by symptoms of comorbid illnesses, side effects of medications that mimic depressive symptoms, and substance use.
5. Lifetime rate of mortality secondary to suicide has been estimated to be 2% to 15% for individuals with mood disorders.
6. Key predictors of suicide for individuals diagnosed with a mood disorder include: previous suicide attempt, family history of depression, family history of suicide, aggressive behavior, impulsivity, loss, separation, comorbid anxiety, and substance use.
7. Practice parameters recommend CBT, IPT, and psychopharmacological treatments.

FURTHER READINGS

Barraclough, B. M., & Pallis, D. J. (1975). Depression followed by suicide: A comparison of depressed suicides with living depressives. *Psychological Medicine, 5,* 55–81.

Bethell, J., & Rhodes, A. E. (2007). Depressed mood in the suicidal population. *Canadian Journal of Psychiatry—Revue Canadienne de Psychiatrie, 52*(11), 744–748.

Bruce, M. L., Ten Have, T. R., Reynolds, C. F., Katz, I. I., Schulberg, H. C., Mulsant, B. H., et al. (2004). Reducing suicidal ideation and depressive symptoms in depressed older primary care patients: A randomized controlled trial. *Journal of the American Medical Association, 291*(9), 1081–1091.

Galfalvy, H., Oquendo, M. A., Carballo, J. J., Sher, L., Grunebaum, M. F., Burke, A., et al. (2006). Clinical predictors of suicidal acts after major depression in bipolar disorder: A prospective study. *Bipolar Disorders, 8*(5 Pt 2), 586–595.

Hallfors, D., Waller, M. W., Ford, C. A., Halpern, C. T., Brodish, P. H., & Iritani, B. (2004). Adolescent depression and suicide risk: Association with sex and drug behavior. *American Journal of Preventive Medicine, 27*(3), 224–230.

Hatcher-Kay, C., & King, C. A. (2003). Depression and suicide. *Pediatrics in Review, 24*(11), 363–371.

Isometsa, E. T., Aro, H. M., Henriksson, M. M., Heikkinen, M. E., & Lonnqvist, J. K. (1994). Suicide in major depression in different settings. *Journal of Clinical Psychiatry, 55*(12), 523–527.

Suominen, K., Isometsa, E., & Lonnqvist, J. (2004). Elderly suicide attempters with depression are often diagnosed only after the attempt. *International Journal of Geriatric Psychiatry, 19*(1), 35–40.

van Praag, H. M., & Plutchik, R. (1984). Depression type and depression severity in relation to risk of violent suicide attempt. *Psychiatry Research, 12*, 333–338.

Vanderhorst, R. K., & McLaren, S. (2005). Social relationships as predictors of depression and suicidal ideation in older adults. *Aging & Mental Health, 9*(6), 517–525.

ELECTRONIC RESOURCES

American Foundation for Suicide Prevention: http://www.afsp.org
http://www.afsp.org/index.cfm?page_id=05678008–958D-8476–7CD04234DBBBFC69
National Institute of Mental Health: http://www.nimh.nih.gov/health/topics/schizophrenia/index.shtml
http://www.nimh.nih.gov/health/publications/older-adults-depression-and-suicide-facts.shtml

Educational and Informative Sites

All About Depression: http://www.allaboutdepression.com/gen_04.html
American Psychiatric Association: http://www.apa.org/pi/aging/depression.html
Ohio State University Medical Center: http://medicalcenter.osu.edu/patientcare/healthcare_services/mental_health/mental_health_about/mood/depression_suicide/
Oregon Health & Science University: http://www.ohsu.edu/health/health-topics/topic.cfm?id=8407
Suicide Prevention, Awareness, and Support: http://www.suicide.org/depression-and-suicide.html
Suicide and Suicide Prevention: http://www.psycom.net/depression.central.suicide.html
Surgeon General: http://www.surgeongeneral.gov/library/mentalhealth/chapter3/sec5.html

■ Knowledge Acquisition Test

True or False

1. Depressed males are more likely to attempt suicide than depressed females.
2. Depressed males are more likely to complete suicide than depressed females.
3. Sixty percent of depressed individuals are likely to complete suicide.
4. Smoking cigarettes is a risk factor for suicide among depressed individuals.
5. Psychopharmacological treatments are more effective than psychosocial interventions for reducing risk of suicide in individuals with depression.

Short Answer

6. List the key risk and protective factors for suicide among individuals with depression.
7. Describe the recommended practice guidelines for treatment of individuals with depression.

Multiple Choice

8. What item in the following list is not a *DSM-IV-TR* criteria for depression?

   A. Sleep disturbances
   B. Suicidal ideation
   C. Loss of appetite
   D. Loss of interest
   E. All of the above
   F. None of the above

9. Which of the following is not a mood diagnosis?

   A. Major depressive disorder
   B. Double depression
   C. Dysthymia
   D. Bereavement
   E. All of the above
   F. None of the above

10. Which of the following items is a risk factor among individuals with bipolar disorder?

    A. Mixed episodes
    B. Depressed episodes
    C. Longer time since diagnosis
    D. Medication nonadherence
    E. All of the above
    F. None of the above

Answer key is available in the Instructor's Manual; qualified instructors may e-mail textbook@springerpub.com *to request a copy.*

REFERENCES

American Psychiatric Association (APA). (2000). *Diagnostic and statistical manual of mental disorders* (4th ed., text revision). Washington, DC: Author.

American Psychiatric Association (APA). (2003). *Practice guideline for the assessment and treatment of patients with suicidal behaviors*. Washington DC: Author.

Appleby, L., Warner, R., Whitton, A., & Faragher, B. (1997). A controlled study of fluoxetine and cognitive-behavioural counselling in the treatment of postnatal depression. *British Medical Journal, 314*(7085), 932–936.

Baldessarini, R. J., Tondo, L., Davis, P., Pompili, M., Goodwin, F. K., & Hennen, J. (2006). Decreased risk of suicides and attempts during long-term lithium treatment: A meta-analytic review [erratum appears in *Bipolar Disord.* 2007 May;9(3):314]. *Bipolar Disorders, 8*(5 Pt 2), 625–639.

Beck, A. T., Rush, A. J., Shaw, B. F., & Emery, G. (1979). *Interview with a depressed suicidal patient*. New York: Guilford Press.

Birmaher, B., & Brent, D. (1998). Practice parameters for the assessment and treatment of children and adolescents with depressive disorders. *Journal of the American Academy of Child and Adolescent Psychiatry, 37*(Suppl 10), 63S–82S.

Blair-West, G. W., Cantor, C. H., Mellsop, G. W., & Eyeson, M. L. (1999). Lifetime suicide risk in major depression: Sex and age determinants. *Journal of Affective Disorders, 55*(3), 171–178.

Bostwick, J. M., & Pankratz, V. S. (2000). Affective disorders and suicide risk: A reexamination. *American Journal of Psychiatry, 157*, 1925–1932.

Brent, D. A., Oquendo, M., Birmaher, B., Greenhill, L., Kolko, D., Stanley, B., et al. (2002). Familial pathways to early-onset suicide attempt: Risk for suicidal behavior in offspring of mood-disordered suicide attempters. *Archives of General Psychiatry, 59*, 801–807.

Burt, V. K., & Stein, K. (2002). Epidemiology of depression throughout the female life cycle. *Journal of Clinical Psychiatry, 63*(Suppl 7), 9–15.

Conwell, Y., Duberstein, P. R., & Caine, E. D. (2002). Risk factors for suicide in later life. *Biological Psychiatry, 52*, 193–204.

Coyne, J. C., Fechner-Bates, S., & Schwenk, T. L. (1994). Prevalence, nature, and comorbidity of depressive disorders in primary care. *General Hospital Psychiatry, 16*(4), 267–276.

Dawson, R., Lavori, P. W., Coryell, W. H., Endicott, J., & Keller, M. B. (1998). Maintenance strategies for unipolar depression: An observational study of levels of treatment and recurrence. *Journal of Affective Disorders, 49*, 31–44.

Frank, E., Kupfer, D., Perel, J. M., Cornes, C., Jarrett, D. B., Mallinger, A. G., et al. (1990). Three-year outcomes for maintenance therapies in recurrent depression. *Archives of General Psychiatry, 47*(12), 1093–1099.

Grunze, H. (2005). Reevaluating therapies for bipolar depression. *Journal of Clinical Psychiatry, 66*(Suppl 5), 17–25.

Isacssona, G., Bergamn, U., & Rich, C. L. (1996). Epidemiological data suggest antidepressants reduce suicide risk among depressives. *Journal of Affective Disorders, 41*(1), 1–8.

Isometsa, E., Henrikksson, M., Marttunen, M., Heikkinen, M., Aro, H., Kuoppasalmi, K., et al. (1995). Mental disorders in young and middle aged men who commit suicide. *British Medical Journal, 310*, 1366–1367.

Ivanova, M.Y., & Israel, A.C. (2005). Family stability as a protective factor against the influences of pessimistic attributional style on depression. *Cognitive Therapy and Research, 29*(2), 243–251.

Jackson, B., & Lurie, S. (2006). Adolescent depression: challenges and opportunities: A review and current recommendations for clinical practice. *Advances in Pediatrics, 53,* 111–163.

Kaplan, K. J., & Harrow, M. (1996). Positive and negative symptoms as risk factors for later suicidal activity in schizophrenics versus depressives. *Suicide & Life-Threatening Behavior, 26*(2), 105–120.

Kendler, K.S., Gardner, C.O., & Prescott, C.A. (1999). Clinical characteristics of major depression that predict risk of depression in relatives. *Archives of General Psychiatry, 56*(4), 322–327.

Klerman, G., & Weissman, M.M. (1993). *New applications in interpersonal psychotherapy*. Washington, DC: American Psychiatric Press.

Klerman, G., Weissman, M.M., Rounsaville, B., & Chevron, E. (1984). *Interpersonal psychotherapy of depression*. New York: Basic Books.

Lehtinen, V., & Joukamaa, M. (1994). Epidemiology of depression: Prevalence, risk factors and treatment situation. *Acta Psychiatrica Scandinavica, 377,* 7–10.

Malone, D.A., & Lartey, P. (2004). *Depression and suicide-recognition and early intervention* (2nd ed.). American Medical Association.

Malone, K.M., Oquendo, M.A., Haas, G.L., Ellis, S.P., Li, S., & Mann, J.J. (2000). Protective factors against suicidal acts in major depression: Reasons for living. *American Journal of Psychiatry, 157,* 1084–1088.

Melhem, N.M., Brent, D.A., Ziegler, M., Lyengar, S., Kolko, D., Oquendo, M., et al. (2007). Familial pathways to early-onset suicidal behavior: Familial and individual antecedents of suicidal behavior. *American Journal of Psychiatry, 164*(9), 1304–1306.

National Institute of Mental Health D/ART Online Public Information. (1998). Depression awareness, recognition and treatment. Retrieved April 15, 2008, http://www.nimh.nih.gov/dart/darthome.htm

Ohayon, M.M. (2007). Epidemiology of depression and its treatment in the general population. *Journal of Psychiatric Research, 41*(3–4), 207–213.

Oquendo, M., Waternaux, C., Brodsky, B., Parsons, B., Haas, G.L., Malone, K.M., et al. (2000). Suicidal behavior in bipolar mood disorder: Clinical characteristics of attempters and non-attempters. *Journal of Affective Disorders, 59,* 107–117.

Pratt, L. A., & Brody, D. J. (2008). Depression in the United States household population, 2005–2006. Retrieved April 17, 2008, http://www.cdc.gov/nchs/data/databriefs/db07.htm

Preston, J., & Johnson, J. (2004). *Clinical psychopharmacology made ridiculously simple* (5th ed.). Miami, FL: MedMaster.

Rihmer, Z. (2007). Suicide risk in mood disorders. *Current Opinions in Psychiatry, 20*(1), 17–22.

Rosse, R.B., Fanous, A., Gaskins, B.L., & Deutsch, S.I. (2007). Side effects in the modern psychopharmacology of depression. *Primary Psychiatry, 14*(7), 50–58.

Shaffer, D., & Pfeffer, C.R. (2001). Practice parameter for the assessment and treatment of children and adolescents with suicidal behavior. *Journal of the American Academy of Child & Adolescent Psychiatry, 40*(Suppl 7), 24S–51S.

Strakowski, S. M., McElroy, S. L., Keck, P. E., & West, S. A. (1996). Suicidality among patients with mixed and manic bipolar disorder. *American Journal of Psychiatry, 153,* 674–676.

Thase, M. E. (1996). *Cognitive behavioral therapy manual for treatment of depressed inpatients*. New York: Plenum Press.

Thase, M. E. (2008). Citalopram-resistant depression: Cognitive therapy and medication similarly effective as second line treatments. *Evidence-Based Mental Health, 11,* 48.

Thase, M. E., Friedman, E. S., Biggs, M. M., Wisniewski, S. R., Trivedi, M. H., Luther, J. F., et al.(2007). Cognitive therapy versus medication in augmentation and switch strategies as second-step treatments: A STAR°D report. *American Journal of Psychiatry, 164*(5), 739–752.

Tondo, L., Isacsson, G., & Baldessarini, R. J. (2003). Suicidal behaviour in bipolar disorder: Risk and prevention. *CNS Drugs, 17*(7), 491–511.

Ustun, T. B., Ayuso-Mateos, J. L., Chatterji, S., Mathers, C., & Murray, C. J. (2004). Global burden of depressive disorders in the year 2000. *British Journal of Psychiatry, 184,* 386–392.

Valtonen, H. M., Suominen, K., Mantere, O., Leppamaki, S., Arvilommi, P., & Isometsa, E. (2007). Suicidal behaviour during different phases of bipolar disorder. *Journal of Affective Disorders, 97*(1–3), 101–107.

Wolraich, M., Felice, M. E., & Drotar, D. (1996). *The classification of child and adolescent mental diagnoses in primary care: Diagnostic and statistical manual for primary care (DSM-PC) child and adolescent version*. Elk Grove Village, IL: American Academy of Pediatrics.

Young, A. H., & Hammond, J. M. (2007). Lithium in mood disorders: Increasing evidence base, declining use? *British Journal of Psychiatry, 191,* 474–476.

14 Substance-Related Disorders and Suicide

This chapter examines the relationship between substance-related disorders and risk of suicidality. Substance use and abuse has been associated with increased risk of suicide attempt and completion (Dhossche, Meloukheia, & Chakravorty, 2000; Maris, Berman, & Silverman, 2000). Diagnosed and undiagnosed substance-related disorders are very prevalent in society. Research recommends that every individual using or abusing substances, not merely those with depression, should be assessed for the presence of suicide ideation and risk (Mino, Bousquet, & Broers, 1999). Similarly, it has been recommended that all suicide attempters be assessed for substance abuse (Dhossche et al., 2000).

■ Goals and Objectives of This Chapter

An understanding of:

■ *DSM* criteria for alcohol and substance use disorders
■ The course of illness of alcohol and substance use disorders
■ The etiology and epidemiology of alcohol and substance use disorders
■ The relationship between alcohol and substance use disorders and suicide
■ Risk factors for suicide unique to individuals with alcohol and substance use disorders
■ Protective factors for suicide unique to individuals with alcohol and substance use disorders
■ Evidence-based practices for alcohol and substance use disorders

INTRODUCTION

Substance abuse is a significant concern across cultures and societies. In the United States, the total economic burden associated with drug dependence is $67 billion annually (which includes the costs of crime, lost work productivity, foster care, and other social problems related to substance use and abuse; McLellan, Lewis, O'Brien, & Kleber, 2000).

The mental health impacts of substance abuse are significant. Alcohol and drug use and abuse have a strong association with major depression and suicidality (Agosti & Levin, 2006; Goldstein & Levitt, 2006). Alcohol dependency is associated with an increased risk of impulsive suicide attempt in individuals both with and without depressive symptoms (Lejoyeux et al., 2008; Modesto-Lowe, Brooks, & Ghani, 2006; Preuss et al., 2003; Sher et al., 2007). Recent or acute alcohol ingestion is also associated with an elevated risk of impulsive suicide completion (Borges & Rosovsky, 1996; Lejoyeux et al., 2008). Research using psychological autopsies has found that individuals abusing alcohol also seem prone to suicide completions, specifically among adolescents (Giner et al., 2007).

In addition, research has found that a significant percentage (40% to 62%) of suicide attempts presenting in emergency departments have recently consumed alcohol, whereas prevalence of alcohol intake among all emergency patients is 2% (Lejoyeux et al., 2008; Saliou, Fichelle, McLoughlin, Thauvin, & Lejoyeux, 2005; Suokas & Lonnqvist, 1995). Further, research indicates that adolescent males may be at more risk of suicidality due to alcohol use, while suicidality may lead to increased alcohol use or abuse among females (Light, Grube, Madden, & Gover, 2003).

Drug use has been associated with an elevated risk in suicide attempts and completions. However, the risk varies across type of drug and nature of use/abuse. There is little published research on marijuana use and suicide risk. The minimal exploratory research that exists suggests that adolescents with a cannabis abuse or dependence from disadvantaged sociodemographic backgrounds may be at higher risk of suicide attempts (Wilcox, 2004). Research findings on opioid use and suicide are also mixed.

Stereotypes regarding individuals with substance-related disorders pervade our society. There are a number of competing and contrasting values, judgments, and beliefs associated with this issue. Consequently, individuals who abuse substances are often unfortunately characterized as weak, corrupt, amoral, unpredictable, unproductive, and dangerous. These assumptions and stereotypes can stigmatize and negatively impact the quality of clinical engagement and treatment with individuals with reorganized mental health disorders. It is essential for clinicians to recognize their personal and professional values regarding substance abusers.

▓ Individual Exercise 14.1

1. When you hear the term *substance abuser*, what are the first words or thoughts that come to your mind?
2. When you hear the word *alcoholic,* what are the first words or thoughts that come to your mind?
3. Are your listed words or thoughts generally positive or negative? Did they surprise you in any way? If so, how?
4. What personal *and* professional considerations and assumptions may make it hard for you to work with this population?
5. What personal *and* professional considerations may make it easy for you to work with this population?

DSM-IV-TR DIAGNOSIS

Substance-related disorders refer to the taking of a number of legal and illegal substances, such as alcohol, drugs, medications, or toxins. There are 11 classes of substances categorized in the *DSM-IV-TR.* In alphabetic order they are: alcohol, amphetamines (and sympathominetics), caffeine, cannabis, cocaine, hallucinogens, inhalants, nicotine, opioids, phencyclidine (PCP; and arylcyclohexylamines), and sedatives, hypnotics, or anxiolytics (American Psychiatric Association [APA], 2000). All substance-related disorders are categorized into two main groups: substance use disorders and substance-induced disorders. Substance use disorders are further subdivided into substance dependence and **substance abuse disorders**, which are described in detail below. Substance-induced disorders are subdivided into **substance intoxication** and **substance withdrawal** disorders (APA, 2000).

Substance dependence is characterized by a cluster of cognitive, behavioral, and physiological symptoms indicating that the person continues to use despite significant substance-related problems (APA, 2000, p. 192). An individual with substance dependence develops a three criterion pattern of repeated self-administration characterized by:

(1) increased tolerance for the substance that requires large amounts to achieve intoxication; (2) withdrawal difficulties that can develop in behavioral, physiological, or cognitive domains that are unpleasant and may require substance use to alleviate; and (3) compulsive drug-taking behavior, where the individual alters their behavior, such as taking more substances or using substances over longer periods of time. According to the *DSM-IV-TR* (APA, 2000), diagnostically substance dependence requires a maladaptive pattern on substance use, leading to significant impairment or distress, and requires three or more of the following:

- **Tolerance** (either increased amounts or diminished effect from the same amount)
- Withdrawal
- Use of larger amounts or over longer period of time
- Persistent desire or unsuccessful effort to cut down
- Large amounts of time devoted to activities to obtain, use, or recover from the substance
- Less time for important social, occupational, or recreational activities
- Substance use continues despite persistent and recurrent problems

The second subcategory of substance use disorders is substance abuse disorder, whose core feature "is a maladaptive pattern of substance use manifested by recurrent and significant adverse consequences related to the repeated use of substances" (APA, 2000, p. 198). Diagnostically, substance abuse disorder involves clinically significant impairment or distress requiring one or more of the following criteria within a 12-month period (APA, 2000):

- Recurrent substance use resulting in the failure to fulfill major role obligations at work, home, or school
- Recurrent use in situations that are physically hazardous
- Recurrent substance-related legal problems
- Continued use despite having persistent or recurrent social or interpersonal problems caused or exacerbated by the substance

Substance-induced disorders are subcategorized into substance intoxication and substance withdrawal disorders. Substance intoxication is the development of a reversible clinical condition due to the recent ingestion or overuse of a substance. The criteria for substance intoxication include (APA, 2000):

- The development or reversible substance specific syndrome due to recent ingestion
- Clinically significant maladaptive behavior or psychological changes due to the effects of the substance, such as mood changes, cognitive impairment, impaired judgment (impaired functioning)
- Symptoms are not due to a medical condition or mental disorder

Substance withdrawal is characterized by maladaptive behavior along with cognitive or physiological changes due to cessation or reduction in substance use. The diagnostic criteria include (APA, 2000):

- The development of a substance-specific syndrome due to cessation or reduction in use
- Causing significant distress or impairment in functioning (e.g., social, occupational, other)
- Symptoms are not due to a medical condition or mental disorder

EPIDEMIOLOGY AND PROGNOSIS

Alcohol dependence is one of the most common psychiatric disorders. In Western developed countries an estimated 90% of individuals have used alcohol, with approximately one-third developing alcohol-related difficulties (Erinoff et al., 2004). It is further estimated that approximately 10% of men and 3% to 5% of women will develop severe alcohol-related life impairments or alcohol dependence during their lives (Sher, 2006).

The National Comorbidity Survey conducted in the United States found the 12-month prevalence of alcohol dependence was 10.7% for males and 3.7% for females, while the lifetime prevalence was 20.1% for males and 8.2% for females (Kessler et al., 1994). In a replication of the National Comorbidity Survey, males continued to have greater rates of substance disorders in comparison to females (Kessler et al., 2005).

Relapse is a common and prevalent issue among individuals with substance-related disorders. It is estimated that between 40% and 60% of individuals treated for alcohol or other drug dependence will relapse within a year following treatment discharge (McLellan et al., 2000). Research indicates that patterns of relapse following alcohol treatment are similar for women and men (Walitzer & Dearing, 2006). However, several studies have found that women are disadvantaged prognostically at pretreatment (Foster, Peters, & Marshall, 2000; Glenn & Parsons,

1991) and that alcohol has a more deleterious effect on women (Graham, Wilsnack, Dawson, & Vogeltanz, 1998; Walitzer & Dearing, 2006). In regards to drug abuse, research findings indicate that women are less likely to relapse post–substance use treatment (Walitzer & Dearing, 2006).

In a review of responses to addiction treatments, most demonstrated significant reductions in drug use, improved personal health, and reduced social pathology; however, most did not attain long-term cure (McLellan et al., 2000). Factors associated with relapse include: problems of poverty, lack of family support, and psychiatric comorbidity (McLellan et al., 2000).

SUBSTANCE-RELATED DISORDERS AND SUICIDE

Suicide among individuals with alcohol use disorders remains underinvestigated. Nevertheless, it is clear that alcoholism poses a major risk factor for suicidal behavior. It has been estimated that the lifetime mortality due to suicide in alcohol dependence is between 2.2% and 18% (Roy & Linnoila, 1986; Sher, Sperling, Zalsman, Vardi, & Merrick, 2006). Approximately 20% to 35% of completed suicides are committed by individuals with alcoholism (Caces & Harford, 1998; Pirkola, Isometsa, Heikkinen, & Lonnqvist, 2000).

The rate of suicide attempt among individuals with alcohol use disorders is also alarming. For example, one study found that 24% of subjects with alcoholism attempted suicide, as compared with 5% of individuals with other psychiatric diagnoses (Weissman, Myers, & Harding, 1980). Among individuals with comorbid depression and alcoholism, 40% of inpatients had attempted suicide in the prior week to admission, and 70% had attempted suicide at some point in their lives (Cornelius, Salloum, Day, Thase, & Mann, 1996).

Research into opioid use and suicide is mixed. Among heroin users, research suggests that lifetime prevalence for suicide ideation is between 50% and 60% (Rossow, Groholt, & Wichstrom, 2005; Vingoe, Welch, Farrell, & Strang, 1999), with approximately one-third attempting suicide (Rossow et al., 2005). Although some investigations have found that opioid dependence was related to suicidal behavior, other studies found that opioid dependence did not make a unique contribution to the risk of suicide attempts (Maloney, Degenhardt, Darke, Mattick, & Nelson, 2007).

One study that investigated cocaine and alcohol use preceding suicide found that more than 40% of White adolescents had used one or both substances within 48 hours prior to suicide, compared with less than 20% of Black youth (Garlow, Purselle, & Heninger, 2007). However, the pattern of cocaine use or abuse before suicide is different in adults; research has found that over 15% of Black adults had used cocaine before death compared with less than 10% in White adults (Garlow, 2002).

RISK AND PROTECTIVE FACTORS

Among the demographic risk factors for suicide among individuals with alcohol use disorders, being male confers significantly greater risk (Sher, 2006). In addition, being older than 50 years of age is associated with increased suicide risk among individuals with alcohol use disorders (Conner, Beautrais, & Conwell, 2003; Sher et al., 2005).

Psychosocial risk factors include:

- Aggression and impulsivity (Greenwald, Reznikoff, & Plutchik, 1994; Horesh, Gothelf, & Ofek, 1999; Koller, Preuss, Bottlender, Wenzel, & Soyka, 2002; Lipsey, Wilson, Cohen, & Derzon, 1997; Mann, Waternaux, Haas, & Malone, 1999; Plutchik & Van Praag, 1989; Sher et al., 2005)
- Life stressors (Conner, Conwell, Duberstein, & Eberly, 2004; Duberstein, Conwell, & Caine, 1993; Henriksson et al., 1993; Lester, 1992)
- Hopelessness (Hewitt, Norton, Flett, Callander, & Cowan, 1998; Kingree, Thompson, & Kaslow, 1999; Wright & Obitz, 1984)
- Living alone (Henriksson et al., 1993; Sher, 2006)
- Unemployment (Henriksson et al., 1993)
- Financial difficulties (Henriksson et al., 1993; Preuss et al., 2002; Sher, 2006)
- Interpersonal losses, particularly the end of a romantic relationship (Conner et al., 2003; Conner et al., 2001; Duberstein et al., 1993; Pirkola et al., 2000; Preuss et al., 2002)
- Younger onset of alcohol use (Cheng, 1995; Conner et al., 2004; Sher et al., 2005)
- Longer duration of alcohol use(Cheng, 1995; Conner et al., 2004; Sher et al., 2005)
- A family history of alcoholism
- A history of substance, especially cocaine, abuse (Sher, 2006)

- Comorbid major depressive episode (Preuss et al., 2003; Sher, 2006)
- Prior suicidal behavior and family history of suicide (Preuss et al., 2003)

In addition, consumption of a greater amount of alcohol when drinking is linked to increased suicide risk (Borges & Rosovsky, 1996; Brent, Perper, & Allman, 1987; Cornelius et al., 1996; Hufford, 2001; Welte, Abel, & Wieczorek, 1988). Research suggests that, in comparison to abstinence, alcohol intoxication increases suicide risk as much as 90 times (Borges & Rosovsky, 1996).

Conversely, a major protective factor against suicide in alcohol use disorders is social support (Galanter, 1988; Sher, 2006). Additional protective factors against suicide in alcohol and substance abusers are effective clinical care for psychiatric and physical illness, access to clinical interventions, support for seeking help, restricted access to lethal means of suicide, strong problem-solving skills, strong conflict resolution skills, and cultural and religious beliefs that discourage suicide (Sher, 2006).

■ Case Example 14.1

Adam is a 19-year-old, single, White, Jewish male. He is a high school graduate and completed 1 year of college. He was raised in an upper-middle-class family where academic and career success was extremely important, as was their Orthodox faith. Adam was the last of five children. Seven years apart from the next youngest of his siblings, Adam was an unplanned child. He was a good student but had to work hard to earn his grades. He had several friends and dated occasionally throughout high school but never had a serious girlfriend or a best friend.

After graduation from high school Adam went away to college. He did well his first semester and passed all of his classes with above average grades, but the adjustment to living away from home and college life was not easy. He found it hard to make friends and could not relax in social situations. During the spring semester Adam began to socialize more, which negatively impacted his studying and class attendance. He began to rely on the use of alcohol to cope with academic stress and to feel comfortable in social situations. When he came home for the summer after his first year, his parents noted that his sleep pattern was disrupted. He was often irritable during the day and would only seem to relax after he had a drink. After some time they asked him about it, and he indicated that he was drinking more than he had in the past but did not think it was a problem. While they were concerned, his parents agreed they would "wait and see if he got any worse" before they "jumped to any conclusions that Adam was in need of help." Adam returned to school that fall, but due to his continued alcohol consumption, he was unable to attend most of his classes and failed the semester, at which point he dropped out of school. Over the next year, Adam became more isolated as friends increasingly commented on his drinking and noted their concerns. His parents finally insisted that he see a mental health professional after an episode during which he disappeared for two days due to a drinking spree.

On mental status exam, Adam is alert and oriented x3. His clothes are disheveled, and his grooming is poor. He has constricted range of affect and acknowledges feeling depressed and, at times, acting impulsively. He denies that his drinking is a problem and reports feeling attacked and criticized by others. According to Adam, it is the unreasonable expectations of others that led him to drop out of school. As for the recent episode, he reports being unable to remember what happened during those two days. He said "this is no big deal. It has happened to me before at school."

▓ Role Play 14.1

Using case example 14.1, in groups of three (clinician, client, and observer), engage the client and conduct an assessment for substance-related disorders and suicide risk. What specific risk and protective factors should you consider? Be aware of your personal and professional attitudes in working with this client. What other information would you need to know?

Case Vignette 14.2

Using case example 14.1 and role play 14.1, change the following:
    Gender: From Adam (male) to Anne (female)
    Environment: Note that Anne was physically abused by her boyfriend while at college.

Case Vignette 14.3

Using case example 14.1 and role play 14.1, change the following:
    Sexual Orientation: From heterosexual to homosexual
    Religion: From Judaism to Catholicism

CURRENT PRACTICE GUIDELINES
AND EVIDENCE-BASED PRACTICE

The main treatment modalities used to address suicidality among alcohol and substance abusers are Alcoholics/Narcotics Anonymous (AA/NA), **cognitive-behavioral therapy (CBT), motivational enhancement therapy** (MET), and psychopharmacological treatment (Sher, 2006). Across modalities, treatment is aimed at achieving abstinence from use, stabilizing acute medical and psychiatric problems, increasing motivation for recovery, assisting the patient in getting social support for recovery, enhancing coping and relapse prevention skills, and promoting maintenance of recovery (Babor, Kranzler, Hernandez-Avila, & Ungemack, 2003; Oyserman, Bybee, Mowbray, & Hart-Johnson, 2005; Schuckit, 2005; Sher, 2006).

Alcoholics anonymous (AA) and Narcotics Anonymous (NA) are well-known established psychosocial treatments for alcohol and substance abusers. The foundation of AA and NA is a 12-step program through which a person with alcohol or substance abuse needs to progress to maintain recovery. Members of AA and NA are able to access help 24 hours a day and are paired with a senior sober member of the group who serves as a sponsor (Sher, 2006).

CBT has been found to be an effective treatment for persons with alcoholism (Feeney, Connor, Young, Tucker, & McPherson, 2004; Sher, 2002). The focus of CBT is on the process of relapse and recovery. Treatment focuses on changing (1) cognitions regarding expectancy of substance effects, self-efficacy for coping, attributions for success or setbacks; (2) behavior such as coping with high-risk situations and developing functional alternatives such as relaxation and exercise; and (3) lifestyle via balancing social relationships and support and spiritual life (Sher, 2006).

Motivational enhancement therapy uses the patient's intrinsic motivation for change as the focus of treatment (Sellman, Sullivan, Dore, Adamson, & MacEwan, 2001). The therapist seeks to develop a discrepancy in the patient's current behavior and their future goals. Emphasis is placed on commitment to change and on recognizing change talk (Sher, 2006).

There has been growing use of medications for the treatment of alcoholism. For example, Disulfiram, an alcohol-sensitizing agent, has been widely used (Babor et al., 2003; Oyserman et al., 2005; Schuckit, 2005; Swift, 1999). Drinking alcohol precipitates an uncomfortable physical reaction, including nausea, vomiting, and changes in blood pressure in individuals taking disulfiram. Disulfiram is effective in individuals with a high level of motivation (Sher, 2006).

Naltrexone helps to reduce drinking and maintain abstinence by reducing the pleasurable effects of alcohol and the craving for alcohol (Babor et al., 2003; Oyserman et al., 2005; Schuckit, 2005; Swift, 1999). Individuals who drink during treatment with naltrexone report experiencing less alcohol high and are less likely to progress to heavy drinking. Naltrexone reduces the craving for alcohol in both patients with alcoholism and social drinkers (Sher, 2006).

Acamprosate reduces craving and distress during early abstinence and thus decreases the need to consume alcohol (Anton, 2001; Babor et al., 2003; Mason, 2001; Oyserman et al., 2005; Schuckit, 2005). Acamprosate is safe for use in conjunction with disulfiram and naltrexone (Sher, 2006).

Research demonstrates that selective serotonin reuptake inhibitors (SSRIs) lead to decreases in alcohol consumption (Anton, 2001; Babor et al., 2003; Corneliuset al., 1997; Oyserman et al., 2005; Schuckit, 2005). Finally, anticonvulsants such as topiramate also have been shown to be effective treatments for alcoholism (Johnson et al., 2003).

Practice guidelines for suicidal patients with alcoholism or substance abuse recommend the following:

1. Patients with alcoholism who report a suicide plan or intent should be hospitalized and observed closely until the suicidal ideation dissipates, even if it is the result of a temporary alcohol-induced depression. Hospitalization should also be considered if an individual with alcoholism exhibits severe agitation, psychotic symptoms, thought disorder, increased impulsivity, hopelessness, and/or has a history of suicide attempt (Cornelius, Clark, Salloum, Bukstein, & Kelly, 2004).
2. When the suicidality has decreased, discharge from in-patient care may be considered. Before discharge, the family of the patient should be advised to remove all items of danger from the home, such as guns and poisons, and to closely observe the patient after discharge. Referral to an alcohol abuse treatment program should be made (Cornelius et al., 2004).

SUMMARY

The vast majority of individuals diagnosed with a substance-related disorder do not complete suicide. It is important to recognize that individuals with a substance problem are at elevated risk for both suicide attempts and completions. Clinicians need to be aware of the unique risk and protective factors associated with suicide in this population.

For engagement, treatment, and long-term management of individuals with substance-related disorders it is necessary to consider the impact of personal stereotypes, assumptions, and bias in working with this population.

■ Key Points

1. Substance-related disorders are often characterized by periods of remission and relapse.
2. Relapse following treatment for substance use has similar patterns for both males and females.
3. Prevalence of substance-related disorders is higher for males than females.
4. Prognosis is complicated by problems of poverty, lack of family support, and psychiatric comorbidity.
5. Individuals with alcoholism have 60–120 times greater suicide risk than the general population.
6. Among heroin users, research suggests that lifetime prevalence for suicide ideation is between 50% and 60%.
7. The main treatment modalities used for substance-related disorders are Alcoholics/Narcotics Anonymous (AA/NA), CBT, MET, and psychopharmacological treatment.

FURTHER READINGS

Brady, J. (2006). The association between alcohol misuse and suicidal behaviour. *Alcohol & Alcoholism, 41*(5), 473–478.

Erinoff, L., Anthony, J. C., Brown, G. K., Caine, E. D., Conner, K. R., Dougherty, D. M., et al. (2004). Overview of workshop on drug abuse and suicidal behavior. *Drug and Alcohol Dependence, 76*(Suppl 7), S3–S9.

Haw, C., Hawton, K., Casey, D., Bale, E., & Shepherd, A. (2005). Alcohol dependence, excessive drinking and deliberate self-harm: Trends and patterns in Oxford, 1989–2002. *Social Psychiatry & Psychiatric Epidemiology, 40*(12), 964–971.

Koller, G., Preuss, U. W., Bottlender, M., Wenzel, K., & Soyka, M. (2002). Impulsivity and aggression as predictors of suicide attempts in alcoholics. *European Archives of Psychiatry & Clinical Neuroscience, 252*(4), 155–160.

Langeland, W., Draijer, N., & van den Brink, W. (2004). Psychiatric comorbidity in treatment-seeking alcoholics: The role of childhood trauma and perceived parental dysfunction. *Alcoholism: Clinical & Experimental Research, 28*(3), 441–447.

Olson, L., Huyler, F., Lynch, A. W., Fullerton, L., Werenko, D., Sklar, D., et al. (1999). Guns, alcohol, and intimate partner violence: The epidemiology of female suicide in New Mexico. *Crisis, 20*, 121–126.

Rossow, I., Groholt, B., & Wichstrom, L. (2005). Intoxicants and suicidal behaviour among adolescents: Changes in levels and associations from 1992 to 2002. *Addiction,* *100*(1), 79–88.

Roy, A. (2000). Relation of family history of suicide to suicide attempts in alcoholics. *American Journal of Psychiatry, 157*(12), 2050–2051.

Roy, A. (2003). Characteristics of drug addicts who attempt suicide. *Psychiatry Research, 121,* 99–103.

ELECTRONIC RESOURCES

Hotlines and Support Organizations

Adult Children of Alcoholics Worldwide Service Organization: http://www.adultchil dren.org
Al-anon/Alateen: http://www.al-anon.org
Alcoholics Anonymous: http://www.aa.org/
Alcohol and Drug Problems Association of North America: http://www.adpana.com
Alcohol Treatment Hotline: http://www.NationalHotline.org
Narcotics Anonymous: http://www.na.org/

Information and Resources

About Alcoholism: http://alcoholism.about.com/mmore.htm
American Foundation for Addiction Research: http://www.addictionresearch.com
Drug Abuse Resistance Education (DARE): http://www.dare.com
Learn About Alcoholism: http://www.learn-about-alcoholism.com/
National Association of Addiction Treatment Providers (NAATP): http://www. naatp.org
National Council on Alcoholism and Drug Dependence (NCADD): http://www. ncadd.org
National Institute on Alcohol Abuse and Alcoholism, National Institutes of Health: http://www.niaaa.nih.gov
Substance Abuse and Mental Health Services Administration: http://ncadi.samhsa.gov

◼ Knowledge Acquisition Test

True or False

1. Females with substance-related disorders have a better prognosis than males.
2. Males with substance-related disorders have a better prognosis than females.
3. Prevalence of substance-related disorders is higher in males than females.
4. The rate of suicide among individuals with substance-related disorders is 75%.
5. Impulsivity is not a risk factor for suicide among individuals with substance-related disorder.

Short Answer

6. List the key risk factors for suicide among individuals with substance-related disorders.

7. List the recommended evidence-based treatments of individuals with substance-related disorders.

Multiple Choice

8. What item in the following list is not a *DSM-IV-TR* criteria for substance dependence?

  A. Tolerance
  B. Withdrawal
  C. Use of larger amounts or over longer period of time
  D. Persistent desire or unsuccessful effort to cut down;
  E. All of the above
  F. None of the above

9. Which of the following is not a major category in substance-related disorders?

  A. Substance dependence
  B. Substance intoxication
  C. Substance recurrent episode
  D. Substance withdrawal
  E. All of the above
  F. None of the above

10. Which of the following items is a risk factor for suicidality among individuals with substance-related disorders?

  A. Impulsivity
  B. Comorbid depression
  C. Hallucinations
  D. Interpersonal losses
  E. All of the above
  F. None of the above

Answer key is available in the Instructor's Manual; qualified instructors may e-mail textbook@springerpub.com *to request a copy.*

REFERENCES

Agosti, V., & Levin, F. R. (2006). One-year follow-up study of suicide attempters treated for drug dependence. *The American Journal on Addictions, 15*(4), 293–296.

American Psychiatric Association [APA]. (2000). *Diagnostic and statistical manual of mental disorders* (4th ed., text revision). Washington, DC: Author.

Anton, R. F. (2001). Pharmacologic approaches to the management of alcoholism. *Journal of Clinical Psychiatry, 62*(Suppl 20), 11–17.

Babor, T. F., Kranzler, H. R., Hernandez-Avila, C. A., & Ungemack, J. A. (2003). *Substance abuse: Alcohol use disorders*. Chichester, UK: Wiley.

Borges, G., & Rosovsky, H. (1996). Suicide attempts and alcohol consumption in an emergency room sample. *Journal of Studies on Alcohol, 57*, 543–548.

Brent, D. A., Perper, J. A., & Allman, C. J. (1987). Alcohol, firearms, and suicide among youth: Temporal trends in Allegheny County, Pennsylvania, 1960 to 1983. *Journal of the American Medical Academy, 257*, 3369–3372.

Caces, F. E., & Harford, T. (1998). Time series analysis of alcohol consumption and suicide mortality in the United States, 1934–1987. *Journal of Studies on Alcohol and Drugs, 59*, 455–461.

Cheng, A. T. (1995). Mental illness and suicide: A case-control study in east Taiwan. *Archives of General Psychiatry, 52*, 594–603.

Conner, K. R., Beautrais, A. L., & Conwell, Y. (2003). Risk factors for suicide and medically serious suicide attempts among alcoholics: Analyses of Canterbury Suicide Project Data. *Journal of Alcohol Studies, 64*, 551–554.

Conner, K. R., Conwell, Y., Duberstein, P. R., & Eberly, S. (2004). Aggression in suicide among adults age 50 and over. *American Journal of Geriatric Psychiatry, 12*, 37–42.

Conner, K. R., Cox, C., Duberstein, P. R., Tian, L., Nisbet, P. A., & Conwell, Y. (2001). Violence, alcohol, and completed suicide: A case-control study. *American Journal of Psychiatry, 158*, 1701–1705.

Cornelius, J. R., Clark, D. B., Salloum, I. M., Bukstein, O. G., & Kelly, T. M. (2004). Interventions in suicidal alcoholics. *Alcoholism, Clinical and Experimental Research, 28*(5 Suppl.), 89S–96S.

Cornelius, J. R., Salloum, I. M., Day, N. L., Thase, M. E., & Mann, J. J. (1996). Patterns of suicidality and alcohol use in alcoholics with major depression. *Alcoholism: Clinical and Experimental Research, 20*, 1451–1455.

Cornelius, J. R., Salloum, I. M., Ehler, J. G., Jarrett, P. J., Cornelius, M. D., Perel, J. M., et al. (1997). Fluoxetine in depressed alcoholics: A double-blind, placebo-controlled trial. *Archives of General Psychiatry, 54*, 700–705.

Dhossche, D. M., Meloukheia, A. M., & Chakravorty, S. (2000). The association of suicide attempts and comorbid depression and substance abuse in psychiatric consultation patients. *General Hospital Psychiatry, 22*(4), 281–288.

Duberstein, P. R., Conwell, Y., & Caine, E. D. (1993). Interpersonal stressors, substance abuse, and suicide. *Journal of Nervous and Mental Disease, 181*, 80–85.

Erinoff, L., Anthony, J. C., Brown, G. K., Caine, E. D., Conner, K. R., Dougherty, D. M., et al. (2004). Overview of workshop on drug abuse and suicidal behavior. *Drug and Alcohol Dependence, 76*(Suppl 7), S3–S9.

Feeney, G. F., Connor, J. P., Young, R. M., Tucker, J., & McPherson, A. (2004). Alcohol dependence: The impact of cognitive behaviour therapy with or without naltrexone on subjective health status. *The Australian and New Zealand Journal of Psychiatry, 38*, 842–848.

Foster, J. H., Peters, T. J., & Marshall, E. J. (2000). Quality of life measures and outcome in alcohol-dependent men and women. *Alcohol, 22*, 45–52.

Galanter, M. (1988). Research on social supports and mental illness. *The American Journal of Psychiatry, 145*, 1270–1127.

Garlow, S. J. (2002). Age, gender, and ethnicity differences in patterns of cocaine and ethanol use preceding suicide. *American Journal of Psychiatry, 159*, 615–619.

Garlow, S. J., Purselle, D. C., & Heninger, M. (2007). Cocaine and alcohol use preceding suicide in African American and white adolescents. *Journal of Psychiatric Research, 41*(6), 530–536.

Giner, L., Carballo, J. J., Guija, J. A., Sperling, D., Oquendo, M. A., Garcia-Parajua, P., et al. (2007). Psychological autopsy studies: The role of alcohol use in adolescent and young adult suicides. *International Journal of Adolescent Medicine and Health, 19*(1), 99–113.

Glenn, S. W., & Parsons, O. A. (1991). Prediction of resumption of drinking in posttreatment alcoholics. *International Journal of the Addictions, 26,* 237–254.

Goldstein, B. I., & Levitt, A. J. (2006). Is current alcohol consumption associated with increased lifetime prevalence of major depression and suicidality? Results from a pilot community survey. *Comprehensive Psychiatry, 47*(5), 330–333.

Graham, K., Wilsnack, R., Dawson, D., & Vogeltanz, N. (1998). Should alcohol consumption measures be adjusted for gender differences? *Addiction, 93,* 1137–1147.

Greenwald, D. J., Reznikoff, M., & Plutchik, R. (1994). Suicide risk and violence risk in alcoholics: Predictors of aggressive risk. *Journal of Nervous and Mental Disease, 182,* 3–8.

Henriksson, M. M., Aro, H. M., Marttunen, M. J., Heikkinen, M. E., Isometsä, E. T., Kuoppasalmi, K. I., et al. (1993). Mental disorders and comorbidity in suicide. *American Journal of Psychiatry, 150,* 935–940.

Hewitt, P. L., Norton, G. R., Flett, G. L., Callander, L., & Cowan, T. (1998). Dimensions of perfectionism, hopelessness, and attempted suicide in a sample of alcoholics. *Suicide & Life-Threatening Behavior, 28,* 395–406.

Horesh, N., Gothelf, D., & Ofek, H. (1999). Impulsivity as a correlate of suicidal behaviour in adolescent psychiatric inpatients. *Crisis, 20,* 8–14.

Hufford, M. R. (2001). Alcohol and suicidal behavior. *Clinical Psychology Review, 21*(5), 797–811.

Johnson, B. A., Ait-Daoud, N., Bowden, C. L., DiClemente, C. C., Roache, J. D., Lawson, K., et al. (2003). Oral topiramate for treatment of alcohol dependence: A randomised controlled trial. *Lancet, 361,* 1677–1685.

Kessler, R. C., Berglund, P., Demler, O., Jin, R., Merikangas, K. R., & Walters, E. E. (2005). Lifetime prevalence and age-of-onset distributions of *DSM-IV* disorders in the National Comorbidity. *Archives of General Psychiatry, 62,* 593–602.

Kessler, R. C., McGonagle, K. A., Zhao, S., Nelson, C. B., Hughes, M., Eshleman, S., et al. (1994). Lifetime and 12-month prevalence of *DSM-III-R* psychiatric disorders in the United States. Results from the National Comorbidity Survey. *Archives of General Psychiatry, 5,* 8–19.

Kingree, J. B., Thompson, M. P., & Kaslow, N. J. (1999). Risk factors for suicide attempts among low-income women with a history of alcohol problems. *Addictive Behaviors, 24,* 583–587.

Koller, G., Preuss, U. W., Bottlender, M., Wenzel, K., & Soyka, M. (2002). Impulsivity and aggression as predictors of suicide attempts in alcoholics. *European Archives of Psychiatry & Clinical Neuroscience, 252*(4), 155–160.

Lejoyeux, M., Huet, F., Claudon, M., Fichelle, A., Casalino, E., & Lequen, V. (2008). Characteristics of suicide attempts preceded by alcohol consumption. *Archives of Suicide Research, 12*(1), 30–38.

Lester, D. (1992). *Why people kill themselves.* Springfield, IL: Charles Thomas.

Light, J. M., Grube, J. W., Madden, P. A., & Gover, J. (2003). Adolescent alcohol use and suicidal ideation: A non-recursive model. *Addictive Behaviors, 28,* 705–724.

Lipsey, M. W., Wilson, D. B., Cohen, M. A., & Derzon, J. H.. (1997). Is there a causal relationship between alcohol use and violence? A synthesis of evidence. *Recent Developments in Alcoholism, 13,* 245–282.

Maloney, E., Degenhardt, L., Darke, S., Mattick, R. P., & Nelson, E. (2007). Suicidal behaviour and associated risk factors among opioid-dependent individuals: A case-control study. *Addiction, 102*(12), 1933–1941.

Mann, J. J., Waternaux, C., Haas, G. L., & Malone, K. M. (1999). Towards a clinical model of suicidal behavior in psychiatric patients. *American Journal of Psychiatry, 156,* 181–189.

Maris, R. W., Berman, A. L., & Silverman, M. M. (2000). *Comprehensive textbook of suicidology.* New York: Guilford Press.

Mason, B. J. (2001). Treatment of alcohol-dependent outpatients with acamprosate: A clinical review. *Journal of Clinical Psychiatry, 62*(Suppl 20), 42–48.

McLellan, A. T., Lewis, D. C., O'Brien, C. P., & Kleber, H. D. (2000). Drug dependence, a chronic medical illness: Implications for treatment, insurance, and outcomes evaluation. *JAMA, 284*(13), 1689–1695.

Mino, A., Bousquet, A., & Broers, B. (1999). Substance abuse and drug-related death, suicidal ideation, and suicide: A review. *Crisis: Journal of Crisis Intervention & Suicide, 20*(1), 28–35.

Modesto-Lowe, V., Brooks, D., & Ghani, M. (2006). Alcohol dependence and suicidal behavior: From research to clinical challenges. *Harvard Review of Psychiatry, 14*(5), 241–248.

Oyserman, D., Bybee, D., Mowbray, C., & Hart-Johnson, T. (2005). When mothers have serious mental health problems: Parenting as a proximal mediator. *Journal of Adolescence, 28,* 443–463.

Pirkola, S. P., Isometsa, E. T., Heikkinen, M. E., & Lonnqvist, J. (2000). Suicides of alcohol misusers and non-misusers in a nationwide population. *Alcohol and Alcoholism, 35,* 70–75.

Plutchik, R., & Van Praag, H. (1989). The measurement of suicidality, aggressivity and impulsivity. *Progress in Neuropsychopharmacology and Biological Psychiatry, 13*(Suppl.), 23–34.

Preuss, U. W., Schuckit, M. A., Smith, T. L., Danko, G. P., Bucholz, K. K., Hesselbrock, M. N., et al. (2002). Comparison of 190 alcohol-dependent individuals with and without suicide attempts. *Alcoholism, Clinical and Experimental Research, 26,* 471–477.

Preuss, U. W., Schuckit, M. A., Smith, T. L., Danko, G. P., Bucholz, K. K., Hesselbrock, M. N., et al. (2003). Predictors and correlates of suicide attempts over 5 years in 1,237 alcohol-dependent men and women. *American Journal of Psychiatry, 160,* 56–63.

Rossow, I., Groholt, B., & Wichstrom, L. (2005). Intoxicants and suicidal behaviour among adolescents: Changes in levels and associations from 1992 to 2002. *Addiction, 100*(1), 79–88.

Roy, A., & Linnoila, M. (1986). Alcoholism and suicide. *Suicide & Life-Threatening Behavior, 16,* 244–273.

Saliou, V., Fichelle, A., McLoughlin, M., Thauvin, I., & Lejoyeux, M. (2005). Psychiatric disorders among patients admitted to a French medical emergency service. *General Hospital Psychiatry, 27,* 263–268.

Schuckit, M. A. (2005). *Alcohol-related disorders*. Philadelphia: Lippincott.

Sellman, J. D., Sullivan, P. F., Dore, G. M., Adamson, S. J., & MacEwan, I. (2001). A randomized controlled trial of motivational enhancement therapy (MET) for mild to moderate alcohol dependence. *Journal of Studies on Alcohol and Drugs, 62*, 389–396.

Sher, L. (2002). Behavioural therapy for the treatment of alcohol abuse and dependence. *Canadian Journal of Psychiatry, 47*, 586.

Sher, L. (2006). Alcoholism and suicidal behavior: A clinical overview. *Acta Psychiatrica Scandinavica, 113*, 13–22.

Sher, L., Oquendo, M. A., Galfalvy, H. C., Grunebaum, M. F., Burke, A. K., Zalsman, G., et al. (2005). The relationship of aggression to suicidal behavior in depressed patients with a history of alcoholism. *Addictive Behavior, 30*(6), 1144–1153.

Sher, L., Sperling, D., Stanley, B. H., Carballo, J. J., Shoval, G., Zalsman, G., et al. (2007). Triggers for suicidal behavior in depressed older adolescents and young adults: Do alcohol use disorders make a difference? *International Journal of Adolescent Medicine & Health, 19*(1), 91–98.

Sher, L., Sperling, D., Zalsman, G., Vardi, G., & Merrick, J. (2006). Alcohol and suicidal behavior in adolescents. *Minerva Pediatrica, 58*(4), 333–339.

Suokas, J., & Lonnqvist, J. (1995). Suicide attempts in which alcohol is involved: A special group in general hospital emergency rooms. *Acta Psychiatrica Scandinavica, 91*, 36–40.

Swift, R. M. (1999). Drug therapy for alcohol dependence. *New England Journal of Medicine, 340*, 1482–1490.

Vingoe, L., Welch, S., Farrell, M., & Strang, J. (1999). Heroin overdose among a treatment sample of injecting drug misusers: Accident or suicidal behaviour? *Journal of Substance Use, 4*, 88–91.

Walitzer, K. S., & Dearing, R. L. (2006). Gender differences in alcohol and substance use relapse. *Clinical Psychology Review, 26*(2), 128–148.

Weissman, M. M., Myers, J. K., & Harding, P. S. (1980). Prevalence and psychiatric heterogeneity of alcoholism in a United States urban community. *Journal of Studies on Alcohol, 41*, 672–681.

Welte, J. W., Abel, E. L., & Wieczorek, W. (1988). The role of alcohol in suicides in Erie County, NY, 1972–84. *Public Health Reports, 103*(66), 648–652.

Wilcox, H. C. (2004). Epidemiological evidence on the link between drug use and suicidal behaviors among adolescents. *Canadian Child and Adolescent Psychiatry Review, 13*(2), 27–30.

Wright, M. H., & Obitz, F. W. (1984). Alcoholics and nonalcoholics attributions of control of future life events. *Journal of Studies on Alcohol, 45*, 138–143.

Special Populations

The risk of suicide varies across individuals and groups. Certain groups of individuals are uniquely vulnerable toward and affected by suicidality. It is important for mental health professionals to have specific knowledge and awareness of these vulnerable populations.

Part V highlights several vulnerable groups. Chapter 15, "At-Risk Groups," focuses on a number of specific groups within society that are at an elevated risk for suicidality: military personnel; Native Americans; lesbian, gay, bisexual, transgendered/transsexual, and queer/questioning (LGBTQ); homeless; and incarcerated individuals. These at-risk groups often experience high levels of stigma and isolation from society, frequently due to disenfranchisement, separateness, exclusion, or sociodemographic characteristics. It is essential for mental health professionals working with suicidal clients to be aware of and understand the larger context with which individuals within these groups interact. Chapter 16, "Survivors of Suicide," examines family survivors of suicide with a special focus on the grief process and approaches to working with family survivors. In addition, the impact of client suicide on treating clinicians is explored.

Suicide can affect anyone. Yet, its impact is not equal across groups. Every death due to suicide has a direct and indirect effect on others.

While this text focuses intensively on the assessment and treatment of suicidality, it is fundamentally important for mental health professionals to work with and support survivors of suicide, be it family members or professional colleagues.

15 At-Risk Groups

Several diverse and unique groups within society are at an elevated risk for suicidality. These at-risk groups are frequently isolated from the larger society, either through stigma, being disenfranchised, exclusion, and/or sociodemographic characteristics. Although a number of at-risk populations exist, this chapter focuses on the following five groups: lesbian, gay, bisexual, transgendered/transsexual, and queer/questioning (LGBTQ) individuals; Native Americans; military personnel; the homeless; and incarcerated individuals. Although each of these populations could be discussed in the context of other chapters, they are highlighted here due to their importance and distinct vulnerability. The prevalence of risk for each of these populations is highlighted as compared to the larger societal norms. In addition, the population specific risk and protective factors are drawn from evidence-based research. Finally, their place in the social fabric or context of U.S. society that may contribute directly and indirectly to their increased risk also is explored.

■ Goals and Objectives of This Chapter

An understanding of:

■ The influence of sexual orientation on suicidality
■ The impact of the general public's and mental health professionals' attitudes, views, and opinions on LGBTQ individuals
■ Native Americans and suicidality
■ Risk and protective factors for Native Americans

- Prevalence of suicide among military personnel
- Risk and protective factors for suicide among military personnel
- Prevalence of suicide among the homeless
- Risk and protective factors for suicide among the homeless
- Prevalence of suicide among incarcerated individuals
- Risk and protective factors for suicide among incarcerated individuals

INTRODUCTION

Suicide is a leading cause of death across countries, cultures, religions, gender, and the life span (Nock et al., 2008; U.S. Department of Health and Human Services, 2001). Although efforts continually need to be taken to address this larger societal and global phenomenon, there exist a number of specific groups and populations at increased risk for suicidality. It is essential for researchers and mental health professionals to understand and investigate these at-risk populations in order to more effectively identify their unique risk and protective factors, as well as their specific societal and cultural contexts. Effective clinical engagement, assessment, and treatment for those at-risk individuals requires specific knowledge and understanding. The ability to effectively work with and treat one population does not necessarily translate into clinical success with another group.

A fundamentally important issue that arises for mental health professionals in working with at-risk populations is the influence and impact of their own personal attitudes, values, beliefs, views, and biases. Most, if not all, of these at-risk populations are treated differently in society. These at-risk groups and their members evoke a number of positive and/or negative ideas, conceptualizations, or stigmas in individuals, including mental health professionals. Each clinician needs to become aware of their own personal and professional perceptions related to members of these at-risk groups. Without such awareness, effective clinical treatment is not possible.

▓ Individual Exercise 15.1

1. What would be the hardest at-risk group (military personnel, Native Americans, LGBTQ, homeless, and incarcerated individuals) for you to professionally work with? Why?
2. What personal and/or professional considerations may make it harder for you to work with this population?

3. What would be the easiest at-risk group (military personnel, Native Americans, LGBTQ, homeless, and incarcerated individuals) for you to professionally work with? Why?
4. What personal and/or professional considerations may make it easier for you to work with this population?

LGBTQ INDIVIDUALS

In considering sexual orientation, it is important to acknowledge that orientation is a broader construct than simply same-sex activity (Cochran, Mays, & Sullivan, 2003; Sell, 1997). The term *LGBTQ* incorporates a number of constructs, including lesbian, gay, bisexual, transgendered/ transsexual, and queer/questioning. LGBTQ is used to more inclusively and accurately represent the diversity of individuals who identify as such or with nonheterosexual orientations.

Same-sex orientation has been associated with an elevated risk for suicide ideation and suicide attempt. In a national longitudinal study, 17.2% of adolescents identified as lesbian, gay, or bisexual reported suicide ideation compared to 6.3% of heterosexual identified adolescents (Silenzio, Pena, Duberstein, & Knox, 2007). A study of 21,927 sexually active youth found that, among LGBTQ adolescents, over half reported suicidal thoughts and 37% attempted suicide (Eisenberg & Resnick, 2006). Studies have found that same sex orientation is an increased risk factor for suicide and suicide attempts (Remafedi, 1999a, 1999b; Remafedi, French, Story, Resnick, & Blum, 1998). It has been reported that gay youth are two or three times more likely to attempt suicide and are 30% of all adolescent suicide attempts (Gibson, 1989); however, this finding has been questioned due to a lack of clear data (Maris, Berman, & Silverman, 2000). Notwithstanding this controversy, a majority of studies has found an increased risk among both LGBTQ males and females, but findings indicate that males have a higher risk for suicidality (Meyer, Dietrich, & Schwartz, 2008; Remafedi, 1999a; van Heeringen & Vincke, 2000). Also, elevated suicide risk in LGBTQ has been found across ethnicity and race, including White, African American, and Hispanic/Latino youth (Consolacion, Russell, & Sue, 2004; see chapter 9 of this book for further information on youth suicide).

Risk factors associated with LGBTQ individuals include the coming-out process, where an individual discloses their nonexclusive heterosexuality to self and others (Bagley & Ramsay, 1997; Fenaughty & Harre,

2003); increased drug use/abuse (Clements-Nolle, Marx, & Katz, 2006; Silenzio et al., 2007); depression (van Heeringen & Vincke, 2000); history of forced sex, discrimination, and victimization (Clements-Nolle et al., 2006); psychological stress; lack of family support (Ploderl & Fartacek, 2005); negative family reaction (D'Augelli et al., 2005); social isolation (Fenaughty & Harre, 2003); being in a hostile environment (Paul et al., 2002); low self-esteem; and increased levels of hopelessness (van Heeringen & Vincke, 2000). Protective factors for LGBTQ include family connectedness, adult caring, school safety (Eisenberg & Resnick, 2006), family acceptance, school and peer support, positive support networks, high self-esteem, and more developed coping mechanisms (Fenaughty & Harre, 2003).

It is important to recognize the influence of the larger social environment on the risk of suicidality within the LGBTQ population. In population studies, research has consistently demonstrated that sexual orientation is associated with elevated risk for mental health disorders, such as depression, anxiety, and substance use (Cochran & Mays, 2000; Gilman et al., 2001; Sandfort, de Graaf, Bijl, & Schnabel, 2001). Research has also indicated that increased risk is not associated with an illness model of homosexuality (Gonsiorek, 1996); rather, elevated risk is likely associated with the theory of social stress (Cochran et al., 2003; Meyer, 2003; Meyer et al., 2008). According to social stress theories, stigma and experiences of prejudice, rejection, and concealing, as well as internalized homophobia and decreased coping skills, contribute to higher rates in certain mental disorder, such as depression, anxiety, and substance use (Cochran et al., 2003; Dohrenwend, 2000). Consequently, an increased risk of suicide may be associated with the LGBTQ population in comparison to heterosexuals.

Stigma remains a prevalent issue for LGBTQ individuals. An early public opinion poll on attitudes, a Harris poll in 1965, found that 70% of Americans had a negative attitude toward gays and lesbians; it was not until 1999 that public support for legalizing homosexual relations between consenting adults reached 50% (Herek, 2002; Hicks & Lee, 2006). Although polls have increasingly found public opinion to be more tolerant, a significant percentage of the population continues to hold negative attitudes toward the LGBTQ population (Hicks & Lee, 2006).

The negativity of public opinions and related stigma exerts a number of direct and indirect influences on the LGBTQ population, specifically in the form of mental health treatment. Mental health clinicians who assess and treat individuals at risk of suicidality may also have personal values, attitudes, and opinions toward LGBTQ clients. Although most mental health professionals recognize the importance of providing treatment for all clients who need it, an individual clinician's opinion can affect his or her work.

Each mental health profession, including social work, psychology, counseling, psychiatry, and nursing, has studied the influence and attitudes of their members toward gays and lesbians (Bhugra, 1990; Blackwell, 2006; Crawford, McLeod, Zamboni, & Jordan, 1999; Crisp, 2006; Crisp & McCave, 2007; Liddle, 1999; Liszcz & Yarhouse, 2005; Newman, 2002; Savage, Prout, & Chard, 2004; Smith, 1993). Although mental health professionals hold less negative attitudes than the general public, each profession has been found to have negative or homophobic attitudes to some degree (Blackwell, Dziegielewski, & Jacinto, 2007; Crisp, 2006; DeCrescenzo, 1984). These studies have also found that education, exposure, and training in LGBTQ issues have reduced negative opinion and increased tolerance in mental health clinicians. Furthermore, research has indicated that members of the LGBTQ population feel that they have different therapeutic needs (Bieschke, McClanahan, Tozer, Grzegorek, & Park, 2000; Silenzio et al., 2007), but some service providers may not consider any differences (Gambrill, Stein, & Brown, 1984).

Individual Exercise 15.2

1. Consider your own values, attitudes, bias, and thoughts toward individuals with a different sexual orientation than yours. What is your orientation? Are you more comfortable interacting professionally and/or personally with those of a similar orientation? Why or why not?
2. Consider some of the following questions in relation to your views, morality, values, or attitudes toward individuals who self-identify as LGBTQ. Do you believe that individuals who self-identify as LGBTQ are able to be effective parents? Should they be able to adopt? Babysit your children? Become teachers? Get married? Join the military? Live in your community? Be entitled to health benefits from their partner's employer? Hold political office? Be treated the same as a heterosexual client? If you are religious, do you believe that your God is accepting of LGBTQ individuals?
3. How did you develop these ideas, attitudes, and perspectives?
4. Have they changed over time? If so, what has changed and why?
5. How have they impacted your clinical practice?
6. Would further training, education, exposure, and/or supervision in this area improve your ability to work with individuals who self-identify as LGBTQ? Why or why not?

NATIVE AMERICANS

Research has found that suicide is a major health problem for Native Americans. There are 4.1 million American Indians and Alaskan Natives in the United States (U.S. Census Bureau, 2002). Native Americans comprise 561 federally recognized tribes, representing a diverse range of indigenous languages and cultural customs (U.S. Census Bureau, 2002). Suicide is the sixth leading cause of death among Native Americans (Andrew & Krouse, 1995), which is approximately 1.7 times higher than the overall U.S. rate (Indian Health Service, 1998–1999). Research investigating American Indian youth has found that more than 24% have attempted suicide one or more times in their lives (Chino & Fullerton-Gleason, 2006), with more than 16% attempting in the past year (Shaughnessy, Doshi, & Jones, 2004). Adolescent males (15 to 24 years of age) are the highest risk group among Native Americans, with a suicide rate approximately 2.5 times higher than same-aged males in the general U.S. population (Wissow, 2000). In addition, Native youth with a past attempt were more likely to engage in violence and sexual risk behavior and to use tobacco, drugs, and alcohol (Shaughnessy et al., 2004). In one study, toxicology detected the presence of alcohol in 69% of all completed suicides by American Indians, with a higher prevalence in males over females (May et al., 2002).

Risk factors associated with suicidality among Native Americans include depression, drug and alcohol use, being a victim of violence (Alcantara & Gone, 2007; Andrew & Krouse, 1995; Chino & Fullerton-Gleason, 2006), previous suicide attempts (Borowsky, Resnick, Ireland, & Blum, 1999; Shaughnessy et al., 2004), friends or family members attempting or completing suicide, physical or sexual abuse, somatic symptoms, health concerns (Borowsky et al., 1999), family disruption, poor social support network, loss of ethnic/native identity, and lack of religious or spiritual identification (Alcantara & Gone, 2007). For younger adult females interpersonal conflict and partner violence are risk factors (Olson et al., 1999).

Spirituality has been posited as an important buffer against suicidality for Native Americans (Alcantara & Gone, 2007; Garoutte et al., 2003). Research has demonstrated that family connectedness, social support, emotional health, and affective relationships with tribal leaders have a protective effect against suicidality, while engagement with cultural practices has yielded mixed findings as a protective factor (Alcantara & Gone, 2007; Borowsky et al., 1999). One study investigating suicidality in sexually abused Native youth found that family attention and caring exhibited by family members, adults, or tribal leaders; parental expectations; and positive feelings toward school were protective factors for females (Pharris, Resnick, & Blum, 1997). For males, involvement in traditional activities, school enjoyment, academic performance, and caring exhibited by family members, adults, or tribal leaders were protective factors against suicidality (Pharris et al., 1997).

It is important to recognize the larger social context that may contribute to an elevated risk of suicidality among Native Americans. The legacy of colonization or historical trauma has been forwarded as a paradigm for understanding and explaining the heightened prevalence rates of mental disorders and social problems, including suicidality among American Indians (Alcantara & Gone, 2007; Duran, Duran, & Yellow Horse–Brave Heart, 1998; Yellow Horse–Brave Heart & DeBruyn, 1998). Several studies have identified elevated suicide rates with acculturation stress and a decreased risk with traditional integration (Lester, 1999).

MILITARY PERSONNEL

Suicide is the second leading cause of death among active duty military personnel (Centers for Disease Control and Prevention, 2007). The overall suicide rate among military personnel is as much as 20% higher than the suicide rate among civilians (Eaton, Messer, Garvey Wilson, & Hoge, 2006; Scoville, Gubata, Potter, White, & Pearse, 2007; Sentell, Lacroix, Sentell, & Finstuen, 1997). However, suicide attempts have been on the rise since the Army began tracking. Approximately 17.3 per 100,000 troops, or 2,100 military personnel, completed suicide in 2006 (Lorge, 2008). This was the highest in 26 years (Hefling, 2008), up from 350 military personnel in 2002. It is anticipated that due to the deployments in Iraq and Afghanistan, suicide rates in the military are higher than ever (Rutherford, 2008).

While suicide rates once varied greatly among the different branches of the military (Helmkamp, 1995), at present, rates among the various branches of the military are similar (Eaton et al., 2006). Suicides among regular-duty military personnel occur at a higher rate than among recruits (Scoville, Gardner, & Potter, 2004). It is suggested that the lower rate of suicide among recruits is due to the close supervision and limited access to alcohol and motor vehicles during the training period (Scoville et al., 2004). Suicide rates among male recruits outweigh the rate among female recruits by 3.5 times (Scoville et al., 2007). Regular-duty military males also have a higher rate of suicide than regular-duty military females (Sentell et al., 1997).

Findings regarding rates of suicide among military personnel by ethnicity vary. Some have found a higher rate of suicide among minority males and females as compared to nonminority male and females (Hourani, Warrack, & Coben, 1999), while others have found a higher rate of suicide among Caucasian military personnel (Helmkamp, 1995). Scoville et al. (2007) found that the most common method of suicide among U.S. Air Force, Army, Marine Corps, and Navy military recruits was firearms. Others have found firearms to be the leading method of suicide among regular-duty military personnel as well (Helmkamp, 1995; Mahon, Tobin, Cusack, Kelleher, & Malone, 2005). Veterans in the United States are at an increased risk of suicide, and veterans associated with the conflicts in Afghanistan and Iraq have higher levels of functional impairment and psychiatric morbidity (Kaplan, Huguet, McFarland, & Newsom, 2007).

Suicides among military personnel most often occur in the morning shortly after duty commencement, most likely because this is the time when personnel gain access to firearms (Mahon et al., 2005). Thus, being on morning duty is an independent risk factor for suicide among military personnel. Receiving a recent medical downgrade is another service-related risk factor for suicide (Mahon et al., 2005), as are receiving a low performance evaluation and having a history of military problems (Holmes, Mateczun, Lall, & Wilcove, 1998).

Other risk factors for suicide among military personnel accrue prior to military service, including younger age (Mahon et al., 2005), male gender (Mahon et al., 2005; Sentell et al., 1997), history of legal problems (Holmes et al., 1998), history of psychiatric illness (most often depression; Mahon et al., 2005; Ritchie, Keppler, & Rothberg, 2003), and history of suicide attempt (Mahon et al., 2005; Ritchie et al., 2003). Protective factors against suicide attempt include positive attitudes toward help-seeking and mental health treatment and increased awareness regarding mental illness (Knox, Litts, Talcott, Feig, & Caine, 2003). Other protective factors include older age, female gender, and military duties with limited access to firearms.

It is important to recognize the influence of the larger social environment to fully understand the of risk suicidality within military populations. In the case of military personnel, the context of the military community is crucial to consider. Although membership in the military would appear to bring along several protective factors, including common values, customs, and traditions; a strong support network; and a sense of common purpose, involvement in the military also requires being separated from family and friends, having restricted independence, being encouraged to be aggressive, and having easy access to firearms (Rosanov, Mokhovikov, & Stiliha, 2002). These factors may promote suicidal behavior in vulnerable military personnel.

THE HOMELESS

The lifetime prevalence of suicidal ideation among the homeless has been estimated to be as high as 66% (Eynan et al., 2002; Prigerson, Desai, Liu-Mares, & Rosenheck, 2003). The lifetime prevalence of suicide attempt among homeless individuals has been found to be as high as 53% (Prigerson et al., 2003). Approximately 8% of homeless individuals report a history of repeat suicide attempts (Prigerson et al., 2003).

Risk factors for suicide among the homeless population in the United States vary from the risk factors associated with suicide in the general population. Although most research examining risk factors among the homeless population focuses on adolescents, research indicates that middle-aged homeless individuals are at the highest risk for suicidality (Prigerson et al., 2003). Additionally, alcohol and/or drug abuse, psychiatric history, and inpatient hospitalizations are also risk factors for suicide among homeless adults (Prigerson et al., 2003).

Among homeless youth, sexual abuse (Molnar, Shade, Kral, Booth, & Watters, 1998; Rew, Thomas, Horner, Resnick, & Beuhring, 2001; Yoder, 1999); physical abuse (Molnar et al., 1998; Yoder, 1999); alcohol and/or drug abuse (Rew, Taylor-Seehafer, & Fitzgerald, 2001; Votta & Manion, 2004); low self-esteem (Yoder, 1999); mental health problems, especially depression (Votta & Manion, 2004; Yoder, 1999); legal and academic difficulties (Votta & Manion, 2004); prior suicide attempt (Votta & Manion, 2004); LGBTQ sexual orientation (Noell & Ochs, 2001; Rohde, Noell, Ochs, & Seeley, 2001); and knowledge of peer suicide attempt (Yoder, 1999) are associated with increased risk of suicide.

Homeless individuals who perceive themselves as resilient engage in fewer life-threatening behaviors (Rew, Taylor-Seehafer, Thomas, & Yockey, 2004) and a higher level of self-reliance is a protective factor against suicide among homeless youth (Rew et al., 2004). Pride, moral principles, determination, commitment to personal relationships

(Montgomery, 1994), self-confidence (McCormack & MacIntosh, 2001), and positive strategies for coping with loneliness (i.e., making friends, having a pet) have also been found to be protective against suicidality among homeless youth (Rew, 2000). Lastly, homeless youth report that finding a family in their community of homeless peers that provides support and understanding often not found in their family of origin is a protective factor against suicidal behavior (Rew & Horner, 2003).

It is important to recognize the larger social context that may contribute to an elevated risk of suicidality among the homeless population. Life on the streets is generally unsafe and is characterized by a lack of basic survival needs, including food, water, shelter, and medical care (Rew & Horner, 2003). Attitudes of the nonhomeless population can help or hinder the homeless. In one qualitative study of homeless youth, homeless adolescents reported that one resource for meeting basic survival needs was trusting strangers who were worried about homeless people finding food and items they needed to survive (Rew & Horner, 2003). These individuals serve as a protective factor against suicidal behavior. However, homeless youth also reported the crucial skill of recognizing who can and cannot be trusted. Homeless adolescents are often threatened and teased by nonhomeless youths. Additionally, they are often exploited (Rew & Horner, 2003). Common misperceptions of the homeless include that they are lazy, unwilling to work to better their situation, drug abusers, or mentally ill. These negative attitudes hinder outreach efforts designed to improve the life circumstances of the homeless. Intervention and prevention programs aimed at alleviating suicide and other mental health problems among the homeless would greatly benefit from incorporating campaigns designed to educate the public and improve public opinion of the homeless.

INCARCERATED INDIVIDUALS

One of every 100 Americans adults will serve time in prison (PEW Center on the States, 2008). Suicide rates in prisons are high. Suicide among death row prisoners is five times higher than the suicide rate among the general population (Lester & Tartaro, 2002). Suicidal ideation and suicide attempts are more common among incarcerated adults than among the general population (Jenkins et al., 2005).

Suicide is the leading cause of death among juvenile detention centers (Roberts & Bender, 2006). The suicide rate among adolescents in juvenile detention centers is four times higher than the rate of suicide among the general population (Gallagher & Dobrin, 2006; Hall & Gabor, 2004; Roberts & Bender, 2006). In addition, incarcerated adolescents use more violent means of suicide than adolescents in the general population (Penn, Esposito, Schaeffer, Fritz, & Spirito, 2003). Research shows that fewer than half of newly detained youth communicate their suicidal thoughts (Abram et al., 2008). Suicide risk among recently released ex-convicts is much greater then the suicide risk among the general population (Pratt, Piper, Appleby, Webb, & Shaw, 2006), particularly during the first few weeks after release when it has been shown that, compared to the general population, male prisoners are 29 times more likely to die and female prisoners are 69 times more likely to die (Farrell & Marsden, 2008).

Risk factors for suicidality among incarcerated adults include psychosis, depression, personality disorder, younger age, not being married, Caucasian ethnicity, fewer years of education, and poor social support (Jenkins et al., 2005). Risk factors for youth detainee suicide include older age, female gender, living with only one parent, and being arrested for a felony or violent crime (Nolen et al., 2008). Psychiatric illness, particularly mood disorder (Nolen et al., 2008; Penn et al., 2003), substance abuse (Nolen et al., 2008), and conduct disorders (Nolen et al., 2008), also increased suicide risk in this group. Among male incarcerated youth, anxiety disorders are also a risk factor for suicide (Nolen et al., 2008).

Unlike in the general population, there is no seasonal impact on rate of suicide in custodial populations (Fruehwald et al., 2004). Few protective factors against suicide among incarcerated individuals have been identified. However, research indicates that programs designed to address the mental health needs and substance abuse treatment needs of prisoners, including specific screenings for suicidality, may reduce the rate of suicide in this group (Goss, Peterson, Smith, Kalb, & Brodey, 2002; Jenkins et al., 2005; Kariminia et al., 2007; Penn et al., 2003; Skogstad, Deane, & Spicer, 2006).

It is important to fully consider the contextual environment of incarcerated individuals, including the unique aspects of prison life that contribute to suicide risk in this population. Prisons are characterized by social isolation and violence (Fruehwald et al., 2004). Incarcerated individuals most frequently have unaddressed mental health and substance abuse needs (Goss et al., 2002; Jenkins et al., 2005; Kariminia et al., 2007; Penn et al., 2003; Skogstad et al., 2006). These factors, combined with the negative attitude the public has toward prisons and incarcerated individuals, greatly influence suicide risk. Considering the larger social environment is particularly important in considering the rate of suicide among ex-convicts. The public at large has a negative attitude toward ex-convicts (Giguere & Dundes, 2002; Thacher, 2008). For individuals dealing with the stress of adjusting to life outside of prison, where schedules are not regimented and imposed, the stress resulting from being stigmatized and marginalized can have serious negative consequences, such as suicide.

■ Case Example 15.1

You are a mental health professional working in a large community treatment agency. Recently, you were referred a new client. Before meeting him for the first time you review the referral and intake forms, which contain the following information:

Your client is a 24-year-old male named Jon. His new medical doctor referred him to you, following a general physical. According to his MD, Jon is mildly depressed, may be using substances to cope, and has reported some suicidal ideation.

Approximately 9 months earlier, Jon moved into the city for a new job. At first he liked his job, but less so recently. Jon has no family in the city and a limited support network. He describes meeting some people in the bar near his house some nights, but he did not endorse having any close friends in the city. Increasingly, he reported thoughts of suicide but feels that he would not attempt. He has no past history of suicide attempts, psychiatric diagnoses, or hospitalization. Jon indicated seeing a past therapist, but he did not provide a description of the reason, services, or outcomes.

When Jon enters your office, he looks exceptionally despondent and depressed. He sits down and places his face in his hands. After a few moments, he lifts up his face and says "My name is Jon. I'm _____. Although, I do not want to commit suicide, I'm not sure I want to live anymore."

Please fill in the blank with either:

1. Gay
2. A military veteran from Iraq
3. Native American
4. An ex-convict
5. Homeless

■ Role Play 15.1

In groups of two or three (clinician, client, and observer), role play the scenario described in case example 15.1. Engage the client and conduct an assessment. What specific risk and protective factors should you consider? Be aware of your personal and professional attitudes in working with this client.

SUMMARY

Membership in at-risk groups, such as the military, Native Americans, LGBTQ, homeless, and incarcerated individuals, poses additional issues and complications for individuals experiencing suicidality. In addition, mental health professionals working with individuals need to become aware of the unique risk and protective factors that may exert further influence on these groups. Professional and personal awareness is essential for mental health clinicians engaging, assessing, and treating members of these and other at-risk populations.

■ Key Points

1. There exist a number of specific groups or populations that may increase the risk of suicide individuals.
2. At-risk populations have unique and specific risk and protective factors.
3. LGBTQ, Native Americans, military personnel, the homeless, and incarcerated individuals are associated with increased risk of suicidality.
4. The attitudes, bias, and opinions of mental health professionals may undermine their ability to effectively work with at-risk populations.
5. Suicide is the second leading cause of death among the military.
6. Current suicide rates among military personnel are higher than they have been over the past 26 years.
7. Suicidal ideation and attempts occur at an extremely high rate among the homeless.
8. Suicide is the leading cause of death of juvenile detainees.
9. The first few weeks postrelease is an extremely high-risk period for individuals who have been incarcerated.
10. The larger environmental context of each of these at-risk groups needs to be fully considered to understand the elevated rates of suicide in these groups.

FURTHER READINGS

Native Americans

Alcantara, C., & Gone, J. P. (2007). Reviewing suicide in Native American communities: Situating risk and protective factors within a transactional-ecological framework. *Death Studies, 31*(5), 457–477.

Andrew, M. M., & Krouse, S. A. (1995). Research on excess deaths among American Indians and Alaska Natives: A critical review. *Journal of Cultural Diversity, 2*(1), 8–15.

Borowsky, I. W., Resnick, M. D., Ireland, M., & Blum, R. W. (1999). Suicide attempts among American Indian and Alaska Native youth: Risk and protective factors. *Archives of Pediatrics & Adolescent Medicine, 153*(6), 573–580.

Olson, L. M. & Wahab, S. (2006). American Indians and suicide: A neglected area of research. *Trauma, Violence, and Abuse, 7*(1), 19–33.

Yellow Horse–Brave Heart, M., & DeBruyn, L. M. (1998). The American Indian holocaust: Healing historical unresolved grief. *Journal of the National Center, 8*(2), 60–82.

LGBTQ Population

Blackwell, C. W., Dziegielewski, S. F., & Jacinto, G. A. (2007). The use of a strength-based approach in addressing discrimination against gays and lesbians. *Journal of Human Behavior in the Social Environment, 14*(3), 1–17.

Crisp, C., & McCave, E. L. (2007). Gay affirmative practice: A model for social work practice with gay, lesbian, and bisexual youth. *Child & Adolescent Social Work Journal, 24*(4), 403–421.

Fenaughty, J., & Harre, N. (2003). Life on the seesaw: A qualitative study of suicide resiliency factors for young gay men. *Journal of Homosexuality, 45*(1), 1–22

Morrow, D. F., & Messinger, L. (Eds.). (2006). *Sexual orientation and gender expression in social work practice: Working with gay, lesbian, bisexual, and transgender people.* New York: Columbia University Press.

Perez, R. M., DeBord, K. A., & Bieschke, K. J. (Eds.). (2000). *Handbook of counseling and psychotherapy with lesbian, gay, and bisexual client.* Washington, DC: American Psychological Association.

Military Personnel

Allen, J. P., Cross, G., & Swanner, J. (2005). Suicide in the army—A review of current information. *Military Medicine, 170*(7), 580–584.

Bodner, E., Ben-Artzi, E., & Kaplan, Z. (2006). Soldiers who kill themselves: The contribution of dispositional and situational factors. *Archives of Suicide Research, 10*(1), 29–43.

Helkamp, J. C. (1996). Occupation and suicide among males in the US Armed Forces. *Annals of Epidemiology, 6*(1), 83–88.

Stander, V. A., Hilton, S. M., Kennedy, K. R., & Robbins, D. L. (2004). Surveillance of completed suicide in the Department of the Navy. *Military Medicine, 169*(4), 301–306.

Thorenson, S., Mehlum, L., Roysamb, E., & Tonnessen, A. (2006). Risk factors for completed suicide in veterans of peacekeeping: Repatriation, negative life events, and marital status. *Archives of Suicide Research, 10*(4), 353–363.

Homeless Individuals

McCormack, D., & MacIntosh, J. (2001). Research with homeless people uncovers a model of health. *Western Journal of Nursing Research, 23*, 679–697.

Montgomery, C. (1994). Swimming upstream: The strengths of women who survive homelessness. *Advances in Nursing Science, 16*, 34–45.

Rew, L. (2000). Friends and pets as companions: Strategies for coping with loneliness among homeless youth. *Journal of Child and Adolescent Psychiatric Nursing, 13*, 125–140.

Rew, L., Taylor-Seehafer, M., Thomas, N. Y., & Yockey, R. D. (2004). Correlates of resilience in homeless adolescents. *Journal of Nursing Scholarship, 33*(1), 33–40.

Suss, A., Homel, P., Wilson, T. E., & Shah, B. (2004). Risk factors for nonfatal suicide behaviors among inner-city adolescents. *Pediatric Emergency Care, 20*(7), 426–429.

Incarcerated Individuals

Baillargeon, J., Ducate, S., Pulvino, J., Bradshaw, P., Murray, O., & Olvera, R. (2003). The association of psychiatric disorders and HIV infection in the correctional setting. *Annals of Epidemiology, 13*(9), 606–612.

Lewis, C. F. (2005). Post-traumatic stress disorder in HIV-positive incarcerated women. *Journal of the American Academy of Psychiatry & the Law, 33*(4), 455–464.

Penn, J. V., Esposito, C. L., Schaeffer, L. E., Fritz, G. K., & Spirito, A. (2003). Suicide attempts and self-mutilative behavior in a juvenile correctional facility. *Journal of the American Academy of Child & Adolescent Psychiatry, 42*(7), 762–769.

Roberts, A. R., & Bender, K. (2006). Juvenile offender suicide: Prevalence, risk factors, assessment, and crisis intervention protocols. *International Journal of Emergency Mental Health, 8*(4), 255–265.

ELECTRONIC RESOURCES

Native Americans

Center for Disease Control: http://www.cdc.gov/ncipc/factsheets/nativeamericans.htm
Healthy Minds: http://www.healthyminds.org/naian07.cfm
Indian Health Services: http://www.ihs.gov/NonMedicalPrograms/nspn/
Minnesota Department of Health: http://www.health.state.mn.us/mentalhealth/indwork group.html
National Congress of American Indians: http://www.ncai.org/Native_Youth_Suicide_Preventio.209.0.html
Suicide Prevention Resource Center: http://www.sprc.org/grantees/pdf/nspl.pdf
U.S. Department of Health and Human Services: http://www.4woman.gov/minority/americanindian/suicide.cfm

LGBTQ Population

Healthy Place: http://www.healthyplace.com/Communities/Gender/gayisok/glbt_suicide _study.htm
The Trevor Helpline: http://thetrevorproject.org/helpline.aspx

Military Personnel

Any Soldier: http://www.anysoldier.com
Hire A Hero: http://www.hireahero.com
Suffolk County United Veterans: http://www.SCUV.org

The Veterans' Voice: http://www.theveteransvoice.com
Vet Friends: http://www.vetfriends.com
Wounded Warrior Project: http://www.WoundedWarriorProject.org

Homeless Individuals

Alpha Project: http://www.alphaproject.org/
Care for the Homeless: http://www.careforthehomeless.org/services/susans_place.html
http://www.geocities.com/athens/agora/7076/hgroups.html

Incarcerated Individuals

Bridging the Gap: http://www.btguk.org/
Department of Corrective Services: http://www.correctiveservices.wa.gov.au/O/offender
servicessuicideprevention.aspx?uid=8391-4809-0958-4989
The Foundation Training Company: http://www.foundation-training.org/
HM Prison Services: http://www.hmprisonservice.gov.uk/adviceandsupport/azofsupport
groups/index.asp?id=3058,90,91,100,0,0
NACRO: http://www.nacro.org.uk/
New Bridge Foundation: http://www.newbridgefoundation.org.uk/
Suicide and Mental Health Association International: http://suicideandmentalhealth
associationinternational.org/preventionprison.html
St. Giles Trust: http://www.stgilestrust.org.uk/

■ Knowledge Acquisition Test

True or False

1. Same sex sexual orientation has been associated with an elevated risk for suicide ideation and suicide attempt.
2. LGBTQ females have a higher suicide risk than LGBTQ males.
3. Generally, the greater the connection for Native Americans with their traditional identity and cultures the greater their suicide risk.
4. Previous attempts among Native American Indians is not an risk factor.
5. Military personnel have a higher rate of suicide than the general population.
6. Suicide is among the leading causes of death among the military.
7. Homeless youth have the highest rate of suicide among all homeless age groups.
8. A major protective factor against suicide among the homeless is self-reliance.
9. Among incarcerated youth, sexual abuse is a risk factor for suicide.

Short Answer

10. Discuss how the larger social environment may influence the suicide risk within the LGBTQ population.

11. How can mental health professionals improve their ability to work within the LGBTQ populations?
12. Discuss how the larger cultural environment influences the suicide risk within the Native American population.
13. What factors in the military community protect against and contribute to suicide risk?
14. What are the main risk factors for suicide among homeless adults?
15. What factors contribute to the increased risk of suicide among incarcerated youth?

Multiple Choice

16. What item may improve the effectiveness of mental health professional working within the LGBTQ community?

    A. Education
    B. Exposure
    C. Training
    D. All of the above
    E. None of the above

17. Protective factors against suicide among LGBTQ include which of the following?

    A. Family connectedness/acceptance
    B. Developed coping mechanisms
    C. Investment in personal relationships
    D. Self-confidence
    E. All of the above
    F. None of the above

18. Suicide is the _____ leading cause of death among Native Americans.

    A. Fourth
    B. Sixth
    C. Eight
    D. Tenth
    E. Twelfth

19. Protective factors against suicide among the homeless include which of the following?

    A. Strategies for coping with loneliness
    B. Resiliency
    C. Having a pet
    D. All of the above
    E. None of the above

20. Suicide is the _____ leading cause of death among military personnel.

    A. Second
    B. Fourth
    C. Sixth

D. Eighth
E. Tenth

Answer key is available in the Instructor's Manual; qualified instructors may e-mail textbook@springerpub.com *to request a copy.*

REFERENCES

Abram, K. M., Choe, J. Y., Washburn, J. J., Teplin, L. A., King, D. C., & Dulcan, M. K. (2008). Suicidal ideation and behaviors among youths in juvenile detention. *Journal of the American Academy of Child & Adolescent Psychiatry, 47*(3), 291–300.

Alcantara, C., & Gone, J. P. (2007). Reviewing suicide in Native American communities: Situating risk and protective factors within a transactional-ecological framework. *Death Studies, 31*(5), 457–477.

Andrew, M. M., & Krouse, S. A. (1995). Research on excess deaths among American Indians and Alaska Natives: A critical review. *Journal of Cultural Diversity, 2*(1), 8–15.

Bagley, C., & Ramsay, R. (1997). *Suicidal behaviour in adolescents and adults: Research, taxonomy, and prevention.* Aldershot, UK: Ashgate Publishing Company.

Bhugra, D. (1990). Doctors' attitudes to male homosexuality: A survey. *Sexual & Marital Therapy, 5*(2), 167–174.

Bieschke, K. J., McClanahan, M., Tozer, E., Grzegorek, J. L., & Park, J. (2000). Programmatic research on the treatment of lesbian, gay, and bisexual clients: The past, the present, and the course for the future. In R. M. Perez, K. A. DeBord & K. J. Bieschke (Eds.), *Handbook of counseling and psychotherapy with lesbian, gay, and bisexual clients* (pp. 309–335). Washington, DC: American Psychological Association.

Blackwell, C. W. (2006). *Registered nurses' attitudes toward the protection of gays and lesbians in the workplace: An examination of homophobia and discriminatory beliefs.* Orlando, FL: University of Central Florida.

Blackwell, C. W., Dziegielewski, S. F., & Jacinto, G. A. (2007). The use of a strength-based approach in addressing discrimination against gays and lesbians. *Journal of Human Behavior in the Social Environment, 14*(3), 1–17.

Borowsky, I. W., Resnick, M. D., Ireland, M., & Blum, R. W. (1999). Suicide attempts among American Indian and Alaska Native youth: Risk and protective factors. *Archives of Pediatrics & Adolescent Medicine, 153*(6), 573–580.

Centers for Disease Control and Prevention. (2007). Web-based Injury Statistics Query and Reporting System (WISQARS). Retrieved October 19, 2008, from http://www.cdc.gov/injury/wisqars/index.html

Chino, M., & Fullerton-Gleason, L. (2006). Understanding suicide attempts among American Indian adolescents in New Mexico: Modifiable factors related to risk and resiliency. *Ethnicity & Disease, 16*(2), 435–442.

Clements-Nolle, K., Marx, R., & Katz, M. (2006). Attempted suicide among transgender persons: The influence of gender-based discrimination and victimization. *Journal of Homosexuality, 51*(3), 53–69.

Cochran, S. D., & Mays, V. M. (2000). Relation between psychiatric syndromes and behaviorally defined sexual orientation in a sample of the US population. *American Journal of Epidemiology, 151*(5), 516–523.

Cochran, S. D., Mays, V. M., & Sullivan, J. G. (2003). Prevalence of mental disorders, psychological distress, and mental health services use among lesbian, gay, and bisexual adults in the United States. *Journal of Consulting & Clinical Psychology, 71*(1), 53–61.

Consolacion, T. B., Russell, S. T., & Sue, S. (2004). Sex, race/ethnicity, and romantic attractions: Multiple minority status adolescents and mental health. *Cultural Diversity & Ethnic Minority Psychology, 10*(3), 200–214.

Crawford, I., McLeod, A., Zamboni, B. D., & Jordan, M. B. (1999). Psychologists' attitudes toward gay and lesbian parenting. *Professional Psychology: Research and Practice, 30*(4), 394–401.

Crisp, C. (2006). Correlates of homophobia and use of gay affirmative practice among social workers. *Journal of Human Behavior in the Social Environment, 14*(4), 119–143.

Crisp, C., & McCave, E. L. (2007). Gay affirmative practice: A model for social work practice with gay, lesbian, and bisexual youth. *Child & Adolescent Social Work Journal, 24*(4), 403–421.

D'Augelli, A. R., Grossman, A. H., Salter, N. P., Vassey, J. J., Starks, M. T., & Sinclair, K. O. (2005). Predicting the suicide attempts of lesbian, gay, and bisexual youth. *Suicide & Life-Threatening Behavior, 35*(6), 646–660.

DeCrescenzo, T. (1984). *Homophobia: A study of the attitudes of mental health professionals toward homosexuality.* New York: Harrington Park.

Dohrenwend, B. P. (2000). The role of adversity and stress in psychopathology: Some evidence and its implications for theory and research. *Journal of Health & Social Behavior, 41*(1), 1–19.

Duran, B., Duran, E., & Yellow Horse–Brave Heart, M. (1998). Native Americans and the trauma of history. In R. Thornton (Ed.), *Studying Native America: Problems and prospects* (pp. 60–76). Madison: University of Wisconsin Press.

Eaton, K. M., Messer, S. C., Garvey Wilson, A. L., & Hoge, C. W. (2006). Strengthening the validity of population-based suicide rate comparisons: An illustration using U.S. military and civilian data. *Suicide & Life-Threatening Behavior, 36*(2), 182–191.

Eisenberg, M. E., & Resnick, M. D. (2006). Suicidality among gay, lesbian and bisexual youth: The role of protective factors. *Journal of Adolescent Health, 39*(5), 662–668.

Eynan, R., Langley, J., Tolomiczenko, G., Rhodes, A. E., Links, P., Wasylenki, D., et al. (2002). The association between homelessness and suicidal ideation and behaviors: Results of a cross-sectional survey. *Suicide & Life-Threatening Behavior, 32*(4), 418–427.

Farrell, M., & Marsden, J. (2008). Acute risk of drug-related death among newly released prisoners in England and Wales. *Addiction, 103*(2), 251–155.

Fenaughty, J., & Harre, N. (2003). Life on the seesaw: A qualitative study of suicide resiliency factors for young gay men. *Journal of Homosexuality, 45*(1), 1–22.

Fruehwald, S., Frottier, P., Matschnig, T., Koenig, F., Lehr, S., & Eher, R. (2004). Do monthly or seasonal variations exist in suicides in a high-risk setting? *Psychiatry Research, 121*(3), 263–269.

Gallagher, C. A., & Dobrin, A. (2006). Deaths in juvenile justice residential facilities. *Journal of Adolescent Health, 38*(6), 662–668.

Gambrill, E. D., Stein, T. J., & Brown, C. E. (1984). Social services use and need among gay/lesbian residents of the San Francisco Bay Area. *Journal of Social Work & Human Sexuality, 3*(1), 51–69.

Garoutte, E. M., Goldberg, J., Beals, J., Herrell, R., Manson, S. M., & AI-SUPERPFP Team. (2003). Spirituality and attempted suicide among American Indians. *Social Science and Medicine, 56,* 1571–1579.

Gibson, P. J. (1989). *Report of the Secretary's Task Force on Youth Suicide: Prevention and interventions in youth suicide, 3* (DHHS Publication ADM 89-1623). Washington, DC: U.S. Department of Health and Human Services.

Giguere, R., & Dundes, L. (2002). Help wanted: A survey of employer concerns about hiring ex-convicts. *Criminal Justice Policy Review, 13*(4), 396–408.

Gilman, S. E., Cochran, S. D., Mays, V. M., Hughes, M., Ostrow, D., & Kessler, R. C. (2001). Risk of psychiatric disorders among individuals reporting same-sex sexual partners in the National Comorbidity Survey. *American Journal of Public Health, 91*(6), 933–939.

Gonsiorek, J. C. (1996). *Mental health and sexual orientation.* Orlando, FL: Harcourt Brace.

Goss, J. R., Peterson, K., Smith, L. W., Kalb, K., & Brodey, B. B. (2002). Characteristics of suicide attempts in a large urban jail system with an established suicide prevention program. *Psychiatric Services, 53*(5), 574–579.

Hall, B., & Gabor, P. (2004). Peer suicide prevention in a prison. *Crisis: Journal of Crisis Intervention & Suicide, 25*(1), 19–26.

Hefling, K. (2008). Iraq war vets' suicide rates analyzed: High numbers found among members of Guard, Reserves. Retrieved August 3, 2008, from http://www.sfgate.com/cgi-bin/article.cgi?f=/c/a/2008/02/13/MNPSV110J.DTL

Helmkamp, J. C. (1995). Suicides in the military: 1980–1992. *Military Medicine, 160*(2), 45–50.

Herek, G. M. (2002). Gender gaps in public opinion about lesbians and gay men. *Public Opinion Quarterly, 66*(1), 40–66.

Hicks, G. R., & Lee, T. (2006). Public attitudes toward gays and lesbians: Trends and predictors. *Journal of Homosexuality, 51*(2), 57–77.

Holmes, E. K., Mateczun, J. M., Lall, R., & Wilcove, G. L. (1998). Pilot study of suicide risk factors among personnel in the United States Marine Corps (Pacific Forces). *Psychological Reports, 83*(1), 3–11.

Hourani, L. L., Warrack, A. G., & Coben, P. A. (1999). Suicide in the U.S. Marine Corps, 1990 to 1996. *Military Medicine, 164*(8), 551–555.

Indian Health Service (1998–1999). *Regional differences in Indian health.* Rockville, MD: Public Health Service, U.S. Department of Health and Human Services.

Jenkins, R., Bhugra, D., Meltzer, H., Singleton, N., Bebbington, P., Brugha, T., et al. (2005). Psychiatric and social aspects of suicidal behaviour in prisons. *Psychological Medicine, 35*(2), 257–269.

Kaplan, M. S., Huguet, N., McFarland, B. H., & Newsom, J. T. (2007). Suicide among male veterans: A prospective population-based study. *Journal of Epidemiological and Community Health, 61,* 619–624.

Kariminia, A., Butler, T. G., Corben, S. P., Levy, M. H., Grant, L., Kaldor, J. M., et al. (2007). Extreme cause-specific mortality in a cohort of adult prisoners—1988 to 2002: A data-linkage study. *International Journal of Epidemiology, 36*(2), 310–316.

Knox, K. L., Litts, D. A., Talcott, G. W., Feig, J. C., & Caine, E. D. (2003). Risk of suicide and related adverse outcomes after exposure to a suicide prevention programme in the US Air Force: Cohort study. *British Medical Journal, 327*(7428), 1376.

Lester, D. (1999). Native American suicide rates, acculturation stress and traditional integration. *Psychological Reports, 84*(2), 398.

Lester, D., & Tartaro, C. (2002). Suicide on death row. *Journal of Forensic Sciences, 47*(5), 1108–1111.

Liddle, B. J. (1999). Gay and lesbian clients' ratings of psychiatrists, psychologists, social workers, and counsellors. *Journal of Gay & Lesbian Psychotherapy, 3*(1), 81–93.

Liszcz, A. M., & Yarhouse, M. A. (2005). A survey on views of how to assist with coming out as gay, changing same-sex behavior or orientation, and navigating sexual identity confusion. *Ethics & Behavior, 15*(2), 159–179.

Lorge, E. M. (2008). Army responds to rising suicide rates. Retrieved August 3, 2008, from http://www.army.mil/-news/2008/01/31/7222-army-responds-to-rising-suicide-rates

Mahon, M. J., Tobin, J. P., Cusack, D. A., Kelleher, C., & Malone, K. M. (2005). Suicide among regular-duty military personnel: A retrospective case-control study of occupation-specific risk factors for workplace suicide. *American Journal of Psychiatry, 162*(9), 1688–1696.

Maris, R. W., Berman, A. L., & Silverman, M. M. (2000). *Comprehensive textbook of suicidology*. New York: Guilford Press.

May, P. A., Van Winkle, N. W., Williams, M. B., McFeeley, P. J., DeBruyn, L. M., & Serna, P. (2002). Alcohol and suicide death among American Indians of New Mexico: 1980–1998. *Suicide & Life-Threatening Behavior, 32*(3), 240–255.

McCormack, D., & MacIntosh, J. (2001). Research with homeless people uncovers a model of health. *Western Journal of Nursing Research, 23*, 679–697.

Meyer, I. H. (2003). Prejudice, social stress, and mental health in lesbian, gay, and bisexual populations: Conceptual issues and research evidence. *Psychological Bulletin, 129*(5), 674–697.

Meyer, I. H., Dietrich, J., & Schwartz, S. (2008). Lifetime prevalence of mental disorders and suicide attempts in diverse lesbian, gay, and bisexual populations. *American Journal of Public Health, 98*(6), 1004–1006.

Molnar, B. E., Shade, S. B., Kral, A. H., Booth, R. E., & Watters, J. K. (1998). Suicidal behavior and sexual/physical abuse among street youth. *Child Abuse & Neglect, 22*(3), 213–222.

Montgomery, C. (1994). Swimming upstream: The strengths of women who survive homelessness. *Advances in Nursing Science, 16*, 34–45.

Newman, B. S. (2002). Lesbians, gays, and religion: Strategies for challenging belief systems. *Journal of Lesbian Studies, 6*(3–4), 87–98.

Nock, M. K., Borges, G., Bromet, E. J., Alonso, J., Angermeyer, M., Beautrais, A., et al. (2008). Cross-national prevalence and risk factors for suicidal ideation, plans and attempts. *British Journal of Psychiatry, 192*(2), 98–105.

Noell, J. W., & Ochs, L. M. (2001). Relationship of sexual orientation to substance use, suicidal ideation, suicide attempts, and other factors in a population of homeless adolescents. *Journal of Adolescent Health, 29*, 31–36.

Nolen, S., McReynolds, L. S., DeComo, R. E., John, R., Keating, J. M., & Wasserman, G. A. (2008). Lifetime suicide attempts in juvenile assessment center youth. *Archives of Suicide Research, 12*(2), 111–123.

Olson, L., Huyler, F., Lynch, A. W., Fullerton, L., Werenko, D., Sklar, D., et al. (1999). Guns, alcohol, and intimate partner violence: The epidemiology of female suicide in New Mexico. *Crisis, 20*, 121–126.

Paul, J. P., Catania, J., Pollack, L., Moskowitz, J., Canchola, J., Mills, T., et al. (2002). Suicide attempts among gay and bisexual men: Lifetime prevalence and antecedents. *American Journal of Public Health, 92*(8), 1338–1345.

Penn, J. V., Esposito, C. L., Schaeffer, L. E., Fritz, G. K., & Spirito, A. (2003). Suicide attempts and self-mutilative behavior in a juvenile correctional facility. *Journal of the American Academy of Child & Adolescent Psychiatry, 42*(7), 762–769.

The PEW Center on the States (2008). *One in 100: Behind bars in America.* Public Safety Performance Project. Washington, DC: PEW Chartable Trusts.

Pharris, M. D., Resnick, M. D., & Blum, R. W. (1997). Protecting against hopelessness and suicidality in sexually abused American Indian adolescents. *Journal of Adolescent Health, 21*(6), 400–406.

Ploderl, M., & Fartacek, R. (2005). Suicidality and associated risk factors among lesbian, gay, and bisexual compared to heterosexual Austrian adults. *Suicide & Life-Threatening Behavior, 35*(6), 661–670.

Pratt, D., Piper, M., Appleby, L., Webb, R., & Shaw, J. (2006). Suicide in recently released prisoners: A population-based cohort study. *Lancet, 368*(9530), 119–123.

Prigerson, H. G., Desai, R. A., Liu-Mares, W., & Rosenheck, R. A. (2003). Suicidal ideation and suicide attempts in homeless mentally ill persons: Age-specific risks of substance abuse. *Social Psychiatry & Psychiatric Epidemiology, 38*(4), 213–219.

Remafedi, G. (1999a). Sexual orientation and youth suicide. *Journal of the American Medical Association, 282*(13), 1291–1292.

Remafedi, G. (1999b). Suicide and sexual orientation: Nearing the end of controversy? *Archives of General Psychiatry, 56*(10), 885–886.

Remafedi, G., French, S., Story, M., Resnick, M. D., & Blum, R. (1998). The relationship between suicide risk and sexual orientation: Results of a population-based study. *American Journal of Public Health, 88*(1), 57–60.

Rew, L. (2000). Friends and pets as companions: Strategies for coping with loneliness among homeless youth. *Journal of Child and Adolescent Psychiatric Nursing, 13,* 125–140.

Rew, L., & Horner, S. D. (2003). Personal strengths of homeless adolescents living in a high-risk environment. *Advances in Nursing Science, 26*(2), 90–101.

Rew, L., Taylor-Seehafer, M., & Fitzgerald, M. L. (2001). Sexual abuse, alcohol and other drug use, and suicidal behaviors in homeless adolescents. *Issues in Comprehensive Pediatric Nursing, 24*(4), 225–240.

Rew, L., Taylor-Seehafer, M., Thomas, N. Y., & Yockey, R. D. (2004). Correlates of resilience in homeless adolescents. *Journal of Nursing Scholarship, 33*(1), 33–40.

Rew, L., Thomas, N., Horner, S. D., Resnick, M. D., & Beuhring, T. (2001). Correlates of recent suicide attempts in a triethnic group of adolescents. *Journal of Nursing Scholarship, 33,* 361–367.

Ritchie, E. C., Keppler, W. C., & Rothberg, J. M. (2003). Suicidal admissions in the United States military. *Military Medicine, 186*(3), 177–181.

Roberts, A. R., & Bender, K. (2006). Juvenile offender suicide: Prevalence, risk factors, assessment, and crisis intervention protocols. *International Journal of Emergency Mental Health, 8*(4), 255–265.

Rohde, P., Noell, J., Ochs, L., & Seeley, J. R. (2001). Depression, suicidal ideation, and STD-related risk in homeless older adolescents. *Journal of Adolescence, 24*(4), 447–460.

Rosanov, V. A., Mokhovikov, A. N., & Stiliha, R. (2002). Successful model of suicide prevention in the Ukraine military environment. *Crisis: The Journal of Crisis Intervention and Suicide Prevention, 23*(4), 171–177.

Rutherford, J. (2008). Soldiers: Long tours create "lot of stress." Retrieved August 3, 2008, from http://fieldnotes.msnbc.msn.com/archive/2008/05/30/1085766.aspx

Sandfort, T. G., de Graaf, R., Bijl, R. V., & Schnabel, P. (2001). Same-sex sexual behavior and psychiatric disorders: Findings from the Netherlands Mental Health Survey and Incidence Study (NEMESIS). *Archives of General Psychiatry, 58*(1), 85–91.

Savage, T. A., Prout, H. T., & Chard, K. M. (2004). School psychology and issues of sexual orientation: Attitudes, beliefs, and knowledge. *Psychology in the Schools, 41*(2), 201–210.

Scoville, S. L., Gardner, J. W., & Potter, R. N. (2004). Traumatic deaths during U.S. Armed Forces basic training, 1977–2001. *American Journal of Preventive Medicine, 26*(3), 194–104.

Scoville, S. L., Gubata, M. E., Potter, R. N., White, M. J., & Pearse, L. A. (2007). Deaths attributed to suicide among enlisted U.S. Armed Forces recruits, 1980–2004. *Military Medicine, 172*(10), 1024–1031.

Sell, R. L. (1997). Defining and measuring sexual orientation: A review. *Archives of Sexual Behavior, 26,* 643–658.

Sentell, J. W., Lacroix, M., Sentell, J. V., & Finstuen, K. (1997). Predictive patterns of suicidal behavior: The United States armed services versus the civilian population. *Military Medicine, 162*(3), 168–171.

Shaughnessy, L., Doshi, S. R., & Jones, S. E. (2004). Attempted suicide and associated health risk behaviors among Native American high school students. *Journal of School Health, 74*(5), 177–182.

Silenzio, V. M., Pena, J. B., Duberstein, P. R., & Knox, K. L. (2007). Sexual orientation and risk factors for suicidal ideation and suicide attempts among adolescents and young adults. *American Journal of Public Health, 97*(11), 2017–2019.

Skogstad, P., Deane, F. P., & Spicer, J. (2006). Social-cognitive determinants of help-seeking for mental health problems among prison inmates. *Criminal Behaviour & Mental Health, 16*(1), 43–59.

Smith, G. B. (1993). Homophobia and attitudes toward gay men and lesbians by psychiatric nurses. *Archives of Psychiatric Nursing, 7*(6), 377–384.

Thacher, D. (2008, June). *Prisoner re-entry and the professionalization of housing.* Paper presented at the Annual Meeting of The Law and Society, Las Vegas, NV.

U.S. Census Bureau. (2002). *The American Indian and Alaska Native population: 2000 (Census 2000 Brief).* Washington, DC: Author.

U.S. Department of Health and Human Services. (2001). Summary of national strategy for suicide prevention: Goals and objectives for action. Retrieved October 20, 2008, from http://mentalhealth.samhsa.gov/suicideprevention/strategy.asp

van Heeringen, C., & Vincke, J. (2000). Suicidal acts and ideation in homosexual and bisexual young people: A study of prevalence and risk factors. *Social Psychiatry & Psychiatric Epidemiology, 35*(11), 494–499.

Votta, E., & Manion, I. (2004). Suicide, high-risk behaviors, and coping style in homeless adolescent males' adjustment. *Journal of Adolescent Health, 34*(3), 237–243.

Wissow, L. S. (2000). *Suicide attempts among American Indian and Alaskan Natives.* Baltimore: Johns Hopkins.

Yellow Horse–Brave Heart, M., & DeBruyn, L. M. (1998). The American Indian ho-
    locaust: Healing historical unresolved grief. *Journal of the National Center,* 8(2),
    60–82.
Yoder, K. A. (1999). Comparing suicide attempters, suicide ideators, and non-suicidal
    homeless and runaway adolescents. *Suicide & Life-Threatening Behavior,* 29(1),
    25–36.

16 Survivors of Suicide

In the United States, it is estimated that nearly 186,000 to 250,000 individuals each year are left to cope with the death of a loved one by suicide (Bailley, Kral, & Dunham, 1999; Peterson, Luoma, & Dunne, 2002). Until recently, it was generally thought that family survivors of suicide experienced no more difficulties than survivors from other forms of traumatic deaths, such as accidents or natural disasters. Recent research now tells us differently. This chapter explores the impact of completed suicide on family survivors. An understanding of the grief process for this unique group is outlined. Family members are not the only survivors; clinical professionals are dramatically impacted by the death of a client. A review of the impact and influence of a client suicide on treating clinicians and an examination of professional important considerations following a client suicide also are explored.

■ Goals and Objectives of This Chapter

An understanding of:

- The stages of grief
- Complicated grief
- Spousal/partner reactions to suicide
- Parental reactions to suicide
- Offspring responses to suicide
- Professional reactions following a client suicide
- Preparing and training professionals for the possibility of a client suicide

- Supporting a colleague, coworker, or team after a client suicide
- Supporting yourself personally and professional following the suicide of a client
- Working with the surviving family members

INTRODUCTION

Every day suicides are prevented. Individuals managing various difficulties—working alone or with the support of families, friends, and/or professionals—no longer consider suicide an option, necessity, or choice. However, for thousands of other individuals every year, suicide does become the final act. It is estimated that for every completed suicide, there are more than 6 to 10 **survivors of suicide**, people closely affected by the suicide (Lukas & Seiden, 1997; Peterson et al., 2002).

To the thousands of family and friends left behind, the suicide of a loved one can be devastating and can cause severe negative consequences. Research has found that suicide survivors are at increased risk for experiencing psychiatric and physical reactions, including grief, complicated grief, stress, depression, rejection, anxiety, stigma, and somatic complaints.

A suicide death has levels of repercussion beyond the surviving family and friends. Research estimates that among individuals who complete suicide, approximately 33% have contact with a mental health professional within 1 year of their death, with 20% having contact within 1 month (Luoma, Pearson, & Martin, 2002). Across their professional career, mental health practitioners are more likely than not to experience the death of a client due to suicide. Thus, professionals also become survivors of suicide. It is important for professionals to not only understand and work with survivors of suicide but to be able to effectively manage personally and professionally the impact of a client's suicide. It is similarly important that mental health professionals be able to support and work with their colleagues following the suicide of a client.

The clinical implications for effectively working with family, friends, and professional survivors requires mental health practitioners to have knowledge, understanding, and awareness of the unique issues confronted by survivors. Furthermore, it is essential for practitioners to be cognizant of their own personal attitudes, thoughts, judgments, and beliefs regarding those left behind following a suicide.

◼ Individual Exercise 16.1

1. A professional colleague and friend telephoned you at home during a weekend to inform you that his spouse completed suicide the night before. After offering your condolences and speaking with him for a few minutes, you end the call. Alone you think of the news and your years of knowing the woman who had suicided, who seemed so content and confident. What are some of your thoughts and reactions?
2. A professional colleague and friend telephoned you at work early Monday morning to inform you that one of her clients just completed suicide the night before. After offering your condolences and speaking with her for a few minutes, you end the call. Alone you ponder the news. What are some of your thoughts and reactions?
3. How are your thoughts, beliefs, assumptions, judgments, and/or reactions the same and how are they different between the two scenarios presented above?
4. Please complete again the first three questions, but instead of a colleague telephoning you, you are telephoning a colleague for consolation. What would you say? What sort of reaction would you expect?

◼ Small Group Exercise 16.1

In groups of two to four:

1. Review and discuss your answers to question three in individual exercise 16.1.
2. What are the similarities or differences in your responses?
3. How may your reactions influence your practice?

STAGES OF GRIEF

The process of grieving in the face of loss by natural and traumatic causes has been the focus of research for many years. Most notable, Elizabeth Kübler-Ross (1969) suggested a model of the **stages of grief** originally proposed to help dying patients cope with their own death. Her model then became widely accepted as a model of grief that individuals experience after the loss of a loved one. Kübler-Ross (1969) suggested that there are five stages of the grieving process: (1) denial, characterized by a refusal to accept that the loss has occurred; (2) anger, characterized by feelings of fury toward the deceased and those around the individuals; (3) bargaining, characterized by searching for a way out of the situation; (4) depression, characterized by feeling to sad to continue with one's own life; and (5) acceptance, characterized by making peace with what has happened.

She explained that not all individuals experience each of the five stages, but all experience at least two stages. She also believes that the order of the stages experienced may vary across individuals. Kübler-Ross (1969) believes that an individual may get stuck in one of the first four stages, and until they are able to reach the stage of acceptance, they may experience unbearable pain and suffering that negatively impacts their personal and interpersonal functioning. The stages of grief proposed by Kübler-Ross (1969) have led to several other models of grieving that describe the emotional processes that individuals experience after the loss of a loved one. The specific processes or stages may vary across models; however, Kübler-Ross's (1969) concept of the grief process as an individual journey through which a range of emotions are experienced ultimately ending in acceptance of reality remains a fundamental component within each model.

COMPLICATED GRIEF

Complicated grief is differentiated from the normal grieving process. Complicated grief is defined as a group of symptoms that include longing for the deceased, preoccupation with thoughts of the deceased, futility about the future, disinterest in others, difficulty accepting the death, feeling a lack of control, insecurity, and anger and resentment over the death (Prigerson et al., 1999; Shear, Frank, Houck, & Reynolds, 2005). Survivors of traumatic death of a family member are at increased risk for complicated grief and bereavement (Clements, DeRanieri, Vigil, & Benasutti, 2004). This is especially true for family survivors of suicide (Bailey et al., 1999; Farberow, Gallagher-Thompson, Gilewski, & Thompson, 1992a; Knieper, 1999; Mitchell, Kim, Prigerson, & Mortimer-Stephens, 2004, 2005;). When an individual completes suicide, severe consequences ensue for the family the individual leaves behind. This may be due to the sudden shock, confusion regarding why the act was committed, and/or the trauma of discovering the suicide. Survivors' grief reactions can become even more exacerbated by negative responses from the community regarding the suicide (Cvinar, 2005; Knieper, 1999).

Closely related survivors of suicide could be at risk of developing physical and/or mental health problems, including suicidal ideation (Mitchell et al., 2004). For example, among suicide survivors, grief and loneliness have been found to rise over time, whereas grief and loneliness decrease over time among accidental death survivors (Kovarsky,

1989). Additionally, complicated grief among suicide survivors is associated with increased suicidal ideation and behavior (Latham & Prigerson, 2004; Mitchell et al., 2005; Szanto, Prigerson, Houck, Ehrenpreis, & Reynolds, 1997; Szanto et al., 2006).

Currently, there is no research that examines how the process of complicated grief varies across ethnicities and cultures. Given that the rate of depression and suicide attempt vary across ethnicities (Brent et al., 2004; Kessler et al., 1994), it is reasonable to expect that the process of complicated grief may vary across ethnicities as well, particularly in respect to survivors of suicide, a group with elevated rates of depression and suicidality. Future research is needed to better understand grief processes of suicide survivors across ethnicities.

▣ Case Example 16.1

On Friday night, at 2:30 A.M., the phone rang and Jessica was awakened. She had been expecting an earlier call from her son, Daniel, with an update on how her daughter-in-law, Michele, was doing. Michele had been struggling with some issues at work, and they had spent many hours on the phone talking about the situation. Jessica tried to be supportive and periodically provided advice to Daniel and Michele. They had a very strong, close relationship, and Jessica always felt like Michele was her own daughter, not just a daughter-in-law.

The phone call Jessica received was not the one she had expected. A male voice explained that he was calling from the police department in the town where Daniel and Michele lived. The officer explained that Michele had passed away. It appeared as though she had completed suicide. After the officer had explained the situation, Jessica hung up the phone in disbelief. She was unable to speak or move. As far as Jessica knew, Michele and Daniel were making plans to have a family and were planning a vacation, a long cruise to Alaska just 2 months away.

Jessica could not understand how this could have happened. Just yesterday she was on the phone with Michele, and they were developing a plan of action for how to deal with what Michele believed to be gender discrimination at work that was affecting her ability to advance in her career. Michele was brilliant. She graduated Suma cum Laude from Harvard as an undergraduate and was first in her graduating class from Harvard Law School. She was recognized in her specific field of practice and should have been on her way to becoming partner in her firm.

Several months later, after Michele had been buried and Daniel had relocated to a new home (trying to forget the life he lost with Michele), Jessica was still desperately trying to understand how and why Michele had completed suicide. She was haunted by Michele's memory and the phone call they had prior to the day that she completed suicide. Did she miss something? Could she have been more attentive? If she had paid more attention would she have picked up on any clues that Michele had been contemplating suicide? She felt tremendous guilt both for not being able to stop Michele and for being unable to console Daniel during his difficult mourning due to her own struggles with Michele's death. Jessica also felt guilty about the anger she felt toward Daniel. Why did he not see the signs? They must have been there, and he was Michele's husband. If he had paid more attention then Jessica would not be in this position now. She often wondered what was wrong with her. How could a mother feel so angry toward her own suffering child? Often, her thoughts were consumed with anger at both Michele and Daniel.

Jessica felt out of control and did not know where to turn. Five months after Michele's suicide, Jessica finally reached out for support and joined Parental Survivors of Suicide, a support group near her home.

1. Does this case represent what is considered the normal grief process or, rather, complicated grief?
2. What factors may help to protect against the development of complicated grief?
3. What areas would you target in treatment with Jessica?

■ Role Play 16.1

Using case example 16.1, engage in a role play in which you would assess for complicated grief and engage Jessica in treatment. Have one person take the role of client and one take the role of Jessica.

FAMILY SURVIVORS

It is estimated that up to 250,000 individuals a year are left to cope with the death of a loved one by suicide (Bailley et al., 1999; Peterson et al., 2002). As mentioned earlier in this chapter, research now indicates that family survivors of suicide experience heightened feelings of rejection and responsibility and may experience complicated grief (Bailley et al., 1999; Barlow & Morrison, 2002; Clements et al., 2004; Farberow et al., 1992a; Mitchell et al., 2005; Smith, Mitchell, Bruno, & Constantino, 1995). Other studies indicate that severe stress results for the family survivors, especially if they find the body of the loved one or witness the final act (Callahan, 2000; Cvinar, 2005; Knieper, 1999; Lester, 1993; Van Dongen, 1991a).

Suicide survivors have an increased risk of experiencing psychiatric and physical reactions. For example, risk of suicidal ideation (Mitchell et al., 2004, 2005), depression, anxiety, posttraumatic stress, and somatic complaints are increased among suicide survivors (Grossman, Clark,

Gross, Halstead, & Pennington, 1995; Jordan & McMenamy, 2004; Rudestam, 1992; Van Dongen, 1991b; Watson & Lee, 1993; Zhang, Hui, & Zhou, 2005).

Family survivors of suicide are also faced with stigma imposed by society (Alexander, 1991; Barlow & Coleman, 2003; Barlow & Morrison, 2002; Cvinar, 2005; Harwood, Hawton, Hope, & Jacoby, 2002; McNiel, Hatcher, & Reubin, 1988; Range, 1998; Range, Bright, & Ginn, 1985; Reynolds & Cimbolic, 1988; Smith et al., 1995; Stillion, 1996; Sveen & Walby, 2008). It has been demonstrated that suicide-bereaved individuals receive more blame for the individual's death from those around them than non–suicide-bereaved survivors (Cvinar, 2005; McNiel et al., 1988; Smith et al., 1995; Sveen & Walby, 2008). Calhoun and Allen (1991) found that suicide-bereaved survivors were thought of as less likeable and more blameworthy than non–suicide-bereaved survivors. Additionally, the range of negative responses to survivors of suicide varies by their relationship to the suicide victim; children survivors are viewed less negatively than parent survivors (Reynolds & Cimbolic, 1988).

Survivors of suicide also tend to experience difficulty resulting from evaluations of their relationships with the suicide victim. They are inclined to appraise their relationship with the deceased relative as less intimate and less satisfactory (Cleiren & Diekstra, 1994). Additionally, self-directed anger for missing possible signs and/or being unable to prevent the suicide is often experienced (Alexander, 1991; Gyulay, 1989; Lester, 1993; Seguin, Lesage, & Kiely, 1995; Silverman, Range, & Overholser, 1994). Many studies also indicate that survivors of suicide suffer heightened feelings of shame (Alexander, 1991; Barlow & Morrison, 2002; Gyulay, 1989; Harwood et al., 2002; Lester, 1993; Seguin et al., 1995; Silverman et al., 1994; Smith et al., 1995; Watson & Lee, 1993).

Research has consistently demonstrated that one of the major factors associated with complicated grief among suicide survivors is being plagued with unanswerable questions (van Dongen, 1990, 1991a). Suicide survivors agonize over why their loved one completed suicide. Family members often struggle to find a reason for the action of their loved one. This searching often results in feelings of powerlessness and helplessness accompanied by feelings of depression (Cleiren & Diekstra, 1994; Seguin et al., 1995).

Limited research has examined protective factors against developing complicated grief as a suicide survivor. Most consistently, having a supportive friend and family network has been associated with a decrease in the likelihood of experiencing complicated grief and an increase in successful resolution of the grieving process (Callahan, 2000; Farbe-row, Gallagher-Thompson, Gilewski, & Thompson, 1992b; Reed, 1998; Seguin et al., 1995; Thompson & Range, 1991).

The Effect of Relationship to Suicide Victim

Research indicates that closeness of the survivor to the suicide victim is related to the degree of distress experienced. Closely related survivors are at increased risk for experiencing complicated grief (Mitchell et al., 2004).

Limited research has examined differences in the impact of suicide across groups of survivors, specifically parents, offspring, and spouses. Research on parental survivors indicates that parental survivors experience decreases in cohesion among remaining family members and decreases in adaptation or the ability of the marital and/or family system to modify roles and relationships in the face of situational and developmental stress (Lohan, 2002).

Among spousal survivors, a study comparing spousal suicide survivors to spousal non–suicide survivors found that women whose husbands had died by suicide experienced more guilt and blame than widows who lost a husband in an accident (McNiel et al., 1988). Additionally, Agerbo (2003) found that mortality in the suicide surviving spouse is heightened.

In one study that examined sibling survivors of suicide (Brent et al., 1993), sibling survivors experienced increased rates of new-onset depression. This risk was increased in those sibling survivors with a history of psychiatric illness and in those with a family history of depression and/or other psychiatric disorders (Brent et al., 1993).

Although the exact number of child suicide survivors worldwide is not known, it is estimated that annually in the United States approximately 60,000 children experience the death by suicide of a relative, 7,000 to 12,000 children experience the suicide of a parent, and 8, 000 experience the suicide of a sibling (Cerel, Jordan, & Duberstein, 2008). Of the limited research that exists examining the impact of suicide on child survivors, findings suggest that suicide-bereaved children and adolescents are at increased risk for anxiety (Cerel, Fristad, Weller, & Weller, 1999; Shepherd & Barraclough, 1976), major depression (Pfeffer, Karus, Siegel, & Jiang, 2000; Pfeffer et al., 1997), posttraumatic stress disorder (Cerel et al., 1999; Pfeffer et al., 1997), impaired social adjustment (Cerel et al., 1999; Pfeffer et al., 1997, 2000; Sethi & Bhargava, 2003), and internalizing problems (Cerel et al., 1999; Pfeffer et al., 1997, 2000). Furthermore, research indicates that male youth suicide survivors more often experience externalizing behaviors than female youth suicide survivors (Grossman et al., 1995). Some research also indicates that surviving suicide as a child is associated with greater risk of unresolved grief that negatively impacts interpersonal functioning into and throughout adulthood (Demi & Howell, 1991).

Empirically Supported Treatment for Suicide Survivors

While there is extensive literature examining bereavement interventions in general, limited research exists examining bereavement interventions specifically targeting suicide survivors (Jordan & McMenamy, 2004). There are several descriptive papers that describe support groups for suicide-bereaved individuals; however, only nine studies objectively assess the effectiveness of specific interventions for suicide survivors, and not all of these studies incorporated control groups and used random assignment (Jordan & McMenamy, 2004). This limited research indicates that group support programs (Constantino & Bricker, 1996; Constantino, Sekula, & Rubinstein, 2001; Farberow, 1992; Murphy, 2000; Pfeffer, Jiang, Kakuma, Hwang, & Metsch, 2002; Renaud, 1995), family treatment with added group support (Rogers, Sheldon, Barwick, Letofsky, & Lancee, 1982), debriefing interventions (Mitchell & Kim, 2003), and writing interventions where individuals write about the suicide of a loved one (Range, Campbell, Kovac, Marion-Jones, & Aldridge, 2002) are effective interventions for treating survivors of suicide.

PROFESSIONALS MANAGING AFTER A CLIENT SUICIDE

What happens to the practitioner when a client suicides? While professionals are very effective in assessing and treating suicidal patients, there will be clients in treatment who successfully complete suicide. This phenomenon is often neglected or minimized in practice and the literature regarding how professionals manage a client's suicide (Gitlin, 1999). Following a client's suicide practitioners' reactions may vary from grief, shock, denial, distress, depression, isolation, self-blame, a sense of failure, strain on their personal and professional lives, fear of another suicide, and loss of confidence, to avoidance of triggering stimuli (Alexander, Klein, Gray, Dewar, & Eagles, 2000; Collins, 2003; Cooper, 1995;

Dewar, Eagles, Klein, Gray, & Alexander, 2000; Eagles, Klein, Gray, Dewar, & Alexander, 2001; Farberow, 2005; Grad, 1996; Grad & Michel, 2005; Halligan & Corcoran, 2001; Maltsberger, 1992; Spiegelman & Werth, 2005; Strom-Gottfried & Mowbray, 2006; Sudak, 2007; Thompson & Brooks, 1990).

A common myth is that all suicides can be prevented. Although professionals work diligently and effectively with individuals expressing various degrees of suicidality, individuals both receiving and not receiving treatment will suicide. Survey research across a number of mental health professions has found that 35% of social workers, 86% of community mental health teams, 46% to 67% of psychiatrists, and 22% to 40% of psychologists have reported having one or more clients suicide (Alexander et al., 2000; Chemtob, Hamada, Bauer, Kinney, & Torigoe, 1988; Chemtob, Hamada, Bauer, Torigoe, & Kinney, 1988; Kleespies, 1993; Linke, Wojciak, & Day, 2002; Ruskin, Sakinofsky, Bagby, Dickens, & Sousa, 2004). Further, quantitative and qualitative studies have similarly found that nurses and social workers experience the difficult reality of client suicides (Brown, 1987; Gilje, Talseth, & Norberg, 2005; Jacobson, Ting, Sanders, & Harrington, 2004; Ting, Sanders, Jacobson, & Power, 2006). Many professionals in training or educational programs will also experience this phenomenon (Coverdale, Roberts, & Louie, 2007; Dewar et al., 2000; Farberow, 2005; Kleespies, 1993; Ruskin et al., 2004; Sudak, 2007).

Even though the literature is limited on the management of this issue, a number of professions, including medical doctors (Alexander et al., 2000; Dewar et al., 2000; Eagles et al., 2001; Halligan & Corcoran, 2001; Talseth & Gilje, 2007), social workers (Feldman, 1987; Strom-Gottfried & Mowbray, 2006; Ting et al., 2006), nurses (Collins, 2003; Cooper, 1995; Gilje et al., 2005), and psychologists (Kleespies, 1993; Spiegelman & Werth, 2005), have begun to investigate the impact of a client suicide on their practitioners. Confronted with the reality that a majority of mental health clinicians will experience working with a client who completes suicide (Alexander et al., 2000; Grad, 1996), professionally, there are a number of areas that warrant consideration, including preparation and training, supporting other practitioners, managing in the aftermath of a client suicide, and working with the surviving family members.

1. *Preparation and training.* It is important to work to prevent every suicide, but it may be unethical not to prepare practitioners and es-

tablish protocols to managing a future client suicide. Preparation can occur on a number of levels (Alexander et al., 2000; Farberow, 2005):

- Training and education on managing a client suicide should begin in educational institutions.
- Intern, residence, and trainee programs for practitioners need to incorporate the realities of practicing with a suicidal client and how others may have managed a client's suicide.
- Supervisors working in this field should be required to have specific training in how to respond, support, and supervise trainees who may experience this event.
- Agencies, institutions, and programs that work with suicidality need to not only develop and implement protocols and procedures to manage the aftermath of a client suicide, but they need to inform and train new and existing practitioners on these procedures.
- Professional bodies may need to become more active in establishing protocols and preemptively reaching out to members who will work with clients who are suicidal.
- Practitioners need to recognize that the suicide of a client may not be evidence of professional incompetence but a reality of their chosen profession and seek to develop various levels of support in their personal and professional lives.

2. *Colleague and team support.* Although, practitioners typically see clients alone, most professionals working with individuals who may be suicidal operate with others or in teams. The impact of a client's suicide affects the entire team. Research has found that following a suicide a most helpful coping strategy is support from colleagues, conversely, formal inquiries, although necessary, were reported as unhelpful (Alexander et al., 2000; Dewar et al., 2000; Linke et al., 2002; Ting et al., 2006). Supervisors and colleagues need to discourage negative and critical comments toward the clinician survivors and discourage the clinician from overworking and/or self-blame (Collins, 2003). Working to develop a supportive, nonjudgmental, and nonblaming professional environment following the suicide of a colleague's client may directly enable the practitioner and the team to manage the suicide while continuing to provide effective services.

3. *Managing in the aftermath of a suicide.* Like a stone thrown into a still pond, each suicide produces waves that continue to exert profound

influence long after the stone has disappeared from view. The suicide of a client will frequently have immediate and potentially lasting emotional and professional impact on practitioners (Alexander et al., 2000; Anderson, 2005; Chemtob, Hamada, Bauer, Kinney et al., 1988; Dewar et al., 2000; Linke et al., 2002). A practitioner's ability to relate to others' emotional states and cognitive processes and her/his clinical effectiveness can all be affected by a client's suicide. Practitioners will often over focus or ruminate on the **psychological autopsy** of their client, that is, a formal or informal procedure of examining a death by analyzing or reconstructing the events and motives leading up to their death. This process can be both helpful and detrimental to the practitioner.

The following suggestions for practitioners managing in the aftermath of a client's suicide are adapted from Spiegelman and Werth (2005, pp. 50–52).

- Meet with your supervisor or senior practitioner in your department.
- Review the case, and if possible, discuss your emotional reaction to the suicide and plan next steps.
- Discuss how to inform other staff members, coworkers, peers, and others.
- Document the event and supervision session.
- Do not make statements that may sound like an assumption of responsibility.
- If able, obtain facts of the event from a neutral party.
- Contact professional supports (legal, insurance, administration).
- Consider personal counseling and/or personal support from others.
- If supervisor and employer allow, consider contacting significant others of the client (e.g., make counseling referrals for the significant others).
- Consider appropriateness of attending the funeral, wake, or other ritual.
- Consider participating in a future psychological autopsy.

4. *Working with the surviving family members.* A client's suicide does not terminate our professional role. Beyond a responsibility to our selves and our team, practitioners must decide how to continue to work with the surviving family members. This is often the most difficult decision and process of professionals; however, it is often

described as helpful and therapeutic to both family members and the practitioner (Alexander et al., 2000; Anderson, 2005; Strom-Gottfried & Mowbray, 2006). Although it is important for practitioners to determine for themselves, with their employer, and, most importantly, the surviving family members on how to negotiate and navigate this role, the following steps may serve as a helpful guide if continued work with the family is possible. Here are some points to consider:

■ Some grieving family members may want to speak with the practitioner; others may not. It is important to respect the wishes of the individual family members. Initially, providing support and condolences can be helpful, but practitioners may want to avoid reviewing client details or conducting a psychological review with family members. The practitioner may also consider recommending counseling and providing referrals (Anderson, 2005; Spiegelman & Werth, 2005).

■ Consider attending the memorial or funeral rituals. Both personally and professionally, grieving rituals and shared grief can be very important (Alexander et al., 2000; Anderson, 2005; Linke et al., 2002; Spiegelman & Werth, 2005; Strom-Gottfried & Mowbray, 2006). Current literature has indicated that both family members and professionals can benefit by the practitioner attending these rituals (Alexander et al., 2000; Anderson, 2005; Strom-Gottfried & Mowbray, 2006).

■ In some circumstances, there may be some value in an ongoing connection or checking in with the family across time (Anderson, 2005).

In a study that surveyed suicide survivors' perceptions of the treating professional who had worked with their loved one at the time of their death, it was found that the majority (74%) knew of the ongoing clinical treatment (Peterson et al., 2002). Despite recommendations that professionals should contact family members regarding the suicide risk of a client (Linehan, 1999), only a few (11%) reported being contacted by the clinician of their loved one's suicidal risk (Peterson et al., 2002). The majority of family members wanted to speak with the treating clinician and have her or him attend the funeral. Survivors who did not consider bringing lawsuits tended to rate the meetings with the clinicians as more meaningful and believed the clinician to be straightforward and open (Peterson et al., 2002).

▓ Individual Exercise 16.2

You arrive to work at an inpatient psychiatry unit Monday morning to learn that the client you and your interdisciplinary team had discharged on Friday had completed suicide the past evening. You hold a leadership position within the team. Like yourself, the other team members are experiencing a range of affect and looking for support, yet concerned about blame.

1. What steps would you recommend for yourself and your colleagues?
2. How may you support your colleagues?
3. How do you manage your own affect, sense of responsibility, and any concerns for the inevitable formal assessment of the client's suicide?
4. Would your answers to these questions change if the client had insisted to being discharged AMA (Against Medical Advice)? Why or why not?

▓ Small Group Exercise 16.2

In groups of three to five:

1. As a group, review and discuss your answers to individual exercise 13.3.
2. What are the similarities and or differences between the responses of the two exercises?

SUMMARY

Following a suicide many family members and friends become survivors devastated by the death of a loved one. Furthermore, mental health practitioners are likely to experience a client who completes suicide. It is important for practitioners to be able to effectively work with the surviving family and friends. It is also essential for professionals to recognize that they themselves and their colleagues may become professional survivors after a client suicide.

▓ Key Points

1. Survivors of suicide often suffer from complicated grief.
2. Grief reactions of suicide survivors vary according to personal and contextual characteristics.
3. Nature of relationship with suicide victim impacts a survivor's reaction.
4. The stigma experienced by survivors of suicide is a major cause of the severe grief reactions experienced by suicide survivors across types of relationships with the suicide victim (parent, offspring, spouse, peer).

5. A major factor contributing to the difficulty that suicide survivors experience in resolving the grief process is the question of *why* their loved one completed suicide.

6. Across a professional career, mental health practitioners are likely to experience the death of a client due to suicide.

7. It is a myth that all suicides can be prevented.

8. Organizations, agencies, and professions may benefit from educating, training, and establishing protocols to manage the death of a client due to suicide.

9. Following the suicide of a client, practitioners benefit from the support of their colleagues, while formal inquiries, although necessary, were unhelpful.

10. A client's suicide does not terminate our professional role. Beyond a responsibility to our selves and our team, practitioners must decide how to continue the work with the surviving family members.

FURTHER READINGS

Barlow, C. A., & Morrison, H. (2002). Survivors of suicide. Emerging counseling strategies. *Journal of Psychosocial Nursing & Mental Health Services, 40*(1), 28–39.

Cain, A. C. (2002). Children of suicide: The telling and the knowing. *Psychiatry, 65*(2), 124–136.

Clark, S. (1995). *After suicide: Help for the bereaved.* Melbourne: Hill of Content Publishing Company.

Cohen, D., & Putney, R. (2003). Suicide website resources for professionals and consumers. *Journal of Mental Health and Aging, 9*(2), 67–72.

Constantino, R. E., Sekula, L. K., & Rubinstein, E. N. (2001). Group intervention for widowed survivors of suicide. *Suicide & Life-Threatening Behavior, 31*(4), 428–441.

De Fauw, N., & Andriessen, K. (2003). Networking to support suicide survivors. *Crisis: Journal of Crisis Intervention & Suicide, 24*(1), 29–31.

Dunne, E. J., McIntosh, J. L., & Dunne-Maxim, K. (1987). *Suicide and its aftermath: Understanding and counseling the survivors.* New York: W. W. Norton & Company.

Farberow, N. L. (2005). The mental health professional as suicide survivor. *Clinical Neuropsychiatry: Journal of Treatment Evaluation, 2*(1), 13–20.

Gross, B. (2005). Death throes: Professional liability after client suicide. *Annals of the American Psychotherapy Association, 8*(1), 34–35.

Jordan, J. R., & McMenamy, J. (2004). Interventions for suicide survivors: A review of the literature. *Suicide & Life-Threatening Behavior, 34*(4), 337–349.

Jacobs, D. G. (1999). *The Harvard Medical School guide to suicide assessment and intervention.* San Francisco, CA: Jossey-Bass.

Kalischuk, R. G., & Davies, B. (2001). A theory of healing in the aftermath of youth suicide. Implications for holistic nursing practice. *Journal of Holistic Nursing, 19*(2), 163–186.

Krysinska, K. E. (2003). Loss by suicide: A risk factor for suicidal behavior. *Journal of Psychosocial Nursing & Mental Health Services, 41*(7), 34–41.

Lukas, C., & Seiden, H. (1997). *Silent grief.* New York: Charles Scribner's Sons.

Mitchell, A. M., Kim, Y., Prigerson, H. G., & Mortimer, M. K. (2005). Complicated grief and suicidal ideation in adult survivors of suicide. *Suicide & Life-Threatening Behavior, 35*(5), 498–506.

Murphy, S. A., Johnson, L. C., & Lohan, J. (2003). Challenging the myths about parents' adjustment after the sudden, violent death of a child. *Journal of Nursing Scholarship, 35*(4), 359–364.

Parrish, M., &; Tunkle, J. (2005). Clinical challenges following an adolescent's death by suicide: Bereavement issues faced by family, friends, schools, and clinicians. *Clinical Social Work Journal, 33*(1), 81–102.

Peterson, E. M., Luoma, J. B., & Dunne, E. (2002). Suicide survivors' perceptions of the treating clinician. *Suicide & Life-Threatening Behavior, 32*(2), 158–166.

Pompili, M., Lester, D., De Pisa, E., Del Casale, A., Tatarelli, R., & Girardi, P. (2008). Surviving the suicides of significant others: A case-study. *Crisis: The Journal of Crisis Intervention & Suicide Prevention, 29*(1), 45–48.

Reed, M. D. (1993). Sudden death and bereavement outcomes: The impact of resources on grief symptomatology and detachment. *Suicide & Life-Threatening Behavior, 23*(3), 204–220.

Rubey, C. T., & McIntosh, J. L. (1996). Suicide survivors groups: Results of a survey. *Suicide & Life-Threatening Behavior, 26*(4), 351–358.

Sandor, M. K., Walker, L. O., & Sands, D. (1994). Competence-building in adolescents, Part II: Community intervention for survivors of peer suicide. *Issues in Comprehensive Pediatric Nursing, 17*(4), 197–209.

Weiner, K. M. (2005). *Therapeutic and legal issues for therapists who have survived a client suicide: Breaking the silence*. New York: Haworth Press.

ELECTRONIC RESOURCES

Family and Peer Survivors

American Foundation of Suicide Prevention, Surviving Suicide Loss: http://www.afsp.org

Friends and Family of Suicide: http://www.friendsandfamiliesofsuicide.com

Parents of Suicide: http://www.parentsofsuicide.com

Peer Suicide: http://www.friendsforsurvival.org

Sibling Survivors: http://www.siblingsurvivors.com

Suicide Survivors Group: http://www.gvsl.org

Support for Survivors

For Suicide Survivors: http://www.forsuicidesurvivors.com

Grief Support Following Suicide: http://heartbeatsurvivorsaftersuicide.org/index.shtml

A Handbook for Suicide Survivors: http://www.suicidology.org/associations/1045/files/SOS_handbook.pdf

Helping Survivors: http://www.suicidology.org/associations/1045/files/HelpingFactShhet.pdf

Surviving Suicide: http://survivingsuicide.com

Survivors of Bereavement by Suicide: http://www.sobs.admin.care4free.net
Survivors of Suicide Factsheet: http://www.suicidology.org/associations/1045/files/Survi
   vorsFactSheet.pdf

Clinician and Professional Survivors

American Association of Suicidality: http://www.suicidology.org
American Foundation of Suicide Prevention: http://www.afsp.org
Suicide Prevention Resource Center: http://www.sprc.org

▦ Knowledge Acquisition Test

True or False

1. All suicide survivors experience complicated grief.
2. Suicide survivors do not experience more stigma than survivors of other forms of traumatic death.
3. There are no differences between parental, offspring, and peer survivors of suicide.
4. There is a greater likelihood of suicidal ideation among survivors of suicide than among survivors of other forms of death.
5. Professionals will rarely experience a client suicide.
6. After a client suicide, a helpful coping strategy for professionals is the support from their colleagues.
7. A practitioner's ability to relate to others, emotional state, cognitive processes, and clinical effectiveness can all be affected by a client's suicide.
8. Practitioners should always attend the funeral rites of a client after their suicide.

Short Answer

9. What is complicated grief?
10. What are the grief reactions that distinguish between survivors of suicide and survivors of other forms of death?
11. What are the five stages of grief proposed by Kübler-Ross?
12. Why are formal inquiries into the suicide of a client not very beneficial to the treating of professional(s)?
13. Should professions/professionals prepare and train themselves to manage a potential future of a client suicide? Explain.
14. In considering question 13, what steps can professions or professionals take to prepare or train themselves for a future client suicide?
15. How can practitioners work with the surviving family members?

Multiple Choice

16. Complicated grief is characterized by which of the following?
    A. Disinterest in others

    B. Lack of control
    C. Preoccupation with thoughts of the deceased
    D. Futility about the future
    E. All of the above
    F. None of the above

17. Compared to survivors of other forms of death, some report that suicide survivors experience greater:

    A Depression
    B. Posttraumatic stress
    C. Anxiety
    D. Impaired social adjustment
    E. All of the above
    F. None of the above

18. Following a client's suicide practitioners reactions may include:

    A. Little affective response due to comprehensive professional training and education
    B. Professional suspension of their license and probable job loss
    C. A potential range of responses including grief, shock, denial, distress, depression, isolation self blame, a sense of failure, strain on their personal and professional lives, fear of another suicide, loss of confidence, to avoidance of triggering stimuli
    D. A cluster of their clients attempting or completing suicide
    E. None of the above
    F. All of the above

19. Following a client's suicide, some recommended management steps that practitioners may want to consider are:

    A. Maintain clear boundaries by not meeting with your supervisor or department head to review the case
    B. If you do meet with your supervisor, do not document this event
    C. Personal counseling or support is not be helpful and may be interpreted as complicity to the suicide if a lawsuit is filed
    D. Avoid any further contact with the surviving family members
    E. None of the above
    F. All of the above

20. Following a client's suicide, professionals may want to consider:

    A. Contact or support surviving family members
    B. Work with their colleagues and team help each other manage this tragedy
    C. Attend memorial or funeral rites
    D. Periodically check in with the surviving family members
    E. None of the above
    F. All of the above

Answer key is available in the Instructor's Manual; qualified instructors may e-mail textbook@springerpub.com to request a copy.

REFERENCES

Agerbo, E. (2003). Risk of suicide and spouse's psychiatric illness or suicide: Nested case-control study. *British Medical Journal, 327*(7422), 1025–1026.

Alexander, D. A., Klein, S., Gray, N. M., Dewar, I. G., & Eagles, J. M. (2000). Suicide by patients: Questionnaire study of its effect on consultant psychiatrists. *British Medical Journal, 320,* 1571–1574.

Alexander, V. (1991). Grief after suicide: Giving voice to the loss. *Journal of Geriatric Psychiatry, 24*(2), 277–291.

Anderson, G. O. (2005). Who, what, when, where, how, and mostly why? A therapist's grief over the suicide of a client. *Women & Therapy, 28*(1), 25–34.

Bailley, S. E., Kral, M. J., & Dunham, K. (1999). Survivors of suicide do grieve differently: Empirical support for a common sense proposition. *Suicide & Life-Threatening Behavior, 29*(3), 256–271.

Barlow, C. A., & Coleman, H. (2003). The healing alliance: How families use social support after a suicide. *Omega: Journal of Death and Dying, 47,* 187–202.

Barlow, C. A., & Morrison, H. (2002). Survivors of suicide: Emerging counseling strategies. *Journal of Psychosocial Nursing & Mental Health Services, 40*(1), 28–39.

Brent, D., Oquendo, M., Birmaher, B., Greenhill, L., Kolko, D., Stanley, B., et al. (2004). Familial transmission of mood disorders: Convergence and divergence with transmission of suicidal behavior. *Journal of the American Academy of Child & Adolescent Psychiatry, 43*(10), 1259–1266.

Brent, D., Perper, J., Moritz, G., Baugher, M., Schweers, J., & Roth, C. (1993). Firearms and adolescent suicide: A community case-control study. *American Journal of Disorders of Childhood, 147,* 1066–1071.

Brown, H. N. (1987). The impact of suicide on therapists in training. *Comprehensive Psychiatry, 28*(2), 101–112.

Callahan, J. (2000). Predictors and correlates of bereavement in suicide support group participants. *Suicide & Life-Threatening Behavior, 30*(2), 104–124.

Calhoun, L. G., & Allen, B. G. (1991). Social reactions to the survivors of a suicide in the family: A review of literature. *Omega: Journal of Death and Dying, 23*(2), 95–97.

Cerel, J., Fristad, M. A., Weller, E. B., & Weller, R. A. (1999). Suicide-bereaved children and adolescents: A controlled longitudinal examination. *Journal of the American Academy of Child and Adolescent Psychiatry, 38,* 672–679.

Cerel, J., Jordan, J. R., & Duberstein, P. R. (2008). The impact of suicide on the family. *Crisis: The Journal of Crisis Intervention & Suicide Prevention, 29*(1), 38–44.

Chemtob, C. M., Hamada, R. S., Bauer, G., Kinney, B., & Torigoe, R. Y. (1988). Patients' suicides: Frequency and impact on psychiatrists. *American Journal of Psychiatry, 145*(2), 224–228.

Chemtob, C. M., Hamada, R. S., Bauer, G., Torigoe, R. Y., & Kinney, B. (1988). Patient suicide: Frequency and impact on psychologists. *Professional Psychology: Research and Practice, 19*(4), 416–420.

Cleiren, M., & Diekstra, R. (1994). *After the loss: Bereavement after suicide and other types of death.* New York: Springer Publishing.

Clements, P. T., DeRanieri, J. T., Vigil, G. J., & Benasutti, K. M. (2004). Life after death: Grief therapy after the sudden traumatic death of a family member. *Perspectives in Psychiatric Care, 40*(4), 149–154.

Collins, J. M. (2003). Impact of patient suicide on clinicians. *Journal of the American Psychiatric Nurses Association, 9*(85), 159–162.

Constantino, R. E., & Bricker, P. L. (1996). Nursing postvention for spousal survivors of suicide. *Issues in Mental Health Nursing, 17,* 131–152.

Constantino, R. E., Sekula, L. K., & Rubinstein, E. N. (2001). Group intervention for widowed survivors of suicide. *Suicide & Life-Threatening Behavior, 31*(4), 428–441.

Cooper, C. (1995). Patient suicide and assault: Their impact on psychiatric hospital staff. *Journal of Psychosocial Nursing and Mental Health Services, 33*(6), 26–29.

Coverdale, J. H., Roberts, L. W., & Louie, A. K. (2007). Encountering patient suicide: Emotional responses, ethics, and implications for training programs. *Academic Psychiatry, 31*(5), 329–332.

Cvinar, J. G. (2005). Do suicide survivors suffer social stigma: A review of the literature. *Perspectives in Psychiatric Care, 41*(1), 14–21.

Demi, A. S., & Howell, C. (1991). Hiding and healing: Resolving the suicide of a parent or sibling. *Archives of Psychiatric Nursing, 5*(6), 350–356.

Dewar, I. G., Eagles, J. M., Klein, S., Gray, N., & Alexander, D. A. (2000). Psychiatric trainees' experiences of, and reactions to, patient suicide. *Psychiatric Bulletin, 24*(1), 20–23.

Eagles, J. M., Klein, S., Gray, N. M., Dewar, I. G., & Alexander, D. A. (2001). Role of psychiatrists in the prediction and prevention of suicide: A perspective from north-east Scotland. *British Journal of Psychiatry, 178,* 494–496.

Farberow, N. (1992). The Los Angeles Survivors-after-suicide program: An evaluation. *Crisis: The Journal of Crisis Intervention & Suicide Prevention, 13,* 23–34.

Farberow, N. L. (2005). The mental health professional as suicide survivor. *Clinical Neuropsychiatry: Journal of Treatment Evaluation, 2*(1), 13–20.

Farberow, N. L., Gallagher-Thompson, D., Gilewski, M., & Thompson, L. (1992a). Changes in grief and mental health of bereaved spouses of older suicides. *Journal of Gerontology, 47*(6), P357–P366.

Farberow, N. L., Gallagher-Thompson, D., Gilewski, M., & Thompson, L. (1992b). The role of social supports in the bereavement process of surviving spouses of suicide and natural deaths. *Suicide & Life-Threatening Behavior, 22*(1), 107–124.

Feldman, D. (1987). A social work student's reaction to client suicide. *Social Casework, 68,* 184–187.

Gilje, F., Talseth, A. G., & Norberg, A. (2005). Psychiatric nurses' response to suicidal psychiatric inpatients: Struggling with self and sufferer. *Journal of Psychiatric and Mental Health Nursing, 12*(5), 519–526.

Gitlin, M. J. (1999). A psychiatrist's reaction to a patient's suicide. *American Journal of Psychiatry, 156*(10), 1630–1634.

Grad, O. T. (1996). Suicide: How to survive as a survivor? *Crisis: The Journal of Crisis Intervention and Suicide Prevention, 17*(3), 136–142.

Grad, O. T., & Michel, K. (2005). Therapists as client suicide survivors. *Women & Therapy, 28*(1), 71–81.

Grossman, J. A., Clark, D. C., Gross, D., Halstead, L., & Pennington, J. (1995). Child bereavement after paternal suicide. *Journal of Child & Adolescent Psychiatric Nursing, 8*(2), 5–17.

Gyulay, J. (1989). What suicide leaves behind. *Issues in Comprehensive Pediatric Nursing, 12*(1), 103–118.

Halligan, P., & Corcoran, P. (2001). The impact of patient suicide on rural general practitioners. *British Journal of General Practice, 51*(465), 295–296.

Harwood, D., Hawton, K., Hope, T., & Jacoby, R. (2002). The grief experiences and needs of bereaved relatives and friends of older people dying through suicide: A descriptive and case-control study. *Journal of Affective Disorders, 72,* 185–194.

Jacobson, J. M., Ting, L., Sanders, S., & Harrington, S. (2004). Prevalence of and reactions to fatal and nonfatal client suicidal behavior: A national study of mental health social workers. *OMEGA: The Journal of Death and Dying, 49*(3), 237–248.

Jordan, J. R., & McMenamy, J. (2004). Interventions for suicide survivors: A review of the literature. *Suicide & Life-Threatening Behavior, 34*(4), 337–349.

Kessler, R. C., McGonagle, K. A., Zhao, S., Nelson, C. B., Hughes, M., & Eshelman, S. (1994). Lifetime and 12-month prevalence of DSM-III-R psychiatric disorders in the United States: Results from the National Comorbidity Survey. *Archives of General Psychiatry, 51,* 8–19.

Kleespies, P. M. (1993). The stress of patient suicidal behavior: Implications for interns and training programs in psychology. *Professional Psychology: Research and Practice, 24*(4), 477–482.

Knieper, A. J. (1999). The suicide survivor's grief and recovery. *Suicide & Life-Threatening Behavior, 29*(4), 353–364.

Kovarsky, R. S. (1989). Loneliness and disturbed grief: A comparison of parents who lost a child to suicide or accidental death. *Archives of Psychiatric Nursing, 3*(2), 86–96.

Kübler-Ross, E. (1969). *On death and dying.* New York: Macmillan.

Latham, A. E., & Prigerson, H. G. (2004). Suicidality and bereavement: Complicated grief as psychiatric disorder presenting greatest risk for suicidality. *Suicide & Life-Threatening Behavior, 34*(4), 350–362.

Lester, D. (1993). The effectiveness of suicide prevention centers. *Suicide & Life-Threatening Behavior, 23,* 263–267.

Linehan, M. M. (1999). Standard protocol for assessing and treating suicidal behavior for patients in treatment. In D. G. Jacobs (Ed.), *The Harvard Medical School guide to suicide assessment and intervention* (pp. 146–187). San Francisco, CA: Jossey Bass.

Linke, S., Wojciak, J., & Day, S. (2002). The impact of suicide on community mental health teams findings and recommendations. *Psychiatric Bulletin, 26,* 50–52.

Lohan, J. A. (2002). Family functioning and family typology after an adolescent or young adult's sudden violent death. *Journal of Family Nursing, 8,* 49.

Lukas, C., & Seiden, H. (1997). *Silent grief.* New York: Charles Scribner's Sons.

Luoma, J. B., Pearson, J. L., & Martin, C. E. (2002). Contact with mental health and primary care prior to suicide: A review of the evidence. *American Journal of Psychiatry, 159,* 909–916.

Maltsberger, J. T. (1992). The implications of patient suicide for the surviving psychotherapist. In D. Jacobs (Ed.), *Suicide and clinical practice* (Vol. 21, pp. 169–182). Washington, DC: American Psychiatric Press.

McNiel, D. E., Hatcher, C., & Reubin, R. (1988). Family survivors of suicide and accidental death: Consequences for widows. *Suicide & Life-Threatening Behavior, 18*(2), 137–148.

Mitchell, A. M., & Kim, Y. (2003). *Debriefing approach with suicide survivors.* Paper presented at the Survivors of Suicide Research Workshop, Washington, DC.

Mitchell, A. M., Kim, Y., Prigerson, H. G., & Mortimer-Stephens, M. (2004). Complicated grief in survivors of suicide. *Crisis: Journal of Crisis Intervention & Suicide,*
25(1), 12–18.

Mitchell, A. M., Kim, Y., Prigerson, H. G., & Mortimer, M. K. (2005). Complicated grief
and suicidal ideation in adult survivors of suicide. *Suicide & Life-Threatening Behav-*
ior, 35(5), 498–506.

Murphy, S. A. (2000). The use of research findings in bereavement programs: A case
study. *Death Studies, 24,* 585–602.

Peterson, E. M., Luoma, J. B., & Dunne, E. (2002). Suicide survivors' perceptions of the
treating clinician. *Suicide & Life-Threatening Behavior, 32*(2), 158–166.

Pfeffer, C. R., Jiang, H., Kakuma, T., Hwang, J., & Metsch, M. (2002). Group intervention for children bereaved by the suicide of a relative. *Journal of the American Acad-*
emy of Child & Adolescent Psychiatry, 41, 505–513.

Pfeffer, C. R., Karus, D., Siegel, K., & Jiang, H. (2000). Child survivors of parental death
from cancer or suicide: Depressive and behavioral outcomes. *Psycho-Oncology, 9,*
1–10.

Pfeffer, C. R., Martins, P., Mann, J., Sunkenberg, M., Ice, A., Damore, J. P., Jr., et al.
(1997). Child survivors of suicide: psychosocial characteristics. *Journal of the Ameri-*
can Academy of Child & Adolescent Psychiatry, 36(1), 65–74.

Prigerson, H. G., Shear, M. K., Jacobs, S. C., Reynolds, C. F., Maciejewski, P. K., Da-
vidson, J. R. T., et al. (1999). Consensus criteria for traumatic grief: A preliminary
empirical test. *British Journal of Psychiatry—Supplementum, 174,* 67–73.

Range, L. M. (1998). *When a loss is due to suicide: Unique aspects of bereavement.* Philadelphia: Brunner/Mazel.

Range, L. M., Bright, P. S., & Ginn, P. D. (1985). Public reactions to child suicide: Effects
of age and method used. *Journal of Community Psychology, 13,* 288–294.

Range, L. M., Campbell, C., Kovac, S. H., Marion-Jones, M., & Aldridge, H. (2002).
No-suicide contracts: An overview and recommendations. *Death Studies, 26,*
51–74.

Reed, M. D. (1998). Predicting grief symptomatology among the suddenly bereaved.
Suicide & Life-Threatening Behavior, 28(3), 285–301.

Renaud, C. (1995). *Bereavement after a suicide: A model for support groups.* New York:
Springer Publishing.

Reynolds, F. M., & Cimbolic, P. (1988). Attitudes toward suicide survivors as a function
of survivors' relationship to the victim. *Omega: Journal of Death and Dying, 19*(2),
125–133.

Rogers, J. R., Sheldon, A., Barwick, C., Letofsky, K., & Lancee, W. (1982). Help for
families of suicide: Survivors support program. *Canadian Journal of Psychiatry, 27,*
444–449.

Rudestam, K. E. (1992). Research contributions to understanding the suicide survivor.
Crisis: The Journal of Crisis Intervention & Suicide Prevention, 13(1), 41–46.

Ruskin, R., Sakinofsky, I., Bagby, R. M., Dickens, S., & Sousa, G. (2004). Impact of patient suicide on psychiatrists and psychiatric trainees. *Academic Psychiatry, 28*(2),
104–110.

Seguin, M., Lesage, A., & Kiely, M. C. (1995). Parental bereavement after suicide and accident: A comparative study. *Suicide & Life-Threatening Behavior, 25*(4), 489–492.

Sethi, S., & Bhargava, S. C. (2003). Child and adolescent survivors of suicide. *Crisis: Journal of Crisis Intervention & Suicide, 24*(1), 4–6.

Shear, K., Frank, E., Houck, P. R., & Reynolds III, C. F. (2005). Treatment of complicated grief: A randomized controlled trial. *Journal of the American Medical Association, 293,* 2601–2608.

Shepherd, D. M., & Barraclough, B. M. (1976). The aftermath of parental suicide for children. *British Journal of Psychiatry—Supplementum, 129,* 267–276.

Silverman, E., Range, L., & Overholser, J. (1994). Bereavement from suicide as compared to other forms of bereavement. *Omega: Journal of Death and Dying, 30*(1), 41–51.

Smith, B. J., Mitchell, A. M., Bruno, A. A., & Constantino, R. E. (1995). Exploring widows' experiences after the suicide of their spouse. *Journal of Psychosocial Nursing & Mental Health Services, 33*(5), 10–15.

Spiegelman, J. S., & Werth, J. L. (2005). Don't forget about me: The experiences of therapists-in-training after a client has attempted or died by suicide. *Women & Therapy, 28*(1), 35–57.

Stillion, J. (1996). *Survivors of suicide.* Washington, DC: Hospice Foundation of America.

Strom-Gottfried, K., & Mowbray, N. D. (2006). Who heals the helper? Facilitating the social worker's grief. *Families in Society, 87*(1), 9–15.

Sudak, H. (2007). Encountering patient suicide: The role of survivors. *Academic Psychiatry, 31*(5), 333–335.

Sveen, C., & Walby, F. A. (2008). Suicide survivors' mental health and grief reactions: A systematic review of controlled studies. *Suicide & Life-Threatening Behavior, 38*(1), 13–29.

Szanto, K., Prigerson, H., Houck, P., Ehrenpreis, L., & Reynolds, C. F. (1997). Suicidal ideation in elderly bereaved: The role of complicated grief. *Suicide & Life-Threatening Behavior, 27*(2), 194–207.

Szanto, K., Shear, M. K., Houck, P. R., Reynolds, C. F., Frank, E., Caroff, K., et al. (2006). Indirect self-destructive behavior and overt suicidality in patients with complicated grief. *Journal of Clinical Psychiatry, 67*(2), 233–239.

Talseth, A. G., & Gilje, F. (2007). Unburdening suffering: Responses of psychiatrists to patients' suicide deaths. *Nursing Ethics. An International Journal for Health Care Professionals, 14*(5), 620–636.

Thompson, J., & Brooks, S. (1990). When a colleague commits suicide: How the staff reacts. *Journal of Psychosocial Nursing & Mental Health Services, 28*(10), 6–11.

Thompson, K. E., & Range, L. M. (1991). Recent bereavement from suicide and other deaths—Can people imagine it as it really is. *Omega: Journal of Death and Dying, 22,* 249–259.

Ting, L., Sanders, S., Jacobson, J. M., & Power, J. R. (2006). Dealing with the aftermath: A qualitative analysis of mental health social workers' reactions after a client suicide. *Social Work, 51*(1), 329–341.

van Dongen, C. J. (1990). Agonizing questioning: Experiences of survivors of suicide victims. *Nursing Research, 39*(4), 224–229.

Van Dongen, C. J. (1991a). Experiences of family members after a suicide. *Journal of Family Practice, 33*(4), 375–380.

Van Dongen, C. J. (1991b). Survivors of a family member's suicide: Implications for practice. *Nurse Practitioner, 16*(7), 31–35.

Watson, W. L., & Lee, D. (1993). Is there life after suicide? The systemic belief approach for "survivors" of suicide. *Archives of Psychiatric Nursing, 7*(1), 37–43.

Zhang, J., Hui, Q., & Zhou, L. (2005). The effect of bereavement due to suicide on survivors' depression: A study of Chinese samples. *Omega: Journal of Death and Dying, 51*(3), 217–227.

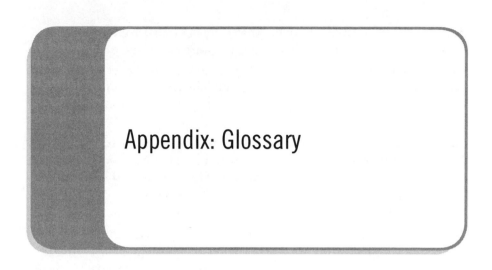

Appendix: Glossary

ABC model: A theory behind **cognitive-behavioral therapy**. ABC refers to antecedents, event, and consequences. The model describes the interconnection among behavior, cognition, and affect. The consequences can be behavioral, cognitive, and/or affective responses to the event.

Acculturation: The process through which immigrants pass as they move to a new country. It is characterized by the struggle to maintain one's cultural identity, traditions, values, and customs while adapting to mainstream culture to which they have emigrated, their **host culture**. This period can, for some, prove to be a time of great conflict that can result in heightened feelings of depression, anxiety, isolation, and suicidality.

Acculturative stress: The heightened feelings (such as depression, anxiety, isolation, and suicidality) that can accompany the process of **acculturation**.

Active euthanasia: An act taken to shorten life.

Activity scheduling: A technique utilized in **cognitive-behavioral therapy** in which the client schedules activities he/she enjoyed in the past in order to change emotions by changing behaviors.

Automatic thoughts: Thoughts that occur automatically without conscious effort or any attention; these thoughts can be true or untrue.

Autonomy: One of the foremost principles that affect a practitioner's course of action regarding a suicidal client. The principle of self-determination involves the client's right to take action rooted in his or her own goals, desires, and wishes.

Behavioral chain analysis (BCA): A technique used in **dialectical behavior therapy**. The BCA begins with identifying a specific situation or event and examining the chain of events leading up to the situation or event and how they may be related. The BCA continues by then exploring alternative solutions and adaptive responses.

Behavioral Therapy: A term used to classify a type of therapeutic treatment that focuses on observing and changing behavior by modifying environmental events and reinforcement, which will impact internal states. Behavioral therapy incorporates a number approaches related to the behavioral learning process, including classical conditioning, operant conditioning, and social learning.

Beneficence: The concept of doing the greatest good possible. Practitioners have an ethical responsibility to strive for the well-being of clients. With regards to suicidal clients, beneficence should take precedence over autonomy because the death of an individual would not generally be considered a "good" action.

Biosocial theory of borderline personality disorder (BPD): The guiding principle of **dialectical behavior therapy**. It suggests that the emotional and behavioral dysregulation experienced by clients with **borderline personality disorder** is both a byproduct of, and reinforced by, the transaction between an invalidating early childhood home environment and an inherent biological emotional vulnerability.

Bipolar I: A condition consisting of fluctuating episodes of **depression** and mania.

Bipolar II: A condition represented by symptoms of **depression** and milder symptoms of mania, or hypomania.

Borderline personality disorder (BPD): A mental diagnosis characterized by a pattern of instability in interpersonal relationships, self-image, affect, and marked impulsivity. It is highly associated with suicide attempts and completions.

Brief psychotic disorder: A condition related to **schizophrenia** in which symptoms include positive psychotic symptoms with a duration under 1 month.

Catastrophic thinking: Assuming or predicting the very worst possible outcome in all situations.

Cluster suicides: A number of connected suicides by unrelated individuals within a given time period in a certain space.

Cognitive-behavioral therapy (CBT): A term used to classify a type of psychotherapy that combines elements of cognitive and behavioral theories. There are several approaches to CBT, including rational emotive behavior therapy, **cognitive therapy**, rational behavior therapy, and schema focused therapy, to name a few. Each approach has its own developmental history.

Cognitive restructuring: A key strategy used in **cognitive-behavioral therapy**. Cognitive restructuring suggests that people can choose to think differently, and this, ultimately, will lead to more constructive behavior patterns.

Cognitive theory: Originated in the field of psychology and the works of Alfred Adler. Cognitive theory is based on the assumption that thinking is a principle determinant of emotions and behavior. A main goal is to help the client identify, challenge, and change thinking.

Cognitive therapy: Commonly referred to under the umbrella term CBT. Refers to a systematic treatment process devised by Aaron Beck, based on Ellis's notion of the importance of irrational beliefs. It is a therapeutic treatment approach focusing on solving problems by modifying dysfunctional thinking and behavior.

Cognitive triad: A term proposed by Alfred Adler that refers to beliefs regarding oneself, others, and the world.

Complicated grief: A group of symptoms that include longing for the deceased, preoccupation with thoughts of the deceased, futility about the future, disinterest in others, difficulty accepting the death, and feeling a lack of control, insecurity, anger, and resentment over the death.

Confidentiality: A major area for practitioners as far as suicide is concerned. Most codes of ethics require a practitioner to breach confidentiality if the client represents a danger to themselves or others.

Core beliefs: An individual's fundamental beliefs that are considered as true regardless of evidence. Core beliefs influence how an individual views oneself and interacts with others and the world.

Crisis: A time-limited response to an event or group of events that significantly disrupts and distresses an individual and overwhelms his/her coping strategies.

Culture of origin effects: Protective or risk factors derived from an individual's culture of origin that are brought with them to the new culture.

Delusional disorder: A psychotic disorder featuring nonbizarre fixed false beliefs.

Depression. See **major depressive disorder.**

Depression not otherwise specified (NOS): Related to **depression**. It includes conditions that display fewer than five symptoms or are of insufficient duration to be considered major depression.

Dialectical behavior therapy (DBT): A therapeutic treatment approach based on the principle that individuals struggle with the dialect of change and acceptance. Rather than emphasizing a purely change oriented approach, DBT recognizes the importance of helping clients accept themselves as they are.

Distress tolerance: Involves teaching clients strategies that help to endure adverse situations, feelings, and/or thoughts.

Double-depression: A condition related to **major depressive disorder**. It is **dysthymia** with a concurrent major depressive episode.

Downward Arrow: A major tool utilized in **cognitive-behavioral therapy**. In the downward arrow method, the clinician and client begin by discussing an upsetting event in which **automatic thoughts** occurred. The clinician then asks the client to consider about each automatic thought, "If this were true, what would it mean to you?" This questioning continues until the underlying automatic thought is revealed.

Duty to protect: Refers to a practitioner's responsibility to protect clients from harming themselves according to various professional codes of ethics.

Dysfunctional thoughts: Can result in an individual distorting and misinterpreting experiences. Examples may include **automatic thoughts, overgeneralizations**, and/or **catastrophic thinking**. Also known as **maladaptive thoughts**.

Dysthymia: A **mood disorder** that features fewer symptoms than major depression and is a chronic illness lasting at least 2 years in adults or 1 year in adolescents.

Emotional regulation: Involves helping clients to manage recent as well as long-standing difficult feelings. Clients are taught to observe their emotions and accept their emotions rather than to push them away. They are also taught to not judge their emotions, not to hang on to them, and not to intensify them. In addition, clients are taught to recognize where their emotions come from and how to describe their emotions. Emotional regulation skills also teach clients how to modulate their emotions should they desire to do so.

Familism: A cultural trait that emphasizes close relationships with immediate family and extended family networks. Can serve as a protective factor against suicide.

Host culture: Refers to the mainstream culture to which an immigrant has emigrated.

Ideations: Thoughts of suicide.

Identity formation: A process of developing a unique or distinct identity and personality, important in adolescent development.

Informed consent: A client has a competent understanding of risks, benefits, and alternatives from which the client can make a decision regarding an appropriate course of action.

Interpersonal effectiveness: A technique that seeks to improve a client's communication skills and the way in which they manage interpersonal relationships.

Interpersonal psychotherapy (IPT): A psychosocial treatment that was developed for adults with depression. IPT is a brief outpatient evidence-based practice. IPT emerged out of **interpersonal theory**. In addition, IPT draws from Adolf Meyer's theory that postulates an individual's psychological disorder comes from his or her adaptations to interpersonal relationships and the larger environment.

Interpersonal psychotherapy for adolescents (IPT-A): A form of interpersonal psychotherapy adapted for and effective with adolescents.

Interpersonal theory: Originated under Harry Stack Sullivan, who hypothesized that interpersonal experiences help in the formation of personality.

Involuntary euthanasia: Intentionally causing the death of an individual, whether, competent, incompetent or unaware, without informed consent or explicit request.

Kantian perspective: A theory that suggests that a person is a rational agent with autonomy of will and that suicide is a violation of one's duty to himself or herself.

Major depressive disorder (MDD): Also referred to as major depression. MDD is generally diagnosed via psychiatric assessment using the *DSM-IV-TR*. Major depression is diagnosed when five or more of the following symptoms are present for at least 2 weeks nearly every day for most of the day. In addition, at least one of the symptoms must be either (1) depressed mood or (2) loss of interest or pleasure in activities. The symptoms include: depressed or irritable mood, loss of interest or pleasure in activities, sudden change in weight or a change in appetite, inability to sleep or sleeping too much, agitation or restlessness, constant fatigue or loss of energy, frequent feelings of worthlessness or inappropriate guilt, difficulty concentrating or making decisions, and frequent thoughts of death or suicide (or a suicide attempt or plan).

Maladaptive thoughts: Beliefs that can result in an individual distorting and misinterpreting experiences. Examples may include **automatic thoughts, overgeneralizations**, and/or **catastrophic thinking**. Also known as **dysfunctional thoughts**.

Mindfulness: Has to do with the quality of awareness that a client brings to what he or she is doing and experiencing. It encourages individuals to live in the here and now, to focus on the present, and to pay attention to what is happening in the moment.

Mood disorders: The most common psychiatric disorders, impacting millions of individuals, their families, and larger society. Mood disorders, such as depression, are the most common psychiatric conditions associated with suicide attempts and completed suicide. Mood disorders are characterized by irritability or depressed mood; loss of interest or pleasure; changes in appetite, weight, and/or sleep patterns; loss of energy; feelings of hopelessness and worthlessness; inappropriate guilt; difficulty making decisions; and mania.

Motivational enhancement therapy (MET): A therapeutic treatment approach that uses a patient's intrinsic motivation for change as the focus of treatment. The therapist seeks to develop a discrepancy in the patient's current behavior and their future goals. Emphasis is placed on commitment to change and on recognizing change talk

Nonmaleficence: Refers to a clinician's duty to minimize or prevent harm. With regards to suicidal clients, it requires a practitioner to take whatever action necessary to prevent a client from taking his own life.

Overgeneralizations: Using a limited negative occurrence to make broad conclusions about a given issue.

Passive euthanasia: The withdrawal or withholding of artificial life-support or medical treatments that may prolong life.

Physician-assisted suicide (PAS): The provision of suicidal means, such as prescribed medications, to an individual who is otherwise able to suicide.

Physiological theory of suicidal behavior: Suggests that differences in suicide rates may be explained by variances in physiology across cultures, specifically regarding the inheritance of psychiatric disorders and concentrations of neurotransmitters.

Protective factors: Factors that may decrease a client's risk of suicide. Protective factors are highly individualized, yet there are several known factors that have been shown to be associated with decreased suicide risk.

Psychological autopsy: A formal or informal procedure of examining a death by analyzing or reconstructing the events and motives leading up to the death.

Psychosis not otherwise specified (NOS): A psychotic condition that includes psychotic symptoms but lacks adequate information to make a specific diagnosis.

Rational suicide: A theory that (despite contradictory evidence) argues that suicide may actually be a rational decision and should be a matter of individual choice.

Risk factors: Factors that may increase a client's risk of suicide. There are several established risk factors for suicidality. It is important to recognize that having one or more risk factors does not make someone suicidal, nor does the absence of risk factors negate the risk. However, the number of risk factors present often correlates with the level of suicide risk.

Sati: A centuries' old Hindu practice, Sati is a ritual act of suicide in which widows self-immolate on the funeral pyre of their husbands.

Schemas: The groups or patterns of cognitions in which core beliefs occur.

Schizoaffective disorder: A psychiatric diagnosis comprised of alternating or co-occurring periods of the psychotic symptoms of schizophrenia and either a major depressive, mixed, or manic episode.

Schizophrenia: A psychiatric diagnosis characterized by grossly impaired reality testing that may manifest as delusions, hallucinations, negative symptoms, highly disorganized behavior or disorganized speech, and impaired interpersonal relationships, schizophrenia has an approximate lifetime risk of 1%.

Schizophreniform disorder: A psychiatric diagnosis that is the same as **schizophrenia** except that its duration is under 6 months, and it may result in less impairment in social/occupational functioning.

Social learning model: A theory that suggests that suicide may be a learned behavior via familial and/or societal modeling.

Social Learning Theory: A theory developed by Albert Bandura that suggests that an individual's behavior is learned through observation.

Stages of grief: A five-stage model suggested by Elizabeth Kübler-Ross of the grief process that individuals experience after the loss of a loved one.

Stress-diathesis model: Proposes that at certain times, triggers or stressors exist that can be considered state-dependent or present only during certain periods of time. Additionally, a threshold or diathesis exists that is more trait-dependent or constantly present. When risk factors from only one of these domains are present, it is not sufficient to elicit suicidal behavior.

Substance abuse disorder: A maladaptive pattern of substance use manifested by recurrent and significant adverse consequences related to the repeated use of substances.

Substance-induced psychosis: A psychotic disorder that features predominant hallucinations or delusions resulting from the use of substances.

Substance intoxication: The development of a reversible clinical condition due to the recent ingestion or overuse of a substance.

Substance-related disorders: Refers to the taking of a number of legal and illegal substances, such as alcohol, drugs, medications, or toxins.

Survivors of suicide: Individuals who are closely affected by the suicide of another person, generally a family member or close friend.

Transcultural protective factors: Protective factors that are generalizable across cultures and ethnicities.

Transcultural risk factors: Risk factors that are generalizable across cultures and ethnicities.

Treatment as usual: Refers to standard care received in the agency where treatment is occurring.

Utilitarian perspective: A theory that considers the consequences of suicide (including the impact on family members, others, and larger society) in determining the moral or ethical judgment of the action.

Voluntary euthanasia: Occurs when an individual requests assistance from anyone in ending his or her life.

Waitlist controls: In research, the waitlist controls are a comparison group of individuals not currently receiving treatment but awaiting service provision.

Index